Praise for David Thomson's

THE WHOLE EQUATION

"The excitement of Mr. Thomson's wild ride is infectious. . . . Thomson's 'mathematics' of myth-building—both Hollywood's and his own—is so compulsively readable." —*Time Out New York*

"Reading *The Whole Equation* resembles nothing so much as being talked to nonstop by a breathless, slightly overdramatizing, but extremely intelligent man, who really does know what he's talking about." —*Commentary*

"Appealing. . . . What Mr. Thomson does most powerfully in this volume is conjure the magic of movies—what Jean-Paul Sartre once called 'the frenzy on the wall.'" —*The New York Times*

"A brilliant attempt to understand the real nature of the dream factory and its role in shaping the lives and beliefs of people all over the world during the past century. . . . After 50 years of film-going, [Thomson] is as shrewd and detached as ever. . . . Wonderful and provocative." —J.G. Ballard, *The Observer* (London)

"A terrific read full of wit and world-weary wisdom about the movies." —*The Orlando Sentinel*

"Thomson analyzes movies as art and business, encompassing 'the wonder in the dark, the calculation in the offices, and the staggering impact on America.' . . . [He] knows, better than most, that the whole equation can include books and films, a comfortable chair in a library and, yes, the aisle seat at the Cineplex." —*The Philadelphia Inquirer*

"David Thomson has the most deliciously riveting style of any critic alive—witty, allusive, with a slithery vivacity and a whip-crack rhythm." —*The New York Observer*

David Thomson
THE WHOLE EQUATION

David Thomson taught film studies at Dartmouth College and has served on the selection committee for the New York Film Festival. He is a regular contributor to *The New York Times*, *Film Comment*, *Movieline*, *The New Republic*, and *Salon*. He was the screenwriter on the award-winning documentary *The Making of a Legend: Gone with the Wind*. His other books include *Showman: The Life of David O. Selznick*, *Beneath Mulholland: Thoughts on Hollywood and Its Ghosts*, and three works of fiction. Born in London, he lives in San Francisco with his wife and their two sons.

ALSO BY DAVID THOMSON

The New Biographical Dictionary of Film

In Nevada: The Land, the People, God, and Chance

The Alien Quartet

Beneath Mulholland: Thoughts on Hollywood and Its Ghosts

Rosebud: The Story of Orson Welles

4–2

Showman: The Life of David O. Selznick

Silver Light

Warren Beatty and Desert Eyes

Suspects

Overexposures

Scott's Men

America in the Dark

A Biographical Dictionary of Film

Wild Excursions: The Life and Fiction of Laurence Sterne

Hungry as Hunters

A Bowl of Eggs

Movie Man

THE WHOLE EQUATION

It was an inadvertent wonder of Hollywood that it mass-produced dreams—the cinema is always a reverie, a dissolve, between the twin poles of fantasy and reality. *(Photo collage © Lucy Gray, 2004)*

THE WHOLE EQUATION

A History of Hollywood

DAVID THOMSON

VINTAGE BOOKS
A Division of Random House, Inc.
New York

The Library of Congress has cataloged the Knopf edition as follows:
Thomson, David [date]
The whole equation: a history of Hollywood / David Thomson.—1ˢᵗ ed.
p. cm.
Includes bibliographical references and index.
1. Motion picture industry—California—Los Angeles—History   2. Motion pictures—
California—Los Angeles—History.   I. Title.
PN1993.5.U65T56 2005
384'.8'0979494—dc22
2004048358

For Steven Bach, Mark Feeney, and Robert Towne,
and for Nicholas and "Nico"

You can take Hollywood for granted like I did, or you can dismiss it with the contempt we reserve for what we don't understand. It can be understood too, but only dimly and in flashes. Not half a dozen men have ever been able to keep the whole equation of pictures in their heads.

—F. SCOTT FITZGERALD, *THE LAST TYCOON*, 1941

There is in Hollywood, as in all cultures in which gambling is the central activity, a lowered sexual energy, an inability to devote more than token attention to the preoccupations of the society outside.

—JOAN DIDION, "IN HOLLYWOOD," 1973, IN *THE WHITE ALBUM*, 1979

I wonder what it's like out there.

—VAN JOHNSON, A CHARACTER ON THE SCREEN IN *THE PURPLE ROSE OF CAIRO*,
1985, BY WOODY ALLEN, LOOKING OUT FROM THE SCREEN
AT THE DARKNESS ONLY WE KNOW

You have the illusion when you're doing things on your computer that you're really out there.

—LAURIE ANDERSON, ON *THE CHARLIE ROSE SHOW*, 2004

Find out the movies a man saw between ten and fifteen, which ones he liked, disliked, and you would have a pretty good idea of what sort of mind and temperament he has.

—GORE VIDAL, "*PARIS REVIEW* INTERVIEW," 1974,
IN *WRITERS AT WORK*, FIFTH SERIES, 1981

CONTENTS

THE WHOLE EQUATION

The tycoon and the private eye (John Huston and Jack Nicholson in *Chinatown*). But in the long term of California's history, which is the hero? "The future, Mr. Gittes—the future." *(Kobal Collection)*

1 · THE GAMBLE AND THE LOST RIGHTS

On a brilliant Saturday morning in late March 2003, warm yet fresh enough to keep many Californians out in the bliss of the air itself, I was invited by the Los Angeles Institute for the Humanities to have a public conversation with Robert Towne, the screenwriter, as part of a weekend conference entitled "From *Sunset Blvd.* to *Mulholland Dr.*: Los Angeles in the Cinematic Imagination."

We were in a large basement hall at the Davidson Conference Center at the University of Southern California, but it was fun, relaxed, and instructive to a degree. I have known Towne for twenty years. We have talked a good deal, and enjoyed it. We are friends, or friendly. We did our best to be serious about the beguiling gloom of *noir* Los Angeles, and the foreboding of Towne's best-known movie, *Chinatown*.

We did a decent job, I hope, yet nothing matched the burnished day outside where, in an urban sprawl far beyond Nathanael West's worst nightmares (to say nothing of the invasion of Iraq that had begun), some people seemed to be having a good time, or as good a time as people have had in human history; that is not to flatter L.A. or the U.S.A., and I hope it's not being silly or sentimental about all the wretchedness there must have been in L.A. that day and others. Still, free people took their leisure—on the beaches, on playing fields, in the shops and open-air restaurants (at the movie theaters even?). Some read books, or wrote them. Some must have married, or been in love.

In the period allowed for questions, a young woman asked Towne whether there was any chance for the completion of the "trilogy" that had been begun with *Chinatown*. For in his mind, at least, there had been a time when Towne had hoped to follow his private eye, Jake Gittes, through the decades—1937, 1947, 1957—tracing the story of water rights, of oil, and of the killing of public transport to let the automobile own Los Angeles. There had been a second movie, *The Two Jakes*—much troubled and not satisfactory, and plainly removed from Towne's control or authorship—but nothing of a third film.

Towne is a successful man as screenwriters go. He has an Oscar and a fine house in Pacific Palisades. He has been involved with the two *Mission: Impossible* pictures (and even a third?) at a very high salary. He has a great dream, to film John Fante's *Ask the Dust,* one of the best novels about Los Angeles in the thirties—and that film has come to pass. Yet I think I know him well enough as a man who would count his losses first if you asked him to describe himself. And he lost Jake Gittes—long ago. "No," he told the questioner. "No chance."

That's what I want to talk about—for if he meant what he said, we are all the losers for it.

Robert Towne is an Angeleno; he has lived there most of his life, and he wears the badge of the city on his sleeve, as it were. In the Preface to a published version of the *Chinatown* screenplay (and very few screenplays get published), he wrote about his memory of the childhood scents of Los Angeles, of a quality in the air now gone in the toxic rush of urbanization. He wrote about it with such warmth and feeling and nostalgia—like a true writer would:

Chinatown is a sort of eulogy for me. It is a eulogy I'm afraid for things lost that would concern others about as much as a missing button or a dead mouse. Easterners, for example, have often tended to be a little snide about the tepid weather and negligible change in seasons—things I have loved perhaps the most about L.A. I've loved the first hint of October nipping thru the sunlight after school, New Year's Day, chilly and clear as crystal as tho someone put the sun in the freezer overnight, the February rains that came with Valentines and would flood intersections with muddy waters rushing around stalled cars, vacant lots in March that overnight sprouted thousands of sharp green spears you could pull and send with a clod of dark earth hurtling at another kid, little ponds of black polliwogs squiggling like animated commas—and then spring and summer with the smell of pepper trees mentholated more and more by eucalyptus, the green lots turning to straw leaving foxtails in your socks and smelling like hay in the morning, the Santa Anas progressively drying the city into sand and summer smells.

The boy noticed; the man learned to write.* Towne's parents were well off, but he attended Pepperdine College, up on the way to Malibu. And he drifted into screenwriting, by way of acting classes—the place where he first met Jack Nicholson. He still likes acting and actors, and even in private talk he has a way of being that is casual but intimate, like the best sort of naturalistic acting. I like this quality in him, and others, but I know some who feel it is just a touch too calculated, too stylish, too unreliable. Make up your own mind. But still its ease and attractiveness, and its worldliness, are deep at the heart of this book's subject.

Towne worked for Roger Corman. He did a few scripts for exploitation films. And then he began to demonstrate, or act out, one of his most vital traits: he made friendships in which his discreet touch, or treatment, was highly esteemed. He had met Warren Beatty—some have said that he and Beatty learned their stylishness in the course of long telephone conversations, absorbing it from each other. Whatever, when Beatty came to make his first movie as a producer, *Bonnie and Clyde,* no matter that he had a highly original script (by Robert Benton and David Newman), and a very

---

*The "thru" and "tho" in that extract are enough to make a copy editor wince. Those new forms are a sign of how screenwriting sometimes rebels against literariness and brings a new kind of sign language—thus *Sunset Blvd.*, the real title, not "Boulevard," and *Mulholland Dr.*, where the abbreviation permits "dream" to slip in.

good director (Arthur Penn), still Beatty hired Towne to go on location with the film to Texas to work on the script, to touch it up, to give it what Beatty wanted, to doctor it. To make sure Warren was in charge.

When that film opened, and eventually enjoyed its outstanding success, Towne had a most unusual credit on it: Special Consultant. I'm not sure that a writer had ever had so secret yet so public a credit, though very often in Hollywood history, writers had done uncredited work doctoring or rewriting scripts. Towne's insider status was confirmed when it became known—and somehow it did slip out—that he had joined *The Godfather* at short notice to "help" with the final scenes of Vito Corleone's life.

It's worth stressing (with what I have in mind) that up to this moment (1972), Towne was most illustrious for his imprecise intervention, doctoring, or help on other writers' scripts. Which would not always have left those other writers feeling better, happy or well treated. But it was Towne's way to success, and I do not doubt the value of what he brought to those two films. Still, I want to underline his ghostly presence, for it is close to the odd avoidance of responsibility in Hollywood.

By the early seventies, therefore, he was in a position where he could expect to get assignments to write whole films, big pictures, worthwhile ventures. In fact, he wrote three scripts in a row—*The Last Detail, Chinatown,* and *Shampoo*—that all received Oscar nominations. It was the peak of his career, with the Oscar going to *Chinatown,* and to him as the sole writer of an original script.

No one has ever argued but that *Chinatown* was his idea. Towne has said that in April 1971 his wife brought him a copy of Carey McWilliams's book, *Southern California Country,* which held the germ of the story of how William Mulholland° had secured water for a growing Los Angeles from the Owens Valley, 250 miles to the north. Around the same time, he saw a magazine article in which a photographer had re-created the late-1930s mood and look of the Raymond Chandler novels.

He had begun work (on spec), or he looked forward to beginning it, when he had dinner with Robert Evans, a key figure at Paramount, and the executive who had had *The Godfather* made. Evans had come to the table to ask Towne to take over the script for *The Great Gatsby,* but all Towne wanted to talk about was *Chinatown.* It's about how Los Angeles

---

°Mulholland is a source for Noah Cross in *Chinatown,* representing the pirate's urge to own progress. But he also contributed to Hollis Mulwray, the Department of Water and Power chief. Mulwray refuses to build an unsafe dam. But Mulholland sanctioned the St. Francis dam, which broke in 1928, killing 450 people.

became a boomtown, he said—incest and water. It's set in the thirties. A second-rate shamus gets eighty-sixed by a mysterious broad. Instead of solving a case for her, he's the pigeon. I'm writing it for Nicholson.

This was more or less so. Nicholson and Towne had talked about *Chinatown*. But Nicholson had not purchased the idea or the script, or Towne's time. I know, that sounds crass when a person is gently nursing a great story and his fondness for a lost city into being. But writers have to eat.

Evans, acting for Paramount, offered Towne $25,000 to do *Chinatown;* he had been ready to pay him $175,000 to doctor Truman Capote's wretched *Gatsby* script.

Towne created it—but Paramount owned it. Yes, such formulae operate all the time in Hollywood, so let me explain the setup carefully. Suppose *Chinatown* was a first novel. That is a little far-fetched, because Towne had done several things already. Nevertheless, in terms of how far the material was autobiographical in feeling, *Chinatown* was like a first novel, in which case he might well have written the book in private, on his own time, and only then offered it to a publisher. Or he might have secured a modest advance on account of promise.

In which case, the deal would have gone thus: for an advance of, say, $5,000 (generous for 1972), Towne would have delivered a novel. When it was published, he would get a royalty of, say, 10 percent of the selling price on the first 5,000 copies; 12½ percent on the next 5,000; and 15 percent after that. There would be provisions in the contract for sales of paperback and other subsidiary rights—including, perhaps, a sale to the movies. Towne would have retained the copyright. That means the author owns the work and is simply licensing the publisher to sell it. His editor at the publishing house might fight tooth-and-nail for a year or more trying to get Towne to rewrite the book, to make it clearer, to make it more saleable. (In fact, on a $5,000 advance, that kind of striving is unlikely—it's not practical or rewarding. An editor works hardest on a book he expects could be a bestseller. If you can't understand a first novel when you read it that first time, why publish it?)

Still, there could be editorial work, and rewriting, and fights before a novel is printed. But they get settled because, once the contract is signed, it is acknowledged that the book belongs to the author. If it goes out of print, and stays out, the author can regain the rights he licensed. He can try to get a new publisher. When he is dead, for at least seventy years, the copyright and any income the book earns go to his heirs or estate. Only after that does a book enter what is called public domain.

The script of *Chinatown* that Towne delivered perplexed its best supporters. Evans and Nicholson joked together how they couldn't follow its twists and turns. Roman Polanski, the director Evans had hired to make the film, was equally at a loss, and sure that he had to take drastic measures to make it "work." Rewrites from Towne didn't clarify enough. Executives at Paramount were advising Evans not to make the picture, or not to attach himself to it so personally. And, of course, Paramount could have elected not to make the movie—they owned it, and thus they had the right of refusal. Evans stuck by it: "I knew I had Nicholson locked, and, even though I didn't understand the script, I knew Towne was a great writer. I felt like a blind gambler wanting to throw back-to-back sevens."

Several important points come from this. Scripts are not easily read, and possibly the richer a film, the harder it is for "outsiders" to detect its quality. It's not going too far to say that in the history of the movies, many semiliterate people (or disadvantaged readers) have had to make a judgment on a hundred or so pages of single-spaced typing, laid out in a strange and inaccessible way. That is one reason why some of those men, the executives, have thrown away scripts in despair and told someone to just tell them the damn story. To this day, "the pitch"—telling a movie story in a few persuasive minutes—is vital to getting projects made. It follows therefore that many scripts are never actually read. In turn, this encourages everyone's assumption, or hope, that they can exist in a state of continual rewrite.

But note Evans's attitude. "I knew I had Nicholson locked. . . ." He saw himself as if not the film's proprietor, then its skipper, assembling units of talent and identifying the picture with his ego and status at the studio. *Chinatown* would not have existed without Robert Towne. Roman Polanski became the project's director, and perhaps the best-known theory of film production is that everything depends on the director, the auteur. When the general public says *Chinatown* to itself, it sees the sour smile on Jack Nicholson's face; not to mention Faye Dunaway or John Huston (hefty presences in its story and mood), Richard Sylbert (its production designer), John A. Alonzo (the cinematographer), or Jerry Goldsmith (who wrote the memorable theme music at the last moment, in just ten days, after another score had been dropped). Still, Evans felt sure and safe in thinking the picture was his because his peers—the power brokers of Hollywood—would expect it of him. Studios own movies. Producers make them.

And then there was the longing in Evans to see the whole enterprise as a gamble: not just in terms of winning big as opposed to losing; but because to gamble is to defy all those sacred American codes of hard work and just reward; it is believing in magic. Nearly everyone important in the old Hollywood gambled several nights a week, as if they dared not lose touch with magic.

Towne and Polanski sat down together to convert the script into a shooting script—the one is a dream, the other is a precise plan of action to determine which sets are built and costumes ordered, and how time and money are scheduled. The two men got on very badly. Towne was hesitant, Polanski aggressive. In a story that had so many hints of rape, Towne felt he was being robbed, or got at. Polanski was intent on the bare practicalities, and he felt Towne was clinging to obscurity and doubt. Writers and directors are not always alike, which is one reason they envy each other.

The decisive battle concerned the ending of the film. Towne's initial concept and the story he had sustained throughout his writing process was gentler than the film we know. Evelyn Mulwray (Dunaway) and her daughter were to get away. Noah Cross (Huston) was to be killed. Jake Gittes was left as the patsy.

Polanski had a darker vision. He believed that Evelyn should die. He reckoned it was truer to the worlds of power and corruption that someone like Cross should survive, triumphant. Of course, Polanski had seen dark things in life. He had been a wanderer in Nazi-occupied Poland as his parents went to concentration camps. His wife, Sharon Tate, had been slaughtered by the Manson gang. You do not have to take pity on Roman Polanski; if you did he likely wouldn't care or notice. You can call him cynical, where Towne was romantic. But in *Chinatown* Polanski smelled a necessary tragedy.

At the last minute, on the nights before the final scenes were shot, Polanski rewrote them to his liking. Towne protested in anger and agony. But he had already been barred from the set. And in the crunch, Evans backed Polanski's instincts.

Now here is a strange thing: a great story (a veiled novel, if you like) on which another voice takes over in the last moments to provide an ending the writer loathes.

History has never seen Towne's ending—it never will, for it wasn't shot. And history has not complained. *Chinatown* was an enormous success at the box office. It was nominated for eleven Oscars, and won just for the screenplay. More important, more than twenty-five years later, it is regarded as an American classic, always playing somewhere on television, and a great American movie. And nowadays, among softer movies, it is the tragic conclusion to *Chinatown* (Dunaway dead, and the daughter in the clutches of evil) that is often held up as a proof of the "grown-up" way in which people made movies in the early seventies.

For years, Towne insisted that his ending would have been better. But that became a hard line to argue as the actual film grew more golden in popular memory, and as *Chinatown* is the first product anyone thinks of when Towne's name is mentioned. In the years since the film opened, its script has been published twice, first in 1983 by Neville Publishing of Santa Barbara, and then in 1997 by Grove Press. On both occasions, it is not actually Towne's script (with his ending), but the cutting continuity of the finished film.

Thus, once a film is done, its script becomes the transcript of the final cut.

The Neville edition was copyrighted to Towne, though that may have referred just to the Preface and Postscript. The Grove edition was copyrighted to Long Road Productions (Evans's production unit within Paramount). And so, more lately, Towne has conceded that the matter is at least arguable. Polanski's version may have been more effective.

But the film survives now in paradoxical form, for a writer whose wishes were thwarted continues to get a credit he doesn't entirely deserve. What could Towne have done as the film was made? I suspect he tried everything, for he is eloquent and resourceful and not above strategy. But he faced this simple fact: he did not own the script or its copyright. The producer was the effective owner and it was up to him to decide on the ending. It was unlikely at that late stage in production that Towne would take himself off the picture, or be fired. But earlier on—after the delivery of the first "foggy" draft, say—he could have been fired and replaced with other writers. He would then have kept a credit (according to Writers Guild arbitration) and shared it with the others. But as sole writer, Towne got the whole Oscar and all of the contracted percentage on profits allowed him by his first contract with Evans and Paramount.

I suspect that Polanski's version is more effective and more successful as a movie than Towne's would have been. Which doesn't mean that, as a novel, Towne's might not have been more enduring. But Towne had given up that chance, traded it away with the copyright for up-front money, the chance of profits later, a shot at the Oscar, and the glamour of a movie. And no screenwriter has any reason to blame anyone but himself for compromises involved in that transaction. In the same way, we as an audience—or a culture—should take such compromises into account when judging the impact or value of movies. They derive from corporations and producers, not individuals or artists.

*   *   *

Still, Robert Towne had thought of *Chinatown* like a creator, or like a writer beginning to open up a private world, albeit one found in such public places that it had meaning for millions. And he could not get it out of his head. Those are conditions, or symptoms, of art or of the aspiration to make something we call art. They are there throughout the history of American film, and as a result something susceptible to being regarded as "just business" is often held in high reverence—not always for what it is, but for what it might be. So Robert Towne fell into the notion that *Chinatown* was "his," and something he wanted to pursue.

He had a simple but legitimate plan—the arc of the whole story—which was that Los Angeles was a natural problem where man's ingenuity and dreams of progress had made a civilization, but at the cost of the sweet air. The state's water was stolen, or redirected, and in time, with the rise of "Big Oil," a vast horizontal city lost its existing public transportation so that the industries of automobile and oil could thrive. Thus a megalopolis stands on deadly tectonic faults, with desert on its three land flanks, with traffic congestion and smog gradually corroding its synapses. Yet it feels like heaven some Saturdays, and still serves as a place many people want to come to.

That isn't just background to this book: the way Los Angeles was and may turn out is crucial to the whole equation of movies, and what they have done for us. And I want to stress the theme of Robert Towne's *Chinatown* "trilogy," if only because that great forsaken dream does not directly address the movies. It knows that other things have always gone on in Los Angeles.

Still, Towne wanted to take Jake Gittes further, and he had a famous hit as his impetus, as well as ongoing friendships with Nicholson and Evans.

Of course, after success, Towne had indecisive years. He touched up other scripts, again without getting credit, but the line of his three-in-a-row stopped. His life was troubled; a marriage was on the rocks; he worried a lot over his own health. He did not easily see a way to build a career. One treasured venture—the script of *Greystoke*, a new approach to Tarzan, which he wanted to direct—had to be traded away (a lost child, in his mind) so that he could finish *Personal Best* (1981), his first film as director, and a tribute to women track athletes.

Meanwhile, Jack Nicholson had become one of the best and most beloved of American actors, while Robert Evans had fallen into ignominy, thanks in great part to his reliance on cocaine and the atmospherics of success. (We will come, in time, to that rather vague sea of calamities. For the moment, trust my suggestion that nothing saps real work, good ambition, and art in Hollywood as much as success—and its money habit. For this reason: Earn more than you are used to, and your personal needs begin to rise in a way that no medication can tame. Make a success and you are no longer simply in the art of making films but in the business of making successes.)

Here, by the way, is a profound contradiction in much of Americana: If, in the pursuit of happiness, you do something grand enough to transform your circumstances, your future chance of happiness may be shot, for you have replaced it with the material of success, with money. You may be doomed. And this can leave you bitter. Was this Marlon Brando's pain?

So Robert Towne wants to return to his poem. His idea for the 1947 stage of the story is that Jake Gittes, still an L.A. private eye, meets up with another Jake, Jake Berman, a charming rogue and a busy Jewish entrepreneur (based in part on Towne's own father, Lou). In turn, Jake Berman will lead Gittes to Katherine Mulwray ("She's my sister, she's my daughter"), the fruit of Noah Cross's rape.

But here's the delicate condition of these characters: Towne imagines their ongoing lives, and feels he has a right to them, while the characters are actually the copyrighted and protected property of Paramount Pictures, where very few have ever given a moment's warm thought to their futures. So how will the deal be done for part two?

Towne talks to Nicholson and Evans—he likely fills their heads with the prospect of the story continued. But those are men in the business beset by so many other, larger problems. It's 1985, and Evans has just come out of the disaster of *The Cotton Club,* during which it was once said that he might be implicated in a real murder. Nicholson can do just about what he likes, granted that it's suitable for a bulkier Jack who now looks close to fifty.

In the truest, most artistic sense of things, you might imagine Jake Gittes in 1937, led away by friends with the warning "Forget it, Jake. It's Chinatown," as a stricken man, ruined, heartbroken, a mess. Whereas the real Jack in the mid-eighties (after *Prizzi's Honor* and *Terms of Endearment*) looks pretty much "Made it, Ma! Top of the world!" We all love Jack. I love Jack. But I don't think he can do David Staebler again, the haunted, depressive failure from *The King of Marvin Gardens* (1972). Success can change an actor.

Still, it has made Nicholson bountiful and impulsive to his friends. And so one night, trying to cheer up a sunken, morose Evans, he says, Why don't we do *The Two Jakes* (that is what Towne wants to call it)? At the start of his career, as a beautiful kid, Evans was an actor—not much of one, but enough to persuade the amiable (and possibly floating) Jack that the two pals on screen with some good lines could carry it off. There and then, Nicholson calls Paramount (for he knows they own the rights) and proposes the plan: Towne to write and direct; Nicholson and Evans acting; Evans producing. The leading parties, the elements, would sign on to do it for "next to nothing" up front, but a big cut of the profits later. Make the flick for ten mill, he says. Just us and you—a one-page memo. A nice friendly get-together, a sort of home movie.

"Next-to-nothing" in Towne's case meant $125,000 to deliver a script, a figure that was by then a modest fee for someone of Towne's standing. It was less than he could have commanded elsewhere. But with an expensive divorce and a new marriage in his list of credits, Towne needed money. The script did not come quickly. Evans, and others in the business, noted that with reputation, Towne had become more reluctant to make up his mind. For some time, he had delivered only 80 percent of the script, enough to remind some people of how Polanski had had to "save" or "doctor" the *Chinatown* script with his savage ending. But Polanski could no longer be a part of the Gittes story. He was living in Paris, having jumped bail before the final plea-bargained settlement in a case where he was said to have drugged and raped a minor. Indeed, he said so himself.

The Two Jakes was in pre-production in 1985: Kelly McGillis and Cathy Moriarty were cast in the female roles. Sets were being built and properties gathered. Evans took a vacation to get as lean and tanned as possible.

Then something started to go wrong, and it may never be possible to know exactly what it was. At least two of the pals and partners, Towne and Evans, were very nervous about the project. Evans had not acted in twenty-five years. Well, not professionally; friends and enemies alike reckoned that in real life he was nothing but an act. But he was uncertainly recovered from his drug habit and he was very anxious about his looks. Towne, not unacquainted with drugs himself, was also becoming more suspicious of whether Bob Evans could play a large part—something he had never carried off before. There was some fuss over hairstyling that Evans required, and stories that Evans had lost self-control as the scissors appeared. There were also feelings that the high-strung Towne was very uncertain of directing this picture; *Personal Best* had been a modest achievement, but even people friendly to Towne wondered about his ability to perform in the spotlight and under stress. He had worked so often in secret and alone; that was part of his habit.

On the point of production, in the summer of 1985, *The Two Jakes* collapsed. The essential point of conflict was Towne's belief that Evans had to be replaced. But any hope he had had that Nicholson might take his side was dashed. Nicholson stood by Evans. He said that if "the kid didn't stay in the picture," then he, Nicholson, was gone, too. Or, according to Evans, Nicholson said that, without Evans, the old deal was off and he would want $6 million against 15 percent of the gross (more or less what Nicholson was used to getting in those days).

This changed the entire nature of the film. It left Paramount very alarmed. It raised Towne's own level of tension and agony. It is not my purpose to say that anyone behaved well or badly, or as anything but a hero. (With most Hollywood stories, that is the real confusion or the insoluble problem.) What I want to stress is that Towne, stretched beyond bearable limits financially and emotionally, could not muster the strength to own his project. He was the "weakling" in view; the writer always is, not just because it's been that way during decades of Hollywood history but because in the American picture business the writers have a union that has always pursued better money deals and never tried to regain copyright. Had Towne owned his characters in this dispute, his power would have been quite different, but he had long since bargained away unique authorship for a few hundred thousand dollars here or there.

Production was halted on *The Two Jakes* and Paramount declared (this is beyond proof) that the project had already racked up bills of $3.5 million. In other words, if anyone—Towne included—wanted to step in and take over the script (there was by then a complete script, a good one), the bill would be $3.5 million. There were rumors of Towne trying to set the film up with Harrison Ford and Dustin Hoffman as the two Jakes. But those guys were as expensive as Nicholson. And the public believed that Jake Gittes was Nicholson.

A few years later, Paramount resuscitated *The Two Jakes*. Nicholson now was the director, and he was to be paid $5 million for acting, just scale for directing. Evans was the nominal producer still, but no one took the idea of his acting seriously any longer. Even Evans came close to admitting that Towne had been right in 1985—the big role was more than the kid could handle. It was still Towne's script, but he was wounded, and angry about the turn of events. When Nicholson asked for rewrites, Towne was so slow that Nicholson was compelled to try writing himself. Both parties believed they had been betrayed. The picture turned out to be a dog. Nicholson has never directed again. And Towne's contribution to the rewriting was impeded by his commitment to *Days of Thunder*, the film on which he met the actor who would become his new patron, when the friendships with Nicholson and Warren Beatty were sundered—Tom Cruise.

And that's how someone who was once among the best writers in Hollywood, and who might have written a fine novel about the life and times of Jake Gittes and Los Angeles, became the man who made a small fortune writing two *Mission: Impossible* pictures.

The gap between *Chinatown* and umpteen possible future *Mission: Impossibles* is the lament of this book.

Good cop, bad cop? Two suits at the start of Metro-Goldwyn-Mayer: Irving G. Thalberg and Louis B. Mayer (*Kobal Collection*)

2 · MAYER AND THALBERG

That Saturday conference was a while ago now. Gray Davis was our governor still in California and Arnold Schwarzenegger was getting ready for the serious disappointment of *Terminator 3*. The anxieties over Iraq that Saturday turned out to be the wrong ones. The movies that ruled that March weekend have passed on. Few could name them now. Which makes movies seem as disposable as the daily newspaper. Still, when the young woman asked about *Chinatown* (and I'm not sure she was alive when it was made), everyone in the room seemed to know what she meant. We had absorbed the story of Gittes, Noah Cross, and Evelyn Mulwray along with the water in Los Angeles. And it isn't only in L.A. that people will sometimes observe something in life and murmur a line from a movie to a stranger—"This could be the start of a beautiful friendship"; "Well, nobody's perfect"; or "Forget it Jake. It's Chinatown"— as if we were both of us looking out at the light and the sky (another kind of screen) and congratulating ourselves on the shared day.

In America, we treasure shared things, as if we had a constant fear of being helplessly divided or scattered. There is the constitution and the president; the one great highway that goes everywhere; the eternal filling station; the songs on the radio, the sky, the fast-food franchises. The movies? Lines of dialogue fifty years old are current still. But in an age when the movies actually begin to supply our presidents (as well as educate their style), and bother less with lines, is the sharing what it was?

So when I talk about "the whole equation" I mean not just the history of American movies, but the history of America in the time of movies. I mean a medium that is reviewed in the arts section, and kept count of in the business pages, but which can easily break onto page one if a celebrity is involved. Trained or not, the president now is a pictured figure; he is the man on television. But the equation also extends to children who have watched twenty thousand hours of moving film by the age of eighteen (if they are restrained in that habit)—more hours than they've spent reading. I mean a kind of mathematics in which nearly everything depends on seeing and being seen.

But there's something else about "the whole equation" that applies especially well to *Chinatown*—it's sinister, yet tidy. The film was set in 1937, but when audiences first saw it in 1974 they had no difficulty in (or no way out of) seeing its contemporary relevance. The water rhymed with Watergate, and even if the film made the dark plot clear finally, still, there was no way of punishing Noah Cross for raping the land, or his own daughter. He was in charge, and he could fend you off with dreamy philosophizing as to what exactly constituted "rape." In very much the same way, the artists—the real and the would-be—in film have always sighed and asked, What chance do I have when the business belongs to others? *Chinatown* is not only tragic and foreboding, not just a parable about the ways in which Los Angeles has relied on exploitation, power, rape, greed, and a sense of the future, but a subtle, magical metaphor for Hollywood and filmmaking in which the lone seeker of truth is told to shut up at the end, to go along with being left alive and (probably) paid off, and accept that the system, the business—"they"—are always going to survive and endure and run the show.

It's Jake Gittes, if you like, going back to the apartment where he lives alone in Los Angeles, finding an ample packet of money waiting for him (provided by the agents of Noah Cross), and then getting into the shower and staying there 111 minutes (or whatever), letting the sluice of water and the occasional squirt of scented shampoo begin to wash away the failure, or incipient madness, and the loss of Evelyn Mulwray, who always had something in the way she was being played that made clear she was doomed. No matter what her writer, or creator, intended. And at 111 minutes, that's a lot of water. And Noah Cross (though he seems to have no interest in the business of movies, beyond just being in one of the best) always understood that, pursuing happiness, every Angeleno wanted to feel fresh, clean, and moist to the touch. Moist is sexy.

If this weighing of a picture sounds simple or simply mathematical, I know it is the most complicated in the field—not just because it requires some way of getting into the minds of movie makers, to be able to observe the deals they make with themselves (as well as the contracts struck with the business), but because it pertains to definitions the rest of us like to keep for such things as "art," "truth," and "integrity" as well as "success," "profit," and "fame."

I need to explain where "the whole equation" comes from. When F. Scott Fitzgerald died, on December 21, 1940, off Sunset Boulevard in Los Angeles, he was working on a novel. It is generally known as *The Last Tycoon,* though his last, working title was "The Love of the Last Tycoon, A Western." He might have changed his mind again—which doesn't mean that the title he left isn't useful or suggestive, not least in its unexpected use of "A Western." We will come to that anon, for the slippage between being eastern or western in the U.S. is important, and far more revealing than the mere wearing of cowboy hats and six-guns. Indeed, the rather camp accoutrements of the "Western" genre have steadily blocked our recognition of the imaginative novelty it was to be Western.

As it developed, *The Last Tycoon* is a novel about Hollywood in which the central character is Monroe Stahr (see how the name mixes classical American history with Jewish immigration and a kind of heavenly light), a producer of films, a famous genius in his world and the creative head of a motion picture studio. Stahr's studio is not named, but readers have always assumed that Stahr is based on the real figure of Irving Grant Thalberg. That's reasonable and correct, up to a point. Thalberg, born in Brooklyn in May 1899 (though the family was from near Coblenz, Germany), was a sickly kid. He never risked tiring himself with college. Instead, at just nineteen, he started working for Carl Laemmle, the head of Universal.

Thalberg ran that large enterprise. He promoted Lon Chaney, the first star of horror, and he reined in the house monster of arrogance and auteurism, Erich von Stroheim. At the age of twenty-three, reluctant to marry or hurt Laemmle's daughter (it was the way of moguls then to want the whole man in an employee), he joined the company of Louis B. Mayer. A year later, Mayer linked up with the Metro and Goldwyn companies. Hollywood had mergers like Texas had oil wells in those days, and most of them faded away, but Metro-Goldwyn-Mayer is something we all know. M-G-M was the studio of studios in what we call the golden age of American film. And Thalberg was its creative boss for some of that time; he was the original for the model that would be Robert Evans one day, so it's downright tidy (as well as crazy) that in 1957, in *Man of a Thousand Faces* (with James Cagney as Lon Chaney), Evans should have played Thalberg.

Irving held his position at M-G-M from 1924 until 1932. He had a serious heart attack that last year, and went to Europe to recuperate. Upon his return, he discovered that his powers at the studio were moderated. Which was also a way of saying that Thalberg, the boy wonder, had by then incurred the envy and the competitive energies of Mr. Mayer—older, stronger, coarser, a winner in most things, no matter the damage left by his victories.

Thalberg married the actress Norma Shearer, just one of the leading ladies at M-G-M. (Surely that shows how much his trim soul was drawn to be wild and "creative.") He did, in great part, supervise the busy creative affairs of the studio, and he was enormously admired for his efficiency, his taste, his relatively gentle ways, and that overhanging shadow, the illness likely to claim him one day. The harder he worked, the more hushed the studio became. Mayer had two daughters, Edith and Irene, and he had warned them not to get romantic about Irving—who was also smart, funny, handsome, and gallant—because he wasn't going to last. Maybe the thing Mayer most loved about Irving was that throb of self-sacrifice—so long as, sooner or later, Irving went.

Fitzgerald, briefly, had been hired and fired as a screenwriter by Thalberg in the days when Scott was a hot novelist. As an employee and a celebrity, he had been up at the Thalberg house. Norma Shearer had been sweet to him. And Fitzgerald had been around the studio enough by 1940 to write those superb passages of *The Last Tycoon* that show Stahr's working day, and the brisk, dispassionate, tireless yet tired way in which he ticked off the unending list of problems, or decisions. Stahr is like Thalberg in that he is quietly spoken, possesses an inward intelligence, is by no means insensitive, but is seemingly unable to get himself out of the cockpit of work that will kill him sooner or later.

Furthermore, Stahr is more than just a studio executive. There is something loftier about him, a presidential vision even, a mind that sees pictures as being vaguely—very vaguely—good for America.

There is another model for Stahr: David O. Selznick, another boy wonder without much formal education, but far brasher, more effusive and arrogant than Thalberg. Selznick talked, and dictated memos, as if he would never run out of energy—and as if there was no end to his superior insights. A noisy upstart briefly at M-G-M, he got himself promoted by way of Paramount to be head of production at RKO, a smaller, cheaper outfit than M-G-M. Along the way, to the melodramatic outrage of Louis B., Selznick married Irene Mayer in 1930. But then, Mayer looked to this unwelcome son-in-law as the instrument that might replace Irving. This maneuvering never dissuaded Mayer from his vast and vulgar public addiction to such things as loyalty and family ties. So, as Irving fell ill, young Selznick was hired on as a producer.

Selznick did well at M-G-M, so much so that in 1935 he formed his own company, Selznick International. One of the great novelties of this venture was its reliance on East Coast, WASP money (from Jock Whitney, whose father had left the largest estate then appraised in America, $179 million; the Lehman brothers, investment bankers; and the financier John D. Hertz) raised through social contacts. In 1936, Selznick bought the rights to *Gone With the Wind* as the project that would determine his equation. And among the many writers he hired and fired on that film was Fitzgerald (by then thought of as a notable "failure"). The novelist couldn't deliver what David wanted. No one could, for David was an egotist armored by never knowing exactly what he wanted.

Selznick was not like Stahr personally, not nearly as efficient or clear-thinking. And to keep up with Stahr's workload, Selznick was a benzedrine addict, as well as a slave to cigarettes, gambling, grandeur of all sorts, and regular, mindless womanizing.

But Selznick had Irene, maybe the darkest, most intelligent, watchful, and conspiratorial woman in Hollywood, a match for her husband's enthusiasm as for her father's Machiavellian sportiveness. Louis B. Mayer said often that Irene—never mind David or Irving—could have been head of the studio if she'd been born a man. Well, sometimes she came close.

And she comes very close to Cecilia Brady, the narrative voice in *The Last Tycoon*, in the way that Nick Carraway serves in *The Great Gatsby.* Cecilia is only of college age as the book begins, but she is the child of the man who holds the position at Stahr's studio that Mayer held at M-G-M. And Cecilia is a movie person—she has been all her life "in a position to watch the wheels go round." She is too practical or too experienced to be excited by Hollywood:

> My father was in the picture business as another man might be in cotton or steel, and I took it tranquilly. At the worst I accepted Hollywood with the resignation of a ghost assigned to a haunted house. I knew what you were supposed to think about it but I was obstinately unhorrified.

That is good writing yet it does not adequately describe many people of Cecilia's or her father's generations. In those times, people were aroused by the power of pictures, as well as the novelty. Their basis for life had been transformed by the movies; they reckoned they had an elixir. By 1940, perhaps, for a broken man like Fitzgerald, and by now surely for us, a more rueful wisdom is necessary. Just as we should never believe in Hollywood's advertising or its worldview, so we should stay doggedly unhorrified at the horror stories in which it takes equal pride. Stay calm and cool—it's your best chance of taking in the history of it all, as opposed to being made giddy by the roller-coaster. And see that, even at college, Cecilia is born with the kind of mind that can see all the way home:

> You can take Hollywood for granted like I did, or you can dismiss it with the contempt we reserve for what we don't understand. It can be understood too, but only dimly as in flashes. Not half a dozen men have ever been able to keep the whole equation of pictures in their heads. And perhaps the closest a woman can come to that set-up is to try and understand one of those men.

We must forgive that last sentence, or hope that Fitzgerald would have dropped it eventually. I can hear the sneer of contempt with which Irene Selznick—the older woman, the one I knew—would have made a show of reading it, and then her theatrical, appalled look as she tossed the book aside. She threw things the way her father had fits, I suspect. Still, the rest of the paragraph is why we're here, for it suggests not just that this under-standing is very unusual because of all the emotional prejudices that get in the way, but that it is fleeting. You can get it, but then you have to keep it in your head, something that growing older, more successful, wiser, or more addled cannot help. You note, too, I hope, how far the general pol-icy—that of survival, living there—is to take it for granted, without asking troubling questions, whether you're in Versailles or Treblinka. Or getting along as best you can.

Of course, Cecilia doesn't say what the whole equation is. It isn't there on the page, the kind of thing a spy could be charged for stealing. She tells us only that it exists, or may once have been known. I'm not sure that I can do much better for you, if you are determined to have a fortune-cookie answer. But if we ask the question in enough ways we may end up knowing so much more.

Actually, I am more hopeful than that, for I am asking for the possibil-ity, the need, even the duty for whole understanding. It can be done; it can embrace the murder and the majesty, the business statistics and millions of us being moved, the art and the awfulness. What I am thinking of is a one-volume account, a history, of magicians, con men, hacks, and scoundrels (and their ladies, too, never fear). Such a book is seldom attempted nowadays. The film bookshelf has become so specialized. No one thinks to try the history of the whole thing in a way that could accom-modate the artistic careers, the lives of the pirates, the ebb and flow of business, the sociological impact—in short the wonder in the dark, the cal-culation in the offices, and the staggering impact on America of moving pictures. Which is also the thunderous artillery of America unleashed on the world. And maybe because it is too hard.

To be whole, the equation needs all of those things. And more.

* * *

I wonder if the smartest thing about Cecilia Brady as a creation isn't that deliberate stress on the humdrum—Hollywood? So what?—as if to say, Don't think it reveals or exposes me. I can only say that Irene Selznick as an old woman was less cautious about revealing herself. So, too many times a day for the comfort of her relatives, servants, and spectators (her audience), you could see the poor child of Russian immigrants raised in strenuous humility yet inwardly on fire because in this new America she was a princess, a kind of daughter to the tsar, with much to be avenged.

When we go to the movies, for good or ill, we are playing with prospects of reinvention or transformation—becoming that radiant figure on the screen, or living as if we inhabited a movie. We aren't just watching actors; we are summoning acting for our very being. Fun? Perilous? It's both, of course, but think of the stress on those first moviemakers, the ones who had risen in a slow dissolve from shtetl to palace. Once upon a time in the long winters and humid summers of the severe and testing East, out of an historical experience of man's meager virtues and many shortcomings, the founding fathers had emerged with a grim, spartan, superb code that culminated in life, liberty, and the pursuit of happiness.

Whereupon, in only a little over twenty years, a band of foreigners, the majority of them Jewish, uneasy with the English language, had arrived and found a trick of the light with which, they said, they could provide the thing itself. Not that they were frauds or hucksters or crooks (though there were traces of those vigorous attitudes), but they were thoroughly alien to the mood of the thirteen colonies, to the tough standards of the New England literary tradition, and the harsh elect of Puritanism. You could say they were un-American—and some did. But the American code was flexible enough to absorb them. Yet still, the country was agitated by the question as to whether it was decent for these newcomers to fulfill the splendid ideals of the Republic.

How easy, how hard, was it for a man like Louis B. Mayer? And how easy, or hard, is it for those of us who love film and the movies—call it cinema, even—to acknowledge that Mayer is one of those with a claim to possessing the equation?

He was a huge storyteller in his own head and a relentless actor, in that he could not leave real life alone. He had to direct it, play it, rewrite it, present it. How easy or natural it was to see himself as a kind of Moses in a great parable and a virgin country. He had come by way of lowly birth in Russia to be a scrap merchant—an itinerant, physical laborer, likely to be thrashed by his illiterate father—in England briefly, then in Canada and New England. Ready to try anything, and already adjusted from changing Lazar Meier into Louis B. Mayer, he began to buy up nickelodeon arcades in the years before the First World War in and around Boston. He had noticed that people liked going into the dark to see the light.

If that seems like a fairy-tale way of putting it, don't rule out the degree to which people were drawn by the vague suggestion of magic, reversal of old orders, or even transformation. The appeal of movies is beyond the sensible, the rational, or the hard-working. Going into the dark, after centuries of progress in which mankind has staggered toward artificial light, smacks of delicious perversity. Maybe it has to do with how many of them there were, how crowded and inadequate "home" was, or some urge to gather in anonymous crowds in the dark of strange palaces. No commentators remarked on such things at the time, certainly not Mayer, if people would pay a nickel each. Five cents, in a room that held 100. Ten shows a day = 5,000 cents = $50. With maybe 50,000 people in the vicinity, you could easily play a show—a collection of bits and pieces—for a week. All you needed was the hall, some chairs, a projection machine, and someone who could handle it. And the films.

Mayer could do the same arithmetic for scrap iron, for rag and bone, waste paper—whatever raw or rank commodity you care to think of—and he wasn't yet convinced that one was superior to another. Getting rid of people's garbage—with all the new people there seemed to be in the cities, with the risks of smell and infection—that could be the winner. Make nice for people! But he was open-minded, and he kept a wad of money in his back pocket, ready to buy an idea if he saw it. Or a person, even.

By 1910 he was a plump, prosperous little tough in a terrific new suit and tie in Boston. And by 1915, without ever having made a foot of film himself yet, he had the wit, the brilliance, to corner the New England distribution rights for D. W. Griffith's *The Birth of a Nation.* He did the sums, and acquired that unprecedented film—the first sensational picture, so extraordinary that people would sit for three hours and more to follow it through. He knew that "everyone" wanted to see it, and he guessed that, whatever the deal they struck, no one in Griffith's organization, least of all the grand man himself, knew how or had the stamina or the time to be everywhere and see how many actually paid to see the film on Thursday in Natick, Newton, Lynn, Saugus, or Woburn, Massachusetts, to say nothing of Manchester, New Hampshire, Rutland, Vermont, or Bangor, Maine.

Mayer and his operatives were the only ones with a need to know, and they would have the paper rolls of coins—unaccounted for, unnumbered and adding weight to a punch if necessary—so they could slip a few back to the arcades and theaters for silence to prevail. Even so, there would still be a fortune going back to Griffith, who was weary and dazed from his Civil War story, and observing how one cut could seem to send a current through the crowd. He was already thinking of his next film—nothing less ambitious than *Intolerance,* a profuse study of man's wrongs to men, the whole of history in a nutshell. Griffith was stunned by the plenty, and he wanted to think pictures—the next picture. If Griffith had been in Natick or Newton every night he'd never have been Griffith. Mayer could see the principle of a new business: a Griffith needed men like Mayer, and had to be prepared to pay for them.

Within ten years, Mayer had been so carried along by the business and the crowd, and by his own elation at having made the right guesses, that he got to mix with beautiful actresses instead of sewage experts, and had strangers in the street stop him and shake his hand and thank him for that week's picture, so he and the stranger, in delighted concert, might reenact its great scenes. He felt he was serving the inner beings of his people— their souls, say—as if his business was akin to a new form of religion. Griffith, meanwhile, was pretty close to being washed up, passed over by rapid history, a drunk, a womanizer, an historical figure.

Mayer could put his wife, his two daughters, and even the wreck of his brutal father in a fine house in Los Angeles, and he could feel that California—sleepy before the movies came—was every bit as fine a place for them as ever Moses imagined. A Western—remember? Goodbye to the dense streets of Boston, made narrower by snow walls, the smoke from factories, and the throngs of the poor. In California, there was sun, space, and fertility. Don't forget the water, please (did Noah Cross ever shake hands with Mayer?). There was still fragrance in the air—Robert Towne was ten years away from being born, the son of a Russian real estate king. Think of the lacy sea unfurling on the hard blond beaches. And if you were a hit you could buy acres of land and put up palaces.

Mayer became in just a few more years not only the highest paid man in America, but a personal friend of President Herbert Hoover. The president of the company? No, the country. As well as Thalberg's boss, he was the stern father figure to lost ladies like Greta Garbo and Jean Harlow (why do you think those names rhyme if there isn't some secret, open-vowel scheme in charge?) and the patron of all the storytelling. He was also the constant advocate of family virtues, on- and off-screen, who could also, any afternoon he dreamed, in his cream-colored office, have some hopelessly hopeful young woman swallow his gray cum and call it cream, because at his level of authority Mayer needed to become sophisticated and compartmentalized. And he could hire the girl as a typist or a message-carrier, which was a good job, with prospects, and all the excitement of working close to the light and the glamour and the magic. If the girl was smart enough, why, she could see the light and even put it to Mayer as a business proposition—he was open-minded with money—that the swallowing of cum could be industrialized in a suitably removed part of town. Why not? For what the story of Louis B. Mayer taught the world—and he was a teacher—was the value of imitation and catering to people. And making nice. Joan Crawford swallowed her share of cum, and her lips shone in close-ups. How do you think lip gloss got invented?*

So, yes, Mayer did the money equations all the time in his head. And he was the first man—maybe the only one—who ever ran a humming factory system that had all its sound stages and its contract artists at work all the time, with one picture coming out a week, and the whole thing profitable. In the 1920s he knew the numbers—the size of the audience, budgets for the pictures, the overhead, the promotion—and M-G-M was secure as a subsidiary of Loew's, Inc., the distribution company, and it was Mayer who would go back east to see and talk to Marcus Loew or Nicholas Schenck, the ultimate powers in the company.

And surely he had reason sooner or later to believe that Nick Schenck for one was plotting against him, if only because the power and the glory were so great. And Irving was a lever that Nick might use—not that Irving knew or helped—to dispose of Mayer one day. So L.B. learned to plot himself, and he got rid of Irving, or leaned on the fragility of his constitution. Irving was never as simpleminded or as treacherous as Louis had taught himself to be. Irving never took the time just to be an emperor in his empire. He was doing things, managing, correcting, helping, editing, tidying up.

Irving Thalberg is still something of a mystery, as if illness had taken away more than anyone guessed, including devil, libido, or malice. And it's not as if Monroe Stahr clears up the mystery. Stahr was married once—to an actress, Minna Davis—who died. In the book he is in pursuit of the flimsy, elusive Kathleen Moore, who stands for little in real life except Fitzgerald's kindness toward Sheilah Graham, the last woman he loved and lived with. He is hopelessly in love with her, in ways that seem to overawe Kathleen and surpass Fitzgerald's skill (or interest?) in describing love. Let's be fair: love is hard to do, and so much less compelling than the way Stahr, the boss, manages to look at pages of script or dailies from several different projects and sniff out where a real movie is coming to life, or going astray. In one passage, he teaches a celebrated English author, Boxley, the possible yet specious secret about how to write for the movies.

That is Fitzgerald at his best, and it shows a great novelist wistful at a new kind of writing, or telegraphese, that had come into being just as he, Scott, was getting started, and might be enough to derail many promising

*There's a real argument about Mayer—whether he dreamed or acted. That's in keeping with the mystery of the movies. Other executives did take advantage, and for women the power was always there—like the creaminess of Mayer's office.

authors. There is even a hint in Stahr, talking to a real writer, of wanting to ask, Why did you ever come here to this godless, bookless place?

Mayer would never have understood that dilemma: he loved to have famous authors at the dinner table. Wasn't it Mayer to whom George Bernard Shaw lamented, Ah, the trouble is, you are interested only in art, while I am here for the money? L.B. wasn't educated; he wasn't a picture-maker. Which isn't to say that Mayer couldn't build a moment in life into a melodrama, or a farce, or a tragedy, so pressured that onlookers could hardly breathe. Whereas Irving would never have had the vulgarity to behave like that—like a magician without a trick. But he had learned enough about movies to see how a certain thing shown provocatively plus information withheld equaled suspense. He had described Hitchcockery before Hitch was famous in America. Yet Stahr tells the story less with relish than suspicion. He knows it is a trick, as opposed to profundity, and he has begun to worry over that gap.

It's as if Thalberg was alarmed by the empty power. I can find nothing in his career to suggest that he was compelled by this insight. He had no passion to be a Griffith or a Hitchcock, and in fact Thalberg is justly known in film history for the various ways in which he controlled wayward directors. Stahr is clearly a good editor and co-writer, a wonderful encouragement to lost, blocked or neurotic people in pursuit of film. His day, so well recounted by Fitzgerald via Cecilia, is a succession of quick problem-solving turns and a portrait of mounting dispassion. One of those problems is guiding a becalmed director away from his own set so that a replacement can take over. Stahr could be—had to be—bleak or cruel, but he has no taste for cruelty, the thing that was sauce in Mayer's daily diet.

Thalberg presided over success for nearly a decade—many stars, high production values, cheerful stories—and he was good or tireless enough to keep the wheels turning. But he did not make piercing or great pictures, and he does not seem to have been touched by the certainty that such things might exist. He is as vital, say, as the chief editor at a publishing house, epitomizing taste and value, able to give key moments—epiphanies, even—to the valuable writers, turning up at openings, parties, and so on, but actually so exhausted that he can hardly read any more.

It's likely that Irving, in practice, defined himself as what he wanted to be, in terms of how he differed from Mayer. Irving was sophisticated, courteous, worldly, meticulous, self-effacing, dutiful, efficient—wonderful qualities, and essential, too, but so remote from the greedy, cruel, vain passion that time and again gets great movies made.

Los Angeles is on the edge. Times change, but the roads always drain away into the desert. David Hockney, *Pearblossom Hwy., 11–18th April 1986* (second version), photography collage. *(© David Hockney. J. Paul Getty Museum, Los Angeles)*

3 · THE PLACE

I wonder if there wasn't a moment in which even the sickly Irving Thalberg reckoned he might beat the odds in California. In his youth, California was endlessly promoted for its health; the orange became an emblem for wholesomeness and vitality, and I suppose that zest lasted until O.J. went to court. In 1872, a New Yorker, Charles Nordhoff, published a book, *California: For Health, Wealth, and Residence,* a model for the new West in that the title does not mention duty, guilt, or community spirit. The West was for anyone who could get there. Arnold Schwarzenegger is just the most recent convert.°

°One who read Nordhoff's book was a Dubliner living in Pittsburgh, William Mulholland, who by 1877 was in L.A. on his way to procuring the Owens River water . . . and *Chinatown.*

As a boy in Brooklyn, Thalberg had spent the better part of his child-hood in bed. He must have heard doctors' talk about a rheumatic heart and a short life. According to Sam Marx, who worked for Thalberg at M-G-M, and loved him, the invalid's mother led a life of "sponging his body hourly, rubbing him down, giving him enemas, placing hot-water bottles by his feet and always encouraging him to believe he was destined to win his battle with the constant pain in his chest."

Well, maybe, but if it's in a Metro movie, sooner or later the young Robert Taylor is going to groan, "Mother! For heaven's sake!" He's going to be out of his bed, taking his chances—which, to me, corresponds with a level, amused, and shyly ready gaze seen in most Thalberg photographs. There's only so much sponging a guy can take. No matter that he was thin and on the cusp, I think Thalberg was brave and hopeful, funny and mod-ern. Try this story: Irving and Norma Shearer had a child, a son. Just back from the hospital, the notoriously intelligent Thalberg came through the studio gates and told the first well-wisher, "Sure, he's fine. And the doctors say he has the intelligence of a three-week-old, already."

How can this Brooklyn boy with a head on his shoulders not be so when he gets the first full-frontal chance to face the great roar of life that is the sun, the light, the warmth, the space, and the "come on, baby" of the West? I can offer you one lovely version of such a scene. It's in *Bugsy,* where Warren Beatty has suggested quite ably (albeit in his clenched, restrained way, too smart really to be a character) the confusion and uncertainty in Ben Siegel, and has even allowed the possibility that the man's shocking violence is a response to his confusion. Then one day he's out driving in Nevada with Virginia Hill and Mickey Cohen, and they argue, and he stomps away from the car in a huff. And as hurt feelings carry him farther into the desert, the long-shot camera sees him stop. Without close-up or heavenly choir (thank you, Barry Levinson), he has a vision or an epiphany: to fill up a little bit of that space, to challenge sun-light with neon, to put the Flamingo and even modern Las Vegas itself there. Where there was Biblical wilderness of the most unpromising kind (125 degrees in the midday summer sun), he sees real estate.

There are strange stories of the light in Los Angeles that ignore the old alarms about smog. David Hockney has spoken of being a child in overcast northern England and seeing Laurel and Hardy movies where "Stan and Ollie, bundled in their winter overcoats, were casting these wonderfully strong crisp shadows." Is it therefore the drama or the accenting of the local light? What is film noir but the night with shadows? Is this a myth? For *The New Yorker,* Lawrence Weschler found cameraman John Bailey

(*American Gigolo*) who said, No, the L.A. light is brighter than else-where—you can measure it on a light meter. And then he found an astronomer, Glen Cass, who said the air is more still, more lucid, more sta-ble. It's as if light is some lovely aspic, purchasable by the pound. L.A.— lies allowed, or light alive?

For years in moviemaking, this exhilarating light was taken for granted, yet it was a gold richer than that found in the Sierra in 1849. Think of all the surfaces California's light could grace—the desert, the ocean, the for-est, the foothills, the mountains, prairie farmland (and even cities as time went by). And now, that light is being discarded as imagery becomes digi-tal, electronic, computer-generated. I don't mean to be religious, but this is a new kind of vanity.

Moviemaking fell in love with love because of California's light. But the escape westward was also the need to shrug off controls and cramping reg-ulators in the East—the Motion Picture Patents Company, a syndicate that tried to monopolize the various inventions that had made filmmaking possible. In the West, the journeying became an epic of pioneering and courage, but it was also an escape from old ways and wearisome ties. It was the start of broken families in America.

In the West, a new business set up its own closed shop. In the burgeon-ing Los Angeles, Hollywood's leaders gained a privileged position with the city's legal system. For decades, the LAPD played ball with the studios, just as Washington overlooked business crimes. Examples will occur in this narrative, large and small, of pictures ignoring the law or remaking it for its own ends. They all contribute to the Eastern wisdom that law enforcement is different in the West. Look at the O. J. Simpson case; look at the wretched tradition whereby Californian celebrities slip away from punishment. Look at the Gray Davis recall—what was that but the West-ern notion that, if you don't like the law, recast it?

You can say that the Western light is medicine for depression, the gor-geous palette in David Hockney's panoramas of pools and canyons, or the blaze of outlaw panache under which Sam Peckinpah's men ride, wild bunches polished by magic hour. It's heady, romantic, and not always that far from craziness, something like those dreams that Joan Didion is coro-ner to in *Where I Was From* (a study in regret that oddly omits the influ-ence of her source of health insurance, Hollywood).

This may sound fanciful, but consider the liberty given to sex and vio-lence (to outlawry, or departures from the staid norm) that have always made the excitement in American movies—with a certain irony, yet thrilled, too, as Jean-Luc Godard would say in the 1950s, that all you needed for a movie was a girl and a gun—or the chance to play freely with those dangerous elements. The light and the pursuit of liberty are intimately connected—they have provided the beauty in American film, and a lot of the lies. There is a glamour, a life enhancement, a romance, in American cinematography that you do not find in other countries, and I think it's because other nations have (or had) an abiding, if sadder, respect for the habit of fatalism or reality.° In American films, the camera tells a certain truth—it records appearance—but then it adjusts the appearance so that it becomes a lovelier version of itself, an ideal often, but a nightmare, too. Anything except the real thing. You have to have had the experience of beholding a pristine landscape, glowing but empty, to know where that betrayal comes from.

Look at Wyatt Earp. In life, Earp was a characteristic new Westerner. Born in Illinois in 1848, he was early on discontented, a wanderer, edging his way westward. He was a gambler and even an owner of casinos, and he was a gunman whose prowess got him into marshalling when that was a way of gaining power in raw, new townships. He passed through Tombstone, Arizona, and became a prospector in Alaska and later a boxing referee—because of his celebrity. Along the way, he abandoned a few wives. And by the end of his life (he died in 1929) he was in and around Los Angeles, "advising" on pictures about the West, men who wore stars, and himself. No wonder we have never had a movie that comes close to the complicated truths of Earp. As Gary Cooper once said to a young screenwriter struggling on a Cooper script, "Look, it works best if you just make me the hero."

But for that alchemy, you need the light. "Put the light where the money is," was a standard rule of Hollywood filmmaking.

That's one reason why this is a history book. For there is an error in conventional film histories in the notion that southern California and El Pueblo de Nuestra Señora la Reina de los Ángeles de Porciúncula began with the movie business. Moreover, to some degree, the whole story of *Chinatown,* and its historical basis, with William Mulholland bringing water from the Owens Valley to Los Angeles in 1913, has added to the illusion.

You see, the place was already hopping in ways that were primed to welcome pictures.

In 1850, as London possessed Dickens, the clamor of Victorian progress and the plans for next year's Great Exhibition, the entire Los

---

°By now, this light, or shining, is universal and taken for granted—it is the desire urged upon us by advertising, or the light that falls on produce in the market.

Angeles area—by which I mean an area that would reach now from past Malibu to Huntington Beach and as far inland as Azusa—had a population of about 2,500. Earlier, in about 1776—the age of Mozart, Samuel Johnson, and Thomas Jefferson—one might ride days in southern California without bumping into scruffy Indians or Spanish priests taking their siesta. Go back to the cockpit of Tudor England, with Shakespeare talking to himself in his Forest of Arden, and California was vacant.

By 1890, the population was 150,000; by 1915, it was a million, more than six times greater. That is an extraordinary jump, the kind of increase that has been counted in Las Vegas in modern times, and in southern Nevada as a whole—the fastest-growing part of the United States for a couple of decades. Yet famously we all know that Cecil B. De Mille (born in Massachusetts) was the first person to shoot a movie in the area—in a barn in Hollywood—in 1913 (the very year Mulholland's fresh water arrived).

Granted, there were film stirrings before De Mille; allow that he, if not truly first, was promoter enough to seize the title. Still, there was something happening in southern California, and it had a lot to do with advertising.

It was in the 1870s and the 1880s that the Santa Fe Railroad and the Southern Pacific opened up the Los Angeles basin. And as any lover of Howard Hawks's *Red River* knows, the railroads made the West possible and permitted sons to outstrip their fathers. The railroad was the mechanics of dreaming; it was a great tracking shot into the future. And because there were competing companies, so there was a price war to get people onto the trains heading West if imagination wasn't quite sufficient. The price went as low as $1 for a ticket from Kansas City to Los Angeles. That's where the multiple of five comes into the history of the equation, and that's how easily the settled population of the Midwest was persuaded to think of a new life.

It seems to me highly likely that there were some Angeleno entrepreneurs in that age who might have tried to influence the railroads. Suppose that Noah Cross is sixty-seven in 1937 (John Huston's age when *Chinatown* was shot); it follows that Cross's father might have helped finesse that deal, with a lanky young son eating up the lessons, and seeing a fine young woman in a white dress with a peach parasol getting off one of the trains— Evelyn's mother? I know in *Chinatown* that Noah Cross speaks of the huge magnetism of the future. But such men have pasts that prove how long ago the future began.

In *Chinatown,* Jake Gittes asks Noah Cross how much he's worth: "Over ten million?" And you have to hear the sweet exhalation of John

Huston's answer, as fragrant and potent as the steam off fresh horse dung: "Oh, my, yes." It's the base fact and the ad, hand in glove, which is itself a working definition of good movie talk: speak the info, but say it with style. Cross was likely oil and water: he owned the Department of Water and Power for a time, and surely he had money in the new oil business. Oil kept popping out of the L.A. basin at the turn of the century, and you can still see the rigs on the flatlands, or even a single machine in a man's backyard, pumping away at the land, as he waits to be James Dean in *Giant*.

What you need to imagine most fully was the sheer sport of Los Angeles around 1890. Strip away all that is there now and just see the landscape: those beaches; the great arc of Santa Monica Bay; the winding shape of the Los Angeles River, meeting the sea at Long Beach; the ridge we now call Mulholland; the forested canyons of Topanga; the rolling, fertile ground in the valley. Yes, I said fertile, because in 1890 there was water enough in the Los Angeles area for people to live and for every kind of fruit to grow easily. There was the the Los Angeles River, there were wells, and there was the runoff from melted snow that came down from San Bernardino. And at nearly every time of year the weather was delightful— three hundred days of sun, they would be saying soon, and desert-hot sometimes. But, truly, it was a place tempered by balmy sea breezes on which you could smell fruit, earth, growth, horses, and the sea. It was a paradise, over which realty advertising could easily enthuse as the perfect place, a place you'd want to be if you got a glimpse or a sniff of it. Come on down! It's so hard to exclude the happy air of advertising because the amiable facts were hyped from the beginning, in the way famous Western characters were asked for their autographs (if they could write).

There are those who lament all that has been lost as eight million or more have crowded into the basin. And, yes, Los Angeles has in its time been afflicted by smog, the collected exhaust from cars trapped in the valley, although no part of the modern world has done more to ameliorate smog with car emission controls. The Noah Crosses of government or industry can get some things right. And though I recognize the use of the railroad at the end of *The Man Who Shot Liberty Valance* as a symbol of crushing progress, I still think it's a bit two-faced of John Ford (born in Maine), who only got out to the West of his dreamworld by train.

So it wasn't a hard sell in 1880. Which didn't stop those sellers and showmen who loved hype and deals for their own sake. And just as selling was recognized as a kind of art, so the properties and the house were an expression of mad, liberated individualism. In the cities of the East people had lived in regimentation: in identical tenements; in apartments in geo-

metrical buildings; as units within superb and often very handsome struc-
tures. But in the West, where space seemed so much more of a raw material, there was a frenzy of self-expression.

Here's a moment from a popular novel of 1910, *The Rules of the Game*
(a poignant title for movie-lovers), by Stewart Edward White. Two heroes,
Bob and Baker, have come at last to Los Angeles:

> At first glance the city seemed to him like any other. Then, as he wan-
> dered its streets, the marvel and vigor and humor of the place seized him.
>
> "Don't you suppose I see the joke?" complained Baker at the end of
> one of their long trolley rides. "Just get onto that house; it looks like a
> mission-style switch engine. And the one next to it, built to shed snow.
> Funny! Sure it's funny. But you ain't talking to me! It's alive! Those fellows
> wanted something different from anybody else—so does everybody. After
> they'd used up the regular styles, they had to make 'em up out of fresh air.
> But anyway, they weren't satisfied just to copy Si Golosh's idea of a Noah's
> Ark chicken coop."

Making it up out of fresh air. And without any concession to taste, overall planning policy, or architectural tradition—but just for the hell of it,
because you can. It's interesting that this surreal variety in Los Angeles
architecture—and it's there still, though disappearing (the city has got
taste lately in a big way)—is so often compared with the classic Hollywood
studio's ability to re-create any place in the world, or in your fancy. Reyner
Banham, a professor of architecture history and one of the better writers
on Los Angeles, wrote in 1971:

> Los Angeles has seen in this century the greatest concentration of fantasy-
> production, as an industry and as an institution, in the history of Western
> man. In the guise of Hollywood, Los Angeles gave us the movies as we
> know them and stamped its image on the infant television industry. And
> stemming from the impetus given by Hollywood as well as other causes,
> Los Angeles is also the home of the most extravagant myths of private
> gratification and self-realization, institutionalized now in the doctrine of
> "doing your own thing."

The willful use of whatever style grabbed your fancy was in vogue
before the movies arrived, and was a big part of the first explosion of Los
Angeles. To assert how deeply Western this is (and again, we do not expect
the Western movie to be architecturally interesting), just look at examples

close to Los Angeles. In San Francisco, a nice compromise was struck between Eastern or European urban planning and Western liberty in that the private residences sit in what seem like neat rows, but it is only on close examination that you find the lust for variation from building to building, allowing you to marvel at a late Victorian city where no two houses are identical. The other example, of course, is Las Vegas, where the emotional atmosphere of a building (its theme) rules, and where one extravaganza can be razed so that another can be erected. Buildings in Vegas are not meant to last longer than moods. Is that insane, or more human?

Bob and Baker, the two guys from *The Rules of the Game*, are staggered by what they see in Los Angeles, and they know that this is a new kind of city, not attempted before in human history. They see that the salesmen are addicted to their own hype, riding very close to fraud. But at the same time, they see that "if all the lots are ever sold, Los Angeles will have a population of five million."

Actually, as the two men explore the young city, White fills us with glee at the sense of the crowd. Somehow, this feels like more than a mere million. This is the eternal, infinite crowd in the total city such as Dickens might have described it:

> Electric signs blazed everywhere. Bob was struck by the numbers of clairvoyants, palm readers, Hindu frauds, crazy cults, fake healers, Chinese doctors and the like thus lavishly advertised. The class that elsewhere is pressed by necessity to the inexpensive dinginess of back streets, here blossomed forth in truly tropical luxuriance. Street vendors with all sorts of things, from mechanical toys to spot eradicators, spread their portable lay-outs at every corner. Vacant lots were crowded with spielers of all sorts—religious or political fanatics, vendors of cure-alls, of universal tools, of marvelous axle grease, of anything and everything to catch the idle dollar. Brilliantly lighted shops called the passer-by to contemplate the latest wave-motor, flying machine, door check, or what-not. Stock in these enterprises was for sale—and was being sold! Other sidewalk booths, like those ordinarily used as dispensaries of hot doughnuts and coffee, offered wild-cat mining shares, oil stock and real estate in some highly speculative suburb.

All of a sudden, you wonder whether maybe the movies were a little late in getting to California.

*   *   *

If there were about 150,000 people in greater Los Angeles in 1890, it's notable that I can find only one of them living there at that time who would have a really significant career in motion pictures: Victor Fleming, a rather forgotten figure now, but the credited director on those two major events of 1939, *The Wizard of Oz* and *Gone With the Wind,* preeminent American movies. Fleming was born in Pasadena in 1883, was alleged to have Red Indian blood, and was a prominent sportsman and gentleman, very handsome and athletic and permanently tanned, typical of a self-created elite in a new land—a man who did not bother to hide his anti-Semitic feelings about the Jews who ran the industry and who had come not just from the East but from all over Europe.

There is only one other comparable Angeleno, and he's a nonstarter really, even if few people in the 1930s caught the aching, apprehensive dream of American pictures as richly as Frank Capra. Francesco Capra had been born in the village of Bisacquino, in Sicily, in 1897. A few days short of six, the boy took a ship from Palermo to Naples and then on to America. Two million Italians left for America in the period from 1900 to 1910, but most of them kept to the East Coast. Capra was in Los Angeles a few weeks after landing in New York. There was then one movie theater in Los Angeles, and its specialty was travelogues. The Capras felt they were living in a small country city, one that was smug, comfortable, and pious, and increasingly suspicious of Sicilians and other outsiders.

There was an aristocracy in Hollywood, or an upper class: the farmers, the early oil tycoons, and the real estate emperors, the generation that had made the place. And they did not invite picture people to join their clubs. They regarded movie success as upstart, the insects buzzing around a fad or a short-lived craze. After all, movie people were a breed already familiar, indulged but guarded against—"theatricals." The Hollywood Hotel (at Hollywood and Highland, built in 1905) was "a glorified theatrical boardinghouse," while Hollywood was "a village. . . . The heat was a clean dark heat. The sky, a strong, deep blue and the mountains like cardboard cut-outs—you could hardly believe they had any backs to them." That was Lenore Coffee, a screenwriter, writing circa 1919; it's striking how early the metaphor got under way that nature itself was like stage décor.

No one observed the scene more sharply than Agnes de Mille (born in 1909), the niece of Cecil B., the daughter of William. She grew up in the town, aware of the place—"Hollywood Boulevard was a shambling, drowsy street of box stores and shingle houses under the dusty, crackling palms and pepper trees," she wrote—and the ideas that were seething among film people: "They sat long after dinner and talked of the studio. I was asleep by then, but I woke to hear their voices. They talked with fervor. They were in love with their new work. In the first year, Pop stayed away from the studio only seventeen days, including Sundays."

That passion shrugged off the contempt of the real estate people, and was hardly fazed by how little there was to do in Los Angeles as a whole. Agnes de Mille attended Hollywood School for Girls, with Irene Mayer. She would become a true artist: she did the exhilarating choreography for *Oklahoma!,* a signal event in the process that brought Western energy and ideals to the East. She later said this of her family and their friends:

> The men who made the early films did not despise their work nor hate their bosses. They had not come to accept frustration as their almost inevitable lot. Each picture was a challenge. They worked as individualists. They worked on their own as artists. And although very few of them were artists, they all had the pleasure and pride of believing they might be and worked accordingly.

You can feel a different yet kindred drive in Noah Cross, with his belief in the thriving world of nature and of what can be done with it; he is just as ruthless with human nature, of course. As late as the 1980s, there were people in California who pronounced Los Angeles with the hard Mexican "g." Mary Frances Kennedy (or M. F. K.) Fisher, the writer on food and other appetites, was one of them, and she had been raised in Whittier since 1912 (when she was four) to levels of bourgeois respectability. Once upon a time, she had her picture taken (she was so beautiful) with a view to getting in the movies. But she came from stock that saw the movies as silly, just too flat-out reckless in their play on the imagination. (Whittier had other moral conservatives, among them the Nixons, and that area, Los Angeles County, bordering on Orange County, is still deeply disapproving of Angelenos trying to get ahead of the future, as opposed to in step with the past.)

Mary Frances was not respectable. I don't mean to say she was a tramp, though I think she enjoyed it if anyone got that impression. She was, after all, a sensualist, one of the first Americans to go crazy about flavor, and to understand that cooking could be as good as the movies and was enough of a converting light to ideals: sun + chard = vitality. She was intensely California in that her very good manners never masked or buried a wide-open attitude, a feeling that there was little point in living life if you were ready to be shocked. Surprised, yes—yes, please—but never shocked.

Is she irrelevant? I don't think so, and not just because of that flirtation with the movies. Rather, it was her happy flirt with just about anything and anyone she found interesting, and her automatic relationship with nature and place, and the world that was for picking and eating. With a few civilized men and fruit trees around, she was content, even if she was maybe too wise to expect to be happy for long.

I have said that happiness is inseparable from the American movie, and surely happiness taken for granted can easily degenerate into stupidity, sentimentality, and absurd overoptimism. All of which became apparent in the American movie very early, and which may kill us yet. But still there are simple yet profound qualities about those movies that I regard as eminently California: action, space, light, movement, rapport with nature, confidence. Not that faith in such things need be simpleminded. Ernest Hemingway identified and treasured all of them, and he was very well aware of the things that betrayed them, detracted from them, turned health into illness. Hemingway was not Californian (if he could help it). He had made up his mind not to like the place, especially Los Angeles. But his attitudes, I feel, were Californian—*Green Hills of Africa* is Californian, with its enjoyment of available space, and the idea of a day handled with honor in pursuit of the animals. There's a moment in Robert Towne's *Chinatown*—cut from the finished film—where Cross admires fresh horse dung. It's Papa-ism, and the film dropped it, I suppose, because audiences cool with killings were squeamish over fresh, sweet dump. That Hemingway, I suppose, has gone out of style, along with John Wayne.

But I want to stress that the movies came to a place uncommonly blessed by beauty and wide open to opportunity, a place that was fifty years or so away from self-doubt. It wasn't a paradise. Where Capra lived, downtown, would turn into a ghetto. The downtown area was the first center of population, because of the railway depot. You meet people in Los Angeles now, and not only those in the picture business, who hardly ever go downtown. But there was always so much left for them. When only downtown streets were paved, when Sunset Boulevard was a dirt road, you could take a horse or a carriage, or you could stroll along in the sunshine, and find places that would be known as Westwood, Brentwood, Beverly Hills, Pacific Palisades, Santa Monica.

I know a producer who lives in Brentwood, and his modest house backs onto a small canyon where he and neighbors have made a Rousseau jungle of great glowing fruits and vegetables in the forest. That wild Los Angeles is still there. And early on, movie people had the money and the privilege

to pick out the best lots, the most fashionable architects and the art deal-
ers and so on who would give them class. They were mocked for that
sometimes, but now Los Angeles is known for modern architecture and
great art galleries. Class is skin-deep, of course, but Los Angeles is one of
the classy places where that notion is owned up to, like courage in a Hemingway story. Some love it; some don't.

The need for water was a close call. The numbers were going up so
rapidly that something had to be done fast. That's when William Mulholland, son of an Irish sailor and absolutely untrained as an engineer, but
head of the Department of Water and Power, saw fit to guide the water of
the Owens Valley, 250 miles to the north, down to the thirsty city by way of
an aqueduct. The marshy dry lake left in Owens Valley is not hideous or
toxic, but Indians and farmers there were put out of business so that the
city should drink, wash its cars, and play. (Robert Towne, a health nut as I
recall, has a lovely long, thin lap pool in his ground at Pacific Palisades.
You could say that *Chinatown* paid for it.)

Later on, of course, the Owens Valley water wasn't enough. In the
1920s, Herbert Hoover, as Secretary of Commerce, organized a meeting
to dam the Colorado River and to use the water that otherwise caused
unholy floods. Hoover was not Californian, but he had attended Stanford
and become fond of the state. He was friendly enough with Louis B.
Mayer to send congratulations in 1924 when the Metro-Goldwyn-Mayer
merger was achieved. The two men must have talked about California's
need. About half the energy supplied by Boulder Dam goes to California,
and the water is now better controlled.

But can it last? Or must some even greater aqueduct go deeper into the
Rockies? And what then? Here we come to a vital, but perilous, thing
about the West—the absence of reasonable answers to those questions,
and they affect Nevada, Arizona, and other places every bit as much. But
Nevada and Arizona do not share the other great risk, the thing that casts
such a gambling light on California. Of course, with Yucca Mountain (the
ultimate depository of nuclear waste) Nevada has its own question marks,
but California, north and south, has tectonic plates in the ground shifting
like lovers in a hot movie.

And not since 1906, at least, can anyone be in doubt about this—there's
no arguing it away as a kind of global warming that may not really work
out. In 1906 the San Francisco earthquake brought down large sections of
the city and caused fires that did far worse damage. There have been others. Los Angeles has had its share, just as it knows the regular danger of
brush fires sweeping through its canyon country. These things will happen

again. The people who know guarantee it. A couple of years ago, a best-selling book, *A Dangerous Place,* written by Marc Reisner as he died, foresaw the results of an ultimate earthquake in northern California. The book was detailed, very well researched, lucid, and alarming. People on the fault line were reading it with their fingers crossed. But still, California is a place where more people wish to come than go.

Is this sensible? My wife and I lived through the 1989 earthquake in San Francisco with our twelve-day-old son. We stood clutching his naked body (he was being changed when the quake hit) and we saw a window and a wall squeeze into a diamond shape and then come back to a rectangle. For a few days we agreed that it was only sane and decent to leave the city we loved, for the sake of the child we love.

We are still in San Francisco, and we still love the fifteen-year-old. I tell this story simply to illustrate the inevitable condition of gambling in so many parts of the West. I do not gamble—as in the Las Vegas fashion—but I am very interested in the practice because I think it has come to be more and more American. And that is where the connection with movies is most disconcerting. For there was in the ordinary lifestyle of the first moguls a steady habit of gambling. I don't know how far this was Jewish, or something picked up in the ordeal of immigration—itself a toss of the dice to see whether new would beat old—but it is implicit in the making of movies, just as it is there in the content of so many of them.

Making a movie is not a wise, judicious use of money. There are so many stocks that are much more reliable and secure. But to make a movie puts one in line, notionally, for a very big hit. Increasingly in the history of movies, as I hope to show, the ethos of the stand-out super-hit has taken over from a policy of steady business. That in itself is a mark of how unbusinesslike the business is. But there have always been individuals in Hollywood ready to wager vast sums at poker or whatever. David Selznick lost a couple of million dollars in two years, as if he couldn't stand success or stability.

Gambling had many sentimental attractions: it could be a simple game with limp cards that could persuade people who knew the president (the president of the country) that they were still from the old country (so long as they wouldn't have to go back to Russia). It was a way of humbling the huge sums of money, the banks, the accountants, and those budgets and annual reports they couldn't read. Gambling was eternal, so nothing had changed; and gambling treated that abyss at their feet as if it were a pool.

Gambling had rules, too, like Russian proverbs. "Don't sell what you haven't seen." That's what Adolph Zukor, the head of Paramount, said at the last moment after Cecil B. De Mille (shooting in the Guadalupe-Nipomo sand dunes near Santa Maria) had spent $700,000 on *The Ten Commandments* in 1923. Zukor worried, so C.B. told him, "I believe it will be the biggest picture ever made, not only from the standpoint of spectacle but from the standpoint of humanness, dramatic power, and the great good it will do."

Well, thank you, said Zukor, and he was reassured for a day.

But then he worried again and the costs went to $1 million.

So De Mille said he'd buy the whole thing back for $1 million. Which he didn't have. So he went to a banker, A. P. Giannini, and asked for the million. I'd need to see a financial statement, said the banker.

No time, said De Mille.

You say it's a good picture? asked the banker.

It's good, said De Mille.

So Giannini made the loan. But when Zukor heard there was $1 million ready, he said, This must be some picture. He stuck with it.

"Production went on under the same banner," said De Mille. "Its final cost was $1,475,836.93. Its gross receipts were $4,168,790.38."

No one in America is totally easy about gambling. Even if it isn't sinful, it is dangerous. It has collateral casualties. And then there is the much larger fear that to offer a nation fantasy, escape, and happiness (or the ghostly chance of such things) is to distract them from reality, from ordinariness and even mortality and morality.° Gambling is a pre-emptive attack on fate. But there we come close to future territory, to the ultimate place of movies in the American imagination. For the moment, let's just say that so many rules of this gaming are there in the landscape and the place—in sunny California.

° Late in the work on this book, I saw Thom Andersen's absorbing and melancholy documentary, *Los Angeles Plays Itself*. He is rueful over what the movies have done with his city, at the way mythic melodrama has suppressed history and so much reality. It's an eloquent and important film, yet maybe finally it would rather have done without the movies. But, in that case, would there be a Los Angeles?

The fever, the rapture, the giddiness of being an audience. Weegee, "Girls Laughing at a Movie," circa 1943 *(Getty Images)*

4 · TO BE IN AN AUDIENCE

D id *The Last Tycoon* have a chance of being an important novel? Not unless Scott Fitzgerald was determined on a load of work that seems beyond his frailty at the time. There are too many things in the novel as we have it that speak to his melancholy—the yearning after a lost love, and the hero worship of Monroe Stahr. But it is only the *plan* for a book, as a script is for a film. And that which is best in the outline—the feeling for power in this dangerous new medium—seems to require that the central people become more important as characters. That's why I don't buy Cecilia Brady's blasé claim that she takes the movies "tranquilly." She could not stay that dull if the novel was to have any chance.

Suppose that Cecilia was born in 1915 (the novel is set in 1935 when she is a junior at Bennington) and grant that she is her father's daughter and sentient (she does fall in love with Monroe Stahr)—how can she be so unstirred? For if this book was ever going to work in a Scott Fitzgerald way then we are waiting for the moment when Cecilia becomes like Nick Carraway, if not rising above the story, then being the last person left, the one who can look back on the relationship between Gatsby and America, the one who can read into the record one of the most foreboding American endings:

> And as I sat there brooding on the old, unknown world, I thought of Gatsby's wonder when he first picked out the green light at the end of Daisy's dock. He had come a long way to this blue lawn, and his dream must have seemed so close that he could hardly fail to grasp it. He did not know that it was already behind him, somewhere back in the vast obscurity beyond the city, where the dark fields of the republic rolled on under the night.
>
> Gatsby believed in the green light, the orgiastic future that year by year recedes before us. It eluded us then, but that's no matter—tomorrow we will run faster, stretch out our arms further. . . . And one fine morning—
>
> So we beat on. Boats against the current, borne back ceaselessly into the past.

The Great Gatsby takes place in 1925, and something central has gone wrong. American energy is betrayed already. The past has been lost, or escaped. But that liberty is a greater loss. Imagine that tone of voice drawing the covers up over the bodies at the close of *The Last Tycoon*—imagine it a woman's voice, dry and tough, but broken—and you see how it might have been an extraordinary novel. The notes that Fitzgerald left for the book have Cecilia telling the rest of the story as she dies in a tuberculosis sanitarium, with Stahr dead and her father remarried. Not unpromising, but some women are made of sterner stuff.

Irene Mayer Selznick (born in 1907, and never allowed anywhere near a college) was not just one of the most devious, artful, savage, and steely people I have ever known, with a seventy-plus-year-old intelligence that got bored with your slowness and sentimentality, and was ravenous for gossip, dirt, talk, ideas, the newest thinking, and how the wheels worked.

That Irene is an important character in this book. She plays a determining part in the equation, and in her one could see and feel how the shtetl and café society held hands under the table. The Irene Selznick I knew, more or less a self-made prisoner of the Pierre hotel in New York thanks to "illnesses" she had elected to accept (or incorporate into her character), possessed a ferocity of mind and claw (I recall the touch of her cold hands) that was constantly educational. You can say she was my Norma Desmond—without a pool, let alone a place on Sunset Boulevard. Terrifying, yet essential. Seeing her was inescapable, because of all the dark stuff she knew, and had done, while feeling herself more lost, or cut off from time, than any Cecilia Brady. Imagine someone raised to honor family ending up in a hotel.

Cecilia Brady says that, at Bennington, she felt that some of the English teachers hated Hollywood "way down deep as a threat to their existence." I should hope so. Because, by that time, by 1935, it was inescapably clear that the movies had altered the world, beyond recall or rescue, in ways that might be appalling, might be lovely. Or, if anything as inanimate as movies cannot have motive or purpose, then they had coincided with other things in such a way as to make for convulsive damage—enough to show politicians and academics alike that things were not under their control, that reason, evidence, argument and so on were chaff in the wind. By 1935, in depression, facing radical political choices, intelligent Americans surely knew that the movies were muddling the argument, just as now we cannot separate political events or the shabby ideas behind them from the media coverage of them. Movies were keeping folks happy, or subdued, when constructive anger was more appropriate.

But in the thirties, America simply reeled from the force of pictures. It did so little to assess the impact. Later on in *The Last Tycoon,* Cecilia's narrative tells us Stahr was "something else again. He was a marker in industry like Edison and Lumière and Griffith and Chaplin." Take the first two, or three.

Cecilia doesn't seem quite sure, but there were two Lumière brothers, Louis (1864–1948) and Auguste (1862–1954), whereas Thomas Alva Edison (1847–1931) was unique. All three deserve credit as inventors, and even as types of businessmen. Which does not mean that they had much in the way of useful understanding. They were contemporaries and rivals in a kind of race being conducted all over the industrialized world. The losers won, and the historic winner came in second. But in remarkable, charming ways, it is apparent that no one in the race could see where it was going.

The Lumière brothers were the sons of a still photographer in Lyons. They worked for their father, and they began to experiment with capturing movement on some photosensitive surface. Edison, with his rather more brilliant assistant, William Kennedy Laurie Dickson, was attempting the same thing in New Jersey. This was in the 1880s and the 1890s, when they, and other racers, were stimulated by the work of Étienne-Jules Marey in France, and of Eadweard Muybridge (in California and Philadelphia). The latter had laid down for public inspection many gravely beautiful series of still photographs of human figures (often nude) going through such elementary motions as walking, jumping, and throwing, pouring water or combing their hair. But Muybridge was characteristic of certain "racers," in that he stepped into retirement rather than carry these still figures into motion and fluidity. So modern in impulse, he had no instinct for change. He gave up America for Kingston-on-Thames, in England, no matter that America had demonstrated every friendly intention by acquitting him of the murder of his wife's lover.

What the trick of movie required was a strip of film, one frame after another, in a mechanism that could pull down each frame, stop it exactly in the gate of the camera, expose it, and then pull the strip forward so that enough frames could be exposed every second to give the illusion of movement and duration if the frames were then projected back onto a flat white surface. This phenomenon, called persistence of vision, occurs when frames run between twelve and sixteen per second. It requires a film strip, with perforated edges, and some sort of claw or hook mechanism so that the claw fits into a perforation, pulls the frame into place, holds it still (this is vital) and does this reliably, sixteen times a second.

Edison was ahead in the race; his film had better perforations—he had far more resources at his disposal, simply because he was by nature and profession an inventor (as opposed to a photographer). But he made a "mistake" (or maybe not; keep an open mind). Once he had a system working, he produced a machine called a kinetoscope whereby one person could step up, look into the eyepiece and watch the film strip run forward for a few seconds. That customer could work the switch or the handle that moved the film and turned on the light that illuminated the film. He could even run it back and forth, if he chose, if he wanted to see the clip again, or if he was delighted by the hitherto unknown beauties (the surrealism) of reverse motion. Edison foresaw a marketplace in which some room or public place had rows of kinetoscope machines so that hundreds of people could have fun. After all, there were hundreds, and far more, who wanted fun, or a chance to whet their curiosity. And if they didn't get "fun," they might run amok, trampling on order and business.

But Edison's "mistake" requires more commentary. I wonder if his way ahead was not helplessly modeled on the experience of reading, for it relied on individual concentration. A reader scans the lines and the page and can pause, to repeat a phrase, or to let meaning sink in. He or she is in charge, or has that feeling. The reader's understanding determines the pace of the experience, or even its continuation, and everything about what is happening encourages the notion of a private insight being gained. By its very nature, reading says we are alone, dependent on ourselves, pledged to the validity of our unique identity. For a moment in history, a dangerous moment, movie will offer an alternative; it will say, "We might all be together!"

One hundred students in the same space (an examination hall), reading their own copy of a standard text may be said to be reading "together." But, in fact, the readings are all proceeding at slightly different speeds or whims. The hundred is (or is not) attending to the same book, but the experience remains solitary.

Take the same one hundred people and put them down in a cinema (no matter how primitive) and something has changed. Attention may vary. Some may close their eyes; some may think of something else; some may conjure up other ways to defy or resist the group experience. But the film ticks over; the light from the screen bathes everyone; the "reading" or the performance of the film cannot be stopped or slowed or adjusted to individual pace. There is no stopping or repeating. More or less, the one hundred are obliged to have a shared experience. This is absolutely fundamental to the beauty and art (and even to the social marvel) of what we call "movie."

But then consider that Edison's mistaken direction lasted only about fifty years. By the 1940s and 1950s, the cinematic experience was challenged by that of television, where many Edisonian circumstances were restored. People watched in their homes; sometimes in family groups, but often alone. At the same time, they knew, say, that on Mondays at 9 p.m. "everyone" was watching, or had the chance to watch, *I Love Lucy*. But still, the experience was not really shared until the next day when strangers might become friendly talking over moments from the same show. At first, television offered no way of stopping or repeating the show, but then came videotape. And in many other ways, the solitariness that Edison adhered to with the kinetoscope was restored by television. What emerges from this is the possibility that movie was a special, short-lived side street, radiant and socially encouraging, but not lasting. The great wonder we are discussing here may have begun to die some time ago.

Somehow—and I don't know enough to guess why, or to be sure it was anything other than chance—the Lumière brothers saw that the machine they had fashioned to photograph things (they called it the *ciné-matographe*) could also serve as a projector if they simply changed the direction of the equation. Thus:

$$\text{Light (of the world)} \rightarrow \textit{cinématographe} = \text{moving picture}$$
$$\textit{cinématographe} \rightarrow \text{light (a bulb)} = \text{projection}$$

And so it was, on December 28, 1895, on the Boulevard des Capucines, in Paris, that the Lumières demonstrated moving pictures for an audience (apparently, thirty-three people). They had a projector and rows of seats (I believe), and they turned off the lights to get the best effect. For his part, Edison had everything except "audience" and the right-direction arrow for the light. His patrons were looking at the light (as we are when we watch television). The movie audience has the light behind them, and it watches that light bouncing off a screen.

What the Lumières showed to those Parisians was a series of brief, fragmentary records of moments from life—workers leaving the Lumières' father's factory, a family picnic, a locomotive coming into a station. They filmed what was at hand without much forethought or planning, let alone "direction," whereas the Edison people were already on to such little scenarios as jokes, surprises, and voyeuristic advantages. Someone who saw the Lumières' show early on, if not the first night, was Georges Méliès, a leading Parisian magician. He was excited, yet probably skilled and cool enough to mask that. But he asked the Lumières if he could purchase their equipment, or borrow it. For he was already aroused by the ways in which it might assist "magic." Oh, save your money, said the Lumières. The *cinématographe* is an invention without a future.

All of which is encouraging to businessmen, as well as a clear warning that whether movie is entertainment, magic, box office, or art, don't expect to get far without shrewdness enough to know an idiot when you see one. Especially if he is a genius, too, as the Lumières were. Their distinction was all the sweeter for being inadvertent, for they had invented, or signaled the possibility of, the movie audience and the thing we would call a mass medium.

I've spelled out some of the ingredients of that breakthrough in comparing the kinetoscope and the *cinématographe*. But we need to go further. For the least of the Lumières' innovations may still be heavy with significance. Suppose that everything that occurred on that December night in 1895 was less part of the invention of cinema, or movies, than the first steps in discovering screens.

It is unlikely that the Lumières' room had a suitable screen; far easier to believe that, as many have done since, they found a large, smoothly ironed white sheet and pinned it, taut and unwrinkled, to the wall. Notice the reversal in popular meaning that was at hand. Until the nineteenth century, a screen was only a piece of furniture, or an adjunct to décor, movable, foldable, a way of cutting off one space from another, a partition. That use is still current. And it is possible, I suppose, in Paris that night that the older kind of screen was put up to serve the function of the newer kind (*l'écran*). But whereas one kind prevented vision, and allowed privacy, the new kind broadcast it and made it public.

There will be more to say about screens later. For the moment, let me add that I am typing these words on another sort of screen. And while in the twenties, thirties, and forties there were academics and teachers horrified at how much time children or young people spent gazing at movie screens—and later with more than horror as these numbers jumped after the introduction of the television screen—consider how, in the early years of the twenty-first century, we are so screen-dependent as to beggar belief. Has the function or the portent (the magic?) of screens altered? Well, maybe—yet maybe the screen has become the preferred medium through which we hope to make the world manageable, and maybe it is still full of irrational demons.

Like the way that as that first Parisian audience saw images of a family eating lunch on the grass, they sighed with pleasure, or rapture, or a kind of primal sentiment that the screen summons. They wanted to be there, in the sunlight, at the picnic. They felt one with the family. They wanted to tickle the baby. And then, when the train pulled into the station, not head-on toward the camera, but coming in its general direction, some in the audience are said to have run screaming from the room, terrified that the actual weight and force of the engine was about to come off the screen and into the room.

Maybe those stories were exaggerated? Maybe some of the Parisians were skittish? Or had they intuited from the start something profound and necessary about these new screens? While 1895 was a thriving period of industrial progress and mechanical invention (what with new cars, aircraft about to be, to say nothing of all the helpful little devices that Edison commanded), it was also the year in which Sigmund Freud published *The Interpretation of Dreams*. Magic acts, hypnotism, séances, and irrational performances were in vogue. And what is sleep but another kind of screen from which figures and phantoms may penetrate the waking world?

Yes, it may have been foolish to get up and run out—it avoids the answer to the question of whether that locomotive is an explosion ready to occur, or Santa's midnight express. We don't run away anymore, though people do sometimes quit movie theatres in distress or outrage. But if you have ever been in the back row of a theater at a screening of Brian De Palma's *Carrie,* and witnessed the mass of people bolt upright, and move vertically a foot or so, as the white hand comes up from the charred grave to grab us, then you know that there can be a convulsive physical reaction in far more sophisticated times. We are very well accustomed to the notion that violence on screen—the plunging knife in the shower scene from *Psycho*—may be doing psychic damage to us. We feel hurt, wounded, victimized—we are changed, there in the secure dark. And violence is only the most overt or apparent intrusion. What of the gentler invasions, like the inducement to be in love or to feel happy? What of those fleeting instants when something like rapture, or complicity, passes over a face thirty feet high, and we sigh, in the deepest pit of our being, "Baby . . ." as if we were being kissed? And kissing?

Was it even that those who ran away were a very enlightened minority, those smart enough to see that our culture had at last reached an extraordinary new kind of predicament and privilege: that of watching heightened things—great danger, great desirability, intense loveliness—without being tied by the responsibilities that attach to real onlookers? If I see real violence in life, should I run away or try to rescue the attacked? If I see loveliness, am I not obliged to wonder if I am in love? Those are the consequences of real space, the companionship of spectacle and viewer. But in the movies, those on the screen do not know we are watching. We are like voyeurs, spies, or peeping toms. We do not quite exist in the old way. Is that what alarmed philosophers? Did they see the coming of humankind's fatal anonymity?

Does the screen indicate to us that we are just dreamers? Cinema is an engine that runs so fluently without our input or labor. And that slipperiness is added to by its capacity to change itself, unimaginably, in a blink: to cut not just from A to Z, but from A to 1—in other words, to reinvent the code or the language—and to say to us the viewer: work it out, relate the violently different things, find the connection. This is how we watch movies, following the old surrealist notion that there are always deep, magical affinities between and among all things. (It is impossible to put two things on a table and for the agile mind not to begin to make a list of connections—physical, formal, humorous, functional, and, above all, poetic.)

Not many movies work that way, perhaps. The surreal potential is alarming, not box-office gold. So movies tell tidy stories; their information needs to fit, to add up, to acquire momentum. That's fine, but in a director like Alfred Hitchcock (crazy for momentum and suspense) there is also an acute eye for formal and subconscious values (like Buñuel, like art film) that sees surreal association, so that a knife is a phallus and a tracking shot toward the old dark house is a kind of sexual or inquiring thrust. In a great movie, those two things work in harmony, and audiences can go crazy with desire and dread.

One day late in 2003, I saw a trailer for a movie called *The Day After Tomorrow*. That film is now old hat; it opened in 2004, so the sensation is a relic now. There was a shot in the trailer of tiny figures advancing across a great polar landscape. Then the camera pans ahead of them to reveal the battlements of Manhattan, covered in more snow, and plainly forsaken. I wanted to see that movie then, even if it proved less impressive than its trailer. You may be laughing at me, but the promise of miracle made real (in this case, with the notion of cataclysmic weather) is what the movies have always been about.

All film has this potential, and its possibility rides like a swimmer on a surface of movement and duration—the flicker of time passing which has the spaciousness of eternity and the desperate need for a last few seconds of life. The threat and the invitation are always there. And if you are in terror—it goes on; if you are in bliss (just before coitus, say)—it will stop. Its tempo and rhythm are playing you, the spectator. Therefore, there is a composer or a player—an auteur—whose presence is automatically indicated in the mechanism and the process. The movie you are seeing has a life of its own that will not stop until it is over. Go away—it carries on; throw garbage at the screen and the image endures, even if scarred. It is oblivious of you—yet it is all *for* you. Dreams have the same contradictory nature.

I think there's something else about this ritual or passion if experienced in intense company—intense as in a packed crowd, but with heightened feelings. There is something sublime and inspiring about laughing as part of an audience. It can renew your faith in human nature and in the power of society to arrive at democratic or fair forms of government. To be in an audience can be a beautiful and blessed state. Yet it may not be that far from the condition of a mob, baying for more blood or cruelty, roaring for violence or stupid answers. And so we come to a very large subject: the clear appeal of movies to totalitarianism, and its natural rapport with the mass, the mob, the crowd.

That said, remember that the movies come along in the crux and the climax of the hard ninety-degree cornering in the graph line that measures population against time. In America, that turn of the century and its drama are all very well, for a naturally empty land needed throngs (and was perhaps unnerved by so much solitude). We already know how much that population surge in the Los Angeles area had to do with a land bonanza and the dream of newcomers reveling in a semi-paradise before the arrival of movies. But the same thing happened all over the world, so that in the period from about 1850 to 1950 the long, slow, gradual uphill gradient turned into the Indian rope trick.

And goes on.

For centuries, most people had lived a life that was indistinguishable from the life of their parents and ancestors. Now, the different generations in a family could only marvel at their transformations, and at the things no longer quite shared. You cannot begin to grasp the equation, or the excitement, that united Irene Mayer Selznick, Charlie Chaplin, and Steven Spielberg—and you—without recognizing and appreciating that convulsion. But convulsions are not always helpful for calm consideration. Life has become a ferment of melodrama, so maybe we are all out of our minds. Does that storm remind you of the movies?

We wrestle with the dilemma: can we sustain our own crowd? Is the world rich and fertile enough for so many? Will there not be the kind of friction or hostility that comes from overcrowding, and from the gulf between privilege and disadvantage? Can "audience" be generous enough to hold off the resentments of the mob?

Can so many be educated, for surely we cannot endure the brutal standoff between the saved few and the wretched many? Can we watch massacres, famines, holocausts, as if we were at the movies watching *Abbott and Costello Meet Frankenstein,* or do we not need to share all things, to move toward equality? In which case, everyone needs education and opportunity, as well as hope. But do the movies offer education, or rather a lifetime of impossible desire?

With education, isn't it essential and inevitable that forms of government become more egalitarian? Will there not be a revolution? Will the great, the rich, and the famous not have to share with the humble, the poor, and the unknown?

In such flux, we will need great things that connect us—the idea of freedom and religion, maybe (though their record of success is poor or mixed). Perhaps there will be things like mass media, the chief purpose of which is to enact or embody commonality and audience. The movies are the first mass medium—projection was that important. And as they came into being they outstripped a feebler, would-be mass medium with the simple assurance: you do not need to be able to read. So Charlie Chaplin was maybe the first human to be recognized or felt for all over the world.

These are large sweeping propositions, but they turn on the most particular timing of the history of the movies. I asked whether Edison was really wrong, or just early. After all, suppose that Edison and the Lumières had lived fifty years later (a blink of the eye in carbon dating terms). Then, surely, the thing we call movies might never have been. The impetus of invention would have gone straight to television, which is all of us watching more or less the same thing, separate yet close in our solitude. Or loneliness. If TV ever smothers film, Edison may only be coming into his own time—for he was an electronics man. Yet the movies did have their window, and they helped reveal us to ourselves at a crucial moment, the one in which we also came so close to destroying the world.

But the educational dispute over the movies was passionate. In 1895, the movies appeared in more or less the same moment as universal education was enacted. For the first time in human history, the most enlightened countries undertook to ensure that every child would learn to read, to count, and to reason—and thus to have a chance to succeed in the world. And then it offered them movies, which allowed them the alternative of dreaming.

At that moment, the state of reading was evolving into what we can regard as the highest flights of the novel—Proust, Joyce, Musil, Henry James, Conrad, Virginia Woolf. (*Mrs. Dalloway* was published the year after the Metro-Goldwyn-Mayer merger, while *Nostromo* and *The Golden Bowl* were published in the age of infantile, one-shot "movies" in nickelodeon arcades.)

Did Virginia Woolf go to the movies? How could a mind as curious as Woolf's have stayed away? Her diaries mention a few films—*Lives of a Bengal Lancer* and *Man of Aran.* She found Chaplin dull. From Henry James's letters we know that he saw newsreel of the Boer War, and of the title fight between Jim Corbett and Bob Fitzsimmons (1897). But James at the movies never sprang to his feet with creative excitement or saw anything to match the subtle dangers Isabel notices in *The Portrait of a Lady* in the way Osmond and Madame Merle are standing together. James had the piercing vision of Jean Renoir, or Max Ophüls, so he settled in his own mind for the movies being a silly marvel. We know that James Joyce actually opened a movie theater in Trieste. And for the New York edition of his novels, Henry James engaged the services of the famous artistic photographer Alvin Langdon Coburn to present illustrations to aid the experience of reading.

But far more significant than those overlaps is the way in which the novel reaches a climax of naturalism and then soars free in "modernism" in the age of the photograph and movie. The novelists at the turn of the century had feasted on the crude film shows, just like everyone else. But they had seen through the speckled, sparkling, herky-jerkiness of it all, the slapstick, the komedy and the krazy kinema, and seen a new model for philosophy. For what the photograph and film offered was a record of the past, in an obliging and patient form that began to invent memory, or point to it as the earth of feelings. To see yesterday or twenty years ago shuffling by was to make time the great new currency. And it was there in film before "plot" or "art." You can feel it in Proust (the close of *Swann's Way*):

> The places that we have known belong now only to the little world of space on which we map them for our own convenience. None of them was ever more than a thin slice, held between the contiguous impressions that composed our life at that time; remembrance of a particular form is but regret for a particular moment; and houses, roads, avenues are as fugitive, alas, as the years.

And it is there in Robert Musil, at the opening of *The Man Without Qualities:*

> So let us not place any particular value on the city's name. Like all big cities it was made up of irregularity, change, forward spurts, failures to keep step, collisions of objects and interests, punctuated by unfathomable silences; made up of pathways and untrodden ways, of one great rhythmic beat as well as the chronic discord and mutual displacement of all its contending rhythms. All in all, it was like a boiling bubble inside a pot made of the durable stuff of buildings, laws, regulations, and historical traditions.

That is Musil's Vienna in 1913, and something more penetrating than any movies have yet managed. Yet I believe it was an intuition that could not have struck Musil without the experience of film slipping through the gate like rain sliding down a window. We have had a great age of story and melodramas in film, but it may yet be that we are getting ready as an audience to grasp the subtler message about time.

For many, movies were a narrative form that came into being to "save" the illiterate from their shortcomings, and to give some small hope of shared experience in new societies. You can dismiss that as a stupid concession to failure or weakness, a way of making hopeless students feel good about themselves, in a mood that struck education sixty years later. But there was an idealism in it, too, a wish to bridge an abyss that might be widening just as universal education offered a chance of healing.

One who held such hopes was the poet Vachel Lindsay, whose book *The Art of the Moving Picture* also appeared in 1915. Lindsay's writing now is charmingly enthusiastic, but his voice spoke for a new age in America, a new language. (Indeed, it was not so far from the enthusiasm that would overtake Soviet Russia just a couple of years later, where the illiterate might become enlightened by a thing called kino, and kino-truth.)

> Patriotic art students have discussed with mingled irony and admiration the Boston domination of the only American culture of the nineteenth century, namely, literature. Indianapolis has had her day since then, Chicago is lifting her head. Nevertheless Boston still controls the textbook in English and dominates our high schools. . . .
>
> Some of us view with a peculiar thrill the prospect that Los Angeles may become the Boston of the photoplay. Perhaps it would be better to say the Florence, because California reminds one of colorful Italy more than any part of the United States. Yet there is a difference.
>
> The present day man-in-the-street, man-about-town Californian has an obvious magnificence about him that is allied to the eucalyptus tree, the pomegranate. California is a gilded state. It has not the sordidness of gold, as has Wall Street, but it is the embodiment of the natural ore that the ragged prospector finds. The gold of California is the color of the orange, the glitter of dawn in the Yosemite, the hue of the golden gate that opens the sunset way to mystic and terrible Cathay and Hindustan.

Think of the wild exhilaration in Lindsay if he'd ever lived to see the bridge—a kind of photoplay, if you like—across the Golden Gate. So he's striving and reaching a good deal. Still, his book was published to considerable acclaim and interest in America and I doubt that any American had ever thought to put "art" and "motion picture" in the same phrase. Irene Mayer was eight when Lindsay's book was published, and she was seeing movies in Boston. What's more she was beholding the business that her father was making of them. How was anyone in that first generation of children who were able to see movies to avoid wondering if the great piled-up columns of what they "knew" and still had to know might be dissolved in their light?

Lazar Meier had been born somewhere in Russia, a hopeless case of history, a reject, human scrap—and maybe that's why he followed that business. His daughter Irene was centuries beyond her father even if, as she found herself a princess in the land of the oranges and thought to go to university (to be a doctor), her father looked at the other young women— the few—she knew of who were going to higher education, and told her off, reasserting the old crushing authority of the Jewish father, "Those girls have to go to college. They don't have your advantages."

"A man beyond the realm of the sacred"—Andre Bazin. Edward Steichen, "Charlie Chaplin," 1925 *(Digital Image © The Museum of Modern Art. Licensed by SCALA, Art Resource, New York)*

5 · CHARLIE

Early in the twentieth century, a few people were taken by the idea of making movies because they felt the urge or the inspiration. Others foresaw a regular business: selling pictures to the public.

But once that trade started, it had to go on every day, all the time. A machine had been set in motion. Could the masters of that grind ever trust the artists to deliver enough fresh product every Monday morning?

Inspired by his success marketing *The Birth of a Nation,* and driven like any hot gas to occupy higher air, Louis B. Mayer decided he would make pictures. It wasn't that he liked movies, or felt any deep urge to make them—he had to be sure of having product to sell. To amplify that rugged ambition, he looked around for personalities, for prettiness, for what might be stars. He developed the idea (just like moviegoers)—"pretty women." And so he made a contract with Mildred Harris Chaplin.

As Mayer's first biographer, Bosley Crowther, put it in *Hollywood Rajah,* Mildred

> was not an actress of any notable talent or popularity. She had knocked about in movies since she was a little girl and had played in several Universal pictures, in supporting roles [she had also played Dorothy in *The Patchwork Girl of Oz*], when Chaplin met her at a very gay house party of Hollywood blades and babes and provided her chief claim to distinction. He gallantly made her his wife.

Charlie, then twenty-nine, married Mildred in 1918—she was sixteen—and the union was one brick in the wall of gossip or moral disquiet (a wall has two sides) that began to figure in America's attitude to Hollywood. Mildred was born in Cheyenne, Wyoming, and uneducated in so many ways before she became a Mayer property. When she heard that her boss was bringing his wife and two daughters out to Los Angeles by train from Boston, she arranged this astonishing welcome, as described by Irene, who was twelve at the time (four years younger than Mildred):

> When we got to the station [in Los Angeles], there was Mrs. Chaplin herself, and we were agog. Waiting was a Marmon tonneau limousine, the closed back of which was upholstered in a soft, pale fabric and boasted a cut-glass vase containing a single rose. This wasn't a make-believe world, this was fairyland.

Of course, it was California, where roses grew, the natural surrealism of bloom and machine was available, and every Eastern or European response could be mocking or condescending. But how does a waif from Wyoming acquire the worldly finesse of just one rose in a Marmon tonneau limousine? The world was changing—décor was coming in, radiating

uneducated minds. You may surmise that Charlie put together that pretty
scene, but I doubt it. After all, Chaplin himself would say of Mildred in
My Autobiography:

> Although she was pretty and pleasant that evening, I lacked the zest and
> enthusiasm that the presence of a pretty girl usually inspires. The only
> possible interest she had for me was sex; and to make a romantic approach
> to it, which I felt would be expected of me, was too much of an effort.

Blessed English honesty, plus our first hint that, when suffering artistic
doubts or fiscal confusion, a young man in the movies could always settle
for sex.

Charles Chaplin, Charlie, Charlot, the Tramp, the little man, kiss-kiss,
was the most important and dynamic figure in the early days of cinema. In
defeat and glory, pathos and aplomb, he was an inspiration to many,
ammunition for the rest, and someone who never knew boredom with
himself. Indeed, following Chaplin's slapstick career, reading the *Autobiography* that could have been co-written by Micawber and Heep, is to
have the sense of someone watching his own show. Surely this is a clue to
filmmaking, direction, or whatever: the ability (or the curse) of being in
life while directing the act at the same time.

On the set or in life, Charlie believed that if things turned stagnant, or
"wrong," he could throw out one idea and start on another, begin again.
He's like the x that can function on both sides of an equation, dancing,
stumbling, skidding from one side to the other. Chasing himself with
attention.

Chaplin had no education, no intellect perhaps. But he was driven by a
brilliant modernism way ahead of Freudian understanding—half narcissism, half utter, cold detachment—that left him as outstanding as Einstein.
And just as the latter now is easily accepted as the epitome of impossible
mathematics or far-fetched intellect, so Chaplin may still be the first image
or name that people would supply in the equation, movies = ...

And if it is wholeness or integration we are after, no one went for more
or for more completeness than Chaplin. He was the director of his films,
and he was at least as much of a pioneer of film grammar as Griffith. He
was the actor, the star, the subject; more than that, his was the range of
feeling being explored. He was also the businessman, a tireless, wriggling,
show-off driven to be in charge of his own affairs. You can call this the
lonely magnificence of art (he saw it that way), but others decided he was
simply a killer at business, taking revenge on his own early poverty.

He could hardly see another person without wanting to conquer them, to envelop them in the need to attend to him. Yet, on occasion, he could be the real fellow, happy to go on a tour, thrilled by the crowd, so ready to be "Charlie" to greet the cry, "Look, there he is!" When great crowds of adoring fans came up to him he held them back a little just by acting out his surprise, his emotion, his being Charlie. The political figure in Chaplin was born very early, for it was a natural response to huge attention: Are you looking at me? Think of all the stars who have been crushed by attention, and remember that Charlie exulted in it and was fueled by it, for he felt he deserved it. From such an early age he was like himself, emblematic—Chaplinesque. Which is not quite being himself, though it may be a hinge of modernism. I mean it as a measure of his greatness (and of his coldness) that when Adolf Hitler came along, Chaplin began to take on the dictator as a subject (or a challenger) because he was his most significant rival.

We will probably never quite know who Chaplin was. Kenneth Lynn's excellent biography (the most recent), *Charlie Chaplin and His Times,* considers all manner of possibilities, in a way that shows how the very range may have been crucial in shaping Charlie's self-awareness. The masquerade, the cover-up of shame or lack of confidence, was to put on the gestures of character. And it worked. Within a decade, Chaplin went from being the workhouse kid of a deranged mother in a wretched part of London, with nothing but his wits and timing, to the image known all over the world: the baggy pants; the out-splayed feet; the jacket too tight; the mustache to make him sneeze; the mascara eyebrows; the dark curls; the battered bowler hat; and the parenthesis of cane. Thus the genius of Edward Steichen who, in 1931, photographed the "real" dainty, elegant, very handsome, silver-haired, tanned spirit of seduction.

In 1915, when he was already a sensation because of his short films at Keystone, and when he was six thousand miles away from the grim overcast of Kennington, in south London, Chaplin told his story to *Photoplay* magazine. It's such a harsh story, yet the telling is blithe and awry, and the hero soars free, flying, with every error of fact:

> I have always worked hard ever since my father died, when I was seven years old. My mother was a wonderful woman, highly cultivated, yet life was hard on her. We were so poor, she used to sew little blouses by hand, trying to earn enough to keep us. That was in England—she died there. Poverty is a cruel thing, and I sometimes think that if I had not worked so very hard as a child, I should be much stronger now than I am, because,

you see, I am not at all strong, physically. I have never had a day's school-ing in my life; my mother taught us [Charlie and his half-brother Sydney] what she could, but after she died, I was an apprentice to a company of traveling acrobats, jugglers and show-people. That was in England, too, and oh, what hard work it was. I have never had a home worth the name. No association that might have helped me when I was young. Looking back upon it is no joke, and that is why it seems so out of place when I am made much of now.

The father? There was a Charles Chaplin, Sr., a music hall singer, who was briefly with the mother, Hannah Hill, though never married to her. Charles was likely the father of Sydney, though the family story was that Sydney was a bastard. Charlie saw Charles Chaplin a few times—as a drunk in pubs, mostly—and the "father" died when the boy was twelve. As for the mother, she did not die until 1928, in California, a hospitalized schizophrenic supported by, but rarely visited by, her son. Her "cultiva-tion" was in Charlie's eyes or memory alone.

In his autobiography, Chaplin remembers having her up to his new house on Summit Drive one day. She gazed at the extravagant property and supposed he must be rich. He told her he was worth $5 million. "So long as you're able to keep your health and enjoy it," she replied.

She died without ever settling for him who his father was. The question remains open because it's likely that she had taken to prostitution to make ends meet. So it could have been anyone—to explain the Italianate looks, or even the Semitic cast (Charlie often said that he wondered whether he was Jewish), the educated voice, and the fastidious air of good manners. I doubt he wanted it settled. Without plain facts, he was so much more mobile and lofty a soul, like any of those foundlings in Dickens. It's a won-der in these days that someone hasn't pinned him down as the love child of some royal figure, or Jack the Ripper.

I do not mean to exclude the chance that Chaplin was simply the son of an unstable music hall singer on the game, and some south London rake. After all, Louis Armstrong, born in New Orleans only a few years after Chaplin, and as tumultuous a genius, was plainly the child of a poor, teenage prostitute. What is more intriguing, with Charlie, is the invented persona that seems to reach from tramp to king. Something in his self-regard accommodated the urchin and a nearly divine grace. I suspect he wondered whether he came from God.

Charlie did get a little schooling, but he went from cheap terraced housing to the Lambeth Workhouse. Still, his mother's connections got him as a youth into the Fred Karno music hall touring company, a first-class operation. That's how he reached America, met Mack Sennett, and was hired on at Keystone, initially at $150 a week (a grand sum of money then). He told Sydney to hurry over: "We will be millionaires before long." In 1916, Chaplin moved to Essanay, at $1,250 a week, and was required to make one one-reel picture every three weeks (a time span that already attested to the care of genius).

The business then was a mass of small companies, and people jumped around (and up). But actors were seldom masters of their fate. (So many other comedian careers are woeful next to Charlie's.) It's as if Charlie moved to *his* plan: when he moved, he transformed his status. Less than a year later, he was at Mutual at $10,000 a week, with a signing bonus of $150,000 and guarantees of a freshly equipped studio for his personal use. (Ten thousand dollars a week in those days is, by today's standards, at least $10 million a year, but this does not adequately convey Chaplin's self-promotion or his wealth. And the top rate of income tax was 7 percent, so Charlie in a week was taxed what a factory laborer might earn in a year.)

That heady salary progression shows not just how brilliant and popular Chaplin was, but how dynamic a medium the cinema was becoming. The history books still ask who went to see the early movies, and they're no more certain of the answer than we know how much money slipped through the cracks. The records were so unreliable. The venues were changing so rapidly. A craze was on, and no one has time to keep proper records during a craze. Still, the best estimates are that in 1907–08, America had about eight thousand nickelodeon outlets—places where films were projected, often converted kinetoscope arcades, as well as shops and theaters. There were still very few "cinemas" or movie houses, places constructed specially for the new medium.

The nickelodeons could seat between 200 and 500 people and they ran a ragbag of one-reel adventures and comedies, with primitive newsreels, sing-alongs (with the words projected on the screen) and live acts such as one might see in vaudeville. Suppose a "show" ran two hours. Suppose a "house" ran five shows a day. Suppose it enjoyed an average crowd of 250 per show. That would produce, very roughly, a box office gross of $500,000 a day across the nation—an annual gross figure of about $180 million.

And, if you're interested in these sums of money, and so much supposing, if you allow a multiplication factor of twenty to approximate today's dollars, that's an annual box office gross of movies in America in 1907–08 of $3.6 billion.

The population of the United States in 1907–08 was about 85 million.

The annual box office gross for 2001 and 2002 was a little over $8 billion each year, with a population of, say, 280 million.

The equation for which these are the raw materials is that a craze and an amusement are different things, and we live with the latter. When it's amusing.

Nickelodeons got their product from local exchanges, and there was a ravenous demand for fresh material. Louis B. Mayer knew the risk in having nothing new to show. The business was chronically unstable and vulnerable locally to gangsterism. The audience often had no idea what they were going to see, but they were disappointed at a familiar film coming back again. The equipment was far from reliable: projection and film perforation were inexact, and could ruin a show. The rooms were poorly ventilated (the bad air at a nickelodeon was proverbial; in some venues perfume was sprayed in the air and disinfectant applied to the scummy floor). The film could catch fire: the stock then was celluloid nitrate, highly inflammable and dangerous at any time if not stored properly. In many respectable households going to the flicks was deemed unhealthy and dangerous. There were several ruinous fires. Projection booths had a bolt on the outside of the door so that management might confine the blaze (and the projectionist).

The old terms of abuse—"the bug hutch," "the fleapit"—denoted how much of a class war hung over movies. The earliest films, those of the years before Griffith, were for the poor, the uneducated, immigrants, and children. Everyone noted, and many were alarmed, how the venues were crammed with children who seemed to have nothing better to do. Social disapproval became tinged with ideas of academic outrage.

Meanwhile, if we are inclined to think that the movies might be an art, let's recall that in the period 1895–1915, they coincided with *The Wings of the Dove, The Ambassadors, The Golden Bowl, Dubliners, Nostromo, Jude the Obscure,* and *Sister Carrie;* with Picasso's cubist onslaught on docile, well-behaved appearance; with *The Firebird, Petrouchka* and *The Rite of Spring* by Stravinsky; with Bartok's *Bluebeard's Castle;* with some of the best plays of Wedekind and Strindberg; and with *The Seagull, The Cherry Orchard,* and *The Three Sisters.*

The connection is this: Charlie Chaplin in the workhouse did not read Henry James, contemplate Picasso, or hear Stravinsky. In later life, though, he met the latter two and chatted with them easily enough, one phenomenon to another. He may even have had the time and the urge to catch up on their work. For all I know, Charlie "owned" Picassos. But the universal education that was being practiced in 1900 was also filled with dismay and disappointment—there were millions of people who could read, but who couldn't read Henry James, couldn't grapple with the pro-longed sentences or the successive qualifying clauses of doubt. Did they fail then? Can America admit that most of us will fail?

The miraculous message borne on the movies—and Chaplin carried it every bit as well as Griffith—was that failures might jump straight from illiteracy to feeling overwhelming emotions at the movies. And the passion that gathered in the medium around 1915 was that here was something not just for the poor, the kids, and the immigrants, but for everyone.

Who knew how far films would go in another decade? So Charlie became universal, an icon for humble and pathetic hopes, yet so distinct, so vivid, so much a character that he helped to make movies palatable for all those who flinched at the fleapit. Such a thing had never happened before, as far as Charlie could tell—or not since Jesus Christ. The com-parison with Armstrong is apt again, for Louis was the man who made jazz into something not simply dirty, black, funky, raw, salacious, but music that white people could feel comfortable listening to. In much the same way, Chaplin redeemed the raw, rowdy medium. The little man, so poor, was so refined that he made the medium feel safe for the bourgeoisie.

There was something helplessly religious about what was happening in our dark, and in the larger and grander movie theaters that began to be constructed to house the audience and all the ambition. It was felt by Lenin, Hitler, Louis B. Mayer, Chaplin, and by just about everyone who went. Woodrow Wilson looked at *The Birth of a Nation.* As a president of Princeton he must have seen that it was trash, racist, sensationalist, and worse. But as one who had some hopes of healing the world, he said (or it became said that he said; he never denied it), "This is history written in lightning."

* * *

Members of Chaplin's family spoke about his fear that his mother's insan-ity might be passed on. But I think Chaplin also was stirred by uncertainty as to who his father had been. He was not shy of the accusation, from his Mack Sennett days onward, that he was a genius, with talents that came from God knows where. And modern movie celebrity is so intimate—that winsome face as big as a house—it can stand to have no credentials or provenance. After all, if Charlie is "ours," or if he is thrilled to belong to us, what do his actual circumstances matter? How does one reconcile trampishness—being at the bottom end of the social scale—with Chaplin's deep design upon us? The tramp act is akin to the gestures of rape, even: it longs to win us, to overwhelm us. But it is also the dandyism that Steichen saw lurking.

The field of silent comedy was ruthless, yet Chaplin soared above the contest. Unequaled at invention and pathos, he was just as obsessed with directing and cutting, with framing and realizing the comic moment. Always aware of his own numbers, he was unsurpassed at taking business control of his whimsical persona. Chaplin was so much his own master that the tramp guise feels like a trick. And he never gave up a speck of ownership of his own films, not even when exile had become his costume, or his latest disguise.

In so many ways, Chaplin ignored the rest of the business, and its odd schemes. It's clear that Chaplin discovered film directing out of his intense, detailed concern with his own performance. More than that, he could not resist the urge to be the very opposite of the persona he had on screen. There may have been no greater artistic ambush for Chaplin than his feeling—gradually developed in the twenties and thirties—that as the spokesman (and creator?) of the little man, he owed it to little men everywhere to speak up for them. And no matter that he had helped invent the self-transportation that could carry one from anonymity to virtually any palace (Chaplin collected celebrity visits), he seems to have had little faith that others could make that shift. He was competitive. And he was always energized and pleased with the idea of an ocean of unknown, loving faces lapping at his upturned toes.

I have stressed the rapidity with which Chaplin went from stranger to center of attention. Effectively, during the course of the First World War, the burgeoning picture business had made him a leading imaginary force in the world. Consider the millions of men during the war years, trying to sleep on the various fronts, and then all those at home in rather more comfortable circumstances. The face and antics of Charlie would have filled the blank screen in more would-be dreams than any other. What's more interesting is that the Chaplin films displayed a mockery of overbearing authority figures, along with a fundamental resignation to fate. The little man knows he's trapped, oppressed, and bamboozled, and he resists in small ways. But in the end he cannot stand up against oppression—man's fate is to be accepting. It is very important to grasp the nature of Chaplin's success, and reassurance, in those terrible years.

Chaplin was ambivalent about war and acceptance. Once America was in the war, he felt a passion for tours selling war bonds. He thrilled at the exposure to adoring crowds, and that's when he made his friendships with Douglas Fairbanks and Mary Pickford. At the same time, in Britain—he was still a British citizen—he was attacked for not coming back home, enlisting, and marching off to that muddy destiny, the Somme. I can't, he answered, my contract with Mutual forbids me from leaving the States. Indeed it did; he had signed such a deal. Which only meant that his image rather than his person traveled in the extraordinary new ways available.

The association with Doug and Mary, and the idea of those icons drumming up war bonds, represented an ideal for Charlie. It was a sign that he had made it, as part of the best company. And it was an alliance of like minds, with the shared experience of being idolized as a test of membership. It was also a model for the notion that the essential people in the movies, those the public bought and loved, should be running the business.

Of course, there is also a fissure in the equation, and in the system of equations. It is a paranoid crack that will run through this book, a fault line for fame, if you like, just as it is at the same time the heady impulse that created United Artists, and helped destroy it. It began not just with the fame and the massive incomes of Charlie, Doug, and Mary, but with the certainty that their human qualities—their transparent identity, the way their radiance prompted dreaming—was what made the movies tick.

There was greed there, too, and the early suspicion that if the system was letting them get away with their vast salaries, it was also because it was screwing them. Consider: if someone offers you a sum of money beyond your imagining, you quickly reason that you are being cheated; there is actually more to be had, more deserved. Nothing was a greater inducement to such paranoia than the chaotic, unrecorded rush in which the business had taken off. Griffith knew, in a vague way, how much he had been cheated over *The Birth of a Nation,* and it was easier to feel aggrieved than to calculate exactly the kind of policy or insurance that would have been necessary to avoid fraud.

Why did the personalities of United Artists come together? You could argue the case of *The Birth of a Nation,* for any idiot saw that it was the start of a business, too. A film that cost $100,000 (more or less) had grossed $18 million in three or four years, yet Griffith had emerged with a profit of about a million because he had been too preoccupied with the picture to take care of his deal.

Equally, it was plain that both Mary Pickford and Chaplin were prepared to go without sleep rather than neglect their own business interests. But there was another pressure. The business, in the years 1914–18, was as disorganized as it was expansive. Paramount led the way as a distribution business, but many smaller operators were fearful of being at the mercy of the rising stars and directors who were capricious in their output, some of them unrestrainedly greedy. (Business people are always shocked to find greed—or the urge to survive—in arty types.) So there was a move to regularize the distribution and exhibition sides of the business, to make a monopoly out of the disarray, strong enough to dictate terms to the artists.

For Chaplin, United Artists was a way out of that fix. He never claimed, or showed himself, to be a devout part of the new company. In his book, Chaplin tells a story of the plot against the artists. So he, Doug and Mary engaged a female detective (attractive) to penetrate the monopoly and find out their plans for a $40 million merger. The detective's contact inside that group—"a glib braggart in an esurient state of libido"—told her that "they intended putting the industry on a proper business basis, instead of having it run by a bunch of crazy actors getting astronomical salaries." That's what guided Chaplin—the proper protection of self-interest (or craziness).

So Chaplin, Fairbanks, and Pickford, with D. W. Griffith and William S. Hart, made an alliance, called United Artists, whereby they would own a distribution company that would market their pictures, allowing them a greater return than if they leased the movies to some outside distributor.

This has always been an intriguing idea that gets at the essential trap in motion pictures, that the business of national, let alone international, distribution of a desirable product is so cumbersome, so obscure, and so mysterious that the producer can easily be deprived of a fair share of his revenue. Plenty of filmmakers over the years, from Griffith to John Wayne to Bruce Willis, have been inclined to say, Well, all right, that's a lot of money I'm getting, so do I have the patience and the stamina to insist that it should be greater? And patience and stamina in this sense are real competitors with such valid alternatives as having fun and making a next picture.

Charlie was very human, a good deal more so than his ethereal screen character. He liked fun, and he was crazy about sex. I cannot find a subtler way of introducing one more part of our equation, which only needs your humanity to understand it. For as the movies are so often about desire, so the world of picturemakers is absorbed in sex. Charlie in 1921 was thirty-two. He was fit, handsome, famous, genuinely charming in person and a hound dog. Moreover, the movies have always been a system dedicated to the transporting (across state lines, let me add) of the image of female loveliness. In turn, that requires a steady process of application, selection, and schooling of female talent. The offices and the corridors may seem thick with flesh, much of it of a level that few of us have been compelled to contend with in our own lives. Not every young woman will make her way to the screen and stardom, but that is no reason not to test and examine her.

Charlie fucked like a very wealthy man with an utterly private life. He could not see that that privilege was going out of style, if only because of the publicity media that helped make him known. And he had acquired a yen for girls. Now, just as fecundity abounds in California, because the growing conditions are so opportune, it is a state that has regularly produced many females developed beyond their actual years, and cute to match. It's not a thing the girls or their parents can restrain, and who would urge that? Nor does warm weather lend itself to body concealment. So the idea occurs that these pretty young things might get into pictures.

Any historian of the movies has observed a phenomenon as evident in life as on the screen: the young women who become the pals, the consorts, and the wives of considerably older men. Inasmuch as young girls are seldom sophisticated sexual partners, I suspect the incidence springs from a deep educational impulse. That, or the wondering in the men whether they may forestall death.

The director Raoul Walsh noted this itch in Chaplin very early on. When the comedian was still at Keystone, Walsh was surprised to discover the studio closed one Saturday. (Saturday was often a working day, further indication of how precious fun could be.) The gateman told Walsh that the closure was an emergency. Some months earlier, a very pretty seventeen-year-old had come to work as an actress. But when she got pregnant, the outraged mother called on the district attorney. Whereupon that officer of the court quietly called Keystone and advised that if anyone had had anything to do with the girl to make themselves scarce, whereupon the whole studio emptied out.

"Charlie?" asked Walsh.

"He was the first to leave," said the gateman, never dreaming that in the decades ahead Chaplin's residence in America would be jeopardized by another pretty girl who had gotten pregnant. Her name was Joan Barry, and Charlie survived (or passed) the blood test. But the facts hardly mattered. His priapic legend was secure by then. Chaplin, unlike Errol Flynn, was never attacked as a rapist, but no one doubted the intensity or the flourish of his need to possess pretty girls not yet of the age of consent.

Remember that very practical way in which Chaplin could speak of Mildred Harris having only sexual interest for him. (Of course, it is a sign of artistry that he could see higher things in a woman.) But sex and romance are not just time-consuming; they eat away at the nervous and creative energies; they promote sleep, so often an enemy of art.

Chaplin was in a position to have a lot of sixteen-year-olds. He married another in 1924: her name was Lolita MacMurray, though she changed it to Lita Grey. They had two children before incompatibility broke through. And if there's anything that can challenge as a thief of the artist's time it is children. They have such sentimental appeal. Whereas famed sexual triumph can keep fading—Chaplin did not have time or space even to mention Lita Grey in his *Autobiography.*

Charlie was neither unkind nor ungallant, but he was a brisk womanizer. As a man of the people, let's say, he preferred pretty girls. A man may march up and down chanting "United Artists" or even "the brotherhood of Man" while secretly hunting for the uniqueness of Woman. Later on in life, with rather comic turmoil as a result, Chaplin attached himself to something like the unity of all souls and little men on earth. Communism! some said, without seeing that Chaplin would do or say anything so long as he had his own way, which is not the worst definition of genius.

When United Artists established itself, the brave partners contributed $100,000 each in the way of capital (against stock) that was meant to set up a distribution organization. They also agreed on a distribution fee of 20 percent for domestic engagements and 30 percent for overseas. This was to assert that the 35 percent charged by Paramount for domestic rentals was an exploitation. But who knew the numbers well enough to be sure? To this day, distribution percentage is the Bunbury for enormous sums of money and the system of accounting is widely and placidly regarded as legalized theft.

One part of the history of business in Hollywood might lead us to think that immense and solemn deliberations led to the demand that the proper return for selling, advertising, or pushing a picture through the system was 20 percent of whatever it grossed at the box office. Yet I suspect the round number was chosen quickly, boldly, and ineptly and that it survived for decades without being reexamined.

Another aspect of the United Artists deal was that the first partners—and anyone else who might be deemed worthy of their company later—were responsible for financing their own pictures. Here is another essential link in the equation, or the chain of production. You will not be in Hollywood longer than an afternoon without learning versions of the wisdom that, whatever you do, don't do it with your own money. For the money can be lost very quickly. Therefore, you get yourself into the position of being able to command money—as advances, or loans, or whatever—from various sources in and outside the business.

On the other hand, there is something essential to true auteurism in resolving to use one's own money. That is the supreme act of self-centeredness, just as it is the gamble that may separate one level of capitalism from another. And if it is your money, you never have to waste time pretending to listen to anyone else, let alone adjusting your script, your casting, your schedule, your final cut. More than any of his partners, Chaplin had known impoverishment, yet he would not proceed without the certainty that the funds were his. He was an immense worrier over many things, including how scenes played, but he never seems to have been disturbed or put off course by worrying about his own money. I doubt if the movies have ever had a maker with more assurance.

Chaplin became, almost immediately, the vital asset and the biggest problem for United Artists. First of all, his prior contract, with First National, and his increasing deliberation, meant that he did not have a picture for UA until 1923, with *A Woman of Paris*. His contract with First National was $1 million and a $15,000 bonus for eight pictures in eighteen months. This sounds like a substantial comedown. But the million was to pay for those eight pictures, and Charlie and First National were fifty-fifty on profits. As to making the films, Chaplin was free as a bird: "He can take any length of time he feels is essential to quality in his releases. He is free to choose his own stories. He is not harassed by telegrams and long-distance telephone calls. . . ."

The pictures he made for First National include *Shoulder Arms* (1918), *The Kid* (1921)—his first full-length feature—and *The Pilgrim* (1923). On *The Kid*, A. H. Giannini and the Bank of America (the Bank of Italy previously) loaned Charlie $250,000 to help make the picture. *The Kid* cost $1.5 million, a third of which was Charlie's own money. It was a monster success, with a gross of over $5 million, enough to give Charlie profits of around $2 million. Observe how far the great popular success of *The Kid* comes from the story of a foundling who makes good—nowhere was Chaplin closer to fictionalizing himself. And all UA could do was watch the bonanza with rueful feelings, and wait for Chaplin to catch up with their contract.

When that day came, *A Woman of Paris* was the greatest departure of his career: it was an attempt at social comedy or satire. It starred one of his discoveries, Edna Purviance, a beauty who never convinced many others or swayed a large audience. And Chaplin appears only in a cameo role, and is barely recognizable. In film history, some critics have praised the film for its stylistic ambitions, and it certainly shows Chaplin as a man who had noticed other directors (like Ernst Lubitsch) and wanted to learn from them. But as far as UA was concerned, *A Woman of Paris* was nearly an act of defiance. The film was politely reviewed, but audiences were perplexed and the picture grossed $643,000 (not an outright disaster, and a tribute to public fascination with Chaplin, but a galling blow to UA).

In its first few years, United Artists had actually reported a loss, though that didn't mean that Pickford and other active producers hadn't done well enough. But the pressure on Charlie was fierce: it focused company politics on the hostility between Charlie and Mary. It was Mary and Doug who in 1924 introduced Joseph Schenck as another shareholder and a management figure. Schenck—"honest Joe" he was called, though he would end in prison—was married to the lustrous Norma Talmadge (he was forty-seven, she was thirty-two in 1925) and he promised her films to the group.

There were arguments in the boardroom: Charlie wanted the number of pictures required of him reduced—he won; he wanted a freer hand in international marketing—he won; he went along with raising the distribution fee to 25 percent. But he lost a protracted argument over funding. Charlie was a privateer: he did it on his own and thought others should, too. But the others didn't always have the money, and they pointed to the unending need for product. Charlie worried that the more UA was run by external financing, the more in jeopardy it was. He was right. But in all things he was solitary first and right second.

What matters is how he rose to the challenge. He would never again be the man who tossed off several short films a year, and maybe those one- and two-reelers were Charlie at his best, or most natural. But he believed in the dignity and the artistic reach of full-length features, and sentiment spread like melting butter to make them large. He made three in the next ten years: *The Gold Rush* (1925), *The Circus* (1928), and *City Lights* (1931). There was no question about them as events, or as prolonged searchings after the hidden picture Charlie wanted.

The Gold Rush grossed $6 million. Charlie walked away from it with at least $2 million, while United Artists had a clear profit of over $1 million. I say "clear profit" as in declared profit. It can never be determined how great the actual profit was—with the 25 percent distribution fee—because no one has ever had a secure hand on keeping track of the real distribution expenses. Of course, the company could claim, with justice, that the same law of elasticity could be applied to its losses on other pictures. And people were still learning how to market a movie, how to finance it, how to present the accounts later. The crucial thing about Chaplin is that as his sense of detail in filmmaking mounted, so his persistence flowered, too.

The climax to this solitary perfectionism is *City Lights,* which remains an exquisite (if nearly excruciating) romance in which the tramp loves a blind girl, a vibrant comedy, and a genuinely interesting look at the phantom barrier between class and classlessness, sight and insight. It is Chaplin's most complex and absorbing film, the one that still repays seeing and which stimulated thought, as well as the most intimate and unguarded revelation of his trembling narcissism.

The making of the picture was astonishing. From start to finish, it occupied him from late 1928 to January 1931, when it opened. There were hundreds of days when shooting was scheduled, but nothing happened because Charlie was lost in various uncertainties: how to play certain scenes; whether his actress, socialite Virginia Cherrill, was good enough. As he never quite knew when "genius" would strike, he kept the overhead standing around and building. And by then, overhead in Hollywood had been institutionalized in the so-called factory system (above all, by Mayer and Thalberg) so that a studio knew it had to make the maximum use of facilities and talent—studio space, crew, star-time—to produce the maximum number of films a year. Chaplin dithered, paying people out of his own pocket, to get things right. Luis Buñuel visited Charlie at the time, and was amazed at his lack of confidence: he had "a good deal of trouble making decisions." But, said Charlie, he was composing the movie's music in his sleep!

The duration of the filmmaking witnessed the clinching victory of sound, and the ruinous crash of the stock market. As it happened, Chaplin had had an instinct to liquidate all his stocks and bonds in 1928, so he remained cash rich. As for sound, he ignored it: there would be no talk in *City Lights,* only music and a few sound effects. He was warned that audience taste was shifting. Joe Schenck told him the film would be harder to sell. He said he was Chaplin, and that was enough. So, for New York, he threw out the UA plan and "four-walled" a theater (the Cohan), which means he paid all the costs of the engagement, and had all the take. He said he spent $60,000—and he took in $80,000 a week for the first three weeks. At the Cohan alone, *City Lights* earned an eventual profit of $400,000. Internationally, it was said, the picture brought Charlie a profit of $5 million.

You may argue that Buster Keaton was the finer artist. But Keaton's perilous survival of physical disaster in his films was matched by the fiasco of his private life. Keaton was a wreck, ruled by others, painfully unable to keep up. Indeed, he was so beaten down in life, one wonders how he mustered the concentration to ensure the serene development of his comic scenes. By the mid-1930s he had gone bust, broken as a man and horribly alcoholic. More to the point, Keaton made a mess of business. Buster Keaton Productions was a company in which 40 percent of the stock was owned by Joe Schenck (Buster's brother-in-law), Nick Schenck, and Nick's wife, Pansy. That arrangement of "relatives," Chaplin might have said, was the funniest thing in all of Buster's work. Buster had no shares himself; he didn't want the worry. Instead, the company paid him—$3,000 a week at his peak—and paid for the pictures. Here is the artist: look after everything, let me concentrate on the picture.

Later on, for a spell, Joe Schenck guided Buster away from independence and United Artists to M-G-M, but great films like *The General* and *Steamboat Bill Jr.* barely made a profit, with box office grosses under $500,000. Today, I think it's fair to say that film history puts Keaton as at least Chaplin's equal. But in their heydays, they were classes apart. Keaton, as many saw it, was a child, unready to take the responsibility of ownership.

He was tenderly reclaimed later in life, not least by Chaplin, who gave him a fond spot and tribute in *Limelight* (1952). And Keaton's work was restored and the films rereleased by Raymond Rohauer, a businessman with taste who bought out what remained of Buster Keaton Productions. Keaton died in 1966 a man of modest means.

Chaplin died in 1977 in Switzerland, where he had retreated after McCarthyite investigation, tax problems, and the paternity suit involving Joan Barry. He made films as late as 1967—*A Countess from Hong Kong* (nearly incoherent)—and he made all but one of them for United Artists. He had been married to Paulette Goddard (his best actress), and he married Oona O'Neill, the daughter of Eugene O'Neill (Charlie was fifty-four, Oona was eighteen). They seemed happy, and they had eight children, one of whom, the actress Geraldine Chaplin, would give a very touching performance as Charlie's demented mother in the dreadful picture *Chaplin* (1992). Charlie was rich, of course. And in 1972, he was allowed back to America to receive an honorary Oscar, "for the incalculable effect he had had on making motion pictures the art form of this century."

That's what the Academy was always for—to blur the equation enough so that profit and fame could be called art.

In movie acting, we discover the divided soul. Adolf Wohlbrück (Anton Walbrook), photographed by Lotte Jacobi, 1932 *(University of New Hampshire, Lotte Jacobi Archives)*

6 · BY A NOSE

These great faces in the movie dark, these moons of becoming, are they one of the few benevolent invasions of the twentieth century, meant to offset all the other images of slaughter, torture, and humiliation? Or is their intense allure just another danger, cunningly disguised? Or is it that the riddles of acting fascinate us at this moment in our history, especially the one in which we discover that we are not simply ourselves?

In other words, in a hundred years or so of marketed movie entertainment and its frequent flirtations with business glory and even artistic distinction, is it possible that the most profound thing that has been going on is the way in which so many of us have been led to think less of reality and more of dream, and the manner in which acting has carried us over that hump? Suppose the whole thing has been designed to make us politely disordered? Or more elastic?

It is as if in the twentieth century, the professional craft of pretending had brushed against our old sense of identity just as it became destabilized by the slippage of religious belief. There's a mixture of thrill and dread in the contact. The possibility of play—of acting—reaches out toward the uncertainty in which we are losing trust with so many of the principles of behavior or being we had been asked to adhere to.

In the age before the Renaissance, individuals possessed an anonymity to which fate was indifferent. There was nothing but types. But in the Renaissance, we discovered character, and with it the need to be true to ourselves—even if the result has been as tragic as it is for Hamlet or Emma Bovary. But then suppose that through photography and movie it becomes possible to step outside our consuming reality, to observe ourselves, to improve our performance. The new model for humanity becomes the actor, with his infinite variety. The center does not hold; possibilities seem to spin endlessly around a nucleic void or uncertainty. The cause of to thine own self being true has turned so treacherous lately that some of us have learned to treasure the assurance with which an actor may settle his own doubts by becoming someone fictitious or lovely.

Yes, of course, this is speculation, science fiction, if you like. But consider the theory for a few years, and look around you. Look at actors closely and wonder if they are not pioneering some perilous process for us.

What happened on the night of the Oscars in March of 2003 reminded me of the first time I saw *The Hours*—and of every time I have fallen for some woman in a movie. This was months before that film opened. A publicist, thinking the film might appeal to me, and hoping I might write about it, arranged a screening in early August 2002. I was alone in the small screening room, and I was shown a print that still had no credits. When I saw the film that first time, I had not read Michael Cunningham's novel. So I did not really know the story, or the casting. This meant that when "Virginia Woolf" first appeared in the film, I was not quite sure who was playing the part. I worked it out, but only on the principle that if Nicole Kidman was in the film—and I knew that in advance—then surely she was playing a leading role. That led to a process of elimination: Woolf had to be Kidman. That was possible, I realized, even though I was busier noticing things unique to this fierce, wounded "Mrs. Woolf" than her resemblances to Kidman.

So I was amused, but full of understanding, when the projectionist came out of his booth after the screening, and asked me, "Well, who was Kidman, then?"

Eight months later, having seen the film again, and having observed its reception, I felt the return of a similar sort of disorientation during the Oscars evening. Kidman was sitting in the front row at the Kodak Theatre as a contender for Best Actress. She was . . . I have to say "recognizable": her customary tall, willowy self, with bright buttery hair pulled tightly back from her very young, if not naïve face. She radiated health; she was peach-like, though maybe "beachy" was a better or more Australian word. She wore an elegant black gown, with three thin straps on one shoulder; there was a lot of bare shoulder and wholesomely glamorous skin on view. (And somehow she did suggest that the dress could just fall off—actresses are close to nakedness; I mean both the prospect of actual nude revelation, as well as the inner uncovering that has to be an actress's metier. But an actress can study an onion, say, as well as anyone; so an actress feels the dread that peeling might end in nothingness, too.)

But there were her happy blue eyes, too, the eyes of an Australian woman who might shrug off the others, her roles, as easily as a beach girl drying in the sun. And her very own nose—that slightly askew button. One doubted that she had had to present credentials to get into the theater. Anyone in security would have known she was "Nicole Kidman." And very nice, too.

I have been a fan of Kidman's ever since I saw her in *Dead Calm* (1989). What do I mean by "fan"? This isn't a coy or facetious question. Rather, it's a way of trying to admit that in searching commentary on films there needs to be some way of accommodating the fondness, the rapture, the attraction (there are other words) the writer feels for an actress, without ever having met or spoken to her. It's a matter of whether there is a candid, useful way of talking about our fantasizing over strangers in what seeks to be "responsible" criticism, let alone the common pursuit of living a good life.

And it's something that affects film criticism most notably. If we go to the theater—to see Kidman, say, in *The Blue Room,* where she was famously nude for a few seconds in London and New York—it's possible for the most reputable critics to talk of her "scorching sexual appeal" or the "undoubted erotic stardom" of the actress, without anyone taking it amiss. Theater is theater. The critic and the naked lady are sharing the same space, but the rules or conventions are clear: we do not advance from our seats to ravish her. We are not so bold, or rude. The arena is arranged for an exemplary performance, or lesson. But in movies, we know how distanced, how sly, how voyeuristic, the whole thing is. We know that she knows we are not quite "there," that we are sheltered in the dark. In other words, there is a built-in furtiveness, a clue to fantasy, and a kind of hushed, woeful lusting after the actress. Woeful in that it will never be realized.

Of course, this has been there with movies from the start. Though at the dawn no one quite grasped the extraordinarily complex gift of self, or persona, or ghostliness that was involved. How do we know that? Because the people in charge of movies were so preoccupied with what they were doing—the machinery, the show, the tickets, the spools of film—that they did not notice what was happening in the dark. They did not appreciate that seeing a woman's face was like a meeting, only a meeting in which the viewer's shyness, modesty, or responsibility was dissolved.

This still works, even if the medium seems bored with it nowadays, and it is still the essential erotic charge in film. A person comes ready to be photographed: he or she is beautiful; every improvement of makeup, hair-dressing and costume adds to the natural glory. The lights are so arranged that not only is he or she perfectly visible, there is also a kind of mood or atmosphere—a desirability—that spills from the skin, like cool water in a desert. Something else begins to occur with the first person given this treatment, and it mounts over a hundred years until it is like a cultural condition: it is that the essence of the person reaches for the surface, for the thing called appearance. Put it all there, where the light is.

But then, as everything seems to be ready, the cameraman or the director makes a small, but momentous adjustment. Josef von Sternberg once described how he had managed it with Marlene Dietrich. He had found her, of course, in Germany. Not that she was unknown or undiscovered, but he saw her, and saw into her. He must have done many real things: he got her to lose weight, and acquire disdain; he surely made love to her, and that may have helped. But eventually, as she stood there waiting, he said, in his autobiography, "Turn your shoulders away from me and straighten out. . . . Drop your voice an octave and don't lisp. . . . Count to six and look at that lamp as if you could no longer live without it. . . ."

Love affairs last about as long as light bulbs? What had happened was that, instead of looking at the camera—which still seems the natural or polite thing to do if you are having your photograph taken—Dietrich turned away a few degrees and looked out into the darkness. That is the shift that turns a snapshot into a dream (if you prefer the latter to the former), for it establishes this unreality: that the woman does not know she is being taken; does not notice the lights, the camera or the crew; she is simply there, for us, patient, yielding, emotionally naked if not always quite the whole thing . . . with this precious extra. She does not refer to our presence. She is as if alone—which, of course, makes her all the more easily ours. In truth, millions of strangers are spying on her, and she is kind enough (or is it something else?) to let us stay as unknown as the dark. Why do the movies take place in the dark? So that the extent to which we are moved, the nature of our voyeurism and the indecent depths to which desire draws us may not be apparent. You see, we have no appearance, no identity, no status. We are the unknown. All of which can be beguiling, but sooner or later we might as well notice the affinity with the crowd in fascist scenarios.

That's what I want to own up to with Nicole Kidman. I apologize if this seems too candid, or mawkish, for upright citizens. I recognize that it is a level of consideration that serious film critics seldom admit to. And, in one obvious way, it is an admission that could rule the critic out of order. Yet, I hold to the admission because it is central to film, and to what happens in the dark. Ever since the beginnings of this strange medium, men and women have been drawn to the screen by feeling "in love with" some of the huge faces (and empty desires) put up there.

Is "in love with" the right phrase? Is it just a matter of the attractiveness of the faces and the great seductive draw of their stories? Is it little more than lusting after such radiant faces and superb bodies that offer themselves to the camera as if unaware that millions will be watching? If we take "unfair" advantage of our secret vantage, well, then, the movies and their people have been tricky, too. They turn a blind eye to what they know, or hope for: that so many peeping toms will be there spying on them. So they let themselves be photographed with the most magical rapture of cinema—the conceit that they are alone. In turn, that strokes another falsehood: that only we—that I alone—am watching Kidman.

Well, you may declare—troubled by this undergrowth—whatever this feeling is, however illicit or perverse, it can hardly be called love, can it? As in love and marriage. Well, "love" is a word and a right we all own, and while we may like to think that it is best restricted to those familial, marital, or friendly ties based on real intimacy and acquaintance, we are troubled, too. After a hundred years of movies, we have discovered the ways in which it may be far easier, and far more beguiling, to be in love with someone you will never meet, as opposed to those raw, awkward customers with whom you can live. Men and women are often unfaithful in life: the awkwardness is too much to bear, or too harsh for our dreams. Yet sometimes we never give up our loyalty to these lovely stars. Isn't this love? Or so like love that "normal" pre-movie notions of that thing have been terribly jeopardized?

Theater critics—reviewers of *The Blue Room,* say—would not be permitted or hired by newspapers to write about a play if they were married or related to the actress (or the actor) in the lead parts. If I review a book, I have to convince the literary editor that I do not know its author—or, if I may have met him or her briefly, that I have no prior commitment of friendship (or enmity). The world of reviewing regards that as proper.

Yet in the matter of the movies, I believe, critics or reviewers are regularly engaged in writing about people on whom they have a crush, for whom they hold a secret torch; there are so many half-shy, half-ashamed ways of putting it. Or not: for, of course, the protective darkness of the movies, the unacknowledged secrecy, means that you do not have to declare your feelings. Which doesn't kill them. In other words, for the critic as for the regular moviegoer, seeing certain films has always been contingent on seeing someone for whom you have these powerful feelings.

For myself, I can't see that the feelings are illicit or perverse—I don't think "love" is very often susceptible to those things, no matter the legal spasms of certain censorious societies. My response is in the nature of the movies and always has been. It can coexist with reasonably happy marriages (for both the critic and the actress). It does not necessarily make for madness, disaster, or murder. We are very clever at learning to accommodate our own tricks, even if we do not like owning up to them.

In social practice, without necessarily sinking to words like "damage," there have been profound consequences. Divorce has flared up, and become commonplace. We are much more aware now of the ease of falling in and out of love. Movies are not the only breath blowing on those fires. But it is foolish to rule out their influence. And if you want to trace just one, active consequence, try this: the movies, I think, were the first permission offered to the masses to "fall in love" with people of their own sex, as well as the opposite one. Does that mean that more of us are homosexual or bisexual? Not necessarily, though the statistics do sustain that conclusion. Above all, it is an indication of how much we exist in our fantasies and, as a result, the degree to which we are beginning to abandon reality. That is the large shift in nature, the great puzzle or predicament, that I referred to earlier.

Now, you may say, it's Nicole Kidman for me, and, say, Russell Crowe for you. Except fantasy is never so restricted; it is a harem, not a conjugal contract. I love hundreds of stars. I suspect that you do, too. That is what really makes movies work, no matter that it's a dynamic that may have sucked us an inch or two closer to madness or muddle or whatever. Why not, we've had fun, too, haven't we? I think we have become more promiscuous, less steadfast in our behavior. I daresay we are more in love now with the idea of love than with the reality. Put it another way—and this is crucial—we have many of us become a little more like actors, waiting for a fresh part, a new start.

Anyway, back to Nicole Kidman at the Oscars. There she was in the front row, looking about as humble and as ready as she could manage. And why not? Even if you thought she was rather far-fetched as an actress in her early days, even if you regarded her as just a pretty attachment to Tom Cruise, many people feel bound to admire the ways her career has developed. She seems older, wiser, more independent, more skilled. Her disentanglement from Cruise was a part of that, maybe. But, really, one had only to list her recent films to see a series of brave, enterprising choices, and increasing range and subtlety as an actress: *To Die For, The Portrait of a Lady, Eyes Wide Shut, Moulin Rouge, The Others, Birthday Girl, The Hours, The Human Stain, Cold Mountain* . . . and the line is hardly over yet.

She was favored to win the Oscar for *The Hours* not just because of her Virginia Woolf (on-screen actually for only about a third of the film, so she could have been nominated for Best Supporting Actress as Julianne Moore was for the same film), but because of the development in her work. There was a feeling that this was her turn, though she was only thirty-five. Without ever seeming gauche or obtrusive, she had contributed to her own publicity campaign with enthusiasm (a very small part of which had been that publicist giving me an early view of *The Hours*). The campaigning, the presentation of self in everyday life, is very much part of the business.

A good deal of that campaigning will be in the contract for a particular film—the obligation to be interviewed and photographed, to give what is called "access" (another word that plays with external and inner presence). But whereas, once upon a time, a studio would have owned Nicole Kidman, and promoted her out of the same office over a stretch of years, now she is her own mistress. And as she moves from project to project, from one studio to another, she needs more comfort than that carousel offers. So she engages a public relations company, and she has someone who "handles" her, on a retainer basis. That person is intimately involved in the mysterious image and identity of a star as well as the sometimes very nervous observer of an unfolding human drama (a peeling) that is not always comfortable.

That process probably would have seemed hideous and unthinkable to Virginia Woolf (though I like the film very much, I was struck to the core by a friend's wicked surmise as to what Mrs. Woolf would have thought about it). Woolf killed herself in March 1941, before she would have had a chance to see *Citizen Kane*. This isn't meant to be flippant or irreverent. Rather it's a way of wondering whether Woolf was a moviegoer from time to time. Did she take for granted that an educated person kept up with exciting things? Would *Kane* have impressed her? Not that I imagine it keeping her out of the River Ouse for long.

Of course resemblance is a peculiar thing. By now, even if you haven't seen *The Hours,* you know some of the things Kidman did to get closer to Mrs. Woolf. She wore a prosthetic nose. She redid her hair. She took on a new voice. And she felt her way toward a far more severe personality than she had offered previously. I gather that in those scenes where she starts to write *Mrs. Dalloway* (and which employ, I believe, photocopies of the novelist's handwriting) Kidman learned to write right-handed instead of left.

Yet she does not look like Virginia Woolf. You would not mistake them—Woolf had a thinner, more elongated, finer face; her mouth was weaker (or more subtle) than Kidman's; her eyes were more remote and less practical. I'm not complaining (though Kidman's Woolf does look quite like Charlotte Brontë). I was astonished by Kidman's performance because of the journey she had made and the amount of self she had abandoned. I suspect she had become a good deal less mercurial and humorous than the real Virginia Woolf, and a little more crushingly aware of how her life was going to end. It's my guess that from day to day, even when struggling to start *Mrs. Dalloway,* the real Woolf was more fun, sillier and less resolved. Real people, even great authors, are like that. Kidman's performance was based upon a huge, tragic respect for writing in someone who likely does very little of it.

No matter (you see, I can tease a beloved), it was a stirring presentation, very much aided by clothes, by the movie's Richmond house, by

Stephen Dillane and Miranda Richardson (as her husband and sister), and by David Hare and Stephen Daldry (scriptwriter and director). Which is all exactly what moviemaking should be in an ideal world. And out of it all, Nicole Kidman had achieved a large gesture toward being Virginia Woolf that many people found moving and interesting. To such an extent, I may say, that I think the film suffered whenever it gave her up for the two other principal women characters and their lives. We wanted more of Woolf and I suspect that Kidman and Hare could have created it.

No matter. I believed I was seeing Virginia Woolf, or the idea of a great and troubled writer who had a hard time creating fiction while staying alive. I identified with the story—to use the language expected of us. And that meant that I wanted to help Stephen Dillane (a dedicated performance) look after his wife. Not that anything like sentimental rescue seemed in sight. Still, his caring was infectious, and it helped build her character that he had such respect for her (that's what drama can do).

But there was something else about Kidman's performance that needs to be talked about, and it hovered over that uncertainty as to whether it was her. It is very rare in movies for stars to be unrecognizable. There are a few treasured instances in the history of the medium—Lon Chaney, the "man of a thousand faces," comes to mind—but he was a pioneer of horror and makeup in a silent medium; Dustin Hoffman putting on all that makeup to seem 103 years old in *Little Big Man;* and Robert De Niro taking on that extra weight to play Jake La Motta years after his boxing career, struggling with a terrible nightclub act.

But the fatso La Motta talked like De Niro. No one ever doubted what we were seeing. Maybe the most remarkable thing about Kidman's Woolf was the voice. Again, I doubt it was like Virginia Woolf's. I seem to remember hearing her once on the radio, and if it was hers the voice was thinner, more upper class, more Kensington, more off-puttingly privileged for today's audience. But Kidman has a very solid Australian accent and she has rarely tempered it. It was all too apparent in her attempt to be Isabel Archer in *The Portrait of a Lady.* And while it wasn't the biggest problem about that odd film, still it was a distraction.

In *The Hours,* her voice was free, unexpected and as helpful to her grim, headachy face as to the idea that that face might be pained by the as yet undelivered *Mrs. Dalloway.* The voice and the attitude together made clear the character's bemusement with so many things in life—nephews and nieces, servants, household, a regular life and Richmond. It was an English voice, plausibly forty or so (the age at which Woolf wrote *Mrs. Dalloway*), bitter and bleak about some things, especially her own health.

What I am trying to get at with Kidman's Woolf is the remarkable way in which she employed the materials and the craft of acting to get at a person whose greatest chance at life was to be someone unreal—like Mrs. Dalloway. And she succeeded. You can look for yourself, and make up your own mind. But whatever you think of *The Hours* as a whole, I think you will feel that Kidman committed herself to a dangerous journey. She had been ready to give up herself, in the way that a novelist wants to escape herself and become a character.

I have remarked on how rare this is in film. On stage, it is quite acceptable that Laurence Olivier, say, can be Hamlet, Macbeth, Archie Rice, Oedipus, all manner of men, varying his look, his voice, his bearing, his stance, his nose (Olivier loved to start with a new nose). But in movies, the great stars were made to look like themselves. Of course, that meant that they needed suitable roles, and their employers were always looking for, say, ideal Joan Crawford material, or a John Wayne vehicle. And it worked: it kept faith with all those lovers in the dark.

To have done otherwise risked a lot. It would have been an experiment with identity or screen personality that might have blocked a career, something that's still true. Screen careers may last less time now. Our promiscuity lets them come and go, and youth becomes an imperative of desirability. But Kidman has taken a risk with Virginia Woolf, I think, in getting far away from the wholesome sexpot that she has done so well for so long she may be bored by it, or aware of how ill-fitting it is.

So it was striking to see the Australian kid back again at the Oscars, her accent like a great sail full of wind. She had had a public life for several years, and she had good reason to think she might win. But she was a mess up on stage. You can argue that it was calculated, but I don't think so. I felt that a not very sophisticated person was trying to quell her own emotions. She turned her back so that we wouldn't see her weeping. She spoke of her mother and her daughter—both there—and of wanting to make them seem proud. It was touching, but trite, and it was shocking to witness after the grave, guarded Virginia Woolf.

For it looked as if, despite her period of immersion in the cold, challenging water of Woolf, nothing had penetrated or lasted in the bubbly Australian girl. She might say not so, and she would be in a position to know. But it might also be that actors and actresses can sometimes find themselves as vehicles for grace or spirit, and then walk away, untouched, unaltered. There are contrary stories of actresses who never got over certain parts—Vivien Leigh is supposed to have hurtled toward her own breakdown with Blanche Du Bois's energy. Maybe such artistic identification seems like a kind of madness.

But what seems more mysterious still, and more of a lesson, is how a cheerful Australian girl could walk in tragic steps for a season or so and then move on, as if the experience were a dream that had slipped away like water. And maybe that is what acting comes to—for the professionals and us everyday amateurs—a majesty that dries in the sun and leaves no trace.

* * *

And yet. . . . If Nicole Kidman can pass in and out of the light of *The Hours* without being altered, I'm not sure that I or this book can get so close to *Mrs. Dalloway* and walk away scot-free. It is all very well to say that Kidman made millions begin to think of the real Virginia Woolf with compassion and insight. I'm sure that happened, and I'm sure that seeing or reading *The Hours* has done wonders for the sale of *Mrs. Dalloway*. But, in truth, *The Hours* settled for a not much more than tender, adult gossip column's sense of Mrs. Woolf. (Oh look! She makes sure lunch is ready—with ginger from town—and still writes the first sentence of her novel!) It does better than that inasmuch as it creates a pattern of lives across more than seventy-five years in which three women grapple with the same kind of dismay, and are borne up vaguely but usefully by the idea of being in some distant, dreaming formation. Like geese flying south?

But it happened, in composing this chapter, that I had a copy of *Mrs. Dalloway* on my desk—sitting on top of Sternberg's *Fun in a Chinese Laundry*—and since writers cannot write every minute and every hour, occasionally I sat back and dipped into what Virginia Woolf had been doing in 1925, with surprising, if not awkward, results. For while *The Hours* presents a compelling portrait of the agony and difficulty of writing *Mrs. Dalloway,* the novel itself seems entirely at ease with its ease, if you see what I mean. It is so beautifully written, I find it a touch excessive or self-pitying to be reminded that it might have been hard. But that is not the worst of it. *Mrs. Dalloway* is so smart, so hip, so cool, so charged with what writing can do, that I found myself pushed back to worrying over what movies had done in 1925.

This harping on what other arts were doing may seem like the thin end of snobbery's wedge. But it's only an attempt to see film as the art it might be. It's an important part of the equation that other things were happening at the same time, just as it's worth stressing that, in 2001–02, the finest minds and operatives in American film sought to do *The Hours* as a way of demonstrating how bold and sensitive they were but still came away with a product that suffers terribly in comparison with *Mrs. Dalloway.* For instance, no mere viewer of *The Hours* would ever know how exhilarating *Mrs. Dalloway* is, or what a sure grasp it has on the particular damage done to the mind by the First World War.

What I really mean by this is that Virginia Woolf is so much smarter than David Hare, Stephen Daldry, producer Scott Rudin, and everyone else who made *The Hours.* It's foolish to deny that gap. It's like settling for a nice, tidy set of quadratic equations when you suspect that calculus is around the corner.

That comparison sounds more alarming than I want it to be. It's not that *Mrs. Dalloway* is so very difficult that many people would have had no chance with it upon its publication and so they fell with glee and relief on what Hollywood had to offer in 1925–26: *The Gold Rush;* William S. Hart in *Tumbleweeds;* King Vidor's *The Big Parade; Ben Hur;* Garbo's *Flesh and the Devil;* or even Sternberg's *The Salvation Hunters* (maybe the most advanced of this group).

Without sound, those films are seldom much more than precocious infants. The quality of life to which they refer or aspire is banal next to the complexities embodied in *The Great Gatsby, An American Tragedy,* or *Mrs. Dalloway.* What's more, somehow a casual filmgoer like Woolf has managed a novel that is already decades ahead of film in the ease with which it tracks through time and space, cuts majestically and shuffles point of view. As early as 1925, *Mrs. Dalloway* is like something out of Antonioni (except that it is more lively and more genuinely anguished than the monotonously depressed Italian could ever manage):

> She stiffened a little on the kerb, waiting for Durtnall's van to pass. A charming woman, Scrope Purvis thought her (knowing her as one does know people who live next door to one in Westminster); a touch of the bird about her, of the jay, blue-green, light, vivacious, though she was over fifty, and grown very white since her illness. There she perched, never seeing him, waiting to cross, very upright.
>
> For having lived in Westminster—how many years now? over twenty,—one feels even in the midst of the traffic, or waking at night, Clarissa was positive, a particular hush, or solemnity; an indescribable pause; a suspense (but that might be her heart, affected, they said, by influenza) before Big Ben strikes. There! Out it boomed. First a warning, musical; then the hour, irrevocable. The leaden circles dissolved in the air.

Such fools we are, she thought, crossing Victoria Street. For Heaven only knows why one loves it so, how one sees it so, making it up, building it round one, tumbling it, creating it every moment afresh; but the veriest frumps, the most dejected of miseries sitting on doorsteps (drink their downfall) do the same; can't be dealt with, she felt positive, by Acts of Parliament for that very reason: they love life. In people's eyes, in the swing, tramp, and trudge; in the bellow and the uproar; the carriages, motor cars, omnibuses, vans, sandwich men shuffling and swinging; brass bands; barrel organs; in the triumph and the jingle and the strange high singing of some aeroplane overhead was what she loved; life; London; this moment of June.

I suppose one either feels the beauty or one does not in the assonance and rhythm of ". . . what she loved; life; London; this moment of June." It's like responding to a tracking movement in one of Jean Renoir's films from the 1930s, with the "spontaneous" tragicomedy of people, rooms, doorways, and space accommodating the camera. But then what is there in movies that can possibly match the richness of "The leaden circles dissolved in the air"? More than seventy-five years later, where has there been a movie that comes anywhere near catching this tapestry of human movement in an actual city, with the flash of ideas and feelings that goes with it? Where is the movie that gives such a feeling of what it is to be alive?

To be more pointed, I cannot help but wonder whether the brimming density of this passage—and of the whole short novel—doesn't reduce the suicide scene in the Ouse in *The Hours* to mere pictorial sensationalism. I still like *The Hours;* I was moved by it. I am still in whatever kind of love it is with Nicole Kidman and the idea she pretends to—of writing. But I cannot hold back the realization that maybe the movies have never been good enough.

Good enough for us and for life. For we deserve more.

* * *

And yet . . . I can't settle for this cul-de-sac, no matter how reasonable it seems. No one ever threatened to put me, or you, in a position where we had to choose—books or films. We can have both, and more. We can hope that there are fresh ways ahead where the one will inform and enlarge the other.

So I looked at *The Hours* once more, having fairly satisfactorily convinced myself of its inadequacy. And I was lucky enough to rediscover the faces, those moons of becoming. I am not sure that the most articulated levels of film language have as yet come anywhere near the intricacy, the subtlety, and suppleness of writing. But still, time and again, the chemistry that exists between photography and the face maintains a depth or mystery in film that is without rival. And so I return to the way Kidman looks in *The Hours.*

And I do mean Kidman. For I find that the other faces have worn themselves out as far as I'm concerned: Julianne Moore, so plucky, yet so inwardly vacant; and Meryl Streep, so valiant, so good-worksy, and so much on idle if she feels she doesn't have a leading role. No, there are only a few faces that are really alive and I find them all in the Virginia Woolf section. I don't mean to take pages spelling out the various looks and transitions that Kidman does. After all, I don't really believe she was doing them. Rather, she had got herself into a state of being where they occurred. So sometimes she is mean, spiteful, nasty, selfish, uncaring; and always there is a frown of effort that you never find in Virginia Woolf's face. I don't think Kidman "did" it, in a way Streep does "do" it. She was possessed, and I (for one) was put in a state of something like love.

This state was there from the beginning of movies, even if, say, Louise Brooks in *Pandora's Box* is the first presence I think I could have fallen for. And Brooks's Lulu is still very dangerous, capable of sweeping pages of description aside with a glance. And the capacity for loving strangers, whether one thinks of them as fictional beings or stars one will never meet, is a profound reflection on the new consciousness whereby every individual leads his or her life while aware of all the billions of other people on Earth. Perhaps it is a fantasy or a fallacy that we can feel for so many strangers. Perhaps it is a mask for our selfishness. But no matter the modern stress on special effects, there isn't a sight in movies as momentous as shots of a face as its mind is being changed. And only movies have allowed that. Still pictures, in contrast, are elephantine studies in sentimentality. But when the face flickers in time—like the woman's face in Chris Marker's *La Jetée*—then the world and its chance of meaning changes.

So maybe movies are always about the faces on the screen, as opposed to the minds that constructed them?

The first dreamer at the movies is the character—Lillian Gish in Griffith's *Broken Blossoms*, 1919 *(Private Collection)*

7 · THE MAN IN THE HAT . . .
A WOMAN IN GLOVES

Last night, April 23, 2003, I attended the San Francisco Symphony, under the direction of Michael Tilson Thomas, in their performance of Mahler's Ninth Symphony. I was there for the music itself, but I was mindful that on the next day (today) I was to begin my effort to describe the evolution of film as a language that occurred in the years just after 1910.

Mahler's Ninth was written in the years 1909–10. It was first performed in Vienna, under Bruno Walter, in 1912, a little more than a year after Mahler's death. (The piece was not performed in the United States until 1931, in Boston, under Serge Koussevitzky.) And in those same years, 1909–12, D. W. Griffith made several hundred short films, one- or two-reelers, among which *The Lonedale Operator, Enoch Arden, The Goddess of Sagebrush Gulch, Just Like a Woman, The School Teacher and the Waif, The Musketeers of Pig Alley,* and *A Corner in Wheat* are the most celebrated.

These were, for the most part, films made for Biograph at their studios on East Fourteenth Street in Manhattan, and then in the Bronx. They were "movies" in which we can trace the many discoveries Griffith was making that might turn film from a mere recording device to a narrative mechanism of some sophistication. In most of the history books, Griffith is identified—and the story of the movies is more easily told because of his presence—as the man who worked out the language of film storytelling, using cuts (or editing) for suspense or for naturalistic smoothness of continuity, and seeing that a variety of shots (or views) could be taken of the same piece of action (a scene or a sequence) so that they could be cut together to make an arresting whole in which the viewer registers both the large action and its emotional details.

It has been orthodoxy for film people to hail Griffith as the essential clarifier of film as a sequential language, instead of a mere wonder—a show of camera magic. James Agee, writing close to the time of Griffith's death (in 1948), said:

> He achieved what no other known man has ever achieved. To watch his work is like being witness to the beginning of melody, or the first conscious use of the lever or the wheel; the emergence, coordination, and first eloquence of language; the birth of an art: and to realize that this is all the work of one man.

Among other things, that suggests that Agee had not seen anything (or even heard of) Louis Feuillade, in France; Victor Sjöström, in Sweden; or even Carl Dreyer, in various European countries. Of course, that is easier to understand when we realize that Mahler's Ninth Symphony (now a standard work) took twenty years before reaching America. Equally, much of Charles Ives's music, intensely American, was not played in his own country until decades after it had been written. In 1910, the United States was not the cutting edge of civilization or modernism. It was a dusty side street next to Paris, Vienna, or even Dublin (where James Joyce was opening a cinema, the Volta).

Griffith fell into his singular reputation: it was the good luck granted him by posterity when he had so much bad luck in life. No one looking at his career as a whole, or at his films in detail, would wish to deny him his place, though Agee's strident, hero-worshipping tones alert us to the chance of there being some others in America who were testing the new ways of filming and cutting. Chaplin was, for one: very often, the sense of timing or uptake he assumed in his viewers is more than Griffith can allow, and in those early years, narrative coherence was the key dynamic. I suspect that historical fairness would have Griffith share his place with several other directors and even with actors and actresses, for these were days when stars in front of the camera could sense how long a look was needed, or from where it might best be filmed.

Still, grant that *The Birth of a Nation* (1915) and *Intolerance* (1916) are worth seeing today as narratives, as demonstrations of cinematic evolution, as "art," but that the viewer who seeks out Feuillade's *Fantomas* (1913–14) or *Les Vampires* (1915–16), or Sjöström's *The Outlaw and His Wife* (1918) may have a better time. The material and ideas are more complex; there is a more modern sense of the leaping potential of the medium; more grown-up people. And Conrad's *Victory* is 1915, too.

To be honest, I don't think any of the films named in the paragraph above really stand up as art, so much as something on the way to art. That can be a fascinating historical inquiry, well worth making. But if you wish to stay a movie "purist," or if you want to cling on to certain sentimentalities and heroes, then don't listen to Mahler's Ninth and its unequivocal revelation of other things felt in 1912. Listen to that music, and you cannot ignore the naïveté, the coarseness, in Griffith.

I am not a musician; I have had no musical education. But that only leaves me in a frustrated or desirous state, for I want to hear more music and find ways of writing about it. Above all, I want here to suggest—as gently as possible—the folly of concentrating on and proclaiming the growing articulation in Griffith's films, their fluency of transition, their range of experience or emotion, their leading us into the mind and the soul, when Mahler's Ninth was their contemporary.

Movies are not novels, and they are not symphonies. Nevertheless, all three work through duration: they ask questions so that we desire the answers; we must apply our time to them—we accept that over the course of one or several hours, the progress of the works (the reading in the novel, the unwinding in the film, the performance of the music) will hold and move us. You may say afterward that you were changed by it; that you were entertained; or that you had an okay time. What that range of response implies is a kind of dramatic effect exerted through time. And whether we describe that shift as narrative or thematic or simply as the forward drive of the music, there are structural affinities, in theme, reiteration, transition; in hesitation, silence, stillness, and ending. Emotionally, and as nervous systems, the three play upon us in similar ways. So the comparison is not out of bounds or irrelevant.

Who then can deny—who would waste his or her own time by entering into argument over it—that the Mahler is possessed by insights into experience rendered as continuation and hesitation that are far beyond the similar effects in Griffith? When people die in *The Birth of a Nation* it is a matter of violence, pathos, and lamentation. When the Ninth Symphony ends, after that slow unwinding of phrases in the cello, the viola, and the violin, it is like sound joining silence, like life accepting death. The Mahler is exquisite, majestic, tragic, accepting—these are the humdrum words of criticism. Griffith, beside him, is a dealer in melodrama and in vastly diminished and inferior notions of life—what it is and might be.

This does not mean that music is always a superior art to film. In the years since 1915, that debate has become so much more challenging, in part, I fear, because music has not developed as richly as film. But that is intriguing, too. Agee said of Griffith, "To watch his work is like being witness to the beginning of melody." Whereas, to hear Mahler's Ninth is often to sense the composer's foreboding that melody itself was stricken, or dying. Yes, there are sustained melodic passages—like the violins at the start of the last movement—but much more often the symphony is built upon the idea of interrupted melody, of fragmentary phrases that are trying to pick up or maintain flow, but which are held back or chilled by other things in the air. What things? Well, I don't think it's too much to say that those things in the air have to do with the dread wars that followed, with the colossal public cruelty of the twentieth century, and even with fears that humanism and knowledge and reason are themselves failing.

And that is why it is so important to say that Griffith and Mahler are contemporary. And just as Griffith's films look helplessly back at recent history in melodrama's lightning, so Mahler cannot help but feel a cold dawn coming up.

Put that way, I think an understanding of Griffith comes into sight. And this is why the aspect of cultural history is so helpful. For Griffith and infant cinema recognize a need in the society of 1910 that amounts to the essential question of that new century, of "modern times": Could everyone in this crowded world be free, mature, and rational? Can egalitarian forms of government and liberal forms of association survive against all the forces of menace, tyranny, fear, paranoia, and totalitarianism that can be felt gathering in Mahler's music, in Cubism, and in some of the great novels of the same period?

Most modern nations had lately achieved the vote and the right for their citizens to be educated—male citizens only, in most cases, but the march was on. We still don't know whether those benefits will save us from ourselves. In 1912, in Great Britain, a country proud of its educational system, there was distress when school inspectors reported that as much as 2 percent of people ranging in age from fifteen to twenty-one were functionally illiterate. That gap had to be repaired.

Allow that the percentage who were only moderately literate was a lot higher than two, and you can feel the great pressure on education. For good and ill, a universal or equal education system does not want to accuse students of being inferior, let alone stupid or inadequate. The psychology of educational systems has become so gentle as to risk being called weak by its critics. Thus, today, in the U.S.A. (the United States of Amnesia), we have grade inflation, much lower levels of general knowledge than were once prevalent (in the time of Griffith, say), the reckless graduation from high school of kids who cannot read properly. The latest finding by those school inspectors in Britain is that the percentage of functionally illiterate people in the age range fifteen-to-twenty-one has risen to 15 percent. We are especially aghast to think that the great experiment of universal education may have been misguided. Do corporal punishment, strictness, stress on "fact," and the kind of competitiveness that keeps some people out of school, or the best schools, work best?

I hope not, for I was a beneficiary of widening opportunity. And I hate the idea of beating sense into children—it is but a first step toward the concentration camp. I am especially fascinated by the place movies held in this great dilemma. And I am very respectful of the idealism displayed by some people who do not seem to me to be helpfully examined as artists. Many early movie people, filmmakers and businessmen, had a vague, innocent dream of improving, or saving, the world. Irene Mayer Selznick would write of that mood: "Movies were like a great cause to us; to be pretentious, you could call it a sense of mission."

No one ever accused David Wark Griffith of a good education. Even Agee said, "He had no remarkable power of intellect, or delicateness of soul; no subtlety; little restraint; little if any 'taste.' " He was born in La Grange, Kentucky, in 1875, part of a poor family given harsher times by the aftermath of the Civil War. He was raised in the countryside (he loved rural society) and moved to Louisville when his father died. He received no education past the age of fifteen. He had a variety of bad jobs before chance led him to the theater, and the idea of being an actor.

This was still the nineteenth century, when no one had any notion of what a film director might be, when movies seemed like a wild craze scooping up the momentary appearance of things, like a blood sample at a crime. Griffith persevered ten years in the theater: he was tall, well-spoken, and handsome in a sad way. He wasn't a leading man. But by 1908, he was a player in movies at Biograph and it was then, to stay employed, that he agreed to serve as a director. The move was forced on him, it seems, for he was known as a bad actor.

It's worth asking what "directing" meant then, if only because the primitive germ of function is very likely still there in the much more elevated job. The director was a manager, a go-between for such elements as the story line, the camera, and the players (apparently self-sufficient tasks). He was there to maintain the efficiency of the enterprise; to school the actors in the action; to make sure the camera was loaded and ready. It was his task to say "Fade in" and "Fade out" (he preferred those genteel orders to "Action" and "Cut"), in the way a starter is essential to a sprint, but then immediately forgotten. He was a supervisor, a time-and-motion nut, a worrier, and a man who ticked off tasks. Very often today, wherever the factory conditions of making film obtain, the director still is. For example, we know the actors in *The Sopranos;* we know David Chase is the creator of the show; but who directs the episodes?

Griffith was one among several people who gradually worked out ways of filming things—he was an organizer, with enough actorly instinct to pick out the key moments in action and to see how a change in camera position might gain a subtlety in short order, as I said earlier. Equally, the camera was the great tyrant in early filmmaking if only because of the ways it might break down or malfunction. Cameramen were gods, in secret conference with the other god, the one who ordered the light. Moving the camera, beginning to take charge of it, was a way of undermining that natural authority. Choosing where to put the camera is a vital element in filmmaking and film art, but it came into being not just for art's sake but as a power play, a way of dominating the set. And in time, Griffith took charge by having a loyal lieutenant, Billy Bitzer, as his cameraman. Griffith made Bitzer famous, but Bitzer knew who was the boss.

I don't think it's frivolous to say that identifying the boss is what Hollywood is all about. It's the lesson Robert Towne learned with *Chinatown* and *The Two Jakes*. And the question remains open enough to have a lot of answers. The business as a whole, with nothing to lose, likes to say that the audience owns the movies. That's a way of giving up responsibility for the product, and of overlooking the common audience pain at feeling screwed, or forgotten. Actors often own pictures: not just as the controlling financial interest involved, but as those ghosts who "own" the screen. Bogart's sour gaze and edgy rhythms patrol *Casablanca,* reason enough for the star's dismay that he made so little on the "classic."

Griffith was not a brilliant man, and not nearly as great a powermonger as many who would follow him. But he was noticeable, if not impressive, physically; and to that he added the simple ploy of often wearing a hat—a broad-brimmed, elegant thing as a rule, a plantation owner's hat, something to make him stand out. He had Southern manners and he liked to indulge his actresses in careful, flattering consultations, tête-à-têtes, about what their characters were feeling. He sometimes danced with "Miss Geesh" before a day's work. He relished that careful intimacy, and was quite happy to go deeper behind the marvelous eyes of the Gish sisters. He regarded such virginal creatures, as he did rural scenes, with guileless fondness and trust. Modern in many ways, Griffith was also a throwback, a man in love with nostalgia and the social values of a pastoral tradition.

There's a fascinating passage from his unfinished autobiography, deeply Victorian in its pleasure at nature and stability, and very instructive as it sees the camera as a box for preserving the past. He was talking about the world of his childhood:

> There was a small field close behind the farmhouse, I went out to it early one spring morning, when a boy, with a little pail to gather dewberries. The berry patch was on a gently sloping hillside. Behind it was a double log cabin where lived two Negro families that had been slaves of my parents. Beside the rambling cabin flowed a small stream and on one side of the patch there was a stake-and-rider rail fence. Several larks were soaring up and down from this rail fence, singing ecstatically in the clear spring morning. In memory I always seem to see around this entire scene a luminous glow of joy. As I walked it seemed that my bare feet hardly touched the ground. Of course, I did not realize that never again would I know such pure joy, such singing, soaring ecstasy. . . .
>
> Often afterwards, I have thought what a grand invention it would be if someone could make a magic box in which we could store the precious

moments of our lives and keep them with us, and later on, in dark hours could open this box and receive for at least a few moments, a breath of its stored memory.

It's like Wordsworth's "Prelude," imitated by a nice little girl, and it's typical of the Victorianism that felt threatened by progress. All of which makes Griffith an unlikely radical or inventor. So many of his movies are set in the past, with a plain wish to return to its simpler values. Not least *The Birth of a Nation,* which has become a revealing definition of cinema in America—an unquestionable landmark, yet unfit to show. Agee said, in its feeble defense, that its racism was faithful to how white men of the South still felt in 1915. Except that Mark Twain's *Huckleberry Finn* was already a classic. If only Griffith had had the wish to make a film of that, instead of Thomas Dixon's odious *The Klansman.*

Nor is it the case that Griffith merely reflected Southern attitudes. It's clear that, in Georgia, at least, the opening of the film and the lynching of Leo Frank (after he had been convicted for the murder of Mary Phagan, and had his death sentence commuted by a governor aware of the shaky case against Frank) revived the Ku Klux Klan. There were twenty-two lynchings in Georgia in 1915, and within a few years the Klan had a membership of 8 million.

When Griffith's young assistant, Karl Brown, read the Dixon book, his heart sank: "The result could not fail to be a complete and crushing disaster." But, not for the last time, literary taste proved misleading.

There's a story about the battle scene that shows how brilliant and how innocent Griffith was. He assigned the young Raoul Walsh (later a great director) to do "pick-up shots," details of small groups of soldiers, Confederate and Yankee, advancing. Just make sure that one side advances one way and the other the other way, Walsh was told. So he went to a field with a few men, a camera, and an assortment of uniforms. First the extras did it one way in blue, then the other in gray. None of them knew what it was for, but Griffith had foreseen that the fragmented dance would cut together. What no one saw then was that the method was in itself a superb, surreal exposé of war.

Let me add this, for it shatters a notion that has often been used to proclaim masterpieces in American film: novelty of technique and radiance of form do not begin to compensate for unholy material. That holds true from *Birth of a Nation* to *Kill Bill;* and it underlines the unusual thematic interest in, say, *Citizen Kane* or *The Godfather.*

I have never heard a satisfactory plea from anyone in defense of Griffith's material. *Intolerance* has staggering scenes, though I am more moved by the still pictures of the Babylon set being built on Sunset than the rather inane balloon shot with which Griffith tried to explore his insanely expensive but unutilized set. But the picture as a whole is foolish and pretentious in a way that only exposes its mind-numbingly blunt message of humanity. In comparison, some of the full-length melodramas that followed are far more watchable. There is a crazy smell of violence and masochism in *Broken Blossoms* (1919), while *True Heart Susie* (1919) and *Way Down East* (1920) are touched by a real charm, chiefly because of that crusty moral realism that kept Lillian Gish from being glamorous. In that respect, too, the great pioneer was hardly ready for his own medium.

But his facility in making a scene (granted it might be a horrible scene) was allied to what I have to regard as commercial, rather than artistic, ambition. Griffith was not fast in his effects, even if he had a taste for hectic cross-cutting; rural pacing prevailed. And you do find him lingering over moments when he's so captivated by the light that he just wants to let it play—now that is real cinema and may be his most innovative sensibility. His films begged to be longer. When he saw that, in Italy, Biblical stories or epics had been made an hour long and more, Griffith thought to test the American bottom. After all, in the theater sometimes people sat patiently for two or three hours. Why not at the movies?

We have seen how rapidly innovation exceeded his grasp, for he was not a grasping man, let alone a decent businessman. It took enormous energy to do *The Birth of a Nation* and then *Intolerance* in a couple of years. No wonder he was exhausted ever after and taken aback, not just by the way he had transformed the mathematical basis of the medium, but in the very mixed reception those two dinosaurs received. *The New York Times*, for instance, was struck by "stupendous" things visually, but refused to ignore the "incoherence" of *Intolerance*.

The financing of *The Birth of a Nation* showed how much Griffith trusted to luck. He had found Harry and Roy Aitken to fund the picture. That seemed reasonable, for they had an operation of film exchanges in the Midwest that seemed prosperous. Not that this picture was ordinary: Griffith had asked for $40,000 straight up, with more likely, and Thomas Dixon was demanding $25,000 for the rights. Dixon came down to $2,000, in return for a big piece of the profits. But the production costs went up and up as Griffith thought of new scenes.

He had elected to film in Los Angeles, at a studio based on Sunset and Vine, while the Aitkens had offices in New York. They had a cash flow problem. They relied on weekly income, so they were Friday-afternoon check-writers: send the check late on Friday and you had the blessed weekend take at theaters to have funds ready on Monday morning. But long before the end of shooting, *The Birth of a Nation* was being funded in dribs and drabs from small private investors or anyone Griffith or the Aitkens could find. It was an improvised method: Griffith asked for money, the Aitkens found it somehow, and Griffith paid the bills. The final budget was about $110,000, serious money for that time.

The biggest film made in America to date (and one of the biggest of all time, in relative terms) had to go begging. Because the people involved had the wrong connections, they ended up relying on small checks from strangers. But one person might have paid for the entire picture, and owned it. If that person had been Griffith, or any large businessman, the outline history of movies would have been different.

As it was, the results were revolutionary. They formed a business. In his 1984 biography of Griffith, Richard Schickel supplies the following figures, which are as stunning as the movie they come from is fussy, muddled, and antiquated. In the years 1915–17, Epoch (the distributing arm set up by the Aitkens) reported net receipts from the box office of $4.839 million. That meant a profit of $1.86 million. Griffith received about a third of that. But then comes the sting. Epoch worked the film according to a states' rights system. They bid out the rights to local exchange groups—like that of Louis B. Mayer in New England—against a 10 percent return. Ten percent of the box office gross. Thus, Schickel estimates that, in all, the picture did $60 million at the box office in those first years. Multiply that by twenty (to get near current values) and you have the most successful film of all time (with an American population of 100 million).

More than that, you have several lessons swallowed whole by a man like Mayer. Here was a new business. The possible payoff from the gamble was so great—from $100,000 you could get $60 million—that it redefined greed. So a right-minded entrepreneur needed to own as much of the package as possible. It proved true as a forecast, for the structure of the business was built along these lines. But it is vital to the gambling spirit, and not just to the funds that a Mayer would need, that a huge success had come so early. The long shot of the blockbuster was laid down as a model. That was juice for gamblers, but it meant that regular business never stood a chance emotionally. The movies were never the kind of business that promised and delivered a steady 4 percent annual growth. They offered a transforming explosion. They needed Hollywood, but they smelled Las Vegas.

Did Griffith get tired? It's not the most far-fetched question. This book will refer to several actors or directors who went on "forever": Fritz Lang, Hawks, Hitchcock, Katharine Hepburn, John Wayne. But among directors there are many who had a brief heyday and never regained it: Griffith, Preston Sturges, Orson Welles, Nicholas Ray, Michael Cimino. Quentin Tarantino? It's too pressing a pattern to ignore, and it speaks not just to work so killing that it can take away appetite. It's a bigger issue than that: on a film set, the director must command 200 people; he must answer all their questions and still hold a creative vision intact. This is prodigious, awful, and inhuman, for it easily encourages tyranny and a woeful exaggeration. Whereas, to be creative, in so many ways, is to stay inward, alone, shy, inarticulate. It's no wonder that so often the spark occurs and then withers in the cockpit of attention. To say nothing of all those things like money, fame, women, and yes-men that come with success. Did the very hat crush Griffith's poor head?

* * *

It's intriguing to see how the American picture business was working out a narrative camera style at the same time it was fashioning the fiscal relationships between production, distribution, and exhibition. It is only by seeing those processes as not just linked, but part of the same organism or bloodstream, that one can trace the peculiar nature of the American movie. What do I mean by that? Reliance on hooks, roller-coasters and big bangs (as the verbal metaphor to describe how the machinery works). Reliance on suspense, on mystery, on what happens next—on our need and right, there in the dark, to see the thing that is being seen and our emotional involvement in getting the answer. In short, as we got our hearts' desire, so the business made its killing. In other words, what propels film narrative is the searching, reactive face. If the face is eager or hooked enough, we want to see what it sees, and thus the gradual disclosure of things becomes the narrative line of a film. And if the narrative holds, the profit will come.

This is as natural, or as unavoidable, as the line in writing having to do with the naming of things or states of feeling, and the way in which an accumulation of naming leads one into the inner workings of the minds involved—those of the characters, the author, and the readers. But if books

are about the possibility or potential of meaning, films are about disclosure, revelation, appearance, the world of visibility, and the fetishization of
appearance. It is a medium most acute when fixed on what happens next;
whereas literature, sooner or later, is about the meaning behind events.

Must those truths always operate? That is a tough question, and one
that only history will answer. The art of film may, one day, find a way of
escaping the crushing restriction of visibility. But nothing makes that less
likely than the simultaneous pressure of money on the nature of the storytelling (or attention). Writing grows out of the simple urge in one person
to tell another a story (and is therefore observable every day all over the
place in very mundane situations). By contrast, film absolutely depends
upon a conceptual process in which production and marketing are the
dynamics. Novels are written in many cases for one person (the novelist)
or a close few; they may find only a few thousand readers in their glory;
later they may become classics, but still are read by less than a million people. American movies have very rarely been set up so modestly. They
require millions at the outset, to raise the money and the confidence in so
large a seduction. They function through their ability to woo a great many
people. Thus the difference between a narrative style that is suspenseful
and one that may be many other things, from poetic to ruminative.

So perhaps you begin to see that the form of a medium and its commerce are linked—certainly, you can admit that in 1915, say, they are con-
gruent: the medium is being defined on-screen and in American cities (in
show business) simultaneously. Still, my task—and it is very close to the
heart of this book; it is the passion in the equation—is to convince you that
the two are one: that the urge to tell these stories is inseparable from the
wish to make money.

The point is very simple yet very complex, and I'm sure Karl Marx and
Walter Benjamin are helpful to making it. But I think I have a punchier
example, and in movies where there is no punch there is no impact. This
story comes some fifteen or so years after the prime of Griffith. The
medium now has sound; sound helps my case a good deal, for it illustrates
the difference between talk that is like life, and talk that simply puts in the
hook. It is the best reason for finding my title in Scott Fitzgerald's *The Last
Tycoon.*

I am putting in the hook—and deliberately holding back. In requiring
your attention, I am exerting power—and power is nearly always close to
fear, or unease. It's worth adding, I think, that Scott Fitzgerald had
insights about Hollywood that he could never apply in practice. As a
screenwriter, he was a failure in the town, not too far from a laughingstock

or an embarrassment. Is that a way of saying that he was a true writer but incapable of acting on his own intelligence?

Enough. In Monroe Stahr's very busy day he has to find time to see George Boxley, a screenwriter, an English novelist hired because his is a famous literary name, because he has a reputation for graceful dialogue, and maybe to show him off at Hollywood parties for one summer. (And because Boxley wants the money that is said to come with going Hollywood. That money may let him go back to Gloucestershire, or wherever, to write his great novel.)

Boxley is seething with awkwardness. There is turmoil inside him—it may be the loss of cricket, Cheddar cheese, and the moist countryside; it may be his meeting with a young girl who is startlingly available. Fitzgerald doesn't say. You could call it "not getting along": being paid a small fortune for being polite to idiots, or even seeing how quickly the small fortune can become a habit that tidies away Boxley's big aim, that great English novel before the lights go out over Europe.

Boxley can't get his stuff, his way of seeing things, on paper. The two guys he's been put with (Pat Hobby types—the hack writer about whom Fitzgerald wrote several short stories) turn everything into their "vocabulary of about a hundred words." (You can smile at that mockery, or feel the idealism of trying to reach the crowd that is not very verbal.)

"Write it yourself," says Stahr.

But whenever he does that, Boxley complains, Stahr tells him it's no good.

"I don't think you people read things," says Boxley. "The men are duelling when the conversation takes place. At the end one of them falls into a well and has to be hauled up in a bucket."

"Would you write that in a book of your own?" Stahr wonders.

"Naturally not," says Boxley. "Movie standards are different."

Whereupon Stahr goes into the lesson. He asks Boxley to imagine that he's gone back to his office at the end of the day, tired out. He's just sitting there, staring, so still that a young typist doesn't notice him when she comes into the office.

She takes off her gloves and empties her purse on the table. These seem ordinary actions, but for the secret viewer, the voyeur, they are implicitly sexual. She has two dimes, a nickel, and a matchbox. (Note: that needs a closeup: as we look at the room, the whole scene, and she empties the purse—the close-up has to be invented; we want to see—it won't take long before we walk out if we don't see the information, the thing itself, that is being referred to.)

She puts the dimes back in her purse, and she goes over to the stove and tosses in her black gloves. She uses the last match to set light to them. She watches the gloves burn. (Do we get a close-up of her face watching? Is it warmed by firelight? Or does it stay cold?)

The phone rings. She picks it up, listens, and replies, "I've never owned any black gloves in my life." She goes back to the stove, and then she realizes that a man, Boxley, is watching her.

Stahr stops. It is very likely the way he dreams, in the shape of beguiling questions that the day must answer. Notice that we don't know anything about the girl, except that she lies (or acts). There is no plot. No society. No history. No sociology. No politics. No web in which all those elements are contained. No *War and Peace,* yet. Just action. Just a hook. Just action on a cold screen.

"Go on," says Boxley, smiling. "What happens?"

Stahr says, "I don't know," and I believe him. "I was just making pictures." Now, that's a cunning play on words, and you can think that it's a very small game in the large enterprise. But he has Boxley's attention.

"It's just melodrama," says Boxley, which is a truth about cinema that human improvement and progress may never overcome.

"Not necessarily," says Stahr. He lies. He has to.

"You were interested," he says, as if reducing his pressure on Boxley's human curiosity.

"What was the nickel for?" asks Boxley.

And here we may be hearing Irving Thalberg, the man himself: "I don't know. Oh, yes—the nickel was for the movies."

The girl, the typist (of course, we don't know she's a typist, she could be a novice running away from a convent), has no history, or backstory. She is less a person or a character than a presence, waiting for texture, a lie calling for explication; and she is someone being watched, who needs the attachment of her voyeur. She comes alive by being spied on. The secrecy of watching is what gives her the chance of an inner life. That is why she lies. And when she does, if she is fool enough to ask a director how to play the "I've never had . . ." line, she may be short-lived. All she has to do is deliver the line like someone betraying or exposing herself. It's like saying "I need you" (if in doubt on-screen say every line as if that were the subtext). It is the attractiveness of dishonesty. Call it melodrama, or a cheap, limiting trick that cuts movies off from so much of the rest of life.

Of course, it means that the girl has to be Nicole Kidman or Julia Roberts or Joan Crawford or Louise Brooks (one of those faces nagged at by frankness yet urged to lie, the eyes that always say "I need you" when they mean "I need need").

But all of this is what makes the girl a possible subject for a film. It is what makes Kim Novak work in *Vertigo* in the moment at Ernie's restaurant, in San Francisco, where her Madeleine pauses for a lengthy heartbeat so that the camera, and James Stewart and all of us, the real suckers, can take her in and begin to fall in love, without ever realizing that she has stopped on the white-tape X on the floor. It is, again, that mixture of honesty and its opposite (look at me, but you can't trust me) that inserts the hook in every fishy mouth. But the essence of the lie, of course, is in the duplicity (or the parallelism) of actress and character. Always, in every movie, we are watching both. But in a hundred years of movies we have learned simply that everyone is an actor, too, which means they are not to be trusted.

This quality of doubt is intensely seductive. I think it is the inherent mystery in far more than mystery movies. It is why we watch, and it is sexual far more than it is intellectual. It is about presence (or allure) as opposed to character. There is a list here of things film has slipped into our culture to replace literary ingredients. And in total, they leave us all as insecure as actors.

Stahr told his story sixty years ago. But the same hook is there in a knockout script I read the other day, Michael Thomas's *Indecent Exposure,* based on David McClintick's book, which has a man arrive at the Century Plaza Hotel in Los Angeles, "a man who can walk on water." He has a "DB" monogrammed on his shirt, but he checks in as "Joseph Fischer." And then he goes to his room, puts a gun in a drawer, tells his mistress to hurry along, writes several letters and signs them "David Begelman." The script is promising because this character is acting out, turning the notion of some secret "in" and putting it into action. Making pictures. And it really is a very good script in that it feels just like a movie. You want to know what happens.

But what the hook eliminates is the chance that we will hold or stop or analyze the drop-dead glamour of this brazen, attractive lying. For by now, the equation—that you are interesting only if you act—has gone all the way down the line, so that it grips guys getting ready to kill themselves and maybe carries them over their own edge. In the late thirties, in the hypothetical match girl scenario, say, Joan Crawford would come out okay, but in real-life David Begelman had a gun so he could blow out his brains at the Century Plaza Hotel. The melodrama has sunk deep. It is a killing thing, a diminution of life.

In Death Valley, California, two seekers of gold are ruined by their link—handcuffs. The end of Stroheim's *Greed* (*Kobal Collection*)

8 · STROHEIM AND SEEING MONEY

A rider appears out of the distance, and where his gaze falls, a story flowers. It could be Shane or The Man from Laramie. It could be Tom Dunson beholding the bare land—and the faraway claim of Don Diego in Mexico—that will become the *Red River* D ranch. Or it could be Noah Cross, on horseback, stopping to smell the orange blossom on some bridle path in what is now Bel Air, and calculating the number of lots he can see and own and sell, just as Monroe Stahr wonders about gloves and a purse. The enterprises are alike, up to their elbows in money, yet romantic enough—the scent of the blossoms, the suspense that clings to that young typist—to make a storyteller out of both of them. The nickel? For the Movies, says Stahr. Why are you doing it? asks Gittes. The Future! says Cross. We may get to the future, the shining white lie that obscures present damage, by the end of this book.

Not that I mean to offer Monroe Stahr or Irving Thalberg as artists or even artist-like. (They were always too eloquent, too tireless, too political in selling pictures—the artists are exhausted, ill-dressed, and incoherent, like actors without lines.) But the two of them, or the one, represented a businessman, a money man who loved to talk the language of art, who liked to hire and own writers (like Scott Fitzgerald) and help fund great museums in Los Angeles. Thalberg never lived long enough for that. He would have been in his seventies by the time Los Angeles became a sleek international city, with superb restaurants and some of the most palatial art galleries in the world—built, and prized by the community, in the ways its ancestors had once treasured great movie studios. But without the vulgarity. I am talking of that time when taste would come to Los Angeles (a terror greater than that of any earthquake). Irving Thalberg would have been crazy about taste.

And in the genteel pursuit of taste, efficiency, and the absence of art, nothing describes Thalberg more fully than his meeting with Erich von Stroheim. He needed Stroheim's absurd obsession and his little-boy ego; and he used Stroheim to help define the ideal nature of the business in just the way Stahr manipulates Boxley.

Anyone in film, or into it, has grown up with the legend of Stroheim, *Greed* (1925), and the film's forty-reel length. Even if, as critics or ordinary filmgoers, we may lament the current engorging trend by which Hollywood tells simpler stories more slowly, so that sometimes it seems impossible nowadays to find a picture under two and a half hours. No matter that, as celebrity gossip hounds, we sniff out the horror stories of this or that director asserting his art, his vanity, in defiance of economic reason and the prospects for making "sensible" pictures (which still leave time for dinner). Still, we picture "the von" himself in Death Valley, in a singlet and riding gear, the beads of sweat like jewels in his cropped hair. We see the footage that this man was obtaining: his two chief characters out in the desert, ironically cuffed together, figures lost in a frame and the furnace of dazzling white gold. And we get drunk on it all, and the grinding naturalistic detail which he lavished on *Greed* (as if all that veracity could ever eclipse or temper its innate melodrama). *Greed* features an astonishing use of real space allied to a nagging view of human nature. Some still say that this was the first adult filmmaking in America, by a man once hired by

Griffith who surpassed the master in terms of both *mise-en-scène* and putting mankind in its squalid place.

Well, maybe *Greed* is high art and great cinema; yet maybe it's just a modern, shrewish Bible warning America (from Cross to Charlie) about gold, and made by a God who is awfully like Theodore Dreiser.

We know that Stroheim yearned to film Frank Norris's novel *McTeague*, and how for the second time in his rebellious career he fell foul of Irving Thalberg and could do nothing as the new genius of M-G-M took his masterpiece and said, very well, but only at two hours. None of this nine-hour nonsense! And we know the moral: that here was the new studio system flexing its muscles so that a slender kid could stand up against the von (a figure of Dempsey-like menace so long as he never smiled, and he had taught himself not to, as part of his solemn Hun act), so that a producer or an executive producer could take over a director's life and cutting room, put them in order, and administer a kind of exemplary spanking.

None of which is wrong, or beside the point. But all of which might be leavened by this last shot from dreaming—of the von, spreadeagled in the Death Valley blaze, looking up at his master (under a pretty parasol) and saying "Yes, yes, spank me, Irving," and the look of deep justice and content in his stricken eyes. After all, anyone who knows Stroheim's work knows how far into sadomasochism he was.

This is not to make fun of Stroheim. Still, those seeking to understand him should be wary of missing his own forbidding, unsmiling dreaming. His great admirer, Jean Renoir, saw a twelve-year-old boy's image of the Marquis de Sade as Stroheim's ideal. This is not to dispute the vitality or significance of either the nine-hour or the two-hour *Greed*. But you can see the two-hour version; you can read *McTeague;* and you can study Herman G. Weinberg's *The Complete Greed,* a book that attempts, with script, stills, and text, to reassemble the elements of the movie Stroheim had originally delivered. That preparation would convince you of Stroheim's eye for action and psychological detail, and leave no question about *Greed* being one of the most impressive achievements in silent film. But I defy anyone to assert that the nine-hour version was automatically, or four and a half times, better. Rather, I ask you to consider that its reputation depends upon its absence.

And here we begin to come to grips with Erich Oswald Stroheim, born in Vienna in 1885, the son of a Jewish hatmaker and a Jewish woman from Prague. No, he was not a Prussian aristocrat, nor a cavalry officer. His greatest skill as a youth lay in making elegant straw hats, and knowing the vanities they appealed to. He was, briefly, a private in the Austrian army, but around the age of twenty (avoiding war), he emigrated to the United States, surfacing in California just as Griffith was making *The Birth of a Nation*. Stroheim acted for the great man in several small roles; he served as a valued assistant director, and we can imagine Stroheim learning at top speed; and he said he was an expert on Prussian uniforms and manners as the taste for anti-German films set in after 1917.

It was in an odd mixture of publicity and propaganda that Stroheim found a new identity and began to add the "von." This famous man is also a mystery in the years 1906–14. And it's very telling of America and the movies that this could be so. For we are dealing with the drastic switch, back and forth, from anonymity to fame, from darkness to light. The deepest appeal of the movies is to suggest that we might escape the dark and the anonymity of "audience" for the light.

Stroheim looked natural in uniform. He loved to act the Prussian martinet, and the sensual connoisseur. He strove to become "the man you [the American public] love to hate." He reckoned he was taking advantage of a gullible system. And he had a cast of mind that enjoyed a certain sardonic superiority; it was what enabled him to look at people in his films (especially the women) with a novel, muckraking point of view. As S. J. Perelman put it, under his gaze "no wife or bankroll must be left unguarded." Call it a lack of sentimentality. Griffith, by contrast, could make himself blind, foolish, and archaic in finding fresh ways of seeing eternal madonnas.

But suppose there was something in the times that added to Stroheim's view of women. Suppose it had to do with the astonishing advances in means of communication, and the relative timidity or ignorance of "the media" to get their hands on stories. The forty years between 1880 and 1920 had witnessed not just the advance of the movies, but the absolute domestication of the still photograph, the telegraph, the telephone, and radio, as well as air flight, the full nocturnal illumination of cities, and even reports of the subconscious mind. There was this constant buzz of static from the new connections, and so little sense yet of how it could be shaped by story or report.

There's no clearer example of that than the Great War (which was also a mass medium—a force that compelled sharing), an appalling, four-year catastrophe (such that the Flanders bombardments could be heard on some days in southern England if the wind was right) that was never adequately reported or mediated (because of political control and censorship) but which destroyed hope. If the existing media had employed a fraction of their power in those years, surely the war would have been shorter. As it was, in Russia, there came a time when unbelievable facts bled into ridiculous hopes, and the country simply shifted its relationship with reality so that war turned into revolution. The energy and the knowledge had to go somewhere. And in the years at the end of the war nearly every nation feared or hoped for the passage from crisis to upheaval.

Never overlook in all of this the new, thumpingly available metaphor—that time was like a film projector, the synchronized advance of two large wheels with the shift of celluloid from one to the other. And whereas, in principle, a film show might go on forever, with one reel leading to another, the projectionist (a figure of the new age) had the nightmare burden of being responsible for it running out. At which point, nothing but the glare of angry white light fills the screen, to be replaced or supplemented by the frustrated fury of the mob. Because their time has stopped.

In that mishap, you can see and feel the power or weight of public attention, itself called into being by the new stress on seeing. It's there, waiting, and it may seize on anyone touched by the light of fame. It's there in the unprecedented adulation (with the terrible threat of rebuke or abandonment) that fell on Doug Fairbanks, Mary Pickford, and Charlie Chaplin (or Fatty Arbuckle). And it's there in the otherwise inexplicable transformation of Stroheim, in a few years, from a sometime hanger-on to Griffith to a renowned image and reputation, a film director in stark conflict with the system of film production.

Just consider that phrase: "the man you love to hate." It was derived from Stroheim's manner on screen, of course. But since when had an entire population been addressed as "you," except by the laws of religion or empire? That "you" is publicity talk, but it is also the fear that an egalitarian mass may get out of control unless its raw power can be identified. Very subtly, a democratic society begins to be treated as an audience or a mass, and so it goes.

Stroheim imposed himself as the image of the recent enemy, in the years 1918–19, in two films, *Blind Husbands* and *Foolish Wives,* which he directed and starred in. He took a remarkable gamble to get *Blind Husbands,* for he offered his services as writer and director for free. All he asked for was $200 a week to act, and that may have been an indication of where Stroheim saw his own destiny: as the first great villain of the movies, a cruel playboy, one in whom a certain sultriness began to supply a strange or perverse seductiveness. For *Foolish Wives,* he was not as generous. On what was notorious as the first film whose budget exceeded $1 million, story and direction accounted for about 35 percent of the costs. Another 35 percent went on sets—most notably the re-creation of Monte Carlo on the rough hillside of Cahuenga where Universal had set up.

It says a lot for Stroheim's personality that he had reached that level of pay so quickly. And when *Foolish Wives* failed at the box office, it was bound to incur the indignation or countermeasures of Universal's new studio manager, Irving Thalberg. Then, as he watched Stroheim's next film, *Merry-Go-Round,* take shape Thalberg came to life. As the picture went over budget, he intervened. This is a signal occasion: *Foolish Wives* had had a budget, but on the strength of one modest success (*Blind Husbands*) Stroheim was allowed to go over budget as he called for more intricate sets, more extras, more authentic uniforms, more of more.

There was a policy in early cinema that you did a thing until you got it right—this clearly came from theater where the process of rehearsal was most easily interpreted as a closing in on rightness or perfection. And since someone has to know or identify rightness, why not the director? In filming, with much more subject to muddle or too many helpful hands, that kind of authority was all the more necessary. With so many different people and skills concentrating on what they are doing, the director is the artistic arbiter, or the manager, who says, yes, we got it, we can move on. If only he'd been called the supervisor he might have had a better time.

This matter of rightness begins to establish the movie as a series of technical quests, most of which can home in on "accuracy." Is the exposure correct? Is the framing exact? Did the characters say their lines right? Did the director approve of their "reading"? All of these questions can be asked, with point. Yet all are open to the chaos of alternatives. For example, in some cases a mistake in exposure (the image too dark or too bright) can be very expressive in result. And if every frame is exact, is there a moment when the movie feels too tidy or too academic? And as some actors surmise, there are many ways of reading a line that are "right" or meaningful. Direction simplifies all that confusion. And it permits the film to be shot in, say, twenty days, as opposed to some infinite number. As every day spent filming is a portion of your final budget, so an equation arises between artistic or interpretative rightness and sound economy.

Put it another way: if you have a hundred or more people on a set making a film (and that number is not unusual), they have to be managed. The instruments of management are the set of contracts by which they are employed; the hierarchy of producers, directors, and assistant directors; and, above all, a script. Without that document, no one knows, or can refer to, the limits of what you are filming. And in a great deal of early moviemaking, the script hardly existed on paper. It was inside the director's head, growing.

Stroheim adored the principle of his own creative expansiveness. His films at Universal, all of his own devising, had been firmly set as tales to appeal to a kind of moral superiority, while indulging the voyeurs in sights of wickedness (this was very much the way Cecil B. De Mille worked, too). But now Stroheim had resolved to adapt a work of literature, *McTeague,* which he had probably read and reread over a period of several years, and which is a classic portrait of character undermined by money. And now his setting was America itself, and rather than build many sets in Los Angeles Stroheim was determined to go to the real places where Norris set his story: the San Francisco Bay area, the California gold country, and Death Valley for the finale. His watchword in so many respects was that ultimately dubious term, "realism."

He had had enough of Universal and Thalberg. He sought freedom. Remarkably, he found it at the Samuel Goldwyn Company. In fact, Samuel Goldwyn had already been eased out of his own company, so Stroheim agreed to terms with two executives, Frank Godsol and Abe Lehr, for a three-picture contract, with the first project to be based on *McTeague.* The film was budgeted at $175,000 and it was meant to be about 100 minutes. But as shooting began, in San Francisco, those two executives approved an astonishing increase—to $347,000—presumably on the basis of Stroheim's shooting script. The director (he does not act in *Greed*) was to be paid $30,000.

As far as can be told, Stroheim did the work for that sum. But the production costs reached $470,000 on a shooting schedule that lasted from March 13 to October 6, 1923. This produced 446,000 feet of film (well over 100,000 more than he had shot on *Foolish Wives*). More or less, Stroheim needed another year to edit that material. There are conflicting stories about the length of his preferred cut, but there are reports of a forty-seven-reel version and some accounts (by eyewitnesses) of a version that required the best part of a working day to be projected.

Stroheim had talked of being exactly faithful to the novel, as if there is ever a way of doing that without actually filming the printed lines on the page. To extract the events (the action or the plot) from literature is to begin to face the question of how far those events depend upon tone, and whether literary voice or attitude can ever be filmed. We do know that Stroheim had added a good deal of material not in the book. (*McTeague* is 442 well-spaced pages in the Penguin paperback.)

Still, it was Stroheim's intent, or his stance, to propose—to the Goldwyn people, he thought—that the film be released at eight hours. He sometimes suggested a screening spread over two evenings. But by the time he had achieved his cut, the Goldwyn Company had been transformed in the April 1924 merger that eventually made for Metro-Goldwyn-Mayer. Thus, his enormous enterprise came under the direct authority of Louis B. Mayer and his lieutenant, Irving Thalberg. As a result, and after the film had been removed from Stroheim, it was released at about two hours in December 1924. By then, with all the work on cutting, the costs had risen to $665,000. In the next six years of domestic release, it earned about $275,000.

Those are the essential facts (or the best one can find) in a business crisis, and plainly Mayer and Thalberg (whose income was related to profits) regarded it as a critical moment in defining their new enterprise. Stroheim did work again for M-G-M. It was never that Thalberg considered him inept or so dangerous as to be avoided at all costs. Indeed, Thalberg seems to have had some fondness for the Austrian. Only a year later, Stroheim made *The Merry Widow* for the studio: cost $592,000, profit $758,000. It was after that, on *The Wedding March* (made for Paramount) and *Queen Kelly* (made for Gloria Swanson Productions, to be released by United Artists), that Stroheim ran into further problems of length and budget that effectively ended his directing career.

Was Stroheim a genius, or a self-destructive poseur? Why not both? Is there that much difference in the world of movies? Shyness in Hollywood doesn't get you in the door. If *Greed* as it now exists is a very good film— some have voted it among the best ten ever made—is it only a quarter of what might have been? Or was Thalberg the cool manager in a hot business, certain that the message in the title needed to be humbled (or reduced to a side issue)? Was he ever heard to murmur, in weird anticipation of Michael Douglas's character in *Wall Street,* that greed is good, or quite good, or good actually, as a way of diverting attention from its immense sermon against greed? Was he on the track of an aesthetic truth? Frank Norris and Erich Stroheim had something in common: they could not take their eyes off the prospect of ordinary Californians destroying themselves for money.

In terms of choice of material, *Greed* was the real thing, a story about one of those abstractions supposed to bind us all, and a topic that so many early filmmakers would have found dangerous or un-American. For just as Norris wrote with what Kenneth Rexroth called "relentless photographic veracity," so he plumbed depths of human nature and social interaction like those recognized by Dickens and Balzac. The thing that Stroheim was most loyal to in Norris was the central depiction of three leading characters all warped and damaged by upbringing. Marcus, McTeague, and

Trina are not paragons of virtue, such as beset (and ruin) silent film in America. They are not figures we are bound to love and admire. We observe them rather than identify with them. They are people you might meet in the Tenderloin on Polk Street, in San Francisco, and be wary of (Norris's first title for his novel was *The People of Polk Street*). Thus, the dominant realism contained in both the film and the novel is to make us feel the way we are on guard in life. This is the line of influence by which Stroheim was so inspiring to Jean Renoir; *Greed* is, in so many respects, a seminal piece of European-style film being made in America where real space, authentic settings, and the rough awkward nature of the people who inhabit them demand scrutiny, not identification.

That is a more useful guide to watching *Greed*, I think, than Rexroth's assertion about "photographic veracity." Norris's stealthy way of observing and absorbing the world goes far beyond the visual; it is a full sensory study. But it is based on something not really possible until the photograph and the movies: the ability to study appearance, without shame. Photography in the late nineteenth century is leaning toward motion in so many ways, from Muybridge to the movies. But it does something else that is vital to our culture, and which actually prompted Muybridge. It isolates the split second (that's how Muybridge established that a racing horse might have all its feet off the ground at one instant). It says to us: Look, here is something you can look at forever, or for as long as you like. Don't blush, you won't run any risk of being picked on as a peeping tom or a voyeur or a busybody. Just feast your eyes on the detail—whether it is an Edward Curtis picture of the Canyon de Chelly, or a loving portrait of a half-clad Lillie Langtry. Let the picture flower and come to life in your mind. Can't you see the pores in her skin; can't you imagine you're catching the warm drift of the desert's scent?

This kind of gaze is the gift of photography, and people knew that it was close to illicit or unfairly privileged, which only made it more alluring. And we find it in the very way Norris writes, with a scrutinizing passion that (I guess) is the one thing above all Stroheim wanted to catch. Notice yet again how easily the thing seen becomes sacred or fetishistic:

> Trina's clothes were hanging there—skirts and waists, jackets and still white petticoats. What a vision! For an instant, McTeague caught his breath, spellbound. If he had suddenly discovered Trina herself there, smiling at him, holding out her hands, he could hardly have been more overcome. Instantly he recognized the black dress she had worn on that famous first day. There it was, the little jacket she had carried over her

arm the day he had terrified her with his blundering declaration, and still others, and others—a whole group of Trinas faced him there. He went farther into the closet, touching the clothes gingerly, stroking them softly with his huge leathern palms. As he stirred them a delicate perfume disengaged itself from the folds. Ah, that exquisite feminine odor! It was not only her hair now, it was Trina herself—her mouth, her hands, her neck: the indescribable sweet, fleshly aroma that was a part of her, pure and clean, and redolent of youth and freshness. All at once, seized with an unreasoned impulse, McTeague opened his huge arms and gathered the little garments close to him. Plunging his face deep amongst them, savoring their delicious odor with long breaths of luxury and supreme content.

To read that passage is to be reminded of so many movie moments: like Dana Andrews being beguiled by the portrait in *Laura;* like the second Mrs. de Winter and Mrs. Danvers in their different responses to the dead woman's room in *Rebecca;* like Jeffrey going secretly into Dorothy's apartment in *Blue Velvet;* or the way a tracking camera and potion-like dissolves take us into Xanadu and the mouth of death in *Citizen Kane.*

So much of what Norris is doing concerns smell, a sensation bungled in cinema. Yet surely that passage is intensely cinematic in that it is founded on the idea of an inquisitive and advancing spectator (it's in the prose rhythms, and its stealth is partly sexual) and the steady fetishization of things seen or perceived, felt or smelled. What that passage urges is: See—and wonder, or imagine! And it is not just something written on the brink of cinema; it is an intense provocation in how to use a camera and a medium.

Alas, that scene is not in the version of *Greed* we have now—the only one we are likely to have. Yet, in a way, that makes it all the easier to see how it might be filmed. And who can doubt that Stroheim, revealed as a fetishist so often in other films, shot it, and reveled in it? For it is a scene about looking (in the broadest sense) and being changed; about the storm of fantasy carrying a character beyond mere reality. It's there, I think, that Stroheim grasped the secret to the equation of film style or film watching, for it is the elasticity of spirit that allowed him a novel sense of continuity in the film strip. In other words, he saw how to film and edit two shots— Trina's empty clothes and McTeague's pregnant gaze—to the point of magic, so that you (you in the audience, so many and so unknown you can be called "you") can smell her, taste her—can have her. For she is a ghost waiting to be possessed. Stroheim knew, in a sexual, possessory way, that something private (and unspeakable) will happen in the world's dark. That is why it *is* dark there: so we can be moved. And it appealed to him. He was good at it. He felt it—after all, he was so much more modern a brute, so much darker and more Continental, than that gentleman, Mr. Griffith.

It was in sensing the change, the exchange, the mutuality between seeing and the thing seen, that he kicked the medium forward. I don't think I can describe it better than the writer and teacher Gilberto Perez. But what Perez is explaining is not just a syntactical bond, it's a fluency akin to the way we do dialogue in novels, something to make a new unity that bases itself in the idea of separate people talking. It's an element of film that was dominant until the 1960s, and by now it looks like the classic style of the medium:

> After watching Griffith, students in my film classes find it striking how much more modern Stroheim looks. Why? The answer is the reverse angle. A shot lets us see a piece of space, the reverse angle shows us the space in which we were standing a moment earlier, and situates us in the space we were just looking at. Such reversal does away with the theatrical demarcation between the space of performance, which belongs to the actors, and the space from which we watch the performance. The reverse angle usually pivots on a character's glance. It identifies the character's eyes with our own by cutting to what is in front of them, so that we see what they are seeing.

Yes, Griffith had made a start in discerning the grammar of shots that linked the viewer and the thing being seen, but there were others who deserved some credit, too. I think it is accurate that Stroheim, and first of all in *Greed,* made this fusion of angles not just magical, but pressing or tumescent. Still, it is premature to say that the medium had yet been identified fully. I am of the opinion that nothing so made the magic, the warm glue that really bound shots together, as sound (and we will come to that). Though sound was clearly a great emotional barrier to many people who had been pioneers in silent film and devótees of mime.

We'll never know how conscious, or articulated, this modernism was, or how far Stroheim owed it to his reading Norris. But there's no question about the impact the novel had on him. He liked the theme, and its mocking disaster—the way in which all human dreams were dashed. There was an essential clash in Stroheim between the romanticism of silent cinema and his own gloomy cynicism; it is the narrative energy of his films. He relished the unglamorous nature of the central characters. He cast not stars but supporting players—it is as if, today, let's say, in a remake of *Greed,*

McTeague were Philip Seymour Hoffman; Marcus, William H. Macy, and Trina . . . well, I'm not sure who, and this is a measure of how bold Stroheim was and how far we have sunk. For we do not really have an actress as odd yet as sexy as Zasu Pitts (the young Debra Winger perhaps).

Pitts's Trina is the first American film depiction of a character worthy of the novel, as plain as she is attractive, as ugly as she is fine. But again, notice how far inspiration carried Stroheim past Norris. In the novel, Trina alone becomes the miser for whom all emotion or sexuality is subsumed in gold. "You beauties!" she says, laying out her coins in rows. "Is there anything prettier than a twenty-dollar gold piece? You dear, dear money! Oh, don't I love you! Mine, mine, mine—all of you mine."

But in the movie, this is carried much further. We see Trina, or Pitts, alone in a mean room at night. We feel the greedy glow of light; Stroheim's plan was to tint every bit of gold in the frame. We see Trina in her underclothes, her dark hair down to her knees, lying on her bed in the moonlight, her body covered and dappled with coins. The eroticism is still disturbing. In 1925, it must have been outrageous in what was still the age of Mary Pickford and Miss Gish.

Stroheim was also thrilled to find a real dentist's office on Polk Street, with the street visible through the window. That depth of focus and reality, that largeness of context, is as moving as it is beautiful. It is also the impetus to the career of Jean Renoir, the brightest heaven of the lifelike ever found by movies. But Stroheim also exulted in the apocalyptic destiny, doom to all dreams, the way in which the thriving, money-grubbing San Francisco could not escape the desert and Death Valley. In that respect, he had understood California and the West and seen through the deluding American dream. He went to Death Valley and did it justice, not just as a surrogate cameraman (a Muybridge) who saw in it the natural metaphor for desolation and failure, but as someone who could embrace the terrible God that ruled there.

Thalberg was too late to prevent *Greed,* and he seems to have never made the case that it was extravagant—Stroheim's old curse, and the easiest reason for curbing a director. Indeed, granted all that was shot, *Greed* was a bargain. But then look at it from the point of view of Thalberg and Mayer.

The merger over which they presided would lead to the establishment of a film factory. It was not there yet, in 1924, but surely the two men had foreseen the necessary patterns of work and the need to keep studio space, equipment, and talent constantly utilized. This was required because they were now allied to the Loew's releasing organization, a gathering of theaters that relied on fresh product. Early equations were in their heads of how many movies they had to make in a year to keep Loew's functioning. Put quality aside for the moment: this is, initially, an unremitting demand for product. It follows from this requirement that all films should be broadly alike: of roughly the same length, and nature. They should be American movies, Metro movies. A ten-hour picture throws the system out of kilter. It is also likely to inspire other directors to be as slow and expansive—and to think that directors are that important!

Now consider "quality." Stroheim's *Greed* was not made to please, to reassure, to entertain, or to encourage the processes of dreaming and fantasy. Instead, it was an attempt to fling odious alternatives in the public's face. I believe that Stroheim meant to film aggressively and offensively, and for 1925, his way of seeing people was as important to that end as the film's length. What I'm suggesting is that Stroheim gambled mightily with this venture; he must have understood the risk he was running of making an impossible, unshowable film. We reckon Stroheim as a very shrewd or worldly man, and he had had ten years to study the emerging personality of the film business. He may not have counted on reunion with Thalberg, but he cannot have thought he would be dealing with anyone better. And Thalberg did reemploy him later.

For those of a mind to believe that the American movie was within reach of "art," it has always been easy to describe *Greed* as a tragic loss. But for anyone willing to allow that American film is something else—not an art so much as a business based on moving us—then what happened is not only understandable but reasonable. It shows Thalberg as a model of fairness. As if fairness had anything to do with art—no, it is the mealy-mouthed language of common sense and business and politics.

It's true that the picture was taken away from Stroheim and given to others to cut, probably under Thalberg's supervision. It's undoubtedly the case that many particular cuts offended Stroheim, just as many of the interleaving titles were not his, but were contrived to cover gaps in the narrative left by the film's truncation. But nearly every picture ever made in Hollywood, to this day, is subject to those intrusions. And sometimes the films are better for them.

I have never seen the entire *Greed;* and, yes, the historian in me would love that opportunity. So I would have welcomed the possibility that Stroheim's first cut might have been laid down in some museum (if in 1925 our museums and great libraries had shown that awareness of film). But the picture business has never taken care of its raw materials. (Stroheim used to tell the story that there was one complete print in existence—owned by

Mussolini!) Yes, it was crass to melt down the discarded footage to recover the silver, though in this particular case no one can fail to appreciate the ironies therein as raw mineral wealth emerges as the final imperative. But what kind of job did Thalberg and his cutters do?

Pretty good, I think. I urge anyone to read the Norris novel and see if they can really hold to the conclusion that the novel has been cheated. In several places, I would argue, Stroheim has improved it. In general, he has captured the key elements of characters, action, and setting. And he has reproduced Norris's fascination with things—things seen. This picture is still watched and appreciated. If it has dropped out of recent top-ten polls that is more because we are fickle and ultra-modern than because *Greed* is in neglect. The movie still works, and leaves one in no doubt about the genius or the devil in Stroheim.

However, I suspect that at ten or eight hours, the passion of the story, its verve, would be smothered by the melodrama, the slowness, the prolixity, the symbolism, and the fatally old-fashioned moral—that greed is bad for you. *Greed* is irretrievably out of date because we no longer think that way. Perhaps we should. Perhaps when under stress we still shelter behind the old moral. Certainly "greed" remains a pejorative term. But in actual practice, we live by a delight in money and possessions that is authentic and American and unstoppable: we are investors, or players. And maybe Mayer and Thalberg sensed that possibility before Stroheim ever recognized it. That is part of the modernity of Hollywood, and part of the ongoing history by which a business may have buried an art, for good and ill.

There are some who said they saw the whole *Greed* once, or a much longer film, and regarded it as astonishing, phenomenal, unprecedented. Then there is this, from Irene Mayer who, at the age of about seventeen got the chance to see the whole damn thing. She may have been ordered into the dark. This is what she said later in her book (and what she confirmed to me in person):

> We went to the studio early one morning to see it and sat through till evening of a very, very, hot day, made no cooler by the final hours of endless footage shot in the blazing sun of Death Valley. It was masterful in ways, and parts of it were riveting, but it was an exhausting experience; the film in conception was a considerable exercise in self-indulgence, and a testament to the incompetence of the previous regime [at Goldwyn]. When it was cut further, it still seemed over-length, except to certain critics who decried the desecration of a masterpiece—and the myth has been carried on by increasing numbers of people who, of course, never saw the

original and who heard about it from others who also hadn't seen it. I was there—and, as it happens, on von Stroheim's side in advance and prepared to do battle. When it was over, nobody said a word—including me.

Of course, she was a company person, with all that entails. She might have been head of the studio, if she'd been a boy. But she later produced *A Streetcar Named Desire,* which I suspect Stroheim would have enjoyed.

Yes, of course, the picture is fake, and the gorilla is like hair growing on the wall. *King Kong,* 1933: the hero eyes Fay Wray and wonders what she wants. *(Private Collection)*

9 · THE FRENZY ON THE WALL

If we imagine the battles between Irving Thalberg and Erich von Stroheim at Culver City in the summer of 1924 over *Greed,* it's easy to hear a moment when the weary Thalberg says, But Erich, if we don't cut it, they will.

He means the theaters, the places where any picture will play, a world and a law unto themselves where often the managers or the owners—the showmen who met the public—might drop a reel or two of film to accommodate their notion of a schedule. Or they could run the projectors faster, so that twenty-four, or thirty-two, frames might hurry through each second instead of the ideal sixteen! Purists of silent film nowadays remonstrate when revival theaters or television mindlessly run silent films at sound speed (twenty-four frames per second). But projectionists in the silent era did it first, if pictures weren't playing well. As for whole reels casually abandoned, it was wisdom among exhibitors that the public wouldn't notice and didn't care. They came just to see something—anything—put up on the screen. They came to see light in the dark, that weird reversal of nature that carried meanings beyond those of story, politics, or sociology.

As a child, in France, Jean-Paul Sartre went to see his first movie. Like 50 percent or so of the audience, he arrived in the middle of the program, feeling his way in the dark, mesmerized by "the frenzy on the wall." It seemed violent, demented, sensational, dreamlike (or nightmarish). In time, of course, this phenomenology (it's the young Sartre thinking) subsided, and story settled in. There were others in France in the 1920s who made it their habit to wander from one theater to another, entering in the dark and waiting until the lovely randomness began to make sense. Then they left for another theater and the same brief miracle of the irrational. "They" were André Breton and his fellow Surrealists.

Today, as story slips away through other drainage systems, it's time to wonder if they weren't aware of a great secret. Kids sitting on today's sofa with a hundred or more cable channels and the remote control trigger in their hands have mastered that surreal haphazard without the exercise. And if you ask them why they are channel surfing they may reply, Because there's nothing to watch on TV. So have they reinvented the frenzy for themselves by other means? Instead of watching, are they editing?

You can say that Sartre was overexcited—where else did "frenzy" come from? Another writer, Gore Vidal, say, might have called film "the sedative on the wall." And anyone who has spent a lifetime at the movies knows that some people do go there to sleep. Which is not quite the same as that well-established and honorable inner motive, going there to dream.

But let's consider what people do in theaters, or what is done to them. I want to examine the nature of movie theaters as well as the kinds of showmanship (or the lack thereof) associated with them. For I am quite certain that the essence of the movies (as business, entertainment, art, show, spectacle, or outrage) once consisted of being gathered in some vast, ornate dark, packed with a thousand or so strangers sitting before and beneath a wall that seemed like the side of a great ship suddenly encountered on a foggy sea, where faces might appear twenty or thirty feet high and then become some hideous, terrifying sight before you had time to close your eyes or put up your emotional shutters. All for a nickel. Or was it $10 the last time you bought a ticket?

I remember that in England during the late 1940s a sixpence—a fortieth part of a pound in days when the pound was worth over $3—was a child's admission price for an afternoon ticket, and I held the small silver coin in my hand till it nearly melted, waiting for some unknown adult to take me into what was then an "A" certificate film. Under fourteen, I could not see such a film without a grown-up, any grown-up. I often had no idea what the film would be; it was whatever picture was on.

This was in Streatham, a suburb of south London that regarded itself as being far loftier than nearby Brixton and Tooting. And perhaps it was. Still, a parent allowing a child to solicit strange adults outside a cinema today could easily end up in court, or before those bristling British Social Services. My mother knew I did this. She was at work and could not take me herself. She was hugely fond of me, and she let it happen, confident that no harm would befall me. Wise woman, she was more anxious about the effect of the films.

In Streatham in those days there were three cinemas within easy walking reach: the Astoria, the Regal, and the Gaumont. No one I knew could say where those exotic names came from, but that only added to the wondrous alien seductiveness of what they offered. Streatham High Road was a long row of shops—separate establishments for meat, fish, bread, fruit and vegetables, ironware, jewels, newspapers and magazines, men's clothes, women's clothes, a thing called haberdashery. I can remember the smell from one small premises that sold only coffee, with coffee being roasted in the window. Yes, Streatham was chic in its own way.

I spell this out because so much has changed. Though there was a large department store (Pratt's), long since closed up and abandoned, there was nothing like a supermarket. The economy functioned with a mass of specialty stores, and most people shopped every day because the refrigerator was still an expensive novelty. And they shopped on foot, for few families had cars. So the High Road was crowded in the mornings, which is when I first encountered these cinemas, from the vantage of a pram.

In the mornings, the cinemas were the only buildings closed. The other "public" places—the library, the post office, the railway station (down the hill)—were all busy. The churches were not crowded, but I knew you could open the door and look into their hallowed gloom without being warned off. I daresay you were welcome if you sought peace or contrition. But the cinemas were closed and resting, like creatures that were essentially nocturnal or too glamorous for the mundane activities of the day. They were also the grandest places on the street, bigger than churches and done with so much more imagination. Suburban churches were all in that dread Gothic revival without fuss, let alone ecstasy. As far as I knew, no one had found a way to design a modern church in Britain—not until Coventry Cathedral, which was close enough to a soulful hotel to tell you that the whole game of religion was up.

The cinemas I frequented were not fabulous, but try telling me then. All three of them were 1,000-seaters (with upstairs and downstairs seating). They had capacious lobbies, and they had decoration. I should add that in the years after 1945 (when I was four), decoration was nearly a decadent thing in Britain. Structure was all anyone asked. Our house had been hit three times by bombs. A part of it was simply lopped off after the war, beyond saving. There were bomb sites everywhere, as well as the prefabricated houses put up as emergency relief, but destined to last a lifetime for some people.

Food was rationed (until the early fifties). People took painful care of old clothes. We were all "hard up" and able to adapt that penury to the natural and eternal self-effacement of Britain's lower middle class. Everyone looked the same; you can see this in photographs of London crowds at the time. There was very little variation in what people wore. Color was looked on as showing off and unnecessary. Nearly every house I knew had net curtains at the windows (so those inside could look out without being seen; do you begin to see how fluently the voyeurism of the movies fed off real life and its rather furtive attitude to life?).

The cinemas had neon, and Britain had Michael Powell's Technicolor. They employed pink, orange, green, and purple without economy or shame. They had heavy plate-glass doors that swung open at midday. There were thick carpets in the lobbies. The air was perfumed, literally. My mother told me that this was done to kill the germs. But I couldn't see the germs and I was romanced by the idea of fragrance in the air. And then the places were decorated—the walls had gold foil on them, or damask velvet. There were designs of warriors and maidens, swans and castles, emperors and witches. It was as if some instinct in the movie business could not tolerate a plain, bare wall. In the broadest sense these designs were fictitious, or fanciful. They were like the threshold to a story. And they were as promising and every bit as vivid as the posters and stills for coming attractions. I knew that word "attraction" before I had a grasp of what attractiveness might be.

Not that even the Astoria (the best of Streatham's theaters) had a unified vision in its design. Rather, it had a little bit of this and a dash of two
or three other things. It was a version of the kind of Hollywood backlot—
that collection of settings and time periods—that you could still find in
Los Angeles in the late seventies and which in so many novels is taken as
the measure of the catalog of history that the studios commanded, and
mocked.

There was a real movie palace nearby, not just fabulous, but ecstatic—
the Granada, Tooting (those two words are still more emblematic of the
sublime and the ridiculous than anything I know). The Granada must have
been a 2,000-seater. Its carpets grew denser and deeper. And its lobby
included huge open spaces, staircases, side chapels, grottoes, and patios
that were, I suppose, all akin to the Alhambra and were about as Spanish
as Sternberg's great Dietrich film, *The Devil Is a Woman* (shot entirely at
Paramount). The Granada was heavenly to me as a child, and when I tell
you that the first film I saw there was *Samson and Delilah* (Victor Mature
and Hedy Lamarr, and a fevered work, jam-thick with wickedness), you
may begin to understand how the place and the movie fused together.
Alhambra—Babylon; it was all the same to me. But when Samson brought
the temple down so that it seemed the structure of the Granada itself
shook, I could believe that God had made both places. That was so much
more likely and encouraging than the churches in Streatham.

It was far from America, let alone Hollywood, but I felt a large fondness
for that place in reaching out to me so early. In fact, the kind of theater I
was discovering was a more or less universal experience. The Granada,
Tooting, since declared a protected landmark, still rates highly in histories
of the movie palace. And in those late forties, when movies were in a box-
office swan song, and there was real anxiety that "we might not get in," I
was going to cinemas designed and built in the late twenties and early thirties, the last great vainglorious age of fantasy architecture—until Las
Vegas and its themed casinos.

We know now how daring or threatening *that* venture was—as if anyone ever doubted America's appetite for gambling, especially after the
success of Hollywood, which was merely another way of imagining yourself in heaven. But such businesses are rarely stable or settled, and even if
there are times when the American movie seems pathetic or dull to a
degree, the picture business never rests. Maybe the best way of defining it
is to wonder whether it ever notices the convulsive changes that beset it,
as they happen.

But in the years between *The Birth of a Nation* and *Greed,* say, the business made great strides in self-confidence, which involved the settling in California, the acceptance of something like a regular length for feature films, the mounting habit of a large audience, and the urge to build theaters for them.

In 1920, the population of the United States was just under 110 million. Admissions, per week, in American movie theaters climbed from a little under 40 million to around 70 million. The average ticket price, in 1922, was actually about 20 cents. Allowing that it had reached a quarter by, say, 1927, and reckoning that the business sold 60 million tickets a week by then, you have a gross annual box office revenue of around $780 million.

If that seems like a prodigious sum to play with (granted that you need to multiply it by a factor of x to match today's money), consider the claims upon that sum. First of all, the theaters (the exhibitors) needed to replenish their "nut," the sum of the legitimate running costs. A financial plan for a 1,000-seat theater in 1928 called for building costs of $150,000 against annual revenues of $54,000, with running expenses of $34,500.

Exhibitors subtracted their nut from the box office, plus whatever percentage agreed upon with the distributor. Those terms varied enormously (they still do), and in the twenties especially, as films played out slowly, working their way from cities to smaller towns, they became more generous to the theaters as time went on. This was and is a cash business, controlled only by integrity at the theaters, some kind of numbered ticketing system, and a proper reporting system by the distributors. Las Vegas is a cash business, too, and we take for granted that "once upon a time" it employed regular skimming practices by which other, non-apparent participants or investors or "friends" might be paid off. Hardly ever in the history of the movies, then or now, has anyone had the time, the patience, the nerve, or the spoil-sport solemnity to instigate a thorough check on its reporting procedures.

Yet, in practice, during the golden era of Hollywood, there were many situations where a parent company owned the theaters that played its films. This was notably the case of Loew's, which owned Metro-Goldwyn-Mayer.

In other words, the game of numbers (more steadily pursued now than it ever was in the golden age, presumably because the public is more interested now) is very artificial. It is a way of ranking films' popularity and success, and it is a broad indicator of a level of business. The numbers that appear in newspapers on a Monday morning to measure success are projections based on just a few case studies. All too many beneficiaries of that glory have later found that the reports on their profit participation are reappraised, and are not so glorious.

Nevertheless, money goes back to the company that made the film. The accountancy procedures applied then are among the intricate marvels of a business-school training, for the direct and indirect costs that can be billed toward a film's production are as a rule more inventive than anything seen on-screen. (I say that with respect and admiration, and because it is instructive to see where the real efforts fall.) Still, there are end results, as witness these figures for M-G-M in the years when Irving Thalberg was instrumental in running its production program:

SEASON	PICTURES	COST (millions)	PROFIT (millions)
1924–25	26	$ 7.9	$ 1.7
1925–26	40	8.8	5.2
1926–27	45	11.6	5.4
1927–28	51	14.1	10.5
1928–29	53	14.6	10.3
1929–30	44	15.6	5.9
1930–31	49	20.7	6.2
1931–32	43	17.6	5.2
1932–33	40	18.5	4.5
1933–34	38	8.8	5.7
1934–35	41	18.8	8.0
1935–36	45	22.9	14.3
1936–37	35	26.8	5.8

There are many film commentators and filmmakers who deplore the kind of film history that is all tables and numbers. They can say that such detail is beside the point if the point is the chance to see and revel in such M-G-M films as *Greed,* Stroheim's *The Merry Widow,* King Vidor's *The Crowd,* Clarence Brown's *Anna Christie* (with Garbo), *Freaks, Tugboat Annie* (with Marie Dressler and Wallace Beery), *Grand Hotel, Dinner at Eight, The Thin Man, David Copperfield, Mutiny on the Bounty,* the Marx Brothers in *A Night at the Opera,* and *The Good Earth*—all of which were items in the Thalberg program. But if you love any one of those films, and feel disposed to write about it, you owe your opportunity to M-G-M and to the balancing economy that could make *Freaks* as well as *Tugboat Annie.* And you cannot grasp the nature of that editorial mind without accepting the test of theatrical exposure faced by the whole program. More or less, for *Greed* to go on for eight hours risked losing *The Crowd*. Someone has to exercise that responsibility.

One of the things best conveyed in *The Last Tycoon* is the rather presidential mood in which Monroe Stahr hopes to maintain profits while drawing the common American forward to something better. Of course, this is the kind of attitude often held by business, religion, education, or politics. Great art, however, seldom has such designs on the people, or much hope for improvement. But Stahr and Thalberg were inspired by an urge to lift the picture business from its grubby origins and to bring it closer to the standard of legitimate theater.

Nowhere was this struggle for dignity clearer than on the exhibition front. One of the trends observable throughout the twenties is to rely on theaters (or cinemas) as places specially designed for the playing of movies, as opposed to the wild collection of converted stores or premises that previously had been adapted for film. But in 1922, among some 20,000 screens in the United States less than 10 percent could seat more than 1,000 people. There were close to 7,000 screens still playing to fewer than 250 people. In 1927, there were only seventeen theaters in the country that grossed over $1 million a year at the box office.

Many of these venues were marginal or inadequate for polite, middle-class entertainment. They were "fleapits" or "bug-hutches," and they were dangerous as well as unhealthy. The provision and servicing of projectors was uncertain. The film was on flammable nitrate stock—several disastrous fires during the early days of exhibition deterred potential filmgoers. In addition, a tradition still held from the earliest years whereby small movie houses often were close to saloons and dangerous urban areas. Country theaters often were makeshift, and in 1922 more than 35 percent of screens in America played four days a week or less. Similarly, in summers, without air conditioning, there was a drastic falloff in business. Indeed, the seasons referred to in the M-G-M table cited above really refer to fall through spring.

But a movie theater has fixed costs whatever its size: two projectors (though many places still had only one, requiring reel-change delays and indicating a fragmented program of shorts and live acts); a projectionist and an assistant; a cashier; a manager; the overhead; someone to play the piano or organ. In becoming larger, a theater needed maybe a second cashier and a few ushers. But the ratio of costs to revenue ran in the owner's favor as the theaters got bigger. In addition, the larger the audience, the more a theater could make on selling "refreshments," the range of snacks and drinks on which it passed on nothing to the distributor.

Audiences were not necessarily well-behaved or attentive. (Are they now?) If pictures didn't talk, they did. In all but the smallest outlets there was some musical accompaniment. The biggest theaters featured small orchestras, sometimes playing scores composed especially for a picture. At the regular theaters, however, piano players were expected to improvise to films they had never seen before. Thus the rapid dependence on coded mood music, and the ease with which rowdy audiences might sing along with a movie. The live music was a throwback to theater, yet it detracted from the magical impersonality that has so much to do with film's power. That authority was further dissipated by the frequency of live acts—singers, comics, jugglers—on the bill. In addition, in theaters that played regularly to immigrant audiences with little or no English, there might be a presenter at the side of the screen, translating the titles and even explaining the action.

There was already a marked disposition toward youth, and children, in the audience. At the end of the twenties, one survey found (with alarm) that 64 percent of children in the United States went to the movies once or twice a week. Already, there was evidence that juvenile delinquents went more often than "nice" children. Some exhibitors admitted that kids were keeping the business alive, and they said it rather shamefacedly—What are you going to do?—because there were worries already, being earnestly expressed, from the churches, the academic community, and from the Boy Scouts, that this exposure to pretty fantasy might not be good for American children. In many cases, it was also reported that women of all ages made up a disproportionate amount of the audience.

But, of course, men went, too. "Everyone" went. By 1928, at least 65 million tickets were sold each week. That was well over half the total population. Subtract the infants and the very elderly, allow that some people went more than once a week, and still it was clear that virtually everyone who could get there went many times a year.

Take *Ben-Hur*, an M-G-M film and a famous disaster in that Louis B. Mayer had observed such confusion and extravagance in the attempts to film it in Rome that he had the production brought home, back to Culver City, where he and Thalberg could watch over the chariot races and everything else and keep the nonsense sensible. (On the same European trip, he picked up Greta Garbo along the way—he was a shopper.) *Ben-Hur* cost nearly $4 million, almost half of the studio's production budget for that year (a year of forty pictures). The studio said the film lost $700,000 on its first release, but that means it brought in revenue (cash flow) of $3.3 million. I don't think it's likely that the studio received more than 25 percent of the box office gross. So that means the original box office take on *Ben-Hur* was at least $13 million. Allow that the average ticket price was 25 cents, and it means that 54 million people saw the movie in its first release.

This strongly suggests that even if you hadn't seen it, you'd been told by others that you should. It's not an exaggeration to say that one in every two people who could have seen it had. And those people had seen it in packed theaters, and they'd be wowed by the spectacle and the drama. They thought they'd seen something great and colossally successful. M-G-M never told them otherwise, and so Mayer and Thalberg watched that epic "disaster" become an emblem of triumph. It was the picture that made the name and prestige of their studio.

We know of one man who didn't go. In *The Last Tycoon,* there is a moment when Monroe Stahr and his beloved take a walk on the beach (they have just made love, and what follows is post-coitally piercing for Stahr). They meet "a Negro man," collecting grunion and reading Emerson. As they talk, Stahr admits he's in pictures and the Negro says, "Oh. I never go to the movies."

"Why not?" asks Stahr sharply.

"There's no profit," says the black man. "I never let my children go." That's all. We could stand a little more; tell yourself that Fitzgerald would have enlarged the moment if he'd lived. But the black man walks away "unaware that he had rocked an industry." Is there irony in that? I doubt it. I think Stahr, like Christ, is ready to agonize over a single atheist. He is exactly like a politician in that every uncertain vote is a ticket to be sold. He wants to win that Negro, and even though Stahr admits, "They have pictures of their own" (there was a secondary film industry for blacks, and in many situations blacks could not enter white theaters), he is troubled. Thalberg let King Vidor make *Hallelujah,* an all-black musical, in 1929. It lost money on a low budget, but it was a famous event and it expressed a certain vague liberalism in Thalberg, if not quite in the system.

But just as the theater crowd was a version of the populist ideal—"everyone"—warmed up by that Chaplinesque conceit that, why, if everyone can laugh at poverty, then maybe we can ease ourselves into social (or socialist) solutions, so did Hollywood have a deeply conflicted attitude toward the crowd, and the implications of audience. There was this moment in film history, above all in the late twenties, when the audience grew steadily, when the business prospered, when the tycoons and the stars built themselves lavish homes in the paradise of California, and hardly knew what to do with the bounty. As if it were a kind of Reich, some of the bosses may have thought it would last for a thousand years, or as long as they lived, just like happy endings.

It's true of both Stahr and Thalberg that they were offended by their own gold rush. They had an innate attraction to taste, academic respect, elitism, snobbery, and a similar kind of primitive aversion to the crowd. You can see it in Chaplin, not least in that dainty, I-swallowed-a-dictionary way of writing that he found for *My Autobiography*. Yes, he kept direct contact with the guts of music hall comedy, its sentiment and violence. But he sounds like the invalid ghost of a rascal actually brought up in that dangerous Lambeth. He was no longer a person of his own class; he lived in walled and gated mansions, to which he had every right. What we're talking about, and it's essential to grasping the history of the movies, is the difference between the classes of success.

Likewise, there's a moment in which we see this dandyism in Monroe Stahr, and again it bears out how closely Fitzgerald had observed Thalberg and thought about his dilemma. It happens that there is a studio lunch, held in honor of a daft visiting dignitary, Prince Agge (Hollywood had become another Grand Canyon tourist spot by the thirties, and everyone with clout wanted a lunch and a photo opportunity with Mickey Mouse or Jean Harlow).

In the course of this meal, a few board members, with suspicious casualness, approach Stahr on "the South American picture idea." It's never spelled out, but it's obviously a kind of *Ben-Hur* with even more risk and cultural prestige—perhaps it's *Nostromo*.

Stahr says he's going ahead with it. Joe Popolos, a theater owner and a lovely caricature of idiocy, laments about the audience: "It's not . . . even as if so you could grab them by the head and push them by and is, is not." (Some board members were not ready for talking pictures.)

And then Stahr spells it out for them, putting his head in the lion's mouth. He can't see any way the picture will gross more than $1.75 million, exactly what he expects it to cost. Except that Stahr actually believes it will gross less than it will cost.

"Excuse me, Monroe," says Mort Fleishacker, the studio lawyer, "I'm fairly new here, and perhaps I fail to comprehend implicitly and explicitly. Do I understand you to say you expect to gross a quarter million short of your budget."

Stahr knows he is being set up. He is about to say things that could weave a noose for his slender neck one day. He is on the point of heresy.

But he is bored and desperate, and dying—allow that Thalberg felt at least two of those three moods. So he answers, "It's a quality picture. . . . It'll lose money. . . . It would be a bigger miracle than *Hell's Angels* if it broke even. But we have a certain duty to the public, as Pat Brady [Cecilia's father] has said at Academy dinners. It's a good thing for the production schedule to slip in a picture that'll lose money."

That duty to the public never goes away as a topic of concern, just as it never surmounts the sensible claims of profit in the business. Today, when most productions are single ventures, not part of a program, there isn't space to be that daring, or socially responsible. But there are leaders in the business—think of Harvey Weinstein—who long to have their (considerable) tastes hailed as socially valuable. And HBO, I'd guess, made *Angels in America* for its own sake, and trusted to other angels.

It is the mystery in our equation. And, to add spice to it all, remember that this Reich did not last. The great surge forward in pictures during the twenties found many rocks along the way. The feverish system, always prey to its own inventiveness and the remorseless draw of technology, got its hands on sound. In one swoop, that apparently modest addition called for a whole series of unforeseen investments: every theater had to be reequipped; most studios had to be soundproofed; many new talents had to be hired—actors who could talk, and writers who could write their talk; old contracts had to be settled. At the same time, the movies that resulted had so much talk that many foreign-born Americans could not keep up with them—no matter that, as I will argue, the enhancement of the medium brought it much closer to magic and art.

Two years after sound became a possibility, and then a necessity, the American stock market crashed, which led to a prolonged Depression in which audience numbers declined and most studios faced the threat of bankruptcy. These were very difficult times for the business, and for anyone who might forgo profit at the outset. After Thalberg had a serious heart attack in 1932, he was never again as powerful. And as befitted a new industry, trade unionism began to knock at the door in the first moves that would undermine the industry's power structure.

Tremors went through Hollywood. On the one hand, the natural populism of the movies edged quite naturally toward socialism, as many Americans saw the dream whipped away from their table. There were considerable doubts as to whether the republic could work decently, without massive suffering. The habitual happy endings of the Hollywood film, and the routine endorsement of civic and family virtues, faced a tough test. Of course, that happiness had always been superficial or brittle or fantastic—it was safely free of any kind of political agenda. The movie business liked to say that it never got involved in politics, as if that were possible in any form with a pretense to art. Whereas a lot more people, many of them white, began to share Fitzgerald's dismay with pictures, and to wonder if their collected fantasies were not part of a grand lie meant to distract the American public from its reality and history. The essence of the movies was a kind of sublime, secret individualism: Imagine you are Garbo, or Joan Crawford, or Gable, or Cagney, or whomever. That was the dynamic transaction in pictures, and it was at odds with any attempt to make you identify with your class, your society, your crowd.

At the same time, and during the very same years, in European countries there was a realization by leaders that the audience was a model for the masses, and that witnessing moral dramas or fables as a group was the beginning of education and national purpose. In political systems as divergent as those of the Soviet Union and Nazi Germany, film was taken up by the leaders (many of whom were genuine film fans) as an instrument of national education and morale. It was a strange endorsement of what Chaplin had felt, and it allowed for that bizarre companionship in Charlie, of being a lonely millionaire and a possible Communist—or, as in the premise of *City Lights,* the tramp and the millionaire who can be buddies so long as the rich man stays drunk.

Hollywood's treatment of the crowd in pictures is in fascinating discord with its need for a crowd at the movies. Indeed, there are few better ways of analyzing its schizophrenia than by assessing its use of the crowd. On the one hand, in most American films there is the sentimental assumption of natural virtue and decency in the crowd; nowhere is this clearer than in the grassroots response to crisis by people in Frank Capra films. Yet, that crowd can just as easily become a mob, spiteful, dangerous, mindlessly insecure—witness its behavior in so many films by . . . Frank Capra.

I think that Thalberg was troubled by the rawness of the movie audience, and by how easily it was taken as the lowest common denominator. His sense that a studio schedule needed a few pictures made "for their own sake" was the gesture of a businessman who aspires to art. It was dangerous not only because of those studio people ready to jump on a sign of weakness, a betrayal of the cause, but because it led Thalberg away from his nature, toward prestige and a notion of art that he did not share or understand, which was anathema. It made him uneasy that he'd made his fortune on the tastes of the mob.

So the mob does not do well in Thalberg pictures. Looking only at M-G-M pictures made during his tenure one finds these unflattering portraits of group behavior: *The Crowd,* King Vidor's extraordinary and beau-tiful picture about a couple striving to retain their individual identity against the drab anonymity of the crowd—a great American picture and a project Thalberg cherished; Tod Browning's *Freaks,* in which the commu-nity of whole, unflawed humans turns so nasty and cruel; Gregory La Cava's *Gabriel Over the White House,* in which the whim or charisma of a president is much more reliable than democratic behavior; and *Fury,* the Fritz Lang film about lynch law, one of the great indictments of savage, popular energy.°

This is only a hint of the steady difficulty faced by our republic in gen-erating a real political hope (as opposed to an advertising battle between warring slogans). But as the audience came under stress in the thirties, Hollywood was torn in different directions. Yes, there are films that make vague gestures of hope and support toward the ideology of the New Deal. But then there are those pictures, like *Fury* (where Spencer Tracy is wrongfully accused and nearly lynched), that give ample reason to be afraid of the mob. This is also the time in which a number of people work-ing in pictures made natural links with the Communist party, or with altru-istic, socialist movements that would incriminate them in the late forties and early fifties, in the age of McCarthyism.

We still often regard that time as a witch hunt against unlucky individu-als, but it was much more. It was a display of the culture of property and power in filmmaking, and of America's larger insecurity as it came into its age of empire.

This insecurity took strange forms. For example, consider two young princes of Hollywood: Maurice Rapf and Budd Schulberg, the sons of Harry Rapf, a leading executive at M-G-M, and of B. P. Schulberg, for a time the head of Paramount. They are childhood pals, growing up on the studio backlots. Then their fathers elect to send the boys east to Dart-mouth College—the Ivy League, respectability, old America, if not the place friendliest to Jews. From there, in 1935, they go together on the kind of trip to the Soviet Union that was available in those days. And they think they see the future. They come back changed, their heads full of Eisenstein and social progress. In time, they will both be blacklisted. And the waywardness of the sons is part of the disgrace (or business failure) that falls on both fathers.

°And when Thalberg was gone, the film he helped set up, and which was made in his honor, *Marie Antoinette,* had his decorous widow, Norma Shearer, humiliated and beheaded by the mob.

Then consider the tone that ends Nathanael West's great Hollywood novel, *The Day of the Locust,* published in 1939, the year before his premature death. West was a New York Jew, a novelist and story writer, who went to Hollywood to do screenplays. He was one among many who accepted that bargain, and I don't think he would have denied the plain fact that he was doing it for the money, for he had no great faith either that good pictures could be made or that writers would be key in their development. While there, he could not stop observing the nature of the city and its communities, and *The Day of the Locust* is most remarkable not for its insider scenes (like *The Last Tycoon*) but because of its loose collection of people who have failed in Hollywood.

His lead character is Tod Hackett, a designer who has been hired straight out of the Yale School of Fine Arts by "National Pictures." And what happens when the Ivy Leaguer goes west is just as intriguing as when a studio brat goes to school back East. Tod sees everyday human wreckage and viciousness; he sees people who will do anything for a break. West does not hate or disapprove of these characters; he simply offers them. But Tod does have an object of dread in his life—the crowd. He is planning a panoramic painting, *The Burning of Los Angeles,* that will nail this mob and realize the natural (or deserved) end of L.A.

The city and its crowd are very important in what follows. By 1939, the year of *The Day of the Locust,* and in many ways the *annus mirabilis* of classical Hollywood, the population of Los Angeles has reached 4 million—up from a million in 1915. This is far ahead of the rate of growth in the country as a whole, faster even than the increase in the size of the national movie audience. It is the vast, sad, mournful move west that characterizes the 1930s, driven by hard times and by the absurd lure of the golden kindness to dreaming that Hollywood represents. And which a man like Nathanael West has come to see as characteristic of America's folly, and damning.

The facts about how many new people came to L.A. are beyond dispute. The majority of them came from the Midwest and from the South as the economies of those regions failed. These were poor people, hoping for the best. You can see their destiny still in the row upon row of small, shabby bungalows that made for the sprawl of Los Angeles and for its lack of architectural distinction before the 1970s.

West's vision is apocalyptic, and that was not general. Hollywood's sense of itself is better conveyed in Preston Sturges's *Sullivan's Travels,* made in 1941, in which a very successful but rather empty-headed movie director (Joel McCrea) feels some vague discontent with his own hit comedies and goes in search of the "real" America. He gets his comeuppance on a chain gang in a southern prison farm where only one thing brings light or relief—the movie show. So he goes home resolved to shut up and make some more diverting comedies.

West sees further, toward a more challenging issue: that maybe Hollywood itself deserves some responsibility for the American malaise that is festering in Los Angeles. Tod Hackett is watching a line of people waiting for a movie premiere:

New groups, whole families, kept arriving. He could see a change come over them as soon as they had become part of the crowd. Until they reached the line, they looked diffident, almost furtive, but the moment they had become part of it, they turned arrogant and pugnacious. It was a mistake to think them harmless curiosity seekers. They were savage and bitter, especially the middle-aged and the old, and had been made so by boredom and disappointment.

All their lives they had slaved at some kind of dull, heavy labor, behind desks and counters, in the fields and at tedious machines of all sorts, saving their pennies and dreaming of the leisure that would be theirs when they had enough. Finally that day came. They could draw a weekly income of ten or fifteen dollars. Where else should they go but California, the land of sunshine and oranges?

Once there, they discover that sunshine isn't enough. They get tired of oranges, even of avocado pears and passion fruit. Nothing happens. They don't know what to do with their time. They haven't the mental equipment for leisure, the money nor the physical equipment for pleasure. Did they slave so long just to go to an occasional Iowa picnic? What else is there? They watch the waves come in at Venice. There wasn't an ocean where most of them came from, but after you've seen one wave, you've seen them all. The same is true of the airplanes at Glendale. If only a plane would crash once in a while so they could watch the passengers being consumed in a "holocaust of flame," as the newspapers put it. But the planes never crash.

Their boredom becomes more and more terrible. They realize that they've been tricked and burn with resentment. Every day of their lives they read the newspapers and went to the movies. Both fed them on lynchings, murder, sex crimes, explosions, wrecks, love nests, fires, miracles, revolutions, wars. This daily diet made sophisticates of them. The sun is a joke. Oranges can't titillate their jaded palates. Nothing can ever be violent enough to make taut their slack minds and bodies. They have been cheated and betrayed. They have slaved and saved for nothing.

If West had lived, he would have been decried as a Communist. You can suppose that he was drunk when he wrote this, or driven half-crazy by personal failure. But West had seen how "personal failure" is a real piece of gravel in the soft oyster of Americana, one that does not readily turn into a pearl. The stunning impact of white lies and golden hopes on American thinking expressed in the sentence "They have been cheated and betrayed" is utterly modern; it could be from Joan Didion's somber *Where I Was From,* published in 2003 (by a movie person and a Californian). It's worth remembering that West, in 1939, could see much of America in an L.A. dream, just as the country was gearing up for its greatest test of faith and unity, the Second World War.

If Monroe Stahr had met West, and understood his message, he might have gone into a rapid decline, or had West killed, in a car crash.

As I said earlier, it's not enough to note that there are passing shapes on the wall at the movies—sometimes strange, sometimes comic and beautiful. You have to ask whether they make a frenzy or a sedative. You have to ask whether the wall is somehow a window on life, or a barrier against it. You have to see how this innocent entertainment is changing the world.

David O. Selznick and his contract player, Jennifer Jones, just after she won the Best Actress Oscar for 1943 in *The Song of Bernadette* (*Harry Ransom Center, Selznick Archive*)

10 · RESPECT

Maybe Nathanael West was a genius—he didn't leave behind quite enough for us to be sure. Nor was he the best guardian of whatever talent he had, or the most hopeful when it came to thinking of posterity. There are so many ways in which he was torn apart, yet desperate to hold himself together. He was a writer of prose fiction, who elected to work in Hollywood. By the end of his life he was writing scripts for $600 a week, yet his publisher's advance on *The Day of the Locust* was only $500—too generous; it sold less than 1,500 copies. He was an active leftist sympathizer, a man capable of referring to "the people" without irony or disdain, yet his head holds that vision of the dark mob and its threatening fuse. He also mocked Hollywood leftists for "the Cadillacs they drove to the political meetings." He loved to drive but he was a terrible driver. Indeed, those people he saw going out to Glendale to watch planes crash might have followed him in his car, waiting for the inevitable.

But what a racetrack Los Angeles was then for driving, and how much that city has done over the decades to sustain luxury and vanity models in the automobile business. To this day, there are eastern Americans who cannot grasp, let alone enjoy, the way in which driving in the West is one of the most commonplace yet exultant liberties, a state of mind, a line of thought, another waking dream.° With the distance from downtown and the rail depot to the Santa Monica shore established, a kind of road circuit was set up (not all of it paved at first). Driving needs friendly weather, open space, and cheap gasoline; the grandeur and wealth of some Angelenos quickly made for exotic cars such as are seldom seen outside L.A., Las Vegas, and certain sheikdoms of the Arabian desert.

In those early days, Wilshire Boulevard was a blacktop strip that reached from Beverly Hills to Santa Monica in 1919, with open rural stretches along the way. Driving was a romance and a sport, and a way of showing off. But the population growth, the crowding of those roads, and the inevitable introduction of new intersections and lights made for desperate accidents. The young John Huston, driving when drunk, killed a passerby in 1933; it was hushed up because he was so promising a kid. His father, Walter, used all his old ties, and a grand jury exonerated the driver. Much the same thing happened to Clark Gable and another pedestrian—M-G-M paid a minor executive to do the year in jail. But on December 22, 1940 (the day after Scott Fitzgerald died), West and his wife, Eileen, hurtled out of a side road onto a main road, running a red light. They were both killed.

In any city as large as Los Angeles, and with such a vast underclass (Midwest immigrants at first, then Okies, then Mexicans, then waves of

---

°In his early twenties, David Hockney flew to Los Angeles—loved it, realized he needed a car, bought one, finessed the test—and only learned to drive going to Las Vegas and back. Was it a dream?

Asian refugees), you might expect a thorough public transport system. After all, what are the movies but a cheap means of imaginary transport? (Producer Jerry Bruckheimer asserted recently, "We are in the transportation business.")

There was a public transport system: the famous "red cars." And there were even attempts by the city in the 1920s to ban parking on the streets so that the trolley system could work to its highest efficiency. Already, car jams were impeding the public vehicles. But automobile users protested, and got organized. The rest of the story is evident in the eventual dismantling of the trolley system and the continuing empire of automobiles. Yes, there is a bus system in L.A. (better than its reputation admits), and there are small stretches of subway now. But the traffic fate of the city was settled in the late 1930s by a commission that outlined a series of freeways, construction of which was not finished until 1950, and it goes on forever, in additions, new lanes, and fresh ramps. But still the newcomer is struck by the lack of public transportation, and by the insistence that even the poor must have cars to survive. Yet if they have cars, how can they be poor? (The vehicle license tax played a part in the 2003 gubernatorial recall elections, at a time when Arnold Schwarzenegger was still regarded as an unstoppable machine himself.)

This, by the way, is the struggle that Robert Towne once intended as the subject for the third part of *Chinatown* (and which is actually pursued in Robert Zemeckis's endlessly appealing *Who Framed Roger Rabbit*), the way in which Los Angeles succumbed to the automobile, to smog, congestion, and all of its vested interests, yet also to the feeling of independence and ownership—the very Americanness—of being in your own car. I still have those mixed feelings, and Towne, I have noticed, drives elegant cars, amused by, yet deeply respectful of, the code that ranks your automobile as a status symbol in the picture business.

You can be a movie tycoon in New York City and never think of owning a car. You use limos or cabs, instead. But in Los Angeles, in the new picture business, the car was the determinant of the good life. On studio lots, to this day, visitors are impressed and delighted to find the parking areas, with famous names painted in the tarmac slots—the measure of achievement. There is even a very funny but hideous story of the supposedly mild, laconic Clint Eastwood being driven to fury and violence when some innocent driver-by parked in his space.

It seems exciting to me still that that first generation in Hollywood realized it was starting not just a business, not just a new gold rush, but a cultural phenomenon that would shape the century. At the very same time, they were laying down roads and buying vehicles to ride them, and they were able to build houses and homes that were so different from eastern homes they might have been in Oz. Everything was starting again.

Not long after the merger that created Metro-Goldwyn-Mayer, Mayer got the notion that he ought to have a new house. He was always reluctant to indulge himself (or to be seen doing so), so he would have depicted it as a pressure building on him. He was an important and successful figure; he deserved a home that showed it. His wife, undemanding to a degree, had always dreamed of a house on a beach, the way she might have dreamed of Rudolph Valentino. And his daughters, Edie and Irene, were teenagers who wanted parties and callers.

Having hesitated at first, Mayer then moved like a studio boss. He acquired a lot on the beach, 60 feet by 180, and then he told his family, "You want to be in by summer? When we need a set at the studio, we build it overnight. We need a big village, we build it in weeks. Don't be at the mercy of those contractors. Don't start with the architects. With us, it's business, it gets done. I will talk to the people at the studio. If it can be done for the summer, we will have the beach house."

He was treating their own home like a romantic, fictional set. And he spared nothing: there was a sea wall and everything on twenty-foot pilings against storm damage. The head of the art department at M-G-M, Cedric Gibbons, was in charge of the plan; the construction was under Joe Cohn, the studio production manager. Crews came in, three a day, working under floodlights, seven days a week to get it done in six weeks.

But it didn't all work out as intended. The labor crews at the studio, along with their brothers at the other studios, were on the point of becoming unionized. As such, they had negotiated overtime rates, and Mayer's home was the living definition of overtime. The construction budget suddenly looked like more than the boss could stomach. So he did the Angeleno thing: he employed cheap Mexican labor and got himself a deal. And a lesson.

So there it was, a new Hollywood palace. It cost a lot, but Mayer was on his way to being the highest-paid man in America. Still, it was Mayer's iron whim that the cost not show. As Irene put it later, "Conspicuous expenditure brought envy and bad luck. Extravagance should be put on the screen where it counted."

Yet the Mayers were having it both ways: this was a picture house in a prize location but Mayer asked his teenage daughters to share a room and to make do with three servants and only one chauffeur. It was a puzzle for the girls: "How could a man of my father's innate conservatism have chosen show business?" asked Irene. "Had he not been as emotional as he was, I don't believe he could have been so drawn to, or have succeeded so well in, the picture business. Certainly he had the necessary gut instinct for it."

If you'd asked Mayer himself, Why the contradiction, I think he would have answered respect, self-respect. But self-respect is odd in a man so crazy for story that people thought he was acting all the time. Somehow, he was too shy, too puritanical or embattled to show his own, hard-earned wealth—it is a key to Hollywood thinking. Here was a man who commanded (quite literally) some of the great beauties of the age: he had brought Garbo from Europe; his studio also owned Joan Crawford, Norma Shearer, Jean Harlow, and many others. Mayer loved to be "father" to these women, and no one quite knows how excessive or prurient that attitude was. It's hard to believe that the plain, squat man and the heartfelt actor was not stirred by their company and the immense, upholstered dreams he put up on the screen with them as protagonists. You cannot do that without being moved by movie. You cannot address the dream without staring at it, and becoming possessed.

But Mayer could feel shame for his own product. On-screen, the women showed skin (a lot of it in the days before the enforcement of the Production Code). They were adulteresses, women who lost their virtue, and sometimes they were whores. But when Stroheim made a joke about that, when he offered the insight that all actresses resembled whores (they performed for the dreams of men), Mayer got up, strode round his own desk and slugged the intimidating Austrian. Knocked him flat on his back. Did that happen? In Hollywood, once told, the tale became fact.

As Bosley Crowther described it in *Hollywood Rajah,* the first book about Mayer:

> Mayer's notions of female propriety included rigid ideas on the not uncommon practice of having dates with boys. He was violently opposed to his teen-age daughters going out at night and forbade such behavior until the girls were virtually grown. Then he diligently screened their venturous escorts and insisted they have the girls home by midnight. His stern and repeated precept was that a woman's place was in the home, and he saw to it that his wife taught their daughters how to cook and sew.
>
> This nigh pathological insistence on the observance of strict formalities was, in part, a carry-over from his own background, in part an accretion from his exposure to middle-class New England gentility. It was, in a sense, a reflection of his own mixed-up morality. He was moved by a pas-

sion for conformance, and also by caution and fear. He felt the worst thing that could happen to him, socially, would be to have his daughters become connected with the fast life of Hollywood.

The very life he was driving! There was a day at the studio when Irene bumped into Joan Crawford. It was the actress's first day on the lot, in 1925. Her new studio name was a month or two away yet; she was still Lucille LeSueur then, or Billie Cassin, the girl born in San Antonio, Texas—that hot, half-Mexican city. Irene was eighteen, Crawford twenty-one. "I thought she was preposterous," wrote Irene, "moon-faced, over-weight, with frizzy hair, and she was wearing a tight black silk dress and an unfortunate pair of shiny black shoes, notable for the pompoms which adorned them."

In a word, vulgar. For years, Joan Crawford was driven to tears and fury by the way her own studio depicted her as less than a lady, not like Norma Shearer. The established star William Haines told her, "You've got to draw attention to yourself. There are fifty other girls trying to get roles in pictures, and the producers don't know one pretty face from another. You've got to make yourself known. Get yourself some publicity. Go to dances and premieres. Let people know that Joan Crawford is somebody."

So to be herself she took all the insults: she agreed to the name change; she had a little surgery, here and there; and she lost the weight that had shocked the boss's daughter—and she kept the weight off, goddamn it! She dieted; she lived a life of self-denial, until her face turned from woe to fury. Irene told me there were cases in the old studio days when actresses with a weight problem were given worms. Crawford? I don't know. And remember that on the publicity side, the studio soon made quite a fuss of the press report that Billie Cassin, in her hard days, might have made a blue movie, a stag film. I think it was a deliberate publicity stunt, but it was humiliating and a way of defining Crawford's slut image. And what did it mean when the reports said that studio executives had looked at the reel of film and established that it was not Joan? What comparisons had that required? Had Mayer been adjudicator?

The rigid compartmentalization of Mayer's own life sometimes terrified Irene, and it was the metaphor for a turmoil that preoccupied America. In quite a few ways, the years after the Great War witnessed headlong liber-alization: women got the vote in 1920; jazz burst forth in a mixture of rage and ecstasy, with very black artists, like Louis Armstrong, introducing a new passion on radio airwaves; the economy boomed and the stock market soared, even if a few critics reckoned it was increasingly unstable; young people became more independent and less schooled by old rules; divorce was on the rise; literature assumed tough voices and sordid material in new ways; dress styles became openly "sexy." And all of these things were broadcast and promoted by the movies—not just by the most dynamic business in the country, but the one with most impact on young minds. At the same time there was a profound fear of Communism taking over the country; there was horror at gangsterism; there was Prohibition. And there was increased anxiety at the dangerous example the movies offered, even the veiled suggestion that they might be anti-American.

You could point to that, if you chose, in the way the Victorian moralism of D. W. Griffith and the iconography of Lillian Gish were so swiftly updated by the fallen women played by Garbo and by the young hustlers in the marriage market, personified by Gloria Swanson. The new woman alarmed as many "old" women as she did men. But there were uglier animosities involved. There was an eastern envy of the sheer ease and sunshine experienced in the West. There is still the notion, and it began in the 1920s, that Californians are sybaritic, flaky, and not serious—please tell that to Mike Ovitz and Jeffrey Katzenberg! And then there was the plain fact that so many of these suddenly potent movie studios were run by foreigners and Jews—this in a country that still took anti-Semitism as much for granted as it did anti-black feelings.

Was it proper or decent for a onetime scrap merchant, without education, to become the highest-paid man in America? Was it wise to let a class of aliens have such influence on the American mind? Did those people deserve all that sunshine, that driving space, those pretentious houses, the chance to compare Joan Crawford's body with a body on film, and all that money? There were not many people, in the twenties, who saw that riot of opportunity as the essence of Americana. All too many found it unfair, for the wide-open country, that place for the huddled masses, could get very edgy if it seemed that nobodies (like Vag, the vagrant in Dos Passos's *U.S.A.*) had ideas and plans of their own. That way lay anarchism, and murder. But the movies traded in desperate transition, and so the Jews in Hollywood walked on eggshells, and were sometimes more virulently dismissive of their own origins than their enemies could dream of being. Remember all of this in the fingers-crossed look worn by the Mayers.

In the early twenties, a series of scandals provided fodder for those ready to think the worst of the movie business. That they were projected so far out of proportion was true to the movies themselves, and to the growing press corps that was attached to them. For the first time, those new beings, stars and celebrities, discovered that just as their adulation was absurd, so there might be a vengeful hatred lying in wait that was equally undeserved.

Over the Labor Day weekend, 1921, there was a prolonged party at the St. Francis Hotel in San Francisco. A lot of those present were lovely young things, too rich for caution, in or hoping to be in movies. At the end of it all, there was a pretty corpse, that of Virginia Rappe, a model and star-let. Rappe's death seemed to be the result of forcible rape, and according to some the rapist was comedian Roscoe "Fatty" Arbuckle. It had been his party, and he had thrown it in San Francisco in order to air out his new $25,000 Pierce-Arrow car.

He was charged with rape and murder and eventually was acquitted after two mistrials (both juries had voted 10–2 for conviction). There was far more hysteria than evidence. One San Francisco paper cried out "Hol-lywood Must Stop Using San Francisco for a Garbage Can." But there *was* a corpse, and there *had* been mayhem at the hotel. Paramount cancelled Arbuckle's contract, and his career was never the same again.

Then, on February 1, 1922, the director William Desmond Taylor was murdered in his bungalow in the Westlake district of Los Angeles. That case was never solved, or brought to court, but ripples of scandalous sug-gestion implicated two actresses, Mary Miles Minter and Mabel Nor-mand, in what was said to have been a circle of sex and drug-taking. By the time the police arrived, Paramount executives were burning papers in the bungalow and Normand was searching for her old love letters. But no one had gotten rid of the pornographic pictures in which Taylor was seen with other actresses.

A year later, in January 1923, the enormously popular star Wallace Reid died in a padded cell in a private sanitarium, a victim of drug addiction. It was said he had started on morphine because of injuries incurred in a rail crash. Barbara La Marr was dead in 1926 from a cocaine overdose, oddly akin to the death "from poisoning" of Olive Thomas, in Paris in 1920, when the young actress was so out of her mind on drugs that she swal-lowed bichloride of mercury. Along with Chaplin marrying the underage Lita Grey in 1924, these were the headline cases as well as the acid subtext to all the sweetness of advertised escapism of the business: "All the adven-ture, all the romance, all the excitement you lack in your daily life are in—Pictures! They take you completely out of yourself into a wonderful new world—Out of the cage of everyday existence! If only for an afternoon or an evening—Escape!"

Threatened by its own excesses, haunted by insecurities, the American picture business reacted cravenly, as it would later under McCarthyism. It tried to avail itself of organization, diligent self-censorship (to forestall the interference of others), and anything that might pass for respect. Institutional cowardice is usually comic; still, its reactions should always be borne in mind whenever claims of art are offered. Business is self-protective, while art is always disinterested and often self-destructive.

In 1922, the industry enlisted Will H. Hays, a lawyer, the former chairman of the Republican National Committee, and postmaster general in the Warren Harding administration. Hays was an ugly weasel and a routine political operator, but he was awarded a salary of $100,000 to clean up the movies and to be the first president of the Motion Picture Producers and Distributors of America, a collection of bosses that included Samuel Goldwyn, Carl Laemmle, William Fox, Adolph Zukor, and Marcus Loew.

The MPPDA was vengeful. Though Arbuckle was acquitted and Minter was never charged, their films were withdrawn; morality clauses were inserted in contracts, a means by which the employers could withhold money, or fire people, if they got involved in scandal; there was a general effort to improve, or cleanse, press coverage that led to sturdier campaigns of lies from the studios on behalf of their stars; and there were efforts to get people to make "improving" films. In a lurid fit of conscience, Cecil B. De Mille, who had waved the movie "flapper" as vigorously as anyone, now discovered religion, and found unexpected showbiz rewards when he realized that Biblical subjects necessarily involved Original Sin, dancing girls, and a good deal of skin. Wallace Reid's widow Dorothy Davenport made a film, *Human Wreckage,* that was a nearly noir study of narcotic destruction.

As for Will Hays himself, he drew up a sort of ten commandments of censorship, a series of "thou shalt nots." Actually, there were thirteen laws; I'll list them here so you can ask yourself how many of them now might qualify as essential ingredients in a production code: do not deal with sex in an improper manner; do not touch white slavery; do not make vice attractive; no nakedness; no prolonged passionate love scenes; no predominant treatment of the underworld; do not make gambling and drunkenness attractive; do not offer instruction in how to commit crimes; do not ridicule public officials; do not offend religious beliefs; do not emphasize violence; cut out those vulgar postures and gestures; and please omit salacious advertising.

Hays was an idiot and a humbug, and he was doing his best to stand up for hypocritical profiteers. But many aspects of the Production Code endured into the 1960s and had a chilling affect on the imagination, the vigor, the candor, and the artistic potential of American movies. Going through that list, one can easily foresee clashes to come. What do we do about the prolonged kissing scenes in *Notorious* and *North by Northwest*? Do we lose them? Or do we thank Alfred Hitchcock's ingenuity for realizing that if the kiss was broken up into many, many short kisses, caresses, nibbles, et cetera, the Code was preserved? What is the record of Preston Sturges in the matter of ridiculing public officials? And suppose the officials do it to themselves? In the matter of minimizing the life of crime, what do we make of *The Godfather, Bonnie and Clyde,* so much of *film noir* and the gangster picture of the early thirties?

Go a little further: how is the treatment of sex improper if it is a driving force in luring people to the movies? And what does restraint have to do with a medium that is founded on the principle—reckless or not—of showing people things they have never seen before?

On the other hand, of course, there is the matter of practical benefit. I don't wish to fall into the bully-pulpit orthodoxy that this country has been depraved, disillusioned, and degraded by the movies, but I do not honestly see how anyone can mount the argument that a single person was ever protected by Hays and his principles. You can ask what did Hays want on the screen (apart from anything that would make money for the business, his cronies) and, unfortunately, the answer comes in some of the most grotesque words ever uttered by what we must recognize as a public official:

> The potentialities of motion pictures for moral influence and education are limitless. Therefore its integrity should be protected as we protect the integrity of our children and our schools, and its quality developed as we develop the quality of our schools. Above all is our duty to youth. We must have toward that sacred thing, the mind of a child, toward that clean and virgin thing, that unmarked slate—we must have toward that the same responsibility, the same care about the impression made upon it, that the best teacher or the best clergyman, the most inspired teacher of youth, would have.

To which, one striking complaint must be added: put aside the cant of such thinking, and ask how else do we account for the realization, a hundred or so years after it all began, that the American movie is far more directed at an audience of arrested and indulged children than at a society of alert, responsible, challenged adults?

Where was Louis B. Mayer when the MPPDA was formed? In 1922, Mayer had his own company but was not yet one of Hollywood's clear leaders. That in itself underlines how striking a promotion he enjoyed when the M-G-M merger was made. Another sidelight on history is that, in 1922, the founding members of the MPPDA included not just Lewis J. Selznick but his son Myron, too. The sudden decline and fall of Selznick's World Film Corporation was only a few months away, but the time lag helps explain Mayer's enormous contempt for the Selznicks.

So, whereas the setting up of the MPPDA was craven, dishonest, and futile, the thinking that led to the start of the Academy was brilliant and full of understanding. For Mayer had foreseen the future of the business, one in which money and the highest earners might take charge. Feeling left out, his response was reactionary, self-interested, and forlorn. But he was right, and he employed a key instrument in Hollywood's search for respect. He firmly resolved that in the competitive arena of filmmaking M-G-M would always have the best, the most stars, the highest production values, the most distinguished novelists and playwrights locked up in the writers' building. And quality must have its rewards. In Oscar's steady shine, it is taken for granted that movies must possess some lasting quality or redemption. In addition, whatever else the Academy has given us, it has provided the best research library on motion picture history.

There was another thorn in Mayer's paw. That problem he had in building his own house was an indication of the potential difficulties that might spread in Hollywood if organized labor ever got fashionable. Mayer had the notion of some lofty organization that might preempt the need for unions to look after the better-paid workers. For there, he was sure, would be the source one day of serious trouble.

In December 1926, Mayer held a modest dinner party at his new Santa Monica house. The guests were actor Conrad Nagel, Fred Niblo (the director of *Ben-Hur*), and Fred Beetson, a producer. Mayer proposed a new organization that might help mediate labor disputes and assist the MPPDA in its clean-up work. But this new organization would be a dining club, too, made up of outstanding figures in all branches of filmmaking. It would be a privilege to belong to it.

On January 11, 1927, thirty-six potential members were Mayer's dinner guests at the Ambassador Hotel. That night the organization was called the International Academy of Motion Picture Arts and Sciences, and Mayer consented to be appointed chairman of the planning committee. On May 4, 1927, at the Biltmore, a more lavish banquet was held at which 231 people signed on for the $100 annual membership, and Doug Fairbanks was made president. The same occasion called for annual merit prizes. At a later meeting, it is said, Cedric Gibbons did a rough sketch of a figure holding a sword that was transfixing a reel of film. No, it's not the cleverest design, for it does carry hints that this strange knight has stopped motion. Never mind. This is probably now the best-known statue in the world: 13.5 inches high; 6.75 pounds; tin and copper, with gold plating. We call it Oscar because . . . well, we're not sure why. But some say it's because Margaret Herrick, the Academy's first librarian, thought the figure looked a little like her uncle Oscar. No one ever said that family life for Hollywood people was straightforward.

We will come back to the Oscars and what they mean. Suffice it to say that eight decades later, the night of the Academy Awards (and the fuss leading up to it) has no equal in preserving the legend that the movies are a binding part of our experience (not just America's, but the world's). Everyone has heard of the Academy, whereas the MPPDA (now the MPAA) leaves most people puzzled. It was a stroke of brilliance, even if its long-term consequences were not quite the ones intended in 1927.

But right from the start the Academy Awards revealed a wound in Hollywood's makeup. The Merit Award Committee was torn over the highest award of all. They recognized even then that there might be a distinction between the picture deemed most successful by the business, and the one that might last the longest and mean the most because something like the idea of art clung to it. If you think of it in terms of 1941, it was the difference between *How Green Was My Valley* or *The Maltese Falcon* or *Sergeant York* and, say, *Citizen Kane*. The first three were box office successes; *Kane* was not. The first three, more or less, pleased the community of Hollywood; *Kane* did not. *How Green Was My Valley* won Best Picture, and it has its admirers still. *Kane* did not win, yet almost by universal assent, it is reckoned the greatest film ever made.

Of course, it doesn't matter too much as long as all the films last so that new viewers can reach their own decisions. But it says a lot about Hollywood's sense of itself that in 1927, the first impulse was to have no single Best Picture. Instead, there would be two awards: one for "the most outstanding motion picture production, considering all the elements that contribute to a picture's greatness"; and the other for "the most unique, artistic, worthy and original production without reference to cost or magnitude." It was having your cake and eating it, cleaning up now, but banking on eternity.

For that first Oscar, *Wings* (from Paramount, directed by William Wellman) was the clear favorite. It was an epic production on the air battle in the Great War, with American heroes. It had been a box office hit. But there were those who argued on behalf of *Sunrise* (from Fox, directed by

F. W. Murnau). Murnau was one of the great artists of German film, recently arrived in Hollywood. As such, he had invested *Sunrise* with extraordinary mood and very beautiful camera movements. It's the story of a married couple, country people, and of how the man is nearly seduced away by a city temptress and urban excitement. Perhaps because the emotional plight was at odds with so much current change in the country, it did not seem like an American picture, despite the presence of stars George O'Brien and Janet Gaynor (one actress who kept up the Gish tradition).

One of its great fans was Louis B. Mayer. It was true that, ultimately, *Sunrise* upheld family loyalty and togetherness along with many rural virtues and pieties. But it also had a pace and a melancholy that were not usually Mayer's meat. In fact, it was a film adored by his intellectually inclined daughter, Irene, and her beau, David O. Selznick. They were moved by it, but they were the next generation and maybe they were being deliberately arty or pretentious to get under Mayer's skin.

In fact, that first year, awards were given to both *Wings* and *Sunrise,* though in nearly all the history books *Wings* is now declared Best Picture. Fair enough, but more people probably still look at, and write about, *Sunrise.* That would have amazed Mayer, I think. For while he was earnest in his quest for respect for the motion picture, I'm not sure that he was ever in favor of reading, or too comfortable with it. Respect is all very well, but take it too far and you may be asleep.

Edward Hopper, *New York Movie,* 1939 *(Museum of Modern Art)*

11 · AT THE PARADISE

I am looking at Edward Hopper's *New York Movie,* a painting from
1939. Over the years, I have spent hours gazing at it, and wondering.
But I cannot decide whether it offers a paradise, or a prison. Yet once
I put it that way, I have to concede that Hopper must have been aware of
a problem, or an ambiguity, in 1939. Would we spend so long with his
painting if it was mere perfection? Was Hopper a realist, or was he dreaming as he painted this picture? Were we asleep at the movies in those days?
Did all of us want to get lost?

It is a picture of an operating movie theater, yet things are wrong. There is that fragment of a black-and-white screen—not really black or white, but gradations of silver light—at the edge of a painting rich in color. There are the red drapes, scarlet, at the foot of the stairs; there are the rose-colored lamps; there is a glow on the brass rails next to the seats; the usherette's suit is midnight blue; and she is such a bright blonde—maybe she ought to be in movies herself. (Is she a premonition of Nicole Kidman?)

All that brave color needs light, and you realize slowly that just about all the house lights are on in this cinema, and maybe some it never had. With a picture playing, whether it is the feature or a preliminary attraction, there would be wounded cries to kill the lights. Darkness is the first fix moviegoers need. And the painting is very specially silent (which is not the same here as being without sound—more of that in a minute).

What has Hopper done? We know he was a moviegoer; as he wandered the city he spent hours in cinemas, for their own sake and to plan works like this. But he has left the lights on, when he could just as easily have painted the real dark. You can imagine that: the composition might be a little different, but every visible detail—the man's cheek in the stalls, the usherette's hair—could depend on the screen's reflected light, that moony spill. Then the painting would be darkness with just those fragments of human attention floating in the gloom, instead of a picture that is like day-for-night, like midnight shot at midday, or like a movie house that is being dreamed.

Then, do you see how the exact center of this strange picture is the least helpful? It is the featureless nothing of a heavy pillar, the thrust that separates the world of the theater (the screen, the seats, the people) from the solitude of the usherette—that quiet, peaceful sidebar where she leans against the wall, her chin resting in one hand. She is not watching the movie. She is not that kind of usherette bursting to get into pictures, a would-be actress studying every tiny gesture on the screen. No, she has her own private movie running, and maybe she is an usherette because in that job you have time to sink into your own thoughts, time to go unnoticed.

Not that she is anonymous or insignificant. Far from it. She'd be tall, I think, even without those high-heeled sandals with their sexy straps. And how does light get to her arched white feet? You can see within those dark blue slacks that she has legs all the way up, a cinched waist and the heave of breasts, as well as that corn-colored hair Doris Day had at Warner Brothers in the fifties, that drops on her shoulders in a wave. And there is light enough to pick out one side of her face—the bone-like flash of wrist and palm. I never saw skin so luminous in a functioning movie house—no, not even one glimpse of pale thigh on a back-row seat in the inadvertent swing of a south London usherette's torch. This girl has such a light strapped to her left wrist; you can see it tucked under the right elbow, thrust up to sustain the head so full of sadness or rapture.

Why watch the movie when that girl is standing there? Is that what the painting is about? Is it Hopper's way of saying that within the crowded, half-awake daydreaming of a packed theater, there may be some pressing loneliness or melancholy, one beautiful girl who doesn't buy the escape of the screen? Yes, that thought is there for sure: Hopper believed in the lonely crowd and urban solitude. He hoped to find drama there, just as his piercing eyes see her feet—put the light where the money (or the sexiness) is. But there's something else going on which has to do with the eternal difficulty in working out what is on the screen.

I mean, this is 1939, so you can propose that the picture playing is something from that famously golden year. Is it *Dark Victory, Love Affair, Wuthering Heights*? I can believe this girl would like those movies and know them well enough so that she could lean against a wall—Hopper is so alert to tiredness—and just listen to its dense soundtrack. I think her eyes are closed—but maybe that's just me—the better to encourage the process of digestion or absorption.

There, that is getting close to something, I think. As I look at the painting I feel myself absorbing its atmosphere, yet being absorbed, so that I wonder if the girl isn't dreaming me as I watch her. Like "Madeleine" in *Vertigo,* declining to notice Scotty, but falling in love with him a little even as he comes under her spell? Don't we fall in love with those who look at us with yearning?

We can see only a fragment of the screen, but imagine Hopper's skill— his deliberate pursuit of solitude or the inaccessible—in that years later we cannot identify the movie. Over the years, I have thought that crest might be a hint of Charles Foster Kane saying "Rosebud." But, again, that's just me—I see that mouth everywhere. And the me writing this book suspects that the film playing in the painting could even be *Chinatown*. Yes, I realize, that's ridiculous—*Chinatown* came more than thirty years later. But *Chinatown* is also about events that transpired just before 1939, and made then it would surely have been in black and white. I can easily imagine Jake Gittes—he knows the story well enough to quit it for a moment—getting up, going over to the usherette and breaking into her detachment with, Excuse me, are you doing anything later? As if a girl who had seen *Chinatown* that often (so she only needed to listen to it) wouldn't know that Jake was bad news. Yes, *Chinatown* is fanciful. But fanciful is all right, too, sometimes. And dreaming seldom honors factual niceties. It just tells you that fusspots after fact are spoilsports, like Jedediah Leland wanting to keep the actual paper with Kane's Declaration of Principles on it when Charlie's already on to his next scene.

That's another reference to *Citizen Kane,* and I know how unsettling it can seem to make such casual, sportive links between a world of history and a world of romance (the real America and its movies). I mean the thought that Charles Foster Kane might have been president, even if George Orson Welles missed the chance to run for Senator from Wisconsin, against Joseph McCarthy. Such games may not fit everybody's taste or experience. At the same time, I think this half-haunted feeling is still very common (and confusing), and it is central to what I take as the whole equation of the movies. "What are you doing after the film?" is a good question to ask of many movie characters.

To put it very simply, and to return to the matter of absorption or direction, I suggest that many people from a certain range of history—people born between about 1900 and 1950—are like screens. That is to say that countless films have played upon our surface, whether we like it or not. And not just many films, but many films many times. Like the usherette, if you will, and in a way that has nothing to do with film scholarship, we have seen *Dark Victory* or *Chinatown* or *Kane* so often we breathe in time with their cuts and we radiate possibility according to the luster of their image. We shuffle them together. They are all in the same pack, and we can do cute card tricks with them. Q◊, anyone?

And because we are screens, helpless gatherers of so many images, we hear a little bit of Bogart's Philip Marlowe in his Dixon Steele (from *In a Lonely Place*), and we are so crowded and so promiscuous that we can see John Wayne kissing Greta Garbo ("How did you like that?" "How did I like what?"), even if such a touch never happened in movie history and, quite likely, never occurred in life. The metaphor of the screen (and its melting pot) is very suggestive, I think, for it lets us see how receptive and yet how superficial we are, like a helpless computer screen that must accept every bit of information put into it.

But our condition is more dangerous or fertile still. For whereas the computer, apparently, has an institutional coldness that can translate everything into 0 or 1 (it tells no jokes), we screens are hideously subject to atmosphere, to irony, to the infinity of suggestion that always lies behind the restricted photographic information of a "shot." And here I come close to what is more obviously the material for film theory than Hollywood history: the matter of how we watch, of how we take in facts (visual things that are fixed and unmistakable) and then interpret them as the tropes of fantasy. But this intense stress on fantasy occurred in fixed years, so that it cannot decently be eliminated from a study of the history of film. And, naturally, the matter is all the more troublesome in that history hopes to establish what happened and why (in rational, evidential ways), when the thing that happened here may yet be judged as a kind of vast collective swoon, a way in which we went mad or gave up the ghost on reason, fact, and the several codes of consequence or responsibility we hope are attached to such things.

This is not easy territory (it is much easier to disapprove of madness than to track it), so let's get back to that Hopper painting (something you can see and hear) as a basis for discussion.

I said "hear" because there are several conventional things to say about sound in the cinema. The medium had often aspired to music. There is a pretty picture of the crew shooting *Greed* in Death Valley, with the Brennan brothers—on violin and harmonium—providing a little mood music as Gibson Gowland (dressed and made up as McTeague) leads a burro into the blasted heat. Such accompaniment was frequent, and it surely follows the notion that the actor would play the scene better if he heard suitable music in the hot air. Similarly, in theaters, in varying degrees of scale, there was often musical accompaniment for the movies. In theaters, this would have added to the communal spirit of the proceedings. Equally (and this is heresy to some), it would have taken away from an ultimate treasure of movies, the condition by which we are alone with the movie.

Then again, sound was a nightmare of invention and a real burden on costs. Sam Warner actually died in the frenzied race in which Warner Brothers would be the first studio to produce talking pictures. But he and his brothers could not foresee that the heavy demands of sound would fall on the business in 1929 and the first years of economic depression.

You can argue that if the men who ran the business had foreseen that problem, they might have denied themselves sound, or delayed it for several years, but that supposes that the fiscal interests in the film business control the technology. Remember how, at the very outset, the technology happened, leaving many business geniuses unaware about what to do with it. Notice how in what is, relatively, America's greatest time of economic crisis during the history of movies (1929–45), the medium took on both sound and color. Ask yourself why and how the allegedly astute movie business could be so clueless about what television would mean, and then the video revolution of the 1980s. For all the talk of synergy these days in the corporate boardrooms that run film and television, and despite the technological availability, consider the trepidation and the delays that attend the introduction of high-definition television as a regular domestic convenience.

In other words, technology seems to respond far more to public curiosity (or readiness) than to business acumen. Film was prompted more by an inchoate public desire (or by the challenge to express desire itself in fresh terms) than by the visionary leadership of inventors and businessmen. A mass medium arose from within a society that was stumbling toward new moods of scale, of crowding, and of loneliness. The future of film technologically, now, I believe, waits on our arriving at some conclusion as to who or what we are going to be, and I fear it may involve the abandonment of some attributes of what we once called humanism in favor of more worrying things. That future might reveal us less as voyeurs than people ready to pay a few dollars for unfair glimpses of others—in surveillance may come spying; in cruelty, torture. What will people sit still for, and watch?* The answer comes into being only as we reach for a switch. Or do not. The shift will occur when a large enough portion of society is not troubled by the loss, or does not notice it. That's as good a way of defining progress as any.

There were declared artists in film—Griffith and Chaplin, and Ozu in Japan—who regarded the loss of silence with distress and defiance. It's a measure of Chaplin's box office power, and his unique mimetic art, that he could ignore sound for so long, and when he did start to talk there were soon plenty of people begging him to stop. As for Griffith, he'd been out-of-date since well before sound came along, and may have elected to blame it for his own shortcomings and for his inability to get past genteel attitudes often protected by silence. For example, the cast-iron innocence and the wronged circumstances of Griffith heroines is reinforced by the way their fervent protestations stay mute. To hear those laments would be to despair of the self-pity and the provincialism involved. The moral imperatives of Griffith's world are more to be asserted than talked about.

I have little sympathy with that attitude: if there was an "art" in silent film, it was too reliant on stilted dance, Victorian theatricality, and the beginnings of Soviet dynamism in composition and editing (the latter generally rejected by Hollywood in that they were too radically intrusive, too dialectical). On the other hand, no one can argue that silent film was not the first great surge forward of a new kind of popular entertainment, with

---

*The TV series 24 was using torture (without much comment) before it came to light in Iraq—in pictures. Torture is photogenic, though no more reliable than depicted sex. In both cases, the burning images leave this question unsettled, "Are they exactly doing it?"

a force that seemed to address the crowd in a way no other medium had managed before.

And in the last years of silence, anyone can see that medium striving for fresh complexity and ambition, moving the camera in pursuit of an emotional intimacy barred by silence, or finding montage forms that made film musical. These notable films were not big hits, but you can watch them still with enormous interest, and with an awareness that a medium is knocking at every door it can find for novelty. I'm thinking of Murnau's *Sunrise* (made by a German invited to America by Fox); of *The Wind* (the Swedish visitor, Victor Sjöström, working with Lillian Gish as her career as a lead actress in film neared its end); Vidor's *The Crowd,* a project initiated and encouraged by Thalberg; and Dziga Vertov's *The Man with a Movie Camera,* a lyrical tribute to the camera and to editing, and a work perhaps more easily seen as the descendant of Constructivism and even Cubism.

Therefore it's not insane that adherents of those films and others cried out, Give us back our beauty! as sound tramped in—and in early sound every footfall was crushing, and as stupid and restricting as it is depicted in *Singin' in the Rain.* But here's the crux of it: with the greatest of silent films, I feel only the prospect of liberation, in that a half-made medium was about to become complete. Whereas I still regard color taking over from black-and-white a few years later (a far more gradual process) as ruinous and unforgivable, as well as conclusive proof that the movies seldom behave like an art form.

What I want to say about sound is not only that a latent art was brought to fruition, nor even that talk promoted a welcome advance in intelligence in American pictures. Rather, it is that the very curious two-way dream in Hopper's *New York Movie* was made possible, just as the depth of inhabitable fantasy became intoxicating. Within a few years, the medium was carried from the necessary belaboring of story and interpretation in even a film like *Sunrise* to the extraordinary prospect of lifelike behavior in, say, Lubitsch's *Trouble in Paradise,* Jean Renoir's *Boudu Sauvé des Eaux,* Sternberg's *Shanghai Express,* Howard Hawks's *Scarface,* Rouben Mamoulian's *Dr. Jekyll and Mr. Hyde,* or Max Ophüls's *Liebelei* (all of which were released in 1932–33).

To be paradoxical, sound pictures allowed characters to be silent, or to be as naturally recessive, as thoughtful, or as mysterious as people we encounter in life. Really as mysterious as life? Well, no, that's another optimistic exaggeration. Still, the advance is astounding, and so modern it altered the very nature of acting. Indeed, eventually it made acting so seductive that that peculiar manner of being has been passed on to nearly all of us, like an infection. Is the only way to behave naturally now to act?

Let me spell that out: In silent pictures characters actually talk a good deal of the time. This is covered in titles, or the things said are so obvious there is no need for titles. Note: whenever obvious things are said in art, art suffers, and is dragged down to the level of small talk. Even when the people are quiet, when they are "thinking," they are like comic-book characters with thought bubbles over their heads. In other words, the focus on thought/talk is narrow, intense, and glaring—it is monotonous and it is one reason why silent films are, literally, fatiguing. So many of the lives on view are shrill, single-minded, and over-emphatic.

Contrast that with, say, the moment in *Morocco* when Marlene Dietrich (wearing a man's tuxedo) has just finished singing to the café audience. In the rush of applause, Amy Jolly (Dietrich's character) fixes on a pretty young woman at one table. She surveys her. The girl is flustered by this cool scrutiny. Then Amy hesitates an instant (Sternberg nearly invented hesitation in the movies) and kisses the girl. What has happened? What does it mean?

Happily, I can say that what has happened is so playful yet so profound that there is no simple way of saying what it means. We have seen and felt a mind at work, a mind and a body blessed by the great advantage of sound, so that Amy may elect silence for a few seconds. And because Dietrich (under Sternberg's fierce, loving gaze, at least) was good enough to fill hesitation with a lifetime of wonder, it is as if a medium has been thrown forward by several centuries in the discovery of doubt and duration. (How long can I watch a movie? Until it solves its mystery and decides on its ending.)

There were silent screen stars, like John Gilbert (who loved Garbo and was loved by Dietrich in life), like Mabel Normand (who sounded like the Bronx), who lamented that sound and its stress on vocal manners had destroyed their careers.° But far more, a generation of favorites slipped away because they did not have access to that emotional quietness, and the allure that attaches to any mystery or reticence in a medium that seems to be giving you all the visual evidence. Now that mystery is usually far more sexual than intellectual, but do not rule out the intellect altogether, or just assume that "art" needs to be intellectual. Sound made movie life more grown-up, more voyeuristic, more sophisticated, more

---

°It was more to the point that Gilbert lost his confidence, and was goaded and hounded by his proprietor, Mr Mayer.

maddening (I think that people were more deluded by the experience). But none of that need have anything germane to do with art—as opposed to magic, extrasensory perception, séance, drug-taking and body-snatching, all of which got a lot of play as story material. And still do. For the movie is a rapture that likes to take other rapturous conditions as its subjects—it is as if only such elements could sustain the folly and the beauty of those lustrous close-ups, or the stealth of tracking shots that thread us into the eye of rapture's needle.

I think that in the silent era, cinema seems to be a storytelling medium in which we and the medium itself are straining against the foolish limitations of the medium so far: the kind of acting that has to signal thought process; the resolve to make story line clear and central (so that people will not lose track); and the way the accompanying music is less authentic and unique than constant reference to the catalog of coded moods—love music, danger music, fight music, chase music.

And then through a simple enough device, that labor and struggle are over, to be replaced by an unease that was never quite anticipated beforehand. Suddenly, we realize that the whole thing is not only about story. It is a kind of séance, or a drug, where we are offered the chance to partake in the lifelike. No, it's not life: we will never meet Joan Crawford or Clark Gable. Yet we are with them. It is surreptitious; it is illicit, if you like, in the sense of being unearned or undeserved. It is vicarious, it is fantastic, and this may be very dangerous. But it is heady beyond belief or compare. And it changed the world. Not even heroin or the supernatural ever went so far.

Is that going too far, too fast? I don't believe anyone has ever tried to explain movies this way; and for good reason: the argument is difficult, and the results are frightening—for you may find that you lose your innocent pleasure at the movies; you may come back with knowledge that damns this lovely magic of ours.

Think of yourself as our usherette, or as someone watching her, waiting for her to yield a clue to herself. The cinema is about seeing and being seen. But hearing is a deeper flow, a more primitive river, one that trusts in persistence—in perceived presence, existence, in continuity—before it tries to fathom story.

When we talked about the beginnings of movie, the phrase "persistence of vision" occurred: it is the phenomenon in our perception whereby enough sequential fragments in a second gives the impression that we have seen real duration, unbroken motion. Yet in fact, as the film strip proved then and still proves, we are seeing a certain number of still pictures (frames) promoted to life and movement. From the outset, in taking pictures, whether the recording system employed a disk or an optical or magnetic track, sound has no such frame divisions. Nowadays, sound is there on the edge of the film strip like a river, or like the transcription of a pulse.

You may ask, what difference does that make? I'd answer, trust your feelings, even if you don't have the knowledge to give a full, neurological explanation—and not even neurologists are that thorough yet. But if, say, the first shot of our invented movie is Hopper's *New York Movie,* then sound has made available possibilities never dreamed of a few years before that innovation. For example, even in 1939 (with good sound), and certainly today, we can hear many things married together: we can hear the soundtrack from the screen at the edge of the painting—it can be "placed," at will, close or far away, not just physically but emotionally; we can hear the ambient sound of the theater—and good sound could let you know how crowded the place is. Do not underestimate that unaccented "room tone," the natural sound going on whenever the world is "silent." In *New York Movie* it would include the collective sighing, murmurs, or shuffling of the audience; it includes the insect-like struggle between true silence and random sound; and it can include the tiny buzzing in your head, for most of our hearing is off a little, because we are a touch deaf or a little emotional.

Different rooms in your house have different tones: try to hear them, and try to recollect how that affects the emotion or the atmosphere of those rooms. Try to grasp how far this texture helps us understand that thing, that place, that state of mind we call "home." Do not underestimate how much you absorb it, like nourishment, or how much your presence, your breathing, your battle with silence, contributes to it for others.

What I am trying to demonstrate is how far sound automatically introduces the enchantment of "you are there" to the witnessed theater or enacted storytelling of silent film. Sound was so sly, so surreptitious. Yes, it enhanced and accelerated narrative. But it made an extraordinary cult out of illusion, or presence. It put us on the lip of another world, in many ways a perfect world (or as lustrous as lighting, décor, stars, and the sheen of the screen could make it). If, with good reason, you quickly seize upon the mockery of that "perfection," then accept this: that it established a fantasy realm, overwhelmingly desirable, a place we longed to be. Going to the movies was a way of being *in* them. It was sound that slipped the engine's tracks, from story to atmosphere, as it were, by suggesting that poised, pregnant hesitation in which something might be said, or uttered, something that came from nowhere known, nowhere yet imagined. It presumes the intense, lovable mystery—the allure—of people on screen that they can say "Rosebud" as their first word, or "What a dump!" or "You do know how to whistle?"

No silent film could stretch to the audacity, the surrealism, or the intimate innuendo of Lauren Bacall's line (which does rely on a huskiness Howard Hawks had built in a nineteen-year-old by having her speak lines so that they would carry the width of Mulholland Drive). The way Bacall talks was in part the way Hawks dreamed of talk (more of that anon). Granted the circumstances of Martinique in 1944 it was fanciful, or dopey. Silent films were always too helplessly sensible to break into that kind of inner talk. And the lines endure, not just for their nerve and their dreaminess, but because they attest to the inner life—libido, or whatever—panting to be released, and inspired by the magical underground sigh of sound that is always there in room tone, in presence, in breathing.

All of a sudden, people on-screen became recessive, ghostly, unknowable yet desirable. I will argue later the case that movies have been diminished (as a passion or a cult) as that superstition has become boring, camp, or foolish. For it is a way of touching fantasy that was always ridiculous, or dangerous, but which held most of the world for a long moment (at least thirty years), a moment some of us can't get out of our heads. And although that moment was also always a creation of business, with price tags on every item, and with treasures to behold if it all worked, still the money, the stardom and so on would not have worked without the new revelation of rather ghastly fake gods, images to worship. I don't think that's too strong. Though once one employs the language of religion, it's easier to see how potentially damaging or misleading the trick could be.

I am not complaining. But I bought the drug or the cult, and I have come to see how far that was an easing of loneliness or a kind of solitude that might have been dealt with in other ways.

And the novelty was quite simply the notion that in a movie you are looking at a real world, palpable, with people thinking of what to say, breathing, and sucking you in. And if you never actually go all the way in, why, that's because of the "real" physical barrier (the screen existing in a different physics from the auditorium), and that is your safety, too. For it was the condition that promises you—the voyeur, the peeping tom, the dreamer—that you would never be identified or accused. And that was necessary and proper, because if you are going to imagine you are James Dean or Loretta Young, then your own identity needs to be put away, set aside, to make room for the dream. So you will not be lonely any longer.

I am no longer sure that young people today feel this stealthy rapture, or are inclined to take it seriously. But the generation of their parents remembers, and even if they sometimes look back on old movies as a guilty pleasure (because it was so deeply furtive, so truly escapist or evasive), there remains fondness and nostalgia. And in some people (the community of film critics and film buffs, though not always filmmakers), the passion insists that the movies then were art, or were within reach of it.

Well, maybe—I don't rule it out and there are still movies that mean as much to me as other arts (I will insist on keeping that level of comparison in mind). But I want to establish here how far the secret, or the trick of movies—the click, if you like, when the drug works—has to do with something that has nothing to do with art. I am talking about this half-magical, half-sinister beckoning to us to be part of that glowing room and its romance. And I know, in my lungs, as well as my head, that it depended on the digestive, breathing flow of continuity that only sound allows.

Of course, sound is now richer still, by far. And more illicit. Consider how sweetly the medium was able to marry (it is still called a married print in the mixing, when all tracks are blended) the talk, the sound effects, and the music in the air. Three tracks? By today's standards, that is primitive. The degree of sound density that people like Walter Murch (an artist, but not a maker of films) has made involves so many tracks and so many aural pressures that even a Murch would have great difficulty translating into words which level gives what meaning.

But nothing is more illustrative of the violent ruptures of meaning allowed in sound film than the way the naturalism of talk, the sound of a sleeve against a face, the moan of a wind, are offset by the orchestral version of melodramatic hopes or fears that is playing. You say, We do not hear that contrast any longer. Maybe, but then look at the intricate interplay of music and "meaning" in advertisements today (maybe the most profoundly pondered movies we ever see), and don't kid yourself that the makers aren't still exploiting that delicious unreason, that madness.

For it seems to me clear now that in the history of the movies there arrives, above all in the 1940s, an exquisite mixture of a lifelike dream world explored through the most refined and elaborate camera styles—with vast sets, insinuating tracking shots, and lighting that throbs with inner life—with the fabrication of music in the air, day-dreamy situations and indulged fantasy. Examples? To find them only in America, and only in the forties, let me list these: *Letter from an Unknown Woman,* by Max Ophüls; *The Shop Around the Corner,* by Ernst Lubitsch; *The Big Sleep,* by Howard Hawks; *Casablanca,* by, well, by Michael Curtiz, but by nearly everyone else on the Warners lot at the time; *Notorious,* by Alfred Hitchcock; *Criss Cross,* by Robert Siodmak; *To Each His Own,* by Mitchell

Leisen; *Daisy Kenyon,* by Otto Preminger; *Mildred Pierce,* by Michael Curtiz, again; *In a Lonely Place,* by Nicholas Ray; *Double Indemnity,* by Billy Wilder; *It's a Wonderful Life,* by Frank Capra; *Meet Me in St. Louis,* by Vincente Minnelli.

I could go on and come to *Citizen Kane,* by Orson Welles. But already I have turned over the ground for later chapters—like the great stress on black-and-white, and all the different meanings "by" can hold in Hollywood.

But don't forget the usherette, that intriguing blonde. Is she listening? Dreaming? Asleep? Terribly tired or in rapture? I still love the way she leans against the wall, bystander at a miracle, nearly oblivious yet so secretly attentive. She could tell you, if any film critic thought to ask, that "by" always had to include the system, the business, Hollywood, the movie theater, the dark. So let her lights be lowered at last, so she can find her unobtrusive way back to the screen where she belongs.

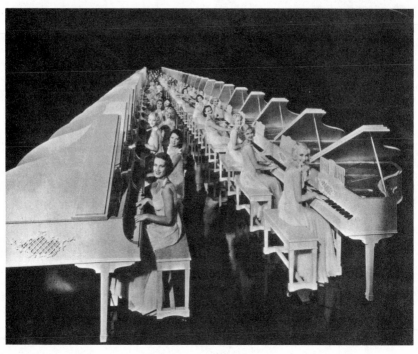

The chorus from Busby Berkeley's *Gold Diggers of 1933* *(Private Collection)*

12 · THE FACTORY

The word "factory" carries little grace or glory these days. Yet wherever a Hollywood movie is made, the comforts of "factory life" come into play. That means strict union controls, lavish catered meal breaks, and immense limos that bring anyone with clout to their place of work. Such things are taken for granted as standard working conditions. Perhaps the last time the word "factory" was used in the film world—with a camp wink and a nod—was at Andy Warhol's Manhattan establishment in the days when he made his films. As far as anyone can tell, Warhol paid hardly a soul, though the drugs were on the house.

"The factory" summons Dickens, Zola, and the legend of satanic mills, of intolerable exploitation by industrial overlords. We think of factories where several hundred thousand chickens jostle, blurting out our eggs— yet we eat the eggs. And the concentration camps are often spoken of as factories of death, places where the urge toward genocide, or unkindness, was subjected to modern ergonomics, the search for greater efficiency. Calling Hollywood a "dream factory" is more sinister now than when the term was first used, in the thirties. We hate to think that we have been enslaved, or that in our most precious inward hopes and fears we may have been especially vulnerable to tricks of conformity and anonymity. We cannot escape the dread that in a factory all the products are alike.

In that sense, it is almost as if humankind preferred to be the opposite of efficient: spontaneous, natural, free, unjudged, uncriticized. But at the same time we hound ourselves with all kinds of imperatives of efficiency: live longer, have a better quality of life, be better educated, be more responsible and responsive, be happier and healthier, be thinner, be quicker, be richer. The grind goes on, an everyday fascism.

And so we come to Hollywood the factory, in which it will be necessary to attend to the real or alleged handicaps and cruelties of such a system, while somehow acknowledging that so many of the films one treasures (and might happily see tonight), like the films listed toward the end of the last chapter, served time in that golden prison, the old Hollywood. Only the other day, I heard a story about how James Stewart in his final years had observed (in those innately Jimmy tones, the voice creaking with wryness and wisdom) that honestly and truly in those bad old days when actors had been "slaves," somehow they had made pretty damn good pictures. Well, yes, indeed. But Stewart omitted to remember that it was he, with his then agent Lew Wasserman, who had made crucial moves to close that old era when he proposed—on *Winchester '73* (1950)—to forgo any up-front salary for a piece of the profits, a kind of ownership.

There's no need to be severe with Stewart (a man who talked to rabbits, after all—a softy when it suited him, and us). But maybe the story offers some instruction in not taking actors too seriously when they have to come up with their own lines. Actors, you see, are not trained to take responsibility for what they say. That's why politics eats them up. (And maybe that's a reason for insisting that those who stand up and perform in politics do write their own material.)

We have seen quite clearly the conditions of choice that led to the factory. A D. W. Griffith could prefer to concentrate on the engrossing task of making a picture, leaving money matters to others, worthy or unworthy of his trust. In the event, for the moment, all parties involved did well because Griffith's hunch paid off—*The Birth of a Nation* was different, novel, and commanding. Best of all, people wanted it, they claimed it as theirs. So he was encouraged to wear the same blinkers in future.

A Louis B. Mayer could see that wondrous charm in the artistic personality—the brilliance and the blindness—and take advantage of it to such an extent that he built a business. Then, with a string of theaters to supply, he grew anxious about the reliable delivery of product, so he took on that duty himself.

Without education, Charlie Chaplin saw that the necessary egotism of creativity demanded nothing less than ownership. Like any artist, good or bad, he would become a world unto himself. He would make his pictures with his money, or with monies he had raised.

And then we have the ordinary way, the way most people took, which is that of Erich von Stroheim, who makes thrilling assertions about his own artistry, genius, and intractability, but elects to do it with your, or our, money, and then finds himself the helpless victim of our taste for economy, common sense, and efficiency.

The outline of choices is more troubling than that. Griffith and Chaplin may display different forms of courage or character, but soon enough their work becomes intolerable, in some part because of the claustrophobic, sheltering privacy of the egotism in which it is made. Meanwhile, Mayer, factory boss for longer than any man in show business, can hardly claim authorship for a foot of film. Whereas, that regular human hypocrisy, self-deceit and public mendacity, having your cake and eating it—the Stroheim method—yes, that has by far the best record at producing pictures you want to see, and see again. Here be liars, scoundrels and cheats— thank God! (So let us beware of the fearsome self-congratulatory virtue that can arise in some modern auteurs!)

All of which may help explain my enduring sympathy for the Thalberg, or the Monroe Stahr, type. Given many of the standards of a society founded in equal rights, common sense, and fairness, Thalberg did his best to organize a mass entertainment as smart as possible. His dilemma, and his opportunity, are very close to those of, say, the leadership of HBO today. There is an ideal, modestly sized but adventurous studio, or cable channel, working to the tight schedules and unyielding budgets of a factory system, that just happens to be responsible for *The Sopranos, Oz, Six*

Feet Under, Curb Your Enthusiasm, Sex and the City, Wit, and *Angels in America. Angels in America* was "big" for HBO: it cost over $60 million. But that is still product at $10 million an hour (two and a half hours of *Cold Mountain* cost over $80 million).

Of course, immense works of art have been made under the tyrannies of some producer, pope, or emperor. But we do not believe in that social bargain any longer, do we? It would horrify us to learn that Frank Gehry's new Walt Disney Concert Hall in Los Angeles, or Clint Eastwood's *Mystic River,* say, had been made thanks to slave labor. We are, more or less, agreed that the welfare of the masses and a semblance of equity are more important than the exercise of Art—aren't we? (Even so, on vacation, we may be in rapture over the pyramids and the cathedrals of oppression. Our political correctness is strained much more by learning how "appalling" Picasso and Gauguin could be. But was Bonnard more dutiful or tender, keeping a wife in cold baths to celebrate her in oils?)

I know, it's risky to tread on such sacred ground, but I have another aim, one so bald or naive you can laugh, which is to wonder what Art might be, especially in a mass society that is as dedicated to doing without elitism as possible. This may seem obvious ground, but that can lead to neglect. Consider these questions.

Art depends on the solitude of inspired, talented, or neurotic egotists. In its expression, it may ease their agonies (for half an hour); it may bring delight and consolation to some—those hearing Mahler's Ninth one night in San Francisco. But Mahler's Ninth on that occasion did not house one homeless person. Renoir's *La Grande Illusion,* unequalled in its antiwar sentiments, was prelude to a fresh war. The moment art finds or claims any utility it is dragged before the court of justification, and that is a forlorn process. I think it is correct to see, and insist, that art demands the single-minded, profitless dedication of time, life, and materials to the quest.

It follows from that proposition that art is not demanding in the way of materials, just as it is remorseless in what it takes from the artist's life. Van Gogh may have killed himself in despair, but the cost of paints and canvas was rarely beyond his poverty. Dostoevsky might have gambled away royalties and been reduced to journalism, but he needed only pen and paper for *The Brothers Karamazov.* I do not mean to fall into the trap of depicting all artists as intense, impossible self-destructives. That is a very tempting role, because of its childishness. But there are other ways. Vladimir Nabokov, for example, taught, maintained a passable set of family relationships, catalogued butterflies, lived in hotels without making a shambles of them, tried to be sociable and amusing a lot of the time, and survived the stupid profit from *Lolita* as well as encounters with Stanley Kubrick. Without being a brute, a savage, or a spoiled baby (moments aside—we all have our moments), he led a decent and orderly life just as he wore smart suits. But despite that bourgeois air he was utterly fixed on art and would have followed much the same course if he had been made tsar of all the Russias, or if he had been a pauper, or if he had been compelled to marry Tuesday Weld (she was a possible Lolita).

All of which is a gentle reminder to my companion film critics to go easily with talk of art in consideration of the movies. Yes, it is very tempting, for it seems to vindicate our profession or our hobbyhorse. But it may not be helpful; it may even help account for the wretchedness of many current films. So it is worth recalling that, at first, Hollywood did not want to have anything to do with art—not even if Irving Thalberg was prepared to slip a few lofty things into his safe production slate that were there because they were different or daring. Art then was what a few actors (like Edward G. Robinson) put on their walls—before L.A. had museums to be proud of.

The factory was meant to be benign, profitable, and useful. Going West had serious impulses of escapism in it: to get away from the Motion Picture Patents Company and the gangsters who had sought to organize filmmaking in the East. Quickly enough, the pioneers found extra pleasure in the chance to make a home and a city in that West. But they also pointed to the sheer utility of 300 days of sunshine a year, plus a variety of locations hardly equalled anywhere else in the United States. In its happy geophysical innocence, nature provided all the backdrops that can now be conjured up through computer generated images, but bathed them in real light. Never doubt the delight those pioneers, and not just the cameramen, took in that real light. Among other things, filmmaking converts light from nature to product.

The factory, or the studio, was a sensible gathering place for people drawn to the light. And do not underestimate the inescapable conditions of collaboration. If you want to write, compose, or paint, the struggle and the responsibility are yours alone, but if you wake up with a movie in your head, you need so many assistants, so many ghosts for your dream. Today, you may need $100 million. There have been astonishing filmmakers who hardly knew how to take a photograph, record sound, or make a cut, let alone draw up a contract or find $500,000. The great cameraman Gregg Toland assured Orson Welles, as they came to make *Citizen Kane,* that he could teach the kid genius all he needed to know about cinematography in a couple of days. This was not literally true, but Toland shrewdly estimated how speed appealed to Welles. By minimizing technology Toland reckoned he could find a mutual trust or confidence, the results of which are there on the screen, and in a credit more generous than Welles gave to his screenwriter.

Chaplin wrote, directed, and cut his pictures; he wrote the music when that came along; he acted out all the roles and told other actors to imitate him. He didn't do the photography, even if he always decided where the camera should be. Some would say his films are clumsy, or restricted, because of that. He did do most of the deals on his pictures. He did the business. He was as much of a dictator as he could manage. It was his mania and his genius.

But few people had Chaplin's energy or insecurity; and no one else had enough money to take their own time. For any young person eager to make films, film school is a sensible destination not so much because of the teaching it provides but because it will offer equipment, film stock, and the support of other people who have skills you lack. The film studio is the same model writ larger, because it offers the best professional company and the resources of basic labor and serious money that you will need. A feature film in the 1920s might be made for a very modest sum, $100,000 or less, but in those days that money was generally beyond the reach of would-be filmmakers. It still is. A studio offered the money, and then provided something far harder to obtain than $100,000: a nationwide system of distribution and marketing, so that your film might be seen by "everyone." In turn, some of the box office revenue would serve to fund your next film.

Does that sound unreasonable, or isn't it the kind of solution any commune of wild artist filmmakers would have come up with, granted the individual urge to make films and the communal pleasure in seeing them? Suppose then that your film is a little bit more demanding than most—suppose it is closer to *Intolerance* or *The Ten Commandments* than to, say, *Way Down East* or *City Lights*. Suppose, casually, that your imagination calls for a few hundred extras here, or an army there—an army that will require weapons and uniforms, things easily conveyed in a sentence from a novel, but coming at $15.75 per head per day, plus the buses to get the men out to the location and the box lunches to feed them (cold chicken, a hard-boiled egg, a piece of tomato, bread and butter, with paper snatches of pepper and salt, please, for everyone on one of De Mille's early pictures).

So you need the bus and the box lunches, the uniforms and the rubber bayonets (real bayonets will raise the insurance cost). Someone has to negotiate the deal with the farm where you are restaging the battle of Gettysburg, Ypres, or whatever. You need latrines, or portable bathrooms—

even if it's only very lately that figures on the Hollywood screen have been to the bathroom (on screen). You need assistant directors to make sure that 300 men tramp past the camera in the proper state of fatigue and despair, without even looking at the embrace of John Gilbert and Renée Adorée (we are in King Vidor's *The Big Parade* for a moment), as if they didn't know yet what stars were.

The Big Parade, done for M-G-M in 1925, cost $382,000. Its controlling executive was Irving Thalberg, who witnessed a mass of footage (involving several thousand extras) of a battle scene, heard Vidor lament that it nowhere featured the long straight road he wanted as an image of implacable destiny, and told him to go shoot the whole damn thing again. The film shot for fifty-six days and ran nearly twelve full reels. (In the end, Vidor agreed to trim it down a little so that viewers could catch the last bus or train.) It was a big picture, expensive, yet it cost less than Stroheim's *The Merry Widow*, Garbo's *The Temptress*, or *Ben-Hur*, all made at roughly the same time. Yet, whereas *The Temptress* and *Ben-Hur* lost money, *The Big Parade* was the movie that established M-G-M financially. Officially, it made a profit after five years of nearly $3.5 million. Vidor claimed that it had grossed $15 million.

Everyone was satisfied: the studio was secure, Thalberg was proved right, millions in the audience were thrilled and moved. And Vidor? Well, perhaps it's worth repeating the director's own words about why he wanted to do *The Big Parade,* for they convey the idealism of early Hollywood:

> One day I had a talk with Irving Thalberg and told him I was weary of making ephemeral films. They came to town, played a week or so, then went their way to comparative obscurity or complete oblivion. I pointed out that only half the American population went to movies and not more than half of these saw any one film because their runs ended so quickly. If I were to work on something that I felt had a chance at long runs throughout the country or the world, I would put much more effort, and love, into its creation.

Notice that money and art are not mentioned. The focus is upon the masses, the mind of the people, in the way of politics or religion. Notice, too, the way Thalberg seems to be in the habit of making time to listen to Vidor, to encourage him, just as he was prepared to let the budget go higher to get a single, poetic effect.

It was another aspect of Thalberg's balance that he encouraged Vidor, just as he reined in Stroheim. Vidor, born and raised in Texas, was an enchanting figure—bold in vision, shy by nature. Vidor had urges in him toward grandeur that were perhaps as dangerous as anything in Stroheim; later on, he would direct *War and Peace* (1956), *The Fountainhead* (1949), *Duel in the Sun* (1946), though he was fired from that one by Selznick for not making it grandiose enough. He also made an astonishing master-piece, *An American Romance* (1944), hardly known today, about the place of wheat and harvesting machinery in a wide open country. He made that film for Metro-Goldwyn-Mayer.

Vidor had too large a vision to rest easily in Hollywood. He was always lunging out in different directions that defy tidy analysis: *Our Daily Bread* (1934) is nearly Communist; *The Fountainhead* is not, it's . . . well, it's Ayn Rand. *Stella Dallas* (1937) is one of the great weepies. And at the very end of his life, Vidor made small films simply for himself and on his own money—*Truth and Illusion: An Introduction to Metaphysics and Metaphor.* You can say he was a studio man, in that Thalberg favored him, but once Thalberg was gone, Vidor became a wanderer, and increasingly an outsider. He was true to himself, and all too often his pictures have the breathtaking energy of Stroheim, but with a faith in people that Stroheim never possessed. Is it to Thalberg's discredit as a man of art that he pre-ferred the optimist? I'm not sure that a great American entertainment—even now—can be made any other way.

But something happened with Vidor on *The Big Parade* that is worth noting. We don't know what he was paid for directing the picture: I'd guess it was in the region of $25,000. But Vidor was a favorite, and Thal-berg (and Mayer) had approved a contract in which he could receive a percentage of the studio's net receipts on a film, if they went over a certain level. There were such participation deals that early.

In the past, despite a few hits, this had not amounted to much. But as *The Big Parade* played to packed houses it was clear that the receipts would not be normal. Vidor reckoned he was due 20 percent of the net (an astonishing sum). M-G-M claimed that few pictures ever grossed more than $1.5 million, so they offered him a cash sum—we don't know how much, but Vidor said "large"—in return for his percentage. Intent on his next project, *La Bohème* (with Gish and Gilbert), he took the cash and lost the chance of earning as much as a million. A future battleground had been drawn, one for which the filmmaker might have to give hours a day to reading the ledger books and doing the math if he was to be taken seriously.

The several factories in Hollywood needed reliable talent, not just tal-ent that could deliver pictures (and audiences) repeatedly, but talent they could count on for years to come. They liked a Cagney because they learned the knack of making his pictures. Some street sets stood for years as the places where Cagney stories took place. This was not anathema to novices knocking at the door. The would-be actor or director may have led a borderline life for several years. He or she wants to do their work, but they want a guaranteed life, too. Accordingly it never seems remotely hostile or menacing when the studio says it would like to take you on, starting at a modest salary (still huge by general American standards), build you, and train you, and see what happens. Say seven years, starting at. . . .

When Greta Gustafsson was recruited by Mayer on his European trip, her deal was mixed up with the one for Mauritz Stiller, the Swedish director who had found her and developed her. Stiller was to get $1,000 a week, whereas Garbo was started at $100 a week for the first year, to be raised to $600 the second year (if she stuck) and $750 the third. At that time, an American factory worker might make $1,200 in a year for a forty-eight-hour week.

By 1926, with her first three-year contract about to end, it was established that Garbo was staying (while Stiller was sent back to Sweden). Her third film at M-G-M, *Flesh and the Devil* (a Thalberg production), made nearly $470,000 in profit. In turn, Garbo was learning the game. Much courted by co-star John Gilbert, she had acquired the advice of Gilbert's manager, Harry Edington (who would negotiate for her throughout her career, for free, but with a per-picture thank-you check from the studio!). Edington told Mayer that $750 was on the comical side, and he suggested $5,000 a week, to see if that got a laugh. In the event, she signed a new five-year contract, starting at $3,000 a week and rising to $5,000.

That contract terminated in 1932, by which time Garbo was at her peak (not that she was ever one of the biggest box office attractions). Her new deal was kept very secret, as if the studio feared it could be infectious. Garbo was given a special production setup whereby she could determine material, director, and starting date—at $250,000 per picture. But from 1932 until her retirement in 1941, she made only nine more films, and on none of those did she have anything like Vidor's notional profit participation. Garbo was very well paid, but the Edington arrangement is fascinating, and one that would be laughed at today, for whereas the actress felt she was secure, her agent (no less) was actually in the pay of the studio.

Of course, these sums are huge; and as Hollywood meant more and more in the world, the scale of the money was fuel to the dream. Garbo's weekly salary in, say, 1931 was four times the average annual wage in the United States. (In 2002, the national median annual wage, $33,000, was at least fifteen times smaller than the weekly income of an equivalent movie star.)

For Garbo's two 1932 films (*As You Desire Me* and *Grand Hotel*) there was a total of ninety-one working days (she might have been called on sixty days; her contract allowed her to stay home when she had her period). What follows from these numbers and the titles of her films (the thinly veiled surrealism of *Flesh and the Devil* and *As You Desire Me*) is the way in which the factory was also making not just stories, shows, or entertainments, but new versions of prostitution fantasies attuned to the mass media. As soon as you ask, Was Garbo popular?, you discover the complexity of the result. Garbo was adored. She was respected, admired, envied. But she did not seem exactly lovable, and her public image (much shaped by studio pressure and publicity writing) was to be aloof, withdrawn, forever unsatisfied romantically. Of course, Garbo was foreign, too, an exotic, someone who often played aristocrats. She was frequently placed way above the masses by her stories, yet the oblique circumstances of whoring were always there. And then there was the enormity of her reward, not for being virtuous or intelligent, but for being beautiful (that alleged incidental to the good life) and being loved by the camera.

Yes, the star's story whispers that you, too, might be Garbo. But it also alludes, mockingly, to those vexing circumstances of the movie theater itself: you can imagine yourself on the screen, but you can't get there. There is no there there.

There is more to the Garbo mystery, and it hinges on money. There have been claims—from Alexander Walker, a Garbo biographer—that M-G-M did a very secret deal with Garbo that did give her some profits on the condition that she would never admit the example. This may help explain her ultimate wealth. Another of her biographers, Barry Paris, reports that her estate was valued at $32 million in 1991 (after trust funds had been set up for her relatives). This for a woman who did not work after 1941! Be generous with her working years and maybe she earned $4 million from salary (in an age when income tax was no higher than 25 percent). Still, the story goes that Garbo lost heavily in the 1929 crash. She had some real estate, and Paris reckons that her investment of $100,000 in paintings turned into $20 million of her final estate. She never lacked for offers: near the end of her life American Express offered her $10 million to do a "Do You Know Me?" commercial.

It's ironic, of course, that someone from the new art may have made her fortune on Pierre-Auguste Renoir. One lesson is that money earned by stars in the twenties and thirties, lightly taxed but well invested, could seem prodigious by the time they died. There were people from that age who became crazily wealthy seemingly without effort. The money details were seldom put to print. But no other section of society aroused such curiosity, or could make such a heady transition from rags to riches. Don't forget, too, that much of this alteration transpired in the hardest economic age America has ever known, the period that produced many signs of a welfare state and many converts to Communism.

So, rapidly, the factory became prized (but suspect) for marketing an impossible dream, the figures in which were always subject to bitterness and rebuke—call it vengeance—because of the scale of the salaries. In hindsight, one can see that the studios prospered as they did in great part because the notion of participation in the profits was not yet widespread.

Income levels for the talent varied outrageously, but a crazy glee barely masked greed and the way people might compromise themselves just to be in Hollywood. A classic example of this is the cable Ben Hecht received in 1926 from Herman J. Mankiewicz. Mank was a new "writer" in Holly-wood. Hecht was a New York author who dreamed of writing novels and plays. This was Mank's teasing message: "WILL YOU ACCEPT THREE HUN-DRED PER WEEK TO WORK FOR PARAMOUNT PICTURES? ALL EXPENSES PAID. THE THREE HUNDRED IS PEANUTS. MILLIONS ARE TO BE GRABBED OUT HERE AND YOUR ONLY COMPETITION IS IDIOTS. DON'T LET THIS GET AROUND."

Such hilarity over $300 a week. The certain, condescending attitude about a society of idiots. Such cables worked, of course. Broke writers need their confidence restored before they can write. They need a couple of martinis and a steak dinner. Yet to their own minds, Herman Mankiewicz and Ben Hecht both died morose and frustrated. Neither of them had written the great books they believed possible. On the other hand, Hecht had had a large hand in writing *Scarface, Nothing Sacred, Notorious, Whirlpool,* and *Monkey Business* (Cary Grant and Howard Hawks), among others, while Mankiewicz has his name on *Laughter, Monkey Business* (the Marx Brothers), *Dinner at Eight, Pride of the Yankees,* and *Citizen Kane.* Indeed, I'd go so far as to say that *Kane* wouldn't have existed without him, and for that job he got $1,000 a week plus a bonus of $5,000 on delivery (to encourage him not to drink), plus his co-writer's earnest effort to screw him out of a credit (and the Oscar that came along later).

But, as someone once said, in Hollywood if you are a writer you stay alive long enough not to write the great books. Until you die. Except Nathanael West, who wrote a great book, and still died.

I don't mean to blame such writers, or organize sympathy on their behalf. There are those, like Hemingway and Margaret Mitchell, who took Hollywood's dollar and stayed home. There are those, like William Faulkner, who generally ignored employment in the factory, and asked to write at home—Faulkner meant Oxford, Mississippi, instead of Brentwood. And even if some careers lapsed, why are writers to be denied their share of stupid reward, sunshine, pretty girls (women even) and the uplifting company of other writers in the same sinking boat? We would have far less gallows humor in this happiest of happy nations (in other words, it's a good thing) if Hollywood hadn't seduced respectable writers.

What all this has done to what the happy nation thinks of writing is another matter.

I find it hard to be simply disapproving of a factory system that steadily hands out big money for very modest work, and which still produces such entertainment. It's surely a more honorable process than the one in Las Vegas, and I'm not against that either.

It is true that, along the way, sturdy souls being paid these hitherto undreamed-of sums (for acting, writing, and directing) turned on the system and charged that it was treating them like trash. The contract system had as one of its ingredients the principle that you did the job to which the studio assigned you. If you were a writer, you wrote or rewrote whatever was put in front of you. If you were an actress, you took the roles offered. I am not profoundly averse to that kind of enforced versatility. In Britain, where I was raised, acting was often subject to a repertory system whereby even a star actor took his share of small parts. In his training years at the Bristol Old Vic, where he played over fifty roles in three years, Peter O'Toole did *Hamlet, Uncle Vanya,* and *Waiting for Godot,* but he was also the Dame in the annual pantomime. And he never complained, or suffered, on fifteen pounds a week.

Not that complaint was disallowed, or unproductive. Consider the magnificent case of James Cagney. We can omit praise or adoration here, I think. Let's just say that the Warner brothers might never have identified the nature of their tough, urban films but for Cagney. With every testy inhalation and snort, with every abrupt motion, he created the world around him. And he set it trembling. As Orson Welles put it, Cagney "displaced air." That extraordinary intimacy I discussed in the last chapter had this effect with Cagney: he sucked in our air—watch him and you have to breathe with him to survive.

How fruitful this slavery seemed. The son of an Irish bartender, Cagney was born in 1899 and raised on the Lower East Side. It was a tough life, though Jimmy was far gentler a soul than the public guessed. To help support his large family, he went into show business and by 1925 was a Broadway dancing star, later signed up by Warners, along with co-star Joan Blondell, for the picture version of their hit show, *Penny Arcade* (retitled *Sinner's Holiday* for the screen).

Talk about a factory. From *Sinners' Holiday* (1930) to *Hard to Handle* (1933) he made ten films. "He still grins that crooked mick grin that made him famous," said his pal, actor Pat O'Brien. On the surface, all seemed productive and tranquil, all of his assignments were for Warner Brothers, and by 1932 Cagney was getting $1,250 a week. However, he complained bitterly about the cheapness and the violence of the films, and he used his kid brother Bill (who was as tough and foul-mouthed as the on-screen Jimmy we "know") to go in and browbeat Warners, especially Jack Warner, for whom the Cagney brothers kept the nickname "The Shvontz" (the prick). Moreover, the Cagney boys were forever threatening legal action, and getting a better deal as a result.

Cagney was not alone among actors in hating to play rotten guys. He wanted to look better. He threatened to walk out over his discontent—but added that he wanted $4,000 a week. He even offered, in public, to do three films for nothing if Warners would then let him out of his contract. He said he reckoned to go back to Columbia University (he had a scholarship) to study medicine or art. Jack Warner refused to cave in. He replaced Cagney in projects (Spencer Tracy got a big break by picking up *20,000 Years in Sing Sing*), until, finally, Frank Capra stepped in as a conciliator (an angel, let's say). Cagney got $3,000 a week. By 1935 it would be up to $4,500.

Nothing changed. Cagney moved leftward: in 1933, he said that Stalin and Gandhi were the best living human beings. He would be an active board member of the Screen Actors Guild. And he continued to agitate against his own studio. He never let up on the Shvontz. It was in this straitjacket that, from 1931 to 1939, Cagney made (among others) *The Public Enemy, Taxi!, Footlight Parade, The Crowd Roars, Hard to Handle, The Picture Snatcher, Jimmy the Gent, Ceiling Zero, Angels with Dirty Faces, Each Dawn I Die,* and *The Roaring Twenties.*

This then culminated in *Yankee Doodle Dandy* (1942), a Warners film but produced by Bill Cagney under the shadow of Jimmy's announced departure from the studio, and as unbelievable yet as exactly right as only Michael Curtiz could pull off. It won Cagney his Oscar, doing George M. Cohan but also bringing together an amalgam of hoodlum, hoofer, and nightmare patriot. Cohan got $125,000 and 10 percent of the rentals for the rights to his life. The film cost $1.5 million and earned nearly $5 million. Still, a charity premiere of the picture, in May 1942, as America took on its own war, raised the astounding sum of $4.75 million in one night.

Thereupon, Jimmy and Bill took leave of Warners and set up as Cagney Productions. They had a bank behind them, with United Artists as their distributor. They would pick and choose, and so they did—four films in seven years, including William Saroyan's *The Time of Your Life,* and every one a dud.

Then, dismayed but still defiant, they staggered back to Warners:

> I sure as hell never expected in the order of things that we'd ever go back to Warners. Our basic reason was a five-letter word beginning with *m* and ending in *y*. But it wasn't just the dough. It's easier to make pictures when you have a factory setup. And I'd never have to face The Shvontz. Brother Bill was there to face the old bastard, and those two money-oriented businessmen could talk on the same level and be perfectly happy together.

Bill had another angle: a top-up fee if Jimmy's old films were reissued (or sold to television). In 1949, and back home, for $250,000, Jimmy did *White Heat.* The screenwriters said it was the old gangster stuff but with some fresh angles—now you could see that the rotten guy was crazy.

Of course, actors—not even ones as air-displacing as Cagney—don't have to be business geniuses or artists. There's no shame in finding shelter in the factory. Temperament or the urge to be "difficult" is the artist's curse or right, and in truth the factory system was pretty good at handling its spoiled babies. Stories abound on how Judy Garland, say, was harassed to her grave by M-G-M, and horribly exploited by men like Mayer. Well, sure, the work was hard. But other child stars, like Mickey Rooney and Elizabeth Taylor (at the same studio), went on and on (and sometimes put executives in the hospital). The person who introduced Judy to drugs was her mother. And if you see fit to cry for Judy then I can only suggest that you take a weekend and read one of the biographies—Gerald Clarke's will do well—and I challenge you on Monday morning to be filled with regret. A lot of artists are pains in the ass, self-destructive beyond the merciful efforts of family and friends, and prepared to get away with anything and everything possible, including the clothes they had to wear in a part.

There were instances of vindictive treatment of wayward stars—John Gilbert had gotten thoroughly on Mayer's wrong side; at the same studio, Joan Crawford's inferiority complex was played like a violin; Humphrey Bogart was for ten years a pretty unsatisfactory villain until happy chance led him into the role of the laconic outsider hero, thus exactly fitting his shy self-image; Louise Brooks went to hell; Gish was "retired" because of steadfast virginalism. But all those cases have explanations in the nature of the person involved. And let us not forget that the factory, the system that Bette Davis believed was fit only for making sausages, gave us the ravishing variety of Katharine Hepburn, Fred Astaire, Barbara Stanwyck, Cary Grant, Cagney, Gary Cooper, Garbo, Crawford, and Davis herself. It gave us Judy Garland in *Meet Me in St. Louis* and *The Wizard of Oz*—more than that, it gave Judy herself those moments, which remained beacons for her (as well as tormenting memories) as she cracked up. The factory had a nearly infinite range of star personalities, and if we have found those people precious and valuable then the factory deserves some thanks. Sausages do not have that range or vivacity.

The more interesting point is how the factory system helped make those people so appealing. The abiding tenor of the photography was not just fond, but glamorous. That sounds simple and even natural until you notice the degrees of normalcy, homeliness, or naturalism that have obtained for decades in French film. It's not that French cinema rejected beautiful people (look at Catherine Deneuve, Gérard Philipe, Alain Delon, or Emmanuelle Béart). But the *beauté* is allowed to be more commonplace: in terms of scenario, it can coexist with inner ugliness; and in the photographed image it is not always as meticulous an arrangement of key light, fill, and backlighting.

In Hollywood there was a saying, "Put the light where the money is," which implied a kind of aura of romance always attending the beautiful people. But there was a corollary: don't bother to photograph those who are not "good-looking." Grant, too, that the attitude conveyed by the lighting was underlined by costuming, by makeup, and by the way of surrounding characters with idealized décor, and you can begin to feel the significance of a way of seeing.

Take two classic films from 1939: Selznick's *Gone With the Wind* and Renoir's *La Règle du Jeu (The Rules of the Game)*. There's room enough to love both films—the all-time success and the box office failure, the landmark and the masterpiece. But observe how fully the Renoir picture is committed to real nature and human nature: the array of characters in which the people seem more from life than from a fashion magazine; the general eschewing of adoring close-ups by Renoir in favor of a camera style that keeps people in groups, in social interaction; the way the French film employs locations, a true out-of-doors and real rooms. Whereas, for Selznick, Georgia was a place not visited until the film's premiere. His southern mansions, his Atlanta, his battlefields are fabricated on sets and on the back lot, or even painted on glass. Studio control attends everything and makes it handsome, significant, or vivid. There is never a dull moment or a plain view in *Gone With the Wind;* is that one reason why it feels so removed from real life? On the other hand, the Renoir film—indeed, the entire body of Renoir's work—makes us feel the relationship between fiction and life, meaning and chaos.

Time and again in his work, Renoir went to places that seemed vital to his stories. Yes, he was the son of one of the most admiring painters of nature, but Renoir the son is a great deal less romantic or sentimental than the father (he is a greater artist), and he knows that nature is often tough, alien, hostile, and at odds with characters. The shooting scene in *La Règle du Jeu* is both a record of how a social group behaved in 1939 and a larger view of natural harshness. In contrast, the operatic closure to the first half of *Gone With the Wind,* where Scarlett is posed against a savage sunset and a crooked tree, vowing never to go hungry again, is a picture of determination or courage or stubbornness in which nature is not trusted. Indeed, it has been submitted to décor, a process true throughout Selznick's work, and in most of Hollywood cinema.

Why not, when the factories had sound stages ready for shooting, brilliant designers, and warehouses full of props, scenic elements and costumes? A factory uses its raw materials, whereas a Renoir sought the elements of life. Famously, the attitude that prevailed in Hollywood that it was possible, with accuracy and flavor, to re-create any place in the world with sets. In that handful of films Sternberg and Dietrich made at Paramount in the thirties, you can see the proof of that confidence: they "did" North Africa and the desert; China; Russia; Spain—and did them all in a Paramount style, a shimmering, half-mocking "perfection" always added to by the irony of Sternberg's gaze and the near insolence of Dietrich's response.

These were not films about the look of the real world. They were pictures about desire and fatalism. And Sternberg was a genius and a great photographer who had come upon a woman, an actress, and a photographed face such as he never found again. I do not want to exclude films like *Morocco, Shanghai Express,* and *The Devil Is a Woman* from history or my pantheon, but they are a triumph of a photographic style that was nearly demented in its taste for artificiality and its steadfast looking away from naturalism (which is, for many, a fundamental power in photography). Sternberg was not just a genius. He was a deliberate outsider who all but plotted his own downfall as a top director. But it is not going too far to suggest that most of the pictures made in his Hollywood aspired to his rare photographic command and its industrial quality.

For his was a style that bespoke control, as well as hours in the studio, fussing with the technique of the dream. There was an endless chess match of the abstract going on in Sternberg's mind as he ruminated over whether the movies were his or Marlene's. She won, finally, by ignoring that game and staring the camera down. But what Sternberg never quite grasped was how far the whole enterprise belonged to Paramount, to a studio with resources of décor, fur, feathers, and gorgeously veiled lights as rich as its command of people like Jules Furthman, Lee Garmes, Hans Dreier, and Travis Banton, the craftsmen or the servants of the dream, all of whom were under the same contract system as owned Jo and Marlene.

A team lay in waiting, and you can find it, time and again, at Hollywood's best moments: there was the crew and cast that was generally available for Lubitsch, Capra, John Ford, Preston Sturges, and even Orson Welles—novice and upstart, but enough of a gang leader to know the necessity of having his people whose Mercury allegiances were mixed (they thought he was either a genius or a monster whose comeuppance they did want to see). Welles and *Citizen Kane* are regularly nominated as a prime example of outsiderism in Hollywood, thankfully free from factory conditions. But any close study of how that film was made shows that Welles relied on the inspired support of people like cinematographer Toland, art director Van Nest Polglase, and special effects expert Vernon Walker (all studio men); that he took every advantage he could of studio tricks with photography and décor. It's not that he filmed in new ways; rather, he plunged into studio style—special effects and matte shots—with the fervor of a kid with a new train set. More than that, he was treated with grace and loyalty by an RKO administration (chiefly George Schaefer, who would be canned because of Orson) who believed in him and never deviated from his contract, not even when he behaved badly.

Citizen Kane was a radical departure in many ways—it was so much more difficult and ambiguous a picture than the studios wanted to make— but it reveled in the factory. Indeed, those haunting Xanadu interiors (the ragbag of culture Kane has collected) are only the most beautiful rearrangement of the standard props barn that Hollywood ever made. Welles adored that spurious cultural catalog and that mocking mastery of all the world's styles; it was so very close to his witty nihilism, his belief that in the end nothing mattered. Perhaps his most striking originality lay in the vision that Hollywood's control was a tyrannous beauty that had actually rendered décor, objects, space, and sheer things null and void. Like a wicked magician, he was ready to say "Rosebud" and have the whole edifice vanish.

In time, that despair at achievement (the secret to Kane's woe, I think) would settle in among American filmmakers, as it became clear that all décor, all wealth, all ownership could be mimicked in the computer. But Welles knew the lovely toy he had, and in *The Magnificent Ambersons*—as he showed himself out of the Hollywood door—he made what is one of the most elegiac tributes to the studio, its dark cavernous interiors and the way a warm world can be constructed there; a place where the camera can prowl and soar, as music does on the grid of the staff. But that is a film about the end of a house and its way of life, and an example of the notion that if you build a great set for a film, you may be obliged to destroy it. Doesn't Xanadu begin to burn?

There were other great directors who made the studio or the factory their implicit subject—Fritz Lang, for one, who hardly noticed fresh air or daylight in America in his more than twenty years here, but filmed a series of airless, enclosed sets that were theorems proving the futility of human beings. Yes, those films often had happy or positive endings, as the studio system ordered, but the cinematic elements were always much more potent than the requirements of the Code. Thus, Lang's work, from *Fury* and *You Only Live Once* through *Ministry of Fear* and *The Woman in the Window* to *The Big Heat* and *Human Desire,* is a model of pessimism poisoning the strenuous claims of virtue, authority, and decency. Time and again in American pictures, the real pulse of a film overwhelms the polite, cheery strictures imposed on filmmakers. Some lamented that Hollywood was a prison, while others quietly filmed the prison. As a result, by the end of the 1950s, American film had helped undermine the specious confidence of the nation. And made prisoners of us all.

The most shocking thing about films made today is how that pulse is gone, that steady, defiant singing of the imprisoned soul. There was an age in which, consciously or not, some filmmakers saw the factory as a metaphor for the state of the nation. And a sufficient number of the movies made then were filled with the passionate responses—whether anger, black humor, violence, or outrage—of prisoners. So, within the genres of Hollywood storytelling, within the confines of censorship and the upbeat ending, within the grid of films as "entertainment," the movies came so close to being an art that the history of it all, the looking back, can still move you to tears.

It was the forties, really, that key moment of world education for the mass of Americans, and the last time our movies were unmistakably on the cusp of feeling for an entire society. And the moment when, implicitly, the factory system stood nakedly as a representation of societies that had fought great wars, exploded unthinkable bombs, and nearly destroyed everything—as if, according to Kane's dream, you could utter your last word and have everything go out, like a light. *Cut!*

The image is from 1934, but the look is timeless. John Gutmann, "Cynics, Hollywood" (the title as bold as the picture) *(© 1998 Center for Creative Photography, University of Arizona Foundation)*

13 · VIABLE BUSINESS

Have you ever considered that it was not really until the nineteenth century that "entertainment" became a worthwhile business? And have you wondered whether, by the start of the twenty-first century, it may not have become so central to our lives that it begins to replace the large, vague territories once left to government, education, or religion? Once you admit to the civil right to be entertained, does the fun ever stop or yield to "higher" causes? Does it even accommodate failure in those loftier areas? For example, if you show prisoners a movie every now and then, does that excuse the condition of death row?

No doubt, esteemed Renaissance painters and eighteenth-century composers were able to exist in a kind of upper-middle-class comfort in which they might carry on their work without distraction. (All they had to worry about was Inquisition, plague, or sheer loss of favor.) The first novelists, in England and France, could become celebrities on the strength of selling a few thousand copies. We may suppose that those theatrical masters, Burbage and Alleyn, did well enough; and Shakespeare did not go unrewarded. But it stands to reason that the eternal human impulse, to put on some kind of diversion, or to watch it, meant humble fare for the providers until the advent of mass media and the industrialization of the audience—until printing, newspapers, and movies. Chaplin became who he was only because the look of his act could be sent around the world. But he had learned to woo laughter with live audiences first, a few at a time. There is a lesson in that history: such things as making a handful of people laugh must be done for their own sake first. Start with your dad if he has a mind to hit you.

The first generation of Americans who set themselves to make an entertainment for all of America had not the least training for what they were about. In the main, they were not educated people, though maybe that lack helped them feel closer to the crowd. If they had anything in common it was having arrived lately from a very different world, in often being Jewish and wary of that distinction, and of having had some experience in the clothing business. It is not even that they were ambitious, inventive souls who had grown impatient with legitimate theater, vaudeville, or publishing. Those neighboring fields did not provide our movie pioneers, just as, only a few decades later, the next novelty, television, was not the natural escape for movie mavericks.

Most people running the movie business in 1940 were blind to television. Most people in "theater" had been dubious about the "flickers." Méliès is one great exception; he seems to have grasped the new ambivalence of reality being made available in another fashion the first time he saw movie. Griffith was a theater person, to be sure, but he only started to direct movies because he couldn't get hired as an actor. So let us proceed with caution over the notion that Hollywood invented a new kind of business efficiency to thrill America. So often, with the movies, things only seem to work in the dark. It was later, in the age of Hitler, Stalin, Roosevelt, and Churchill, that film found real fans, guys who had grown up in the dark, as its proponents.

Back at M-G-M, in Culver City, a few years after the merger, Mayer and Thalberg had to schedule and budget their factory operation, and then cooperate with the marketing operation that was Loew's in New York. Memos mounted. Meetings took place. Flow charts could not be denied. There was no choice. Without a plan they would have had so many lost souls asking, Where do I go? Emotionally, in crowds, most people want to be assigned. For every haggling with Garbo or Crawford over what their contract should be, someone at the studio had to know the total annual commitment of all the contracts—not just of the stars and the directors, but of the army of craftsmen, too. And someone had to see that all those talents were kept employed. Although some stars might go on suspension if they hated the scripts offered, the studio still had to carry on paying its other contract artists, whether or not there were projects that suited them. Every week in which a sound stage was empty, or a star idle, was a misuse of resources. Not that rest was ruled out, but the factory workers of America in the twenties and thirties were not spoiled for vacation time, and in those heady days it was not uncommon for some stars to make four or five pictures a year.

The output of James Cagney, that personification of energy, in the thirties is: two films in 1930; five in 1931; three in 1932; five in 1933; four in 1934; six in 1935; one in 1936; one in 1937; two in 1938; and three in 1939. (Warren Beatty has made twenty-two in forty years.)

That's thirty-two films in a decade, most of them routine no-nonsense Cagney vehicles. Of all those pictures, only seven ran over ninety minutes (and the longest was the highly exceptional *A Midsummer Night's Dream*, where Cagney played Bottom for Max Reinhardt). Fifteen of them were under eighty minutes. Very few were "big" ventures, and I suspect that the budgets and profit margins were modest. The stories were formulaic, something Cagney disliked. But the formula worked, and who knows if Cagney's insolence wasn't best suited to short, explosive setups? He had sixteen different directors, with deft hacks like Lloyd Bacon (nine pictures) and Roy Del Ruth (four) the most frequent. Certain writers figured regularly: Kubec Glasmon, John Bright, Robert Lord, Warren Duff. But so did the same hats, guns, and push-around dames. Then notice the decline in the late thirties, when Cagney's pictures became bigger or more important, and there were fewer of them. Was the audience becoming more discriminating? Was the public weary of gangster violence? Or was it just that Jimmy—a rebellious fellow, one of Hollywood's leftists—was naturally "uppity" and belligerent? All those answers apply, and all would require the scrutiny and adjustment of a studio controller.

What tipped Cagney from uppity to organized was his discovery that, at a cost of $150,000, *The Public Enemy* had made $1 million. Cagney felt himself squeezed on the money and confined as an actor—yet, granted his freedom, he found only a dead end. It's very hard to determine what the profit margin of the studio system was; it's not even clear that the business employed people skilled enough to know where it was going, let alone guide or steer it. The movie business began as a craze. Throughout the twenties, the audience built steadily; in the thirties, it declined and then built again more slowly, staying loyal through very difficult times; in 1946–47, it reached a peak; then suddenly it began to fall—and, really, has never stopped falling, despite the way today's figures can be made to seem overwhelming. As a result, there has never been such a thing as stability in show business; that is part of its excitement. But it is also a warning to the numbers men against being too dogmatic. Sooner or later, the bean-counters know, some wild, headstrong passion will insist on making an unreasonable movie—*Gone With the Wind* and *The Passion of the Christ* were the perfect examples of not going by the rules.

Still, in the early thirties, the Mayer-Thalberg years, Metro's product seems to have made a profit of around 25–35 percent on the costs of production (assuming that those costs assessed a proper overhead factor in recognition of the costs of building and rental). During some years (see the table on p. 123) the profit went far higher: in the period 1927–29 (the first impact of sound) it was about 70 percent; in 1935–36 (just before Thalberg's death), it was 60 percent. Those are astonishing figures, and they may be underreported. After all, Metro's fiscal operation involved releasing through its own releasing organization. The opportunities for "adjustment," for skimming money in several different ways, were untold. Here are words of wisdom from Aubrey Solomon, author of *Twentieth Century–Fox: A Corporate and Financial History*:

> In the golden years of Hollywood, when Twentieth Century–Fox, as well as the other studios, owned its own theater chains, the entire business was a closed circle. Only studio bookkeepers knew for certain whether a picture made or lost money and even then they were never sure. The more money a movie grossed, the more overhead a studio lopped off that gross. With such practices, most movies never showed more than meager profits.

If the small-timers could not stop boasting, it's safe to bet that Mayer and Thalberg knew how to shut up and keep a steady expression. Don't go crazy, don't spend like an idiot, don't give away the fact that there were millions to be made (at a time when income tax was in its infancy—the top rate was 7 percent in the twenties). Mayer knew how easily the world could be turned upside down; his own eminence was the proof. And so we come back to that strange, tortured contrast between the expressive explosion of the movies (the liberation of fantasies) and the repressive impulse of those who counted the booty so secretly and dreaded the chance that fantasy run amok could scatter this rich new order.

Soon enough, authentic lifestyle differences emerged between Mayer and Thalberg. Instinctively and innately, Thalberg positioned himself next to Mayer as the quieter, the dryer, the more restrained, the more thoughtful of the two—the good cop. It followed from this self-image that his disciplining of Stroheim led to a culture at M-G-M in which directors were put under the authority of producers—a group of young suits hired by and loyal to Thalberg and supposedly touched with his taste and coolness. It was a team a little like the band of formally dressed athletes that J. Edgar Hoover hired to make the F.B.I. seem like a knighthood of honor, straight haircuts and conformist thinking (and no more successful).

But the producer figure was also a natural consequence of the way emerging studios needed the routine of factory life, of control, schedules, and budgets. It was a way of insisting that you can't allow a director to make it up as he goes along, if only because that leaves you no way of controlling the expenditure on a film when (even if it loses money) it must fit into the overall pattern of many hits and a few adventurous failures. What meant far more in the way of control—but which I think remained beyond Thalberg's understanding—was the manner in which the screenplay itself became a managerial tool, a set of plans, insurance that the system would be upheld.

As I said earlier, in the early days of silent film, the "script," as we know it today, did not yet exist. The sources of money were often happy to have someone tell them the story, or act it out, over dinner. The actress Constance Collier observed Griffith working on *Intolerance* in a style that would have horrified a Thalberg: "He never had a scenario, but would take miles and miles of film that never saw the light of day. . . . How he held in his brain the continuity of the story was absolutely beyond understanding."

Cameraman Karl Brown saw the same thing through the lens: "Instead of working with pen or pencil, or through the mind and artistry of a professional writer, however skilled, he sculptured his thoughts in living flesh. . . ."

This is the nightmare of Hollywood production, from *Intolerance* to *Heaven's Gate,* the fear that a project is so out of control it exists only in the mind of its genius and his unrestrained experimenting with very expensive elements. Yet in the history of world film, there are many occasions on which a kind of improvisational liberty has delivered something remarkable; you can find this approach in Griffith, Chaplin, and Stroheim from one era, in Renoir, Godard, and Antonioni from another. Perhaps it all depends on how far you care to believe in the mind of a genius—and the people who run pictures can never make up their minds about that. So sometimes geniuses get taken to dinner and hacks get the plum jobs.

The script in Hollywood is now regarded as a sacred thing: time and again, the emptiness of modern movies is blamed on bad scripts, and with ample reason. Too many of our modern pictures have no story to tell, nothing remotely like "good" dialogue, no interesting characters. There are warnings in the business, such as not beginning to shoot until you've got the script problems worked out, that coexist oddly with the knowledge that many films that had "problem-free" scripts still end up being reconstructed and endlessly reshaped in the editing process (with new lines dubbed on resistant lips). To be brief, I don't know that there is any reliable correlation between scripts and films. I'm not even sure that there should be in a medium so open to the vagaries of performance, accident, shifts in the light, or improvisational brainstorms.

But the script gained credence and authority in the age of Thalberg because it was a factory-friendly document. What am I doing tomorrow? was a question that nagged at everyone, and it could be answered with the script and the production schedule—that crucial framework, devised by a production manager, that works out in advance the order in which different scenes will be shot, and thus determines the décor and the sound stages (to say nothing of the personnel and the limos) that will be required tomorrow and the day after.

A production manager, maybe the most influential job in real factory control, cannot function without a script, or the certainty that the script will be adhered to. Of course, a script can be changed, rewritten, reappraised suddenly. That's how, as *Chinatown* proceeded, Polanski could assert that Towne's ending was wrong, that he would write a new ending and the picture would proceed accordingly. But even then, new pages were needed if only to know just what kind of street was required, which actors, how many cars, and what crew resources.

Writers in Hollywood believe that they are the abused creative force in picture-making, and I don't mean to say that they haven't been trashed and exploited. Few of them were born with the urge to write screenplays. Instead, they had the profound desire to play with words, a way of passing the time that can go on, irrespective of work or employment. William Faulkner, apparently, managed to write a good deal of *Absalom, Absalom!* while being paid by Twentieth Century–Fox to work on Hawks's *The Road to Glory.* This is a measure of the implacable deceit in real writers. Still, it is vital to an understanding of what has happened to see that the script became a production tool, a built-in part of the schedule/budget process, a lever of control—and a way of claiming money. Who knows whether a script is "real writing"? Still, it's the delivery that triggers a check. In turn, the value placed on the script helped raise the status of writers, while sapping their creative risk-taking and independence. The writers who got ahead (Darryl Zanuck went from screenwriter to studio boss) were those who saw how far scripts were the structure of practical business management.

But Mayer was out of control—he didn't like to read. I don't mean that he behaved like a savage. Still, he favored emotional instinct, and offered it to novices as a policy. He dressed better as he rose in the world; he worked out the strict style for his home, his wife, and his daughters; he insinuated himself with political leaders; he learned to deliver a good speech for a variety of occasions, even if he seldom wrote at length. He was strong, stalwart, ever-present. At the same time, he was intensely emotional, confused, and impulsive, a demon of temper or sentimentality, driven with reckless force in contrary directions, always likely to turn straight talk into a melodramatic scene. Never mind looking at a screen, Mayer was turned on by watching life. And he could never quell thoughts of envy, rivalry, and even distaste when he watched the cool, controlled performances of Irving. They were made for each other in so many business ways, but they couldn't endure the fit.

By the end of the twenties, Thalberg (who married Norma Shearer in 1927) had extra feelings of family responsibility, allied to that constant fear of his own demise. His base salary was $400,000 a year ($8 million today), and his reputation was as high as it would ever be. But he was muddled in ways that might have startled his business colleagues. Forever in doubt as to whether to settle for cash or take Loew's stock, he had gotten into serious trouble with the IRS for giving stock away to family members and not reporting it properly. To add to the dismay, he had turned to Mayer and to Nick Schenck for help or advice. This was a new Irving in Mayer's eyes, one he was happy to see—a guy in a mess. It seems to have initiated a growing emotional pressure (his forte) that Mayer now exerted on Thalberg, and which exacerbated Irving's breakdown in the thirties.

This is a part of the human truth and maneuvering that lay behind the habit and efficiency of the factory. There was much more. In September

1926, Mayer had been persuaded to invest $50,000 in the Julian Petroleum Corporation. Courtney Chauncey Julian was a Canadian who struck oil in the Los Angeles area in the early 1920s, and thereafter raised vast funding on the mere promise of more oil. It was a scam, with different levels of shareholding and the fraudulent report of great profits by the inner circle to hook suckers. But by 1927, the name Julian was an object of scandal and Mayer was one of several people charged with usury, for apparently lending money to Julian at inflated levels of interest. Mayer repaid the interest and the case against him was dropped, but the Julian scandal dragged on and he remained fearful of fresh charges.

It was a warning to a man as easily frightened as he enjoyed intimidating others. And it persuaded Mayer to put more of his money in land, property, and such things as racehorses, instead of dangerous paper that he scarcely understood. But by 1928, Mayer was earning $800,000 a year (twice Thalberg's salary). Of course, the Thalberg household brought in Norma's salary, too, plus the $10,000 Thalberg had asked from Marcus Loew as a wedding present for her. (Shortly after that fairy-tale generosity, Loew died.)

Yes, these were titans of a new industry, the most talked about business in America, and it was beyond their vision to see much danger on the horizon. But they were also a gang of hoodlum boys caught up in a desperate rivalry for prestige and bragging rights that usually was resolved through money. That said, the picture business was a headlong success on which they had little to do except keep their places.

In a way, Marcus Loew's surest place in this history occurs with his death. But let's give him more room: he was the son of an Austrian immigrant, a waiter, and he was born in New York in 1870. Without education, he was a teenager selling furs who went broke a couple of times before he joined his pal, Adolph Zukor, in buying up nickelodeon arcades. Remember, this was the scruff end of an upstart craze, with one or two outlets coming at a time. But within a few years, partnered by Nick and Joe Schenck, the company was Loew's Consolidated. Zukor went his own way, to help found Paramount. And thus it was Marcus Loew who had determined on the 1924 merger of Metro (his production arm) with Mayer and Goldwyn. When he died, in September 1927, Loew left a fortune of $35 million (over $700 million by today's values).

Now, that's a business history, sure enough. But is it reliable?

Loew did not leave a tidy estate. A large portion of Loew's shares, enough to control the company, went to his widow. Whereupon, several self-improvers in the business made clear their eagerness to take over the company. I stress this natural enough fierceness as a way of pointing out its marked absence in a decision still to come (see p. 232).

The most significant attempt to take over Loew's came from William Fox, real name Wilhelm Fried, born in Hungary in 1879, brought to New York as an infant, the senior among thirteen children, and working in a clothes factory from the age of eleven. He shifted over into buying arcades and by 1912 had entered production as the Fox Film Corporation. Fox's taste ranged widely, from Tom Mix westerns to Murnau's *Sunrise*. By 1927 his company was worth about $200 million, and all of a sudden he made his moves on the widow Loew. He raised a loan from Chase Manhattan and offered to buy out her shares. His next step would be to gain effective control of M-G-M, and a chance to oust Louis B. Mayer.

Loew's direct successor, Nick Schenck, played a very devious game suggestive of his own equal wish to get rid of Mayer. Indeed, Thalberg was bribed to stay quiet when he got wind of the plan. It's hard to know what Schenck's plan was (apart from terminating Mayer), but the plan came close to fruition. In 1929, it was critically interrupted by the crash of the stock market and by a serious car accident that put Fox out of action. In addition, Mayer pulled strings in Washington to put antitrust threats in the way of Fox's move; the gang fight had reached all the way to the White House. Fox's ploy was defeated. His company drifted for a few years, before succumbing to its own merger in 1935 with the young, energetic Twentieth Century company (and there Mayer took his sweet revenge on Fox by becoming a significant investor). But this had been one more step in the increasing animosity and distrust that held Mayer, Thalberg, and Schenck in place.

* * *

Apart from each other, the movie moguls had several other things to fear: there was the chance that movies might outrage or offend American sensibilities. Already in the twenties, the country was changing at a pace never seen before; the possibility existed that the U.S. Justice Department might recognize tendencies toward monopoly; there was, in theory, at least, the risk of some comprehensive technological change sweeping away prior investments; and there was the drastic decline in the American economy that began in 1929, but set in more seriously a couple of years later. Fox and Paramount lost money in 1932; Warners had three bad years in a row,

1932–34; Universal sustained losses throughout the early thirties. In those same years, the average weekly attendance in U.S. theaters was as follows:

1928	65 million
1929	80 million (the biggest one-year jump ever recorded and striking proof of the audience for sound)
1930	90 million
1931	75 million (the biggest one-year decline)
1932	60 million (the same again)
1933	60 million

The loss of a third of the audience in two years was alarming. Yet the business had regained those losses by the end of the decade. This was enough to suggest that the ticket price itself had been tougher to afford in the early years of the Depression. There again, the business had reason to fear a widening gap between its prosperity (especially its scale of living) and that of the audience. The most alarming cross-cut of the 1930s was between the images of natural American poverty and Park Place, the incomes in Hollywood and the surge of unemployment across the nation. It's worth adding that some very daring films, including comedies like *My Man Godfrey,* did risk depicting the savage contrasts between the rich and the poor. In hindsight, *Godfrey's* sardonic observance of social chaos, typified in the arched but calm eyebrows of William Powell, seems like one of the great achievements of American film.

Still, the sharpest fears harbored in Hollywood were for any forces that might think of redistributing the existing wealth. For the generation of leaders that had witnessed (and had their lives transformed by) the early riot of the picture business, nothing was more ominous than a reappraisal of ownership. The films were by and from the studios, the product of a factory system.

But suppose that balance shifted? Suppose organized labor or better legal representation for the artistes took hold? What was to be done with unions and agents, or with anyone who had a plan to spirit away some of the gold the business had mined, and then protected? (I have to say that because, in any book that uses Hollywood numbers, and which has tried to test their veracity, the writer must admit limits in the scrutiny.)

In 2003, there was a case in the trade papers to make old-timers smile. It concerns *My Big Fat Greek Wedding,* a rather nicely independent project, a film from the fringes of live comedy performance, a rowdy but unlikely outsider's venture that was taken up by such altruists as Tom

Hanks and his wife Rita Wilson. "Wouldn't that make a good movie?" she said to him, after seeing Nia Vardalos's live show.

So it did. And in a year of splendid domestic performance, the film had numbers attached to it of $240 million, to say nothing of foreign earnings. The picture had been a sleeper hit, the kind everyone in the business says they love and long for. Why? Well, maybe because, after a year, the picture that apparently cost $5 million was still in the red by $20 million or so—a wonderful write-off.

I don't know what happened on *My Big Fat Greek Wedding*, and even if I did I doubt that my publisher's lawyers would be prepared to let me repeat it. I don't even know that "anything" happened, in the sense of anything untoward, granted that the total number of producers, co-producers, and executive producers on this picture was ten. Counting credited producers is a key to accounting genius.

These days, it's a safe assumption that everyone who has such a credit on a film is taking away a piece of the action. They may have worked night and day for two years to achieve that reward; or they may have done no more than make an introduction. Not even Irving Thalberg believed ten producers were necessary, let alone useful, on a project. But Thalberg didn't have to raise the money for his movies. He simply got a production number, and charged everything on the picture to that number.

In other words, the accounting procedures available now, and the coming together of the financial interests that get a picture made, are very complex and mysterious. Any independent project today that avails itself of studio facilities is likely to incur an "overhead" charge. Every picture Thalberg made eventually had an overhead charge. But in the ultimate consideration of whether a picture was in the black, it has always been very hard to define the overhead, or to be sure that it wasn't as infinitely flexible as Hollywood's ideas of what a "good girl" might do. For example, suppose Irving and Norma Shearer occasionally took a trip to Europe. And reason that, along the way, the chronically fertile mind of Irving thought about his many projects, maybe a hundred. And let us accept the legend of his brilliance enough to believe that, in Paris and Rome, he had decisive insights on fifty of them. Then ask against which project should the expenses of that trip ($20,000; I'm making it up) be charged? Why dump on one unlucky title? Suppose they charged it against all of them? Fifty times $20,000—that's $1 million being soaked up right away. Which doesn't mean that Irving didn't also put in for expenses.

Actors and crew sometimes worked on different pictures the same day. Block-booking procedures (illegal but common) meant that a theater wanting two or three big pictures had also to take twenty minor ones. That packaging allowed for a generous spread of costs.

All of this is to say nothing about the basic cash business whereby a theater (many of them owned by Loew's, the same company that made the films) could say, well, we didn't do as well as expected last weekend. We've seen the massive gap between what *The Birth of a Nation* took in at the box office and what it returned to Griffith and his partners. We know that Louis B. Mayer came to life in that gap. We know that in the early days gangsters would threaten theaters and arcades with violence in return for a cut as protection. We know that the American gangster is always looking to be more businesslike. And we know, time and again, over the history of the movies, that people like Nia Vardalos cry out, Where did the money go?—only to have someone come up to them and whisper, "Forget it, Jake. It's Chinatown." She got her movie made, the way another Jake, La Motta, got his shot at the title, and for such things you accept compromises.

The two Jakes are supposed to reason thus: You want to keep working, don't you? So next time get yourself a better deal. Because while you think you're making pictures, they believe they're making deals. A writer may flinch from that cynicism, but then he or she must ask why they are writing pictures. After all, one paints or photographs pictures; one writes novels. This is one of the dark closed circles of film culture, exactly the fruit of the voyeuristic fantasizing I have talked about. For it is the movies that have made the gangster—from Tony Camonte to Tony Montana, from Joe Schenck to Michael Corleone—villains or cynics we love to admire (from the dark). The screenwriter nowadays must come equipped with sardonic drop-dead lines that cover his own compromise. It's the last charm left to Joe Gillis in *Sunset Blvd.*

It's also naughty or provocative to jump from talk of unions and agents to mention of gangsters. Still, there is a point: it is that every fresh interest coming to the pie has taken the attitude that sharp practice has been at work, and that only sharper practice will lead to a "fair" share. In every American gold rush, the same sort of momentum has been at work. Gold diggers rewrite the laws to suit their business, and sooner or later only lawyers can restrain them. When it comes to the precious numbers, what are we dealing with? Informed estimates, you will be told—approximations; a jungle of detail (often with disclaimers, doubts, and footnotes) that litigious parties may examine and check out, if they have the time or the money to pay the lawyers, and if they are prepared to run the risk of being proved correct. In the end in such disputes, you sue and settle. It is the way things are done. Unions and agents in Hollywood have learned that same lesson.

The leaders of the business were flat-out opposed to unionism. It seemed too close to the Communism that had plagued some of them in Soviet Russia. It was plainly a plot to get at their money. But as it turned out, the business was at a great advantage as long as it could confine the contentious issues to money. Still, Mayer and his colleagues had taken up the cause of an Academy in the hope that it might pass muster as a benign, industry-wide union or forum, a place where business could be promoted and disputes settled.

The first large union in Hollywood was the International Alliance of Theatrical Stage Employees (IATSE), a body that included ordinary studio laborers to theater employees (like projectionists). This was a union, founded in 1893, that began in the theater and then extended itself to all the "little" people in the business. But it was tried and tested, hard core (in several ways), and it did use the threat of strikes (at the theaters) to leverage better deals for people who in the early thirties were being paid around $50 a week (a perfectly manageable wage by national standards).

Granted the presence of IATSE, it says a lot about the command of the moguls, the conservatism of the talent, and the sheer amount of money being spread around that there were no other active unions in Hollywood until 1933. When President Roosevelt closed the banks that year there was dismay in the movie business, a trade where cash flow was vital, and momentarily in decline. At M-G-M, Mayer ordained a 50 percent pay cut across the board, for at least eight weeks. There was much protest, and IATSE and the Academy together managed a compromise in which the lower earners were spared the cut, while it applied on a sliding scale to higher earners. But it was in this sudden turmoil that the two most important unions came into being, the Screen Actors Guild (SAG) and the Screen Writers Guild (both established in 1933).

Historically, these are the unions that have struck most often, and that have tended to gather the most radical thinking in the picture business (do not expect to be inflamed by its rhetoric). They have had their victories. In the thirties, for instance, actors boycotted the Academy for a while, and as a result they gained the concession whereby as of 1935 Oscars would be awarded to supporting actors as well as to leads. Moreover, SAG has fought for very decent minimums in the way of payment for film and television, and in repeat screenings. If you are a working actor, SAG has made your life comfortable. If you are out of work, like the majority of actors, you are hard-put to maintain your dues payments.

The Writers Guild has much the same story to tell. As a member, I can report that the union health plan, the pension plan, and the minimums are impressive (though the health plan, like all others in America, is under fire). All of which make it very important for the screenwriter to stay employed. Health coverage goes if your employment stops, and in these days that can be difficult and expensive to replace. Moreover, the basic contract of the Writers Guild has called for profit participation for writers as a standard procedure, even if it is points on the profit, as opposed to points on the gross. Note that such extras are still not available to cameramen, editors, composers, designers, not even special-effects geniuses, though sometimes particular contracts may call for them, and surely we are about to see a legal rush in which such experts cash in.

But the Writers Guild has protected its members at the cost of writing. Here I touch upon a subject that many screenwriters may resent: the matter of how far writing has been able to determine and characterize the adventure in our movies, or whether it simply serves the factory process. Screenwriters are better paid now than Herman Mankiewicz dreamed. There are million-dollar deals all over the place. There are even cases of writers getting several hundred thousand dollars a week, plus lavish expenses, to come in and doctor a script as it is being shot. And with writers' contracts offering points, writers do eventually get money on the points.

They are, I suppose, the most protected class of writers in the world—I mean compared to novelists, biographers, and poets. But unlike those authors, they do not own the copyright on their work. It is automatic in the writers' contracts as recommended by the Guild that the absolute rights to the material and the characters remain with the purchasing party, that is, with the production company or the studio. Most screenwriters will tell you that this does not compromise their degree of caring, or pain, over what happens—which is polite hogwash. The culture in which films are written requires that writers move on, that they need not care for their work (because it is not theirs), that they are technicians as opposed to authors. Such writers need to live with half a dozen scripts never made— as queasy a trick as keeping all your children in love. That is the way it has worked out, and there are a few hundred writers in Hollywood who earn good livings, own ample houses, send their children to private schools, and look forward to fat pensions. Good for them. But that is not writing, and it has been a disaster for spirit and risk in American films, for character and story. It is why the *Chinatown* trilogy will never be made.

Not that the Writers Guild is relied on in big-money crises. The Guild does lay out minimal contracts, and it offers assistance in negotiating deals, but few writers take themselves that lightly. Instead, they employ agents and/or lawyers to handle documents that often are as long as (yet more heavily pondered than) the scripts that will emerge.

What a word—"agent"—with its suggestions of espionage! Yet, in truth, in modern times, hardened spies have turned into talk show veterans and tell-all authors while show business agents go to their graves silent. Who can deny that money and the deal are now more sacred even than homeland security? But let's take a moment to marvel at the enterprise, the nerve, the redefinition of so much in that thing called agenting.

Perhaps skilled historians of social and economic process could point to the existence of agent-like beings before the twentieth century, go-betweens who might eventually gather a firkin of ale for word that this play called *Othello* had legs, or whatever. It is not that money or business transactions suddenly crossed the path of art in recent times. It is more than likely that helpful intermediaries have often attended the birth of the many shows we have had. Still, the scale of money in the last hundred years, and the way in which the show has become a business, are beyond dispute. As we shall see, it is not simply that agents saw for themselves a narrow window of opportunity. In fact, agents have made a reappraisal of the business so sweeping that one might sympathize with the breakfast conversation overheard (or dreamed) at Cantor's delicatessen on Fairfax between two agents in which the younger asked the elder:

"Who decided that we get 10 percent?"

"It was a mistake."

"How's that?"

"We were meant to get the 90, the schmucks the 10. It was all bad grammar."

Enter Myron Selznick, short, muscled, belligerent, handsome in a depressive way, very smart, very bitter and seeking vengeance. There are contests over who deserves the title of the first Hollywood agent, but no one disputes that Myron was the first powerful agent and a seminal figure in the brief, startling history of that type. He was the middle of three Selznick brothers, four years older than David, but a couple of years younger than Howard, who loomed over them, not just in height, but because of his problematic condition. Some said he suffered brain damage at birth; others argued that he was not quite sane. He would outlive both Myron and David, and he had the kind of abject, disappointing life that

affects many. He was in and out of a few institutions, and he got in trouble
with the police for harassing women. For the same offense, his brothers
became famous.

Myron was the valued assistant to his father, Lewis J. Selznick, in the
short-lived glory of Selznick's World Film Corporation, one of those far-
reaching business promises that came and went in the decade after *The
Birth of a Nation*. In that position, Myron was not just a business executive
and a producer of many films. He was also, thanks to his father's introduction, on the original board of the Motion Picture Producers and Distributors Association. Myron was only twenty-five when World went bust in
1923, and he then gathered David up in his plan to make good in the picture business, to redeem the family name, and to screw the cabal of executives (that included Mayer, Zukor, the Warners, the Laemmles, Fox, and
Goldwyn) he insisted had screwed his Pop.

David and Myron fought steadily. Myron beat David up, needled him,
teased him, and generally made a fool of him on account of David's physical clumsiness, his daydreaming hopes, his lack of worldliness. Many people mistook Myron for a gangster—he had that bearing, that attitude. In
truth, I think Myron envied David deeply for his capacity for hope, his
chronic delight in creative thinking, and his winning of Irene Mayer.

I mention this because it is necessary backstory for what is to come.
Myron and Irene were alike in their dark, gloomy intelligence; their readiness to plot and intrigue; their strategic instincts; and their fond dismay over
David's shortcomings. I suspect there was a physical attraction between
them, never indulged in anything but sardonic flirt, but a bond, a kinship.

Once Lewis Selznick's fall was finalized, the two Selznick brothers had
a brief fling in the Florida land rush of 1924–26 before going to Hollywood. At first, they lived together, and worked as a team. But then it
became apparent that David had embarked on a career not just as a producer and an executive but as a true filmmaker, someone who would as
soon die as not make his movies his way. Myron was contemptuous of that
passion, but he was respectful of it in this case because it was his brother's.
For himself, he needed another way: he would sooner die than take decisive, positive action. At first, acting simply as an advisor to pals, he saw
there was space and leverage for the right kind of shameless, aggressive
person to march into the office of, say, a Zukor, and cry out, You can't treat
William Powell like this any longer! And squeeze more money for him.

Of course, studio policy dictated long-term contracts (five or seven
years), which meant that "renewal" or negotiation occurred seldom. There
were, however, exceptions—shorter-term deals—and Myron found that

even regular studio contracts sometimes allowed loopholes (especially in the suspension clauses) where aggravation might begin. He had natural advantages: he had been trained in the business; he was innately tough; he knew the lying ploys of the studios (he had used them himself not long ago), and, through David, he had social involvement with many actors, writers, and directors. He also had motive: he wanted to squeeze the men and the type of men who had brought his father down. He wanted revenge. And he knew enough to realize that the business was so awash in money that skimming could be managed quite easily.

People would pay Myron to get rid of him. But he saw the two vectors that could sustain him: first, he could easily get a better deal for clients, many of whom had no previous representation and who were helpless when dealing with experts who offered money beyond their dreams; and, second, if he could acquire enough clients then he had to be dealt with by the studios. Indeed, in subtle ways, he became a kind of surrogate studio, an organization of talent. Myron Selznick was the first person to see that if he placed Loretta Young in this film, say, then it needed a writer, a director, and a co-star, and maybe he could supply those, too. Today this is called packaging.

Myron had famous successes negotiating for director Lewis Milestone and actress Constance Bennett. In 1931, in his first great coup, he took William Powell, Kay Francis, and Ruth Chatterton away from Paramount and delivered them to Warners. He was a great success story of the 1930s, building his list of clients, hiring on junior agents (some of whom would leave to populate the business), and in 1938 moving into a smart, custom-made building at 9700 Wilshire. At the very same moment, Myron was also preparing his next moves: to secure profit participation for some clients, and to make himself the producer of their films.

He failed eventually because of his despairing nature. He was immensely successful, with a house at the beach and a famous ski lodge at Lake Arrowhead that was the site of weekend parties for the stars. He was only forty. He had a wife (the actress Marjorie Daw), and a daughter, Joan. Yet nothing moved or impressed him, not even his own exceptional efficiency. He succumbed more and more to drink despite every effort by David and Irene to put him into treatment. (He would be dead in 1944, looking twenty years older than his real age.) As he declined, his own agents and clients left him. It was a Selznick pattern: Destroy what you have built. In time, David would follow suit.

But Myron had set an example. (Leland Hayward was one of those agents raised and trained by Myron.) Music Corporation of America

(MCA) had gone beyond its early roots in Chicago and the music industry to set up in Hollywood to develop resources in the movie business. It was in 1939 that Jules Stein, the founder of MCA, sent Lew Wasserman from Chicago to Los Angeles to see what he could do. Wasserman lacked all of Myron's flaws and neurotic drive. He was a man who lived by the motto "A tidy desk and a tidy mind," whereas Myron was a more complex human being who believed that outer decorum could never mask inner turmoil. Wasserman hardly took a drink and he would become for a time the most powerful and feared person in Hollywood. He certainly deserves to be among the elect who may have understood "the whole equation," except that he had not so much as a glimmering about the purpose or beauty of the mathematics. No one would do more to take the show out of the business.

*   *   *

One word more on agents: it's nothing less than magic, the way that talent agents, between about 1940 and 1960, just as the movie business declined, asserted, defined, and enlarged their own role in the entertainment industry in so breathtaking a way. I've stressed already the extent to which their ability to spell out a new kind of ownership—indeed, a new structure to the old business—changed all the other factors, and inflated the cost of making a movie. Agents had only a meager 10 percent to play with for themselves so it had to become 10 percent of something bigger. But agents picked up another duty, too, vital to what I mean by the whole equation. They introduced themselves as the new breed that saw the "whole picture." In time, this would lead to their packaging entire pictures (with their own talent) and being the effective decision-makers on a lot of what got made. Such is the power that made Michael Ovitz, once a maverick from the William Morris Agency, the founder of Creative Artists Agency (CAA), and unquestionably the most decisive person in Hollywood in the eighties.

Ovitz carried himself quietly and cautiously for the most part, as if he could hardly believe what had happened. (The writings of Joe Eszterhas, from memos to "books," do speak to a more melodramatic strain in Ovitz, one that might have been learned from watching Rod Steiger's performance as the studio chief in *The Big Knife*.) So, in general, Ovitz doesn't fit this last observation: about the way in which agents became the voice of the business, the unstoppable, half-smart, half-caustic, half-comedian patter (agents are always looking for three halves in one whole). Agents famously never write books (because of confidentiality, discretion, and trust—pause for laughter). But agents are the talkers in the business; they are the running commentary, often foul-mouthed, invariably hilarious, and always alarming. They tell the stories—word of mouth. They remind me of the role Joe Pesci has played in some Martin Scorsese pictures, especially *GoodFellas* and *Casino*, a force of words, taking over the picture and its world, until, at last, there has to be a merciful execution.

Clive Brook and Marlene Dietrich in Josef von Sternberg's *Shanghai Express*, 1932
(Private Collection)

14 · GOLDEN?

Gold rushes aren't what they used to be. In 1848–49, in California, gold was a provable item: you could take it to an assay office and have it verified; you could carry it down to San Francisco and buy yourself a hotel and a wife. There was a gold standard. A little less than a hundred years later, we say that a "golden age" occurred in Hollywood.

These days, 1939 is regularly hailed as the *annus mirabilis,* with a mass of solid, entertaining (or better) pictures, topped off by *Gone With the Wind,* which established new marks for success, the most dramatic since *The Birth of a Nation.*

Not everyone saw 1939 the same way. If *Gone With the Wind* now seems like the emblem of the studio system, the truth is that it was violently independent, the love child of a man quite ready to see his studio (and his backers) go down.

As he tried to plan *The Last Tycoon,* Scott Fitzgerald wrote to a friend about his own rocky state:

> Very much against my will, I was persuaded to take a job to which I felt spiritually inadequate because I needed a rest from pictures and because my health was going steadily worse. I was going to sleep every night with a gradually increasing dose of chloral—three teaspoonfuls—and two pills of Nembutol every night and forty-eight drops of digitalin to keep the heart working to the next day. Eventually one begins to feel like a character out of *The Wizard of Oz.* Work becomes meaningless and effort a matter of the medicine closet.

That last job was an attempted rescue on *Gone With the Wind* (three weeks at $1,500 a week; for sixty million Americans that was more than they earned in a year), the last straw of humiliation for Scott. The same year, another great man, D. W. Griffith, met another kind of dismay on a project called *One Million B.C.,* for which the kindly Hal Roach had hired him as a "producer," or as the collector of a rescuing pay packet. But Griffith failed again, amid talk of trying to draw the medium back to its precious silence.

Nineteen thirty-nine had so many other bad moments: at the preview of *The Wizard of Oz,* there were many studio experts who urged that that gloomy song, "Over the Rainbow," be cut from the picture. There was real doubt, until Louis B. Mayer said, "Keep it." He trusted instinct. Orson Welles was put under a "carte blanche" contract in that year, which most people around town thought was a terrible sign of the times. (It suggested a new kind of hero: immense, charismatic, and as fascinating as Welles, yet unsound.) As for *Gone With the Wind,* well, Irene Selznick reckoned that if the ordeal of making it didn't destroy her husband, David, then its success surely would. And a war began in 1939, a war that sharpened the meaning of *Gone With the Wind* when it opened in December 1939, but which alarmed every executive in the business: What if we lose the foreign market?

Few people saw gold anywhere. Until the last moment, there were those who thought *Gone With the Wind* would explode like a balloon of hype and Selznick's hot air. The picture had cost over $4 million! Essentially no movie ever made back that kind of sum. The numbers seemed a flagrant indulgence or miscalculation—the new scales in Hollywood always do (it was reported in 2003 that Peter Jackson will get $20 million and 20 percent of the gross to remake *King Kong*).

The entire tone of *The Last Tycoon*, written in 1940, but set in 1935, is about the crisis that faced American film—not just whether the relatively benign Monroe Stahr could hold off his barbarian board, but whether the medium and the business could retain any kind of social contract with America. The last pages of *The Day of the Locust* foresee a dire collision between the fantasy factory and the public enduring hard times and crushed hopes. Even if Fitzgerald had sold out to the movies, even if he could guess the sarcasm in his own obituaries, he was still the author of *The Great Gatsby*, that unchangingly alert study of Americans caught between wild hopes and blunt truth. And Fitzgerald knew, in the end, how perilous it was to try to be Monroe Stahr.

I'm not sure that Nathanael West wasn't closer to the truth. Maybe 1939 is too soon yet to tell just what the movies did to America—especially when the likes of Peter Fonda, Peter Bogdanovich, and Francis Ford Coppola were born only that year. But an era arrived—call it nostalgia, call it enlightened criticism—in which the thirties and even the forties came to represent a golden age of film. At the same time, looking at the intense commercialization of that era, and the disagreeable elements of factory production, some wondered: Can gold result under such conditions? Or is it quartz? That question is even more pertinent today, when production costs have risen out of all proportion, and when so few films, compared with 1939's crop, hold or entertain the "whole" audience, let alone speak for the nation.

To start with, there are the attendance figures for those years of economic depression and war, average weekly attendance at American theaters at a time when the population went from 120 million to 150 million:

1929	80 million
1930	90 million
1931	75 million
1932	60 million
1933	60 million
1934	60 million

1935	65 million
1936	65 million
1937	75 million
1938	75 million
1939	85 million
1940	80 million
1941	85 million
1942	85 million
1943	85 million
1944	85 million
1945	85 million
1946	100 million
1947	90 million
1948	85 million
1949	70 million
1950	60 million

So much in those figures is remarkable. Take the surge following the introduction of sound—was that simply curiosity for a new craze, or am I right in feeling that the medium had been made pregnant? Was there also that much of an appetite for the splendid fast-talking comedies, screwball and romantic, of Preston Sturges, Leo McCarey, Gregory La Cava, Frank Capra, Howard Hawks, and others? There's a faltering during the very hard times of the early thirties, but attendance picks up again and achieves that phenomenal level during the war years, and greater heights still right afterward. But what is that dramatic decline at the end of the decade? It isn't television, for that competition came a little later. We have to see that in the late forties some decline set in of its own accord, no matter that those are the years of *The Treasure of the Sierra Madre, Red River, All the King's Men, Twelve O'Clock High, All About Eve, In a Lonely Place, Sunset Blvd., The Third Man, White Heat,* and *The Asphalt Jungle,* to say nothing of the best years of film noir.

We'll come back to those years. For the moment, I think the appraisal of the golden years owes a great deal to the nostalgic feeling that a way of life and family structure had held together during the Depression and the Second World War, and saw the movies as one of the liveliest flags flying over our stockade. Perhaps it was wishful thinking. After all, many people were beaten down by economic hardship. You can argue that the pressure on blacks was building the great anger that would erupt in the fifties and sixties. Equally, though a just war was won, the years of war accelerated divorce at lower social levels; it shattered family life in obvious ways and in many others more subtle; and it provided ample sources for pessimism. The illusion that human violence and difference had been eliminated quickly faded. It wasn't long after the war that the rugged, grudging heroism of Rick Blaine in *Casablanca,* say, had turned into the neurosis and the bureaucratic confusion of the Cold War years.

I feel compromised myself in making these judgments in that, born in 1941, I started being taken to the movies in the midst of that extraordinary postwar boom when a child could feel comforted by a great mass of strangers enjoying themselves in the same way. I don't think I'd had any notion of what community might mean or offer until I started going to the movies. My timing was lucky, and I was lucky, too, in that many of the first films I saw would later be confirmed (by Andrew Sarris and by *Cahiers du Cinéma*) as great, or very good, or even just "lightly likable" (I was happy with that). However, I know that today there is a younger generation that resents this stress on the long ago, and which prefers to argue that *Jaws* and *Star Wars* were the dawn (because they were kids when those suns came up)—which suggests how far the movies have always belonged to young people, and may seem precious or strained when enthused over by their elders.

The stability in audience numbers in the thirties and forties was borne out in other ways. The array of studios essentially stayed intact between 1930 and 1950: M-G-M was in the same place—it led most of the way—and Louis B. Mayer was a constant. Moreover, while there had been natural attrition (Garbo had retired; Jean Harlow had died so very young), many of the studio's stars lasted: Gable, Tracy, Crawford (even though she moved to Warners in the mid-forties), Robert Taylor, William Powell, and Myrna Loy. Warner Brothers was still run by the brothers, and it had its own core of attractions: Cagney, Bogart, Bette Davis, Gary Cooper. You could say the same for Paramount, where Hope and Crosby had dominated the forties at the box office. Universal, Columbia, and RKO remained in business. The one great casualty of the depression, Fox, had been rescued by the merger with Twentieth Century, led by Darryl F. Zanuck, who had previously been the head of production at Warners.

Zanuck, Goldwyn, Selznick, Disney, and Warner were names that meant as much (or more) in 1950 as in 1930, even if some were ready for easier times. There were other stars who had weathered all changes without losing their audience: Cary Grant, John Wayne, Henry Fonda, Fred Astaire, Ginger Rogers, James Stewart, Ingrid Bergman. Directors who did their best work in this period, and who still seemed ready for more by the late forties, included John Ford, Howard Hawks, John Huston, Frank Capra, William Wyler, Billy Wilder, King Vidor, George Cukor, George Stevens, Michael Curtiz, Alfred Hitchcock.

Plenty of the stars and directors listed above had careers of thirty years or more. It's worth asking how or why that longevity functioned, especially when we may doubt that some of today's wonders will stay at the top for even ten years. There was a club, a social organization, that extended the seven-year contract: the same people stayed around because they had been invested in, and enhanced by, the star-making machinery. Directors tended to learn their craft and earn their opportunities slowly. It was hard to argue that people like Howard Hawks, or at a lower level, William Wellman, Henry Hathaway, and Michael Curtiz, couldn't do anything and everything. They had proved it. But then there's one other thing worth stressing: most of the people named here had been born and raised with the new medium. Nothing yet disputes the notion that the first wave of moviemakers had the surest instincts about the new medium—because they were audience as well as practitioners.

Along with the personnel, the nature of movie fiction had not changed that much. By the early days of sound, a set of genres (many with roots in the silent era) existed that lasted through the forties: the Western; the costume adventure; the crime movie; the horror picture; the women's picture; the literary adaptation. You can come up with movies that don't fit into those genres, though not as easily as you might think. It follows from that, and from the factory system, that pictures had recurring patterns and motifs, among them the unambiguous hero and villain; the idea that good-looking equals good; the dynamic of suspense; the happy ending. I would place alongside these stereotypes a range of behaviors or situations, well worth considering for a moment if you care to reflect upon the cultural influence of movies: How do people kiss, or smoke cigarettes? What do they say when they're in love? What does a "nice" bedroom look like? What does the city look like when crime is in the air, or romance? How are wars fought? What is courage, and is it necessary? Ditto honor? What do women want if not merely to be photographed looking gorgeous? (If that code seems quaint, don't forget how it persists—in advertising.)

I do not mean to underestimate the seeds of doubt and cultural self-destruction that could be found in a searching analysis of such things. But just because so many people went to the movies, and were in awe of them, the influence was enormous. It's been popular for decades to argue that violence on screen is itself dangerous in that it may be imitated, or may be so absorbed that it affects our behavior. The matter has never been set-

tled. I suspect that a greater and more insidious influence may lie in what
movies tell us about being in love, and how to conduct ourselves while in
that condition. And although it may seem comic or foolish now—for our
young are more cynical—I think it is hard to overestimate the effect
movies had on lifestyle in the thirties and forties. If I had to point to one
singular yet typical instance of how an amiable yet vacant selfhood on
screen took over the whole of America, I would say "Ronald Reagan."

All of this is to suggest a vulnerability to uniformity in the factory product and to a kind of servitude in its employment of would-be artists. But
there are numerous cases that prove something close to the opposite. For
example, Frank Capra worked for Columbia (and only for Columbia) from
the last days of the silent era until the outbreak of World War II (after that,
his employers were Warner Brothers, the U.S. Army, his own Liberty
Films, M-G-M, Paramount, and United Artists). Films from the Columbia
years include *The Miracle Woman, Platinum Blonde, The Bitter Tea of
General Yen, Lady for a Day, It Happened One Night, Mr. Deeds Goes to
Town, Lost Horizon, You Can't Take It with You,* and *Mr. Smith Goes to
Washington.*

I leave it to you to judge whether that list constitutes art or just a terrific
body of entertaining films (and a fascinating insight into American ideals
and self-deception). While they were being made, Capra was battling with
Harry Cohn, the boss of Columbia, a man of infinite vulgarity, incipient
brutishness, and thug-like ego. As Capra put it, "It was fight, fight, fight,
fight. Even after it was proven that if they left me alone they would get a
better picture. I was the toughest bastard you ever knew. I had to be.
Because if you give in you've lost your position. You're lost."

No one lost in this deal. If Capra felt besieged, that pressure fed his
innate jitteriness—it's the tension in his parables between virtue triumphant and the world going to hell. For all the fighting, Capra never
enjoyed such security again. At Columbia he found many of his best col-
laborators: writers Robert Riskin and Sidney Buchman; cameraman
Joseph Walker; to say nothing of Barbara Stanwyck, Jean Arthur, and
James Stewart. As for Columbia itself, the studio was promoted to major
status just because of Capra, when *It Happened One Night* swept the 1934
Oscars. Columbia had never won Best Picture before; they won again in
1938 with Capra's *You Can't Take It with You*—and they did not win again
until *All the King's Men* in 1949.

The numbers in the Capra era at Columbia are fascinating. When
Capra came to the studio, in 1928, Columbia was far from a major outfit:
its average budget was $18,000 per picture, with a couple of "prestige"

productions at $30,000. Capra was hired to direct for $1,000 a picture. Even on *It Happened One Night,* the budget was only $325,000 (including the fabulous bargain of Gable and Claudette Colbert, both on loan, for $60,000—no wonder that "King" Gable felt he was a slave ready to be bartered).

A word more about Colbert and Gable, and Capra's instinct that they would work well together. It was an early form of "chemistry," and proof of the sort of reaction that was enhanced by sound. She sounded so proper, and he so rough: that was the imprint of her classiness (Colbert really was Parisian, a socialite, and about to marry a leading Los Angeles doctor), while Gable was "bad," lower class, with a scarred past and a terrific confidence that his grin and his snarl mustache would help him get away with anything. In sound pictures, differences worked better than similarity: that's how Fred gave Ginger class, while she dragged sex under his haughty nose.

Capra, a magician of such pairings, was by then earning $3,000 a week, plus 10 percent of the profits on his pictures. *It Happened One Night* did at least $1 million in rentals, very likely more, but the numbers were depleted by the illegal block-booking techniques so that some of *It Happened One Night*'s revenue could be assigned to other, lesser films.

Still, Capra received some profit money, and then he got a much better deal: $100,000 a movie and 25 percent of the profits. Fighting to the end, Capra declared in his autobiography, *The Name Above the Title,* that Cohn and the studio had cheated him out of any actual profits. This was all part of the legend that profits were written in mist, and of Capra's sorrowful legend of integrity being beaten down. But Joseph McBride's Capra biography, *The Catastrophe of Success,* makes clear that over the years Capra earned almost $1 million on his profit participation, a benefit he had negotiated personally with Cohn, so there was no agency cut, either.

On his last Columbia film, *Mr. Smith Goes to Washington,* Capra's profits never paid off well: he would pocket about $42,000 in forty years, no matter that the picture eventually amassed $3.8 million in rentals. But since the picture cost $1.9 million (about $280,000 over budget), the result would seem to indicate some vengeance on Cohn's part at seeing the last of Capra. So Capra had a grievance, after all. Still, the profit participation he enjoyed was not just a healthy pension. It was an early measure of the recognition that directors did determine the fate of films, and it was a mark of Cohn's crooked trust. Capra was a rare case (five nominations for Best Director while at Columbia), and in the end he surely benefited from allegiance to a studio that had seemed so inferior when he arrived there. The loyalty paid off as Columbia rose in the world. But never at Columbia did Capra have absolute authority over material, casting, or cut. He could suggest; he could maneuver; he could fight. And he was good on all fronts. But he felt at the mercy of Harry Cohn, and he was always eager to please or outwit the boss.

All the same, the Capra films of the thirties mean more than the numbers. Their whole equation must also look to the strange social dynamics that Capra felt (and these are very emotional pictures) and how that appealed to the public. For these are films set amid hardship and recession, yet urging the noble individual to make good on the original promise of America, even if that means driving corruption out of the Senate itself. This is populism of a precarious order in that Capra always felt the speed with which a crowd could shift from a collection of lovable character actors to a cruel mob. Moreover, the strain of nobility often tells on his heroes: they break down, they weep, they are exhausted by their ordeals.

For myself, I don't think Capra is an artist so much as someone desperate to do contrary things: to be noble, but to please people; to do the right thing; and to be famous. In a way, the most intriguing thing in his work is the very question he faced: What is a film director? Can he be all these things? Can he stand up to the alleged tyrannies of Harry Cohn? The thing that Capra's films are most hysterically afraid of, the regular compromise in democratic process, is actually the very thing that made the partnership with Cohn function so successfully. Capra was a fine popular storyteller who needed to be told to behave himself if his natural mischief was to show. He needed the system he hated to be at his best.

After the war (during which he made stirring propaganda documentaries), Capra sought a new way. With colleagues William Wyler and George Stevens (all of whom had seen the war firsthand and been altered by it) he formed Liberty Films, a small version of United Artists, except that it was a production company. It was for Liberty that Capra made *It's a Wonderful Life* (his best-loved picture and the most ambivalent). At last he was his own producer and part of the production company, working on loaned money from the Bank of America. He would own *It's a Wonderful Life*.

In fact, United Artists declined the opportunity to distribute the picture. It went to RKO. That was a sign that some wondered if Capra was too locked into the spirit of the thirties. In other words, the war made moneyed interests ask, How much has the public mood shifted? *It's a Wonderful Life* was budgeted at $1.5 million, but it cost $2.8 million, nearly a million dollars more than *Mr. Smith Goes to Washington*. Production costs had shot up during the war as munitions factories vied for labor. But there were other elements of inflation: on *Mr. Smith*, Columbia had borrowed Jimmy Stewart cheaply from M-G-M but by the time of *Wonderful Life*, Stewart (and his agent Lew Wasserman) negotiated a deal that paid a fee of $162,000 against 10 percent of Liberty's share of the gross receipts. Stewart walked away with about $400,000 on the picture.

I stress this because, as mentioned previously, it was only four years later, on *Winchester '73*, that Wasserman and Stewart got such a deal. But the agent's grip had actually tightened earlier; America's great guy was the blunt end of asking for much more. Stewart would later say that, depressed after the war (he had flown bomber missions), he was thinking of giving up the movies, but then Capra called and sketched out the role of George Bailey, whereupon Jimmy was an actor again. Details to follow.

It's a Wonderful Life seems to me an advance, and Capra's best film. The plight of idealism pitted against a corrupt commercial system is nearly tragic now. Despite the formal happy ending, the vision of what can happen to Bedford Falls without George Bailey is unforgettable. *It's a Wonderful Life* is meant to be another inspirational romance, but it is more undercut by traces of film noir, by dread and anxiety, than Capra could control. In part that may have been his worry at being boss. He went over schedule and over budget. George Stevens, writing the checks, warned him of where they were headed. But was a director the best person to rein in another director? In going independent, was Capra missing a tough production manager? The film got Capra another Best Director nod and a Best Picture nomination.

It's a Wonderful Life could not quite cover the costs of production and marketing (in total, nearly $3.8 million). Moreover, Capra was stung when one of his Liberty partners, William Wyler, defeated him at the 1946 Oscars for *The Best Years of Our Lives*, done as a prior commitment to Goldwyn and a smash hit. It had cost $2.1 million, and Goldwyn put another $400,000 into advertising. In other words, while being nearly forty-five minutes longer than Capra's film and taking an extra month to shoot, *Best Years* was more than a million dollars cheaper. Not that this mattered too much in the end, for *Best Years* earned nearly $11 million. Wyler had been paid $2,500 a week (so he probably earned only half of Capra's $156,000 on *Wonderful Life*), but he had 20 percent of Goldwyn's profits, too (well over a million dollars after accounting).

Why was *The Best Years of Our Lives* so much cheaper? Samuel Briskin, another Liberty partner, argued that production costs had escalated terribly during the war. But the money paid to the talent in *Wonder-*

ful Life was way up. On *Best Years,* Goldwyn took the view that the film had no star roles, and was well suited to young contract players. Briskin could have added that *Life*'s night scenes were done at night; that the call for snow was enormous and costly; or that, a free man, Capra insisted on shooting in sequence. That was part of the indecision, or second-guessing, that had overtaken Capra once he became an owner and his own boss. More and more, it was evident that the old studio overhead had been kind to directors in that it relieved them of many tasks. At Columbia, Capra had called for what he needed and it was delivered. As his own producer, he had to hire people to find the extras, the properties, or whatever, or obtain them himself. Granted freedom at last, he felt insecure.

The onetime spokesman for the ordinary guy who goes to Washington and speaks to the nation fell into the kind of neurotic inertia that lurks in the dark for all Capra heroes. He concluded that Liberty wouldn't work. So the new company would be broken up. Partner George Stevens, who felt that *Wonderful Life* was a good film that had done well, was against this drastic move. Capra thought otherwise:

> We didn't have enough capital, so we decided to sell Liberty Films, which was a very, very hopeless thing to do. My partners did not want to sell. But I got cold feet, and I'm the one who insisted that we sell. And I think that probably affected my picture-making forever afterward.
>
> Once you get cold feet, once your daring stops, then you worry a little bit. And when you worry about a decision, then you're not going to make the proper film anymore. That is, I couldn't. And I think that was the start. When I sold out for money, which is something that I had always been against anyhow, and security, I think my conscience told me that I had had it. . . . And it was a thing in my life I've regretted ever since.

Capra never made another film anywhere near as good as *It's a Wonderful Life.* And here is an example from life of the riddle of art, money, and a job to do. At Columbia, Capra had been a regular complainer, yet he had felt free to express himself—to do his best, to take risks—just because he lacked any final responsibility. Put to the test of liberty, he decided to sell the company. Jules Stein, the head of MCA (and thus Lew Wasserman's boss), was assigned to sell Liberty and he did, to Paramount (the studio his agency regularly favored): $4.1 million in Liberty assets going for 135,000 shares of Paramount stock (assessed at $23 per share).

The fact that stock was involved raises a crucial point, one that changed the film business. Income tax rates rose sharply in the late thirties and during the war. Thus the lavish Hollywood salaries were undercut by tax rates as high as 75 percent. But on capital gains, the same people paid only 25 percent. And so, all across the business, rewards were translated as quickly as possible from salary to shares. And thus, ownership became a much more urgent issue—but ownership for mere reward, as opposed to the burden of responsibility. Owning nearly a third of Liberty, Capra took Paramount stock he could sell for $1 million. In turn, he became a Paramount contract director at $3,000 a week, with no cut of the profits. Mr. Deeds had decided to stay home.

The story is sadder still with Preston Sturges, perhaps the most appealing director of the same era. Sturges was a sophisticated man, with business training: he had lived in Europe, and worked for his mother's cosmetics company. He was drawn to writing, first for the stage and then the movies, and as he watched his own scripts directed, he reckoned he could do that, too. He had just turned forty when he got the chance at Paramount. At $2,500 a week, rising to $3,250, he wrote and directed a string of pictures that still glow with good humor, affection, and a vivid sense of creeping madness: *The Great McGinty, Christmas in July, The Lady Eve, Sullivan's Travels, The Palm Beach Story, The Great Moment, The Miracle of Morgan's Creek, Hail the Conquering Hero.*

Not all of those films are equally good, but Sturges enjoyed several things at Paramount, beyond the resources of a great studio: the benevolent attentions of a fond production chief, William LeBaron; a fairly steadfast crew; and a house gang of supporting actors, to say nothing of Paramount contract stars as expert as Joel McCrea, Veronica Lake, Barbara Stanwyck, and Eddie Bracken. The budgets on the pictures stayed safely beneath a million dollars. The pictures flourished at the box office. That large thing, the war, was only a lever for farce.

"I loved Paramount," Sturges would write later. He also did what he could to develop the career of Billy Wilder at the studio, and to welcome French exile René Clair to America. In 1941, William LeBaron was replaced as production chief by Buddy DeSylva, and thereafter every decision seemed like a battle. A climax came when DeSylva wanted Ella Raines replaced on *Hail the Conquering Hero.* Sturges was devoted to his players and believed that the director should cast a picture. (Raines stayed.) Then there was the cutting. Paramount had the final cut on all Sturges pictures, and he wanted equality. It wasn't the money, Sturges said, and perhaps it wasn't, though cash flow was a recurrent problem in a scapegrace life that could easily have been material for one of his pictures. As Sturges put it:

My real contract with the studio was the loyalty and affection I felt for it; the privilege of thirty days' notice was protection for both of us. I said that I realized that I could not demand the decision on the final cut of a picture because that would make the picture my property, which it was not. On the other hand, I said I thought that they should recognize that I worked very hard to make a picture, spent many months with it before it was shot and was certainly closer to it than anyone else.

There's a nub of irresistible sense: Isn't it business wisdom to trust a director once you've hired his expertise and judgment? Who else has as much of the picture in his head all at once?

Sturges was too reasonable a gent. He agreed to a new seven-year contract, if after every picture he had a two-week window to end the contract. He asked for that "to cause their production head, whoever he might be, to treat me with the courtesy due a grown man of known integrity and not like an irresponsible child. I said no man of value could stand the existing situation very long. If he could stand it, he would no longer be a man of value."

Paramount declined this qualification. They offered more money instead. But Sturges was firm. A Paramount executive, Frank Freeman, made a small bet that if the director quit, a year later he wouldn't have made a film. A grim prophecy. Sturges went into misguided alliance with Howard Hughes, one result of which was the travesty *Vendetta*, a film of many directors, including Max Ophüls (at $750 a week), all in the attempt to reveal Faith Domergue as a beauty and an actress. These years, Sturges would say, with a humor the screen begged for, were "accompanied by the gentle laughter of the I.R.S." Sturges's marriage ended. His popular Los Angeles restaurant, The Players, was forced to close. He did find a new deal, at Twentieth Century–Fox, for the prodigious sum of $8,750 a week, to do *Unfaithfully Yours* (which cost $2 million).

Nearly bankrupt, Sturges was released by Fox because he had been so thoroughly at odds with Darryl Zanuck, and so nostalgic for Paramount. Just a few years before, much had been different, he lamented to Zanuck:

> When I remember that I made *The Lady Eve* for $666,000 and *The Miracle of Morgan's Creek* for $775,000, I am outraged to see the slow, demoralizing, enthusiasm-sapping, absurdly expensive methods of film production that are growing like a cancer in the heart of this industry, making ruinously dangerous, as you said yourself a year ago, all the forms

of interesting experimentation and removing all the long shots from a business that always has been and always will be a gamble.

What did Sturges mean by this "demoralizing" process in such a short space of time? Union demands for money, overtime, and prerogatives were more intrusive. The big-name talent was exerting new leverage. Sam Briskin, at Liberty, had voiced the new equation: "It is no longer possible to make cheap films, and there is no point in making expensive films without aiming for the highest attainable qualities because they will not return a profit." But there was also the sudden falloff in audiences, a move away from pictures which no one could explain. But Sturges was also exposed by postwar peace. The self-contained farce of his wartime movies was a precious consolation during the war, but comedy after 1945 suddenly faced a new kind of existential dismay. It was not until *Some Like It Hot,* in 1959, that Billy Wilder got close to the spirit of Sturges's best films.

By then, Sturges was dead, after several years in France looking for a way out. It is one of the saddest of Hollywood endings, and one that presents filmmaking not just as a gamble, but as a precarious sanity prey to the seething human misunderstandings that make Sturges's films so funny still. If there is a lesson, it may be just to seize your moment in Hollywood and let the future go hang. Preston Sturges never quite knew what he had, let alone how he lost it.

Capra and Sturges were would-be artists more reliant on the factory system than they knew. Still, they are both celebrated in film history—Capra as a hero in his own time, Sturges as one of those masters who, somehow, someway, never got an Oscar nomination as director. *The Lady Eve,* I'd suggest, is one of those movies fit to be seen today or tomorrow without a word of qualification, without even the admission that it is sixty years old. To be that age and still so smart and sexy!

Now consider another career from the golden age, that of a man who seldom had a home to call his own. This man worked in Hollywood from 1936 for twenty years. His pictures, in order, had these owners and distributors: M-G-M; Walter Wanger and United Artists; Paramount; Twentieth Century–Fox (three films in a row); Arnold Productions and United Artists; Christie Corporation, International Pictures, and RKO; Paramount; Diana Productions and Universal; United States Pictures and Warner Brothers; Diana and Universal-International; Fidelity Pictures and Republic; Twentieth Century–Fox; Superior Pictures and Columbia; Fidelity and RKO; Wald-Krasna Productions and RKO; Blue Gardenia

Productions–Gloria Films–Warner Brothers; Columbia; M-G-M; RKO for two.

In his American career Fritz Lang visited every major and minor distributor. It is a classic story of instability, hustling, and Lang's unique, impervious self-assertion with hardly an emphatic box-office hit to his name. Seldom seen without his monocle, autocratic and even cruel in his manner to actors, Lang held himself in Hollywood as one of the masters of cinema history. He was the most prominent figure from the great age of German Expressionism, the director of *M*, of *Metropolis* (a futuristic vision that cost $1 million in 1927, and might have been four times that sum if shot in America), and the Dr. Mabuse films. Hollywood, he implied, was lucky to have him.

At the same time, he was forced to take on rank assignments, inflated B-pictures, and minor players. Mocked behind his back for being so "Teutonic," he was a Hollywood character without ever being accepted or welcomed. By contrast, Ernst Lubitsch, who had come to America ten years ahead of Lang, rose to a position in charge of production at Paramount, made a string of hits, and was universally popular and invited out. You can argue that Lang never captured or cared about American moods and idioms. He simply transferred his stark, pessimistic view to American assignments and survived as he was bumped from one place to another.

Apart from the brief period at Diana Productions (where Lang was a partner with Walter Wanger and Wanger's wife, Joan Bennett), Lang was never paid more than $50,000 for doing a picture. On *Moonfleet* (in 1955 at M-G-M) he was paid $48,000; twelve years earlier, on *Hangmen Also Die!*, he got $45,000. Again, except for the Diana pictures, Lang never qualified for a single percentage point. He did his job and hurried on. When he died in 1976 (still living in Hollywood, which he regarded as home), his house was worth about $700,000 and he had another $200,000 in the bank. These are the numbers you might expect of a crew member, not a director.

He was too proud, too fierce to admit to being disappointed, let alone crushed. And he had a strange comfort: humiliated in status, reduced in money, treated like an outcast, Fritz Lang never yielded in his way of seeing. To step quickly from business to art, the pictures Lang made in America include ten that are riveting, chillingly ambivalent, works of "pure" cinema inasmuch as they depend on composition, lighting, the sheer structure of the image. Lang was a genius, and I suspect he would have done it all for free—*Fury, You Only Live Once, Man Hunt, Hangmen Also*

Die!, The Woman in the Window, Ministry of Fear, Scarlet Street, The Big Heat, Human Desire, Beyond a Reasonable Doubt.

In all those movies, the language is American. The actors—Edward G. Robinson, Glenn Ford, Ray Milland, Joan Bennett, Sylvia Sidney, Gloria Grahame—are American. Yet they are taking place less in a fixed locality than on a universal sound stage and in the cold mind of a camera. If you want to try one, and be surprised, see *Ministry of Fear,* a lesser-known film, ostensibly placed in wartime London, yet actually a study in doorways, thresholds, entrances, and exits. Lang is as unattractive personally as Preston Sturges is winning. Yet I'm not sure if Fritz Lang isn't one of the best examples of people who simply sacrificed themselves to their art.

You can argue that Lang never appreciated the golden nature of his Hollywood, just as he never grasped (or was impressed by) the nature of America. But Howard Hawks is his obverse: a man insouciant about where he worked, yet equally confident that in any factory or range he would re-create his world and vision. Hawks made many films touched by darkness, yet taken as a whole his work is more than golden. It is a paradise. This is not just because of the optimistic, fantasizing vision of men and women; it's because Hawks sees movies as a garden of delights, a playground, a way of holding back mortality even. Hawks was a man who rode in his own aura of success and happiness, as much as Lang was forever cornered by darkness and dismay. He was also a natural businessman and a lifelong winner. As Quentin Tarantino put it, "He's just too damned enjoyable."

After the great success of his flying picture *The Dawn Patrol* (1930), Hawks made a directing deal with First National for $25,000 a picture (the results were *The Criminal Code,* on loan, *The Crowd Roars,* and *Tiger Shark*). His rate jumped up when Goldwyn gave him $60,000 to do *Barbary Coast,* which turned out to be one of his duller efforts. By the late thirties, he had a new contract with RKO at $130,000 a year.

Part of that deal was the undying *Bringing Up Baby,* where the blithe sublimity of the picture makes a pretty contrast with its financial turmoil. With Cary Grant hired in for $75,000 and Katharine Hepburn at $72,500 (plus 5 percent of the gross from $600,000–$750,000 and 7.5 percent after that—a lady, but a careerist, too), the picture was budgeted at just over $767,000. After all, it was a small comedy to be filmed entirely on sound stages. But Hawks fell in love with its rare madness and fussed no end to get the dream just right. RKO did not stop him. There were overages for the stars (they ended up taking $120,000 each) and the picture finally went over $1 million.

But it did disappointing business from the start. Hawks guessed that it was because there was no one normal in the film (though the leopard is like most leopards you meet). Today that is regarded as the brilliance of the film. Still, it did only $715,000 domestically, with another $390,000 from foreign. The studio lost money (after the marketing costs), and it was a principal reason why Katharine Hepburn was labeled "box-office poison."

As a result, *Only Angels Have Wings* and *His Girl Friday* (both at Columbia) were done a touch more modestly. They are masterpieces of the factory system, in which there is a kind of exultant, enclosed bliss to the pictures, as if to say how blessed we are to be shut up in this kind of factory. The newsroom in *Friday,* the South American airfield in *Angels,* are both cloud-cuckoo island settings (patently fabricated) for Hawks's dream of how he wanted the world to be. But they are also containers for some of the best, subtlest talk and interaction ever put on the American screen.

So Hawks's reputation was strong again. For *Sergeant York* (in truth a dud, but his biggest hit) he got $85,000 and for *Ball of Fire,* at Goldwyn, he was paid $100,000. That led to the Warner Brothers contract that gave him $100,000 a picture for doing *Air Force, To Have and Have Not,* and *The Big Sleep;* I'm not sure if anyone has ever made pictures that are such smart fun (and with Lauren Bacall a discovery of Hawks and his new wife, Nancy "Slim" Gross, and under personal contract to them, starting at $750 a week).

With steady box office success, Hawks then came to what I think he anticipated as the climax of his career, *Red River.* For the first time, he went independent. He, Slim, and his agent Charles Feldman set up Monterey Productions for the picture. Feldman (one of the great Hollywood operators, and a terrific character—poker-player, womanizer, bon vivant, and producer of *A Streetcar Named Desire* and *The Group*) raised the money from a variety of sources, including a big loan from the Security-First National Bank. Hawks was paid $125,000 to produce and direct. But as majority owners of Monterey, he and Slim were to get 57 percent of the film's profits.

Everything seemed poised. (I think it's worth noting how far *Red River* itself is about a hazardous business venture—getting cattle to the railhead. Still, cattle *are* tricky.) The Arizona location had mixed weather. And Hawks was at his dream again. A picture initially budgeted at $1.25 million went as high as $2.8 million. Feldman yelped but he could not restrain Hawks, who felt he had a masterpiece in the making, especially with the bold, clashing casting of John Wayne and Montgomery Clift. Talk about chemistry: the Duke looked at Clift and thought the stripling bisexual was feeble. But Clift had a New York acting style that only pushed Wayne into working harder on his greatest performance.

Can anyone now say Hawks was wrong? My own devotion to *Red River* is too strong to hear protests. It is the first film I saw twice. Its domestic rentals (released by United Artists) were $4.15 million—a smash hit. Alas, all manner of trouble (and extortion) came with the extra loans needed to get done. Then Howard and Slim broke up. There were intense cash flow problems. Hawks directed *A Song Is Born* for $250,000 in order to get by. But the business of *Red River* was prolonged and full of trouble. For years, creditors pursued it and blocked any profits. In the end, as part of Monterey, Hawks got just a few thousand more. So the picture ranks in history as both a smash and a dud. It doesn't matter. You can see it. Hawks had gone for his dream. He had labored to make it "right" and beautiful. And he paid for it.

So, yes, there was gold to be had, but what's so tricky to grasp today is the curious way in which money could betray such things as honest, forthright, independent ambition, and hide within the forms of factory filmmaking that were allegedly uncongenial. Yet nothing would slow the urge to independence, and maybe every reader's temperament must decide how far that urge was driven by hopes of art or dreams of money.

It's obvious, I think, that the factory could be a very warm and supportive place, just as freedom could add more burdens to the ordeal of making a film than many "artists" could endure. But the factory system was losing power and confidence for other reasons, yet to be described. And in the end, the studios would push most filmmakers out into the cold of going it alone. Enough of them would make fortunes so that nothing can kill the legend of "independence" in American filmmaking, or in America as a whole. It's something we love to believe in, just as Hawks was drawn to the flame of happiness. But have no doubt: in the hills that are the thirties and forties there is gold still (I have picked out only a fraction of it), a study of which can reorient your ideas of what the cinema is, and ought to be.

What is fascinating still, in an illustration of American energy as much as Hollywood ambition, is how it was possible to persuade yourself that you were mainstream, professional, businesslike, and "Hollywood" while being defiantly personal. But such figures were really producers more than directors. We are coming to the greatest, and the most self-destructive (he would have wanted every title): David O. Selznick.

Divorce as a bond in DNA: Max von Mayerling (Erich von Stroheim) attends his ex-wife, Norma Desmond (Gloria Swanson), at the close of *Sunset Blvd.*, 1950 *(Kobal Collection)*

15 · DIVORCE, HOLLYWOOD STYLE

L ove and marriage are the inevitable destinations of so many movies. As late as 1955, in *Our Town* on TV, there was Frank Sinatra being as wide-eyed as possible, singing "love and marriage . . . go together like a horse and carriage" (a rather clunky, lurching song by Sammy Cahn and Jimmy Van Heusen—one wheel seems to be coming off), and hoping to have us overlook his tempestuous and recent history with Nancy Barbato and Ava Gardner. Indeed, he was trying to let himself forget it—so that he might start again. And again. Sinatra may be the mythic instance of erotic impulse (Gardner remarked that though he weighed only 110 pounds, 105 of that was cock), still he had the modern itch, the movie urge—why not fuck everyone?

Already, that way of putting things points to a large rift (or explosion) in the way movie follows other narrative arts. The history of the novel observes it catering to a new middle-class interest in the questions Whom shall I marry? and Should I seek "love" or "gratification" in those unions, or "security"? Those questions combine an interest in the individual need for happiness and a larger notion of a respectable and respect-worthy society, where marriage may hold people in place, in self-respect as well as good social standing, even in an age that is losing its religious imperatives.

The proper pursuit of marriage (managed as comedy or tragedy) is something that binds Jane Austen and Tolstoy, George Eliot and Proust. The reunion of union, and its sexual affirmation (albeit in language that troubled censors) is the conclusion to *Ulysses;* it is the question left hanging at the end of *The Portrait of a Lady;* and it is the wretched social noose that strangles the romanticism in *Madame Bovary.*

Of course, there is more to those novels than love and marriage. But the novelists seem to have leaned toward the lifelong preoccupation of so many readers—and female readers, allegedly (Am I happy? Is it folly even to ask that question?)—just as they are working out an intricate social morality supple enough to accommodate human weakness (or is being helplessly in love a strength?).

The novel is a fixed thing: a block of paper and binding, held in two hands, resting in the lap—solid, graspable, immediate. Its type is set; its pages cut and numbered; its end is white space. A book is an object, a piece of property; the act of reading is drawn forward by human attention and understanding. That is another model for our responsibility in life, and in love. Just as our gaze moves over words progressively (in advance and accumulation), scanning them, registering them, and determining meaning, so we are encouraged by the fact of the book to see, identify, grasp, and choose. Books teach us to talk, to think, to be literary; thus novels school us through the lives of characters.

Transfer this formula to the movies, and strange things begin to happen. The "thingness" of a movie is largely absent for the audience. It is a phantom imprint of light so powered that we feel our own insignificance. The show turns over without us. We cannot lay hands on it. Because it keeps moving on, we are under no burden to recognize, grasp, identify, and choose. We can let it wash over us, just as a voyeur need take no responsibility for the things he can see. And because our conscious decision-making power is less involved, so another part of ourselves emerges—passive, pliant, thrilled, fantasizing, drawn to witness wild, dangerous, impossible things, and to be thrilled by the rare advantage we have gained over physics, consequence, and damage. Not really there.

We are, therefore, less inclined to fix upon the means of choice in love and marriage than yield to the parade of dreams that are more likely to become glamorous and sexual, as opposed to matters of character and context. We have found another level of consciousness: to pass through shared reality well enough, but to keep a special private room alive behind our eyes, the one where anything is permitted, the one where every dutiful husband may be a Bluebeard. More than that, we may be inclined to give up on the old real life because of the infinite glories of the fantasies, the dreams.

I have compressed this argument, though I hope you can see how far it extends matters to do with the nature of viewing, the dark, and cinemas that I have already discussed. It is not a small extension either, for it has to do with the speed with which a rational, humanist society might give up on its own codes. And that is a terrible insight into the technology of all media, and the way their innate messages may overwhelm the things authors believe they are saying.

Why do we divorce more now? How do we feel about it? We are very proud of being cool, modern, and up to date, but if we are attached to a medium which in its deepest being urges detachment I am very afraid. The English literary critic and teacher F. R. Leavis spoke of "the common pursuit." He believed that to read was to examine moral life (as opposed to being merely entertained). He was severe and humorless about it, and chronically elitist. Whereas education has everyone to deal with. That's one reason why, after 1950, entertainment came to be welcomed as art. That made for great benefits and one real problem: that movie hardly cares if we are in pursuit. What follows in this chapter, and in the book as a whole, is an attempt to account for the anxiety this causes, and to wonder whether it is avoidable.

Take Howard Hawks and Nancy "Slim" Gross. Hawks had been married first to Athole Shearer, the sister of Norma, which made him Irving Thalberg's brother-in-law, not a bad spot to occupy in terms of career, and proof that Howard was "in" as far as Hollywood society was concerned. These were chums who played fierce croquet together on the rolled lawns of Bel Air. But Athole was not well. No one exactly knows what the problem was; she had some kind of disturbed mind—which isn't to say that Howard's fucking around didn't disturb her, too.

On August 30, 1938, at the Clover Club (off Sunset), the town's most prestigious gambling establishment, Howard met Nancy. She was twenty-one, tall, blonde, very smartly dressed, and devastatingly attractive—"like a knife," Irene Selznick would say. She was attended that night by two men, the actor Bruce Cabot (dumb; you recall *King Kong,* where he is the hero) and Albert Broccoli (smart; he would later launch the James Bond pictures). These guys fell back as Nancy met Hawks. Howard was tall, urbane, handsome, classy, intimidating—everything about him was trained for that last quality. He was a knockout who hid behind his own suave façade. He would have been laughable if the screen hadn't redeemed his coolness. Her autobiography takes up the story:

"Do you want to be in movies?" he asked her, dancing. It was his regular come-on; it still is for countless would-be seducers in the picture business.

"No," she told him.

"You don't?" he said. That quickly, she took control. It was a flip-flop that Hawks did on-screen more deftly than anyone, which was not always the case in life. But the charm of meeting your own ideal character can be enormous.

Though he was old enough to be her father, it was a meeting of well-matched adversaries. Love followed, with sex. And there was a period of several years when "Slim," as he called her, was not just Howard's fashion plate companion, wife, and partner, but his muse. You can feel her behind Jean Arthur and Rita Hayworth in *Only Angels Have Wings,* Barbara Stanwyck in *Ball of Fire,* and Joanne Dru in *Red River*—attractive, talkative, smart, feisty, intelligent. And it was "Slim" who first saw Betty Perske's picture in a magazine, proposed her to Hawks, and then served as model for the clothes and the insolent back-chat that established Lauren Bacall as that stranded yet very sophisticated figure in *To Have and Have Not.*

But don't forget the lovely, sinister ambivalence of that title. Isn't it the mood and the predicament of the usherette in Hopper's *New York Movie*—being at the movies, yet not quite having them; watching fantasy, without owning it? (But if you owned fantasy, might that kill it, like marriage?) Slim was too smart for Hawks. She came to realize that her lover, husband, and partner was a devout fantasist: he looked at you but he saw the screen of possibility. They were happy for a while, but he wanted more, the impossible, or anyone he noticed. He had wanted Bacall (he did own her), but she had a choice and preferred the guy in the toupee, Bogart. In the end, Howard's wandering eye (a camera term, if you like) proved too much for stability or trust. He was always moving on, looking farther ahead. And though he got older, the girls he noticed stayed the same age. So there was a divorce, and in California, that land of communal property in marriage, it was an item significant in depriving Howard of his full rewards on *Red River*.

I do not intend to waste time "proving" some connection between the movies and divorce. Even if you are inclined to see the movies and divorce as very American habits, still the connection is persuasive. So let us just notice that, in the years from 1900 to 1950, the incidence of divorced men rose in America from 0.3 to 2 percent. In the next fifty years, it leaped ahead from 2 to 8.6 percent. Yes, of course, divorce had operated earlier, in the famous "Western" era when families could be broken up by pioneering journeys and bigamous ties entered into. (Natalie Wood in *The Searchers* surely marries the Comanche chief "Scar" before her uncle Ethan—John Wayne—springs a pragmatic divorce.) By 1915, when one in seven American marriages ended in divorce, the figure was one in five in Los Angeles (and one in four in San Francisco). Open space and a relative absence of law stimulated breakups. But give some credit to the infinite space of the screen's suggestion in so many ways—be someone else, start again.

And certainly divorce was affected by the separations caused by war, and by the decline in religious faith. It was also a taboo practice that accelerated the more generally it occurred. And for many people, divorce was most observable in that most publicized version of pioneering, Hollywood lifestyle. Let us simply refer to that enormous extra, tidal pull toward new dreams—how next week's picture could seem more lustrous than this week's—and the way the whole dynamic of the movies played upon romantic transformation.

That is too imprecise to prove, yet too suggestive to forget. And let me point to an intriguing instance of what can happen in the willful ignoring of such things. One of the best academic books on the movies published in America is Stanley Cavell's *Pursuits of Happiness*. Cavell is a philosopher, but a man crazy about movies—and with great taste. His book dwells with affection and great value on *The Lady Eve, It Happened One Night, Bringing Up Baby, The Philadelphia Story, His Girl Friday, Adam's Rib,* and *The Awful Truth*. In the course of its argument, it suggests that there was a genre, fit to be compared with late Shakespeare or Mozart opera—the "Hollywood comedy of remarriage."

If I look closely at just one of Cavell's group of films, it ought to be *His Girl Friday*, one more Hawks film made under the sign of Slim. It's very telling that Hawks had taken the setup from its literary original—*The*

Front Page, a play by Ben Hecht and Charles MacArthur—and added marital confusion. This time the editor's (Cary Grant's) crack reporter is also his wife (Rosalind Russell)—his ex-wife, actually—a woman who has despaired of his trickery, his chauvinism, his steady overlay of fiction on the fact of marriage, and opted instead for a plain, decent husband (a role wickedly lampooned in the casting of the cheerful Ralph Bellamy).

The editor and the reporter have work to do, and Grant's first ruse to keep Russell is simply to point her at the reporting job that only she can do. She falls for this—or is she merely admitting the very odd rules of their game? For affinity and love shine out of this couple. The bond is heard and felt in the way they quarrel and argue (the best evidence of love in Hawks's world). Have they divorced just to ensure the need for a fresh wooing? Is their love contingent on the endlessly renewable fantasy of breaking up so that they can find each other again? Is this love's shrewdest response to the slipperiness of film?

Cavell sees the new "affair" they have as a step toward maturity. I'm not so sure that it isn't dire evidence of the way Grant has found a game (a kind of moveable croquet) he and Russell can play that puts off real life. Whatever your shading to that answer, *His Girl Friday* remains not just the fastest-talking romantic comedy ever made, but a very tricky inquiry into love's need for a chase (or a dream) and the sharpest pointer to uncertain gender roles. It is also one more film that functions like an elaborate closed box, looking in upon itself; it is a model of film's self-reflexive attitude and its impenetrable paradise.

There are many other movies from the golden age that deal in some way with "remarriage," and thus with divorce. Cavell ably demonstrates how often the best of these pictures move from an immature love or marriage to one that is more mature. Excellent both as criticism and as a new model for life, his book is too bound to academe to venture to Hollywood itself. (Though Hawks came close to that subject—the professor in the madhouse—in *Ball of Fire.*) Many of our film critics have been similarly timid of having their judgment warped or stained by contact with the actual world of filmmaking. So Cavell never once asks us, or himself, what all this talk of remarriage has to do with the high hopes of a community increasingly reliant on divorce. Well, let's just say that in this book I have done what I can to persuade Cavell to sit down at Spago, watch the girls drifting by on a summer evening, and feel the air fragrant with opportunity and danger.

Not that love, marriage, and divorce are always user-friendly or damage-free. Terrible human energies and needs are expressed in them. What follows is the story of one divorce, presented to show that movies were still a family business, with its historical destiny worked out in terms of unhealed domestic wounds in a city that still felt like a village seething with rivalries, competition, and the urge to triumph. It is also a chance to examine one film, a notable film, and trace the interaction of money and art, business and dream.

In 1936, David and Irene Selznick had their second son, Daniel; Jeffrey had been born in 1932. They were established in their fine new house on Summit Drive (designed by Roland Coate) in the twisty lanes of Beverly Hills. This was also the first full year since David's new company, Selznick International, had been established—the move into independence that he had always promised himself, after years at Paramount, RKO, and M-G-M as a successful production executive. Here was a producer determined to own his own pictures, to make the things he wanted to make and to do so with the greatest care possible. Selznick did not think of himself as an artist, but he believed in first-class entertainment and showmanship.

Put that way, it all seems admirable and in the realm of perfection. But life had been more muddled or stormy. Louis B. Mayer despised the very name "Selznick"; he believed that David's father, Lewis, had behaved like a rogue, a pirate, and a shameless hustler in a business that cried out for dignity and propriety. There was much humbug in Mayer's attitude, but any crack in his soul was masked by anger and his overwhelming self-dramatizing.

This does not imply simple dishonesty. Mayer was a natural actor; he did it all the time, without planning, rehearsal, or script. He needed to propel life into melodrama. In this frame of mind he caused a tempest of alarm when he heard that David wanted to marry Irene. Irene was his favorite: she was smarter and stronger than her sister Edie. He admired her more. He saw more of his own intelligence and severity in her. He talked to her more. And he put on her a greater load of attention and expectation. He left her profoundly uneasy about letting him down, and that trauma remained, years after David and Mayer were both dead. I think Mayer loved her. Well, of course, you say, he was her father. More than that. There was an oppressive tension between them, expressed as respect, duty, and obedience. Mayer was sexually very confused: he was "owner" of so many young women, their master for seven years. He knew that other executives, his son-in-law included, took advantage of that. But he was also pledged to family, decency, and propriety. He did flirt with some actresses, but he went in dread of being discovered with them. I say this to convey the emotional prison in which Irene grew up, no matter that it looked like the beach house in Santa Monica.

David liberated Irene from that prison, and gave her a hope of freedom from her father, but not without terrible disputes in the Mayer house, prolonged scenes where Mayer deplored David and asked her not to leave. She would not give in; she was smart and modern enough to know she had to leave.

But then David betrayed her, in all the ways a casual egotist could find. He had a flirty eye, and he was of that moviemaker disposition too good-natured to let all those aspiring actresses throw themselves at you without dallying here and there. Irene could handle that. She found it harder to accept that David was also a helpless gambler (Irene was the kind of hawk who could wait days, expecting to find someone's lost dime), so she did all she could to keep that under control and to keep him working. Because when David worked, things happened: at RKO alone, when he was head of production for a couple of years, he made or initiated *Symphony of Six Million, What Price Hollywood?, Bird of Paradise, A Bill of Divorcement, Topaze, King Kong,* and *Little Women.*

But in 1933, as his father died, and David felt very insecure, he yielded to an offer to join M-G-M, to work for his father-in-law, and to be the lever that might be used in ousting Irving Thalberg. Irving, by then, was too fragile for Mayer to count on, and too difficult. So "the son-in-law also rises" (as one trade paper put it) was a way of intimidating Thalberg and humiliating David. Irene was violently opposed to that move, and so angry that the marriage nearly ended. For she felt that she was the person most emotionally threatened and compromised by it. Like her father, she needed to be a center of attention.

At M-G-M, Selznick actually made friends with Irving, and did very good work by the studio's standards: *Dinner at Eight, Dancing Lady, Viva Villa!, Manhattan Melodrama, David Copperfield, Anna Karenina, A Tale of Two Cities.* But he was irked and wounded by the weakness that had made him cave in to L.B. He said he longed for independence. In fact, I suspect that any real solitude terrified him. However, he was nowhere near rich enough to buy freedom. Instead, he took a step never really attempted by Hollywood before. He looked to get funding from old money, East Coast society people amused by the movies and ready to take a flutter. In particular, and very much with Irene's help (she was deeply moved by WASP respect), he made friends with Jock Whitney, heir to one of America's largest fortunes. They became the leading partners in Selznick International, though two smaller backers of note were Irving Thalberg and Myron Selznick.

And it was in 1936, without really reading the book, but on advice from a couple of readers and secretaries, that David paid $50,000 for the film rights to a forthcoming novel, *Gone With the Wind*, by Margaret Mitchell.

For over a year, he underestimated that project; then it began to overwhelm him, so that he put it off. Without intending it, the delay contrived to increase public anticipation for the film. Waiting for *Gone With the Wind* became a sport, especially when the book proved a mighty bestseller. And to capitalize on that mood, while holding off the dread day of actual filming, Selznick launched a search for the "ideal" Scarlett O'Hara, sorting through the cities of the South as well as the talent agencies of Hollywood. George Cukor, a chum to the Selznicks and David's favorite director, was hired to run that search and to supervise the tests of possible candidates. Meanwhile the noted playwright Sidney Howard was engaged to do a screenplay.

Howard was paid $2,000 a week to do that screenplay. A draft was delivered by February 1937, surprisingly close to what was filmed in the end. But between then and the close of production, many other writers were hired to add their improving touches, so that the final sum paid to writers was $146,000 (still well under 5 percent of the total costs even if one adds in the $50,000 paid to Mitchell). I stress that because at every stage Selznick was adamant about his desire to stay faithful to the novel.

Cukor's deal was a mark of Selznick's affection, yet it also made clear the high status of the director under the factory. Cukor had been Selznick International's first employee: offered $3,250 a week plus 5 percent of the producer's gross, he settled for a flat $4,000 a week (Myron was his agent). Ironically, he never made a picture for Selznick International, but the company loaned him out on other projects (at a profit). By the time shooting began (January 1939), Cukor had received over $300,000 for being "on" the project, organizing the search and shooting the many tests. To this day, I'm not sure if any director has been as well compensated without directing the film.

By mid-1938, therefore, *GWTW* had not only direct costs to meet, but had signaled a clear warning that it would be a very long film (well over two hours). The prospective budget was above $2 million; $3 million was more likely. Yet Selznick had no cast. And he faced the fact that, no matter who played Scarlett, the widespread public wisdom was that Clark Gable (who belonged to M-G-M) was nature's Rhett.

Selznick had considered others—Gary Cooper, Errol Flynn, Ronald Colman—but every pondering came back to Gable. There was another consideration. Selznick International had a general agreement with

United Artists to distribute its pictures. But *GWTW* had been held back from that arrangement. Thus it was that Selznick got back into discussions with Mayer for a large deal that might bring him Gable (and some needed production money) and give M-G-M (through Loew's) the right to distribute the movie. By this time, of course, it was clear that *GWTW* had to be a major success. Anything less would likely destroy Selznick International.

It's not clear what part Irene played in these talks. But David needed some coaxing, and L.B. had to be told not to say I told you so. The negotiations were handled as regular business. But a father and daughter do not easily abandon their private lines of communication, and Irene always felt troubled that she was being used by both the men in her life as a go-between, in danger of betraying their trust and losing her own integrity. The matter was the more complicated in that, just as Selznick International considered the Metro offer, it was discussing a deal with Warner Brothers, too, which would have supplied Errol Flynn and Bette Davis, along with Olivia de Havilland for Melanie, and a cash contribution of $2.1 million. In addition, Warners was asking a distribution fee of only 17.5 percent (not just very low, but an indicator of how inflated distribution fees were in general).

That was a very good deal. Flynn and Davis would have worked, and Selznick stood a better chance financially. M-G-M offered Gable (though Selznick would have to pay his fee of $150,000), money, and a 50-50 share of profits.

Selznick chose the Mayer deal, and one can point to several reasons: Gable was a compelling choice—as yet, Selznick had not realized that it was a story about Scarlett; Loew's was the outstanding distributor in the world; and it was family. We'll never know exactly what pressures were exerted, but the terms of the deal are known: Selznick got Gable (whether he liked it or not, and he didn't) plus $1.25 million toward the budget. In return, Loew's would distribute, charge a 20 percent distribution fee, and then take 50 percent of the profits. The contract was for seven years: after that, the split would be 75 percent to Selznick International and 25 percent to M-G-M.

Such wrangling was novel in 1938, but it represented the future of the film business. Selznick's discussions with Warners and Metro are typical of the arguments that go on to this day when most films are set up on a unique, independent basis. The haggling over points here and there; the reckoning on distribution deals and terms of contract—these things are vital. And if directors do not work as often as they once did it is because they are struggling with such things, because those matters have become as important as the dream of the project itself.

The "King" was loaned out: the $150,000 Selznick paid M-G-M to get
Gable was money that represented more than half of his annual salary of
$272,000 (almost certainly the top in the business then). This is important
backstory for what followed, and a signal of how feeble star power might
be. Metro appreciated Gable's pull at the box office. But in the class system that obtained at the studio, Gable, as well as Joan Crawford and Jean
Harlow, was from the wrong side of the tracks, whereas Norma Shearer,
Garbo, Jeanette MacDonald, and Spencer Tracy were socially acceptable.

Gable, the son of an oil rigger, was obliged to give up school at age fourteen. He spent years as a laborer, roaming the country, before some deep
resolve to act got him into acting classes. Or was it that the teacher,
Josephine Dillon, had an eye for the young lout? Whatever, though fourteen years older than he was, she married him. A career was under way,
but it fed the legend early on that Gable might have been a gigolo, or
worse. It was a shady aura that he had in common with Joan Crawford
(and they responded with a decade-long affair, often palpable on screen).

With both Leslie Howard and Olivia de Havilland, Selznick was able to
make bargains in kind: Howard would play Ashley Wilkes for a modest fee
if he could co-direct *Intermezzo;* and de Havilland was essentially traded
for a one-option deal on Jimmy Stewart held by Selznick International.
(You can see how indignant the amiable Stewart might be by then, being
treated as a get-out-of-jail card.) As a result, by the start of shooting on
GWTW, the entire star and cast budget was only $290,000. Which lets you
know how cheaply the greatest coup, Scarlett, came.

The search for Scarlett had been both a publicity campaign and a true
neurosis on Selznick's part. He tested a great many people, from Tallulah
Bankhead to Jean Arthur, who were hardly plausible in the part. He very
seriously considered Katharine Hepburn, and she was anxious to do it, but
he doubted she could be sexy enough. By late 1938, the most promising
contender was Paulette Goddard (Chaplin's wife and the Selznicks' neigh-
bor). She is funny, sexy, and cunning in her tests. She could have done it.
Nor can anyone question Bette Davis's cool estimate: "It could have been
written for me. . . . It was insanity that I not be given Scarlett. But then,
Hollywood has never been rational."

Selznick was still holding out as the day approached, December 10,
1938, on which he would do the picture's first shoot: the burning of
Atlanta. For that, he intended putting the match to most of the old sets on
his lot, with stand-ins as Rhett and Scarlett desperately fleeing in a horse
and carriage. The main shoot was still over a month away. Paulette Goddard was the favorite. Hepburn was there. But Selznick was a gambler in

all things, and for once in his life he was about to win. (And gamblers need just one big win to persuade them that risk is a norm.)

Yet again, family rivalry played its part. The London office of the Myron Selznick agency had heard about a Vivien Leigh. She had done a few films only, sounding very South Kensington. But her greater claim to fame was as Laurence Olivier's mistress. Olivier, too, was a Myron Selznick client and in the fall of 1938 he came, alone, to Hollywood to play Heathcliff in Goldwyn's *Wuthering Heights*. Vivien Leigh arrived later, on her own—or prompted by Myron. And on the night of December 10, after dark, so that Selznick first saw her face in the glow of the fire, Myron introduced the two of them, with his usual needle: "Hey, genius, here's your Scarlett O'Hara!"

Selznick was impressed. That night, Leigh and Cukor read over a few scenes. She knew them by heart; she had bought the novel the day it came out in London; her belief in her right to the role was as strong as Bette Davis's. She was cast. In effect, the famous search had found an unknown. And to top off the search, and in one of the great pieces of Hollywood casting, Vivien Leigh was to be paid $1,250 a week for a guaranteed sixteen weeks. It was less than the weekly rate Scott Fitzgerald got for trying to improve the script.

Even at the end of production, the above-the-line budget costs were only as follows:

Story	$50,000
Script	46,196
Cast	358,556
Direction	363,596
Total	818,348

Yes, it's a lot of money for 1939, and more than the total cost of production of either *The Lady Eve* or *Citizen Kane*. But out of a final budget of about $4.1 million on *GWTW*, the main talents amounted to less than a quarter. The whole cast was cheaper than the direction, and recall that not one cast member on the film had a fraction of a point of profit participation. If the picture was going to succeed, then all the rewards were due to Selznick International and M-G-M. I stress that because in the fascinating comparisons between *GWTW* and today's blockbusters, the fiscal structure of the modern deal is so drastic. Never mind the numbers, if you were to make *GWTW* today (but *don't*), with, say, Russell Crowe, Nicole Kidman, two other stars, a big name director and a top screenwriter, the deal would look something like this:

Crowe and Kidman	$35 million
Two lesser stars	10 million
Script	3 million
Direction	5 million

That's $53 million before you turn over a foot of film, but it's also a very substantial percentage bargained away in advance—maybe as much as 20 percent of the gross; or 40 percent of the producer's profits. And, if in 1939 the actual costs of physical production amounted to another $3 million, what would they be today? Selznick made his film in Culver City and he had no Civil War battle scenes. Today, the movie would be shot in convincing locations (the real Georgia or Romania, say), and I can't conceive that a three-and-a-half-hour film would pass without scenes of massive on-screen slaughter. It would be at least a $150 million production, likely more. Which means that, after costs of marketing, it would need to earn about $400 million to show a profit, except that maybe 20 percent of the gross (the first dollar onward) would already be earmarked. So the profit point would be higher. Selznick's gamble, much mocked in its time, seems relatively carefree.

The film was shot. Cukor was fired, early on. Gossips say that was because Gable was irritated, or threatened, by Cukor's gay manner. I think that's silly prurience. Not even Gable had such power. More to the point, Cukor was bored stiff with the heavy, sentimental material (think of doing those Scarlett scenes so many times in tests!) and with Selznick's helpless interference. His footage lacked energy. So Victor Fleming was brought on (from M-G-M). Yes, he was a Gable chum, and a man better at action scenes. He was also a bloody-minded driver who would get the thing done—in those costumes in the terrible heat of Technicolor lighting, shooting six days a week. By the end of it all, Vivien Leigh was a wreck, hardly recognizable. But she had delivered a great performance, and in Scarlett's determination to survive at all costs, Selznick had found his model and become the film's true auteur.

Gone With the Wind is not art, not anywhere near it, but Selznick had come to identify with Scarlett O'Hara in a manner not unknown in art. And this is worth noting, for Hollywood, then and now, was horribly male-dominated and staunchly blind to the repeated evidence that women made up a majority of the audience, and apparently determined the choice of what film to see. It speaks to Hollywood's true horror of anything like a feminine sensibility that American moviemaking has been so defiant in overlooking that preponderance. Thus, the voyeuristic thrust of the medium stays male, and the employment of women in decisive jobs is risible. As a general principle, I would suggest that any potential reawakening of American film as a mainstream current may turn on how far the country can ever admit its feminine side. Of course, it was often necessary to be brave and manly on the frontier, but at the cost of eternal stupidity?

By December 1939 (with Europe at war), *GWTW* was ready to open—first in Atlanta, then in New York and Los Angeles. I think that opening must have felt like the climax to a great era just because of the uncertainty in Europe. By now, it is much more: *Gone With the Wind* is the movie of movies (so long as we don't have to sit through it again ourselves). Younger generations keep discovering it. One of the marvels of that picture is that its commercial life seems as endless as Scarlett's neediness, just as its striking definition of a smash hit (beyond ordinary, apologetic "success") has become not simply the El Dorado of the movie business, but its *raison d'être*. The movies shifted closer than ever toward gambling when they took the long-shot blockbuster success as a regular model.

How do we convey the empire of *Gone With the Wind*? As *GWTW* opened, it was calculated that Selznick International was in the red by nearly $2 million. In the United States alone in one year the film had rentals of $14 million. In its first run (extended by war), the picture had rentals of $31 million. Officially, in 1989 its rentals were estimated (in actual dollars) at $77.6 million, this after several reissues, but before its fiftieth-anniversary restoration. At that time, with the aid of A. D. Murphy of *Variety* and the finance department of Turner Entertainment (the owners of the film), it was estimated that (in 1987 dollars) *GWTW* had earned worldwide rentals of $841 million. In turn, that sum was said to be only 40 percent of the actual box office receipts.

This was a new kind of money: *How Green Was My Valley* (Best Picture of 1941) had rentals of $2.8 million; *San Francisco* (1936) had earned $2.7 million; *Snow White and the Seven Dwarfs,* Disney's first feature, did $8 million; *Going My Way* (1944) was at $6.5 million; *Casablanca* brought in $3.7 million.

There's another important point to be made: I'm not sure that any film ever made in Hollywood was more cared about by its maker. I've looked closely at the making of both *Gone With the Wind* and *Citizen Kane,* and I suspect that Welles shepherded his masterpiece with more insouciance than Selznick could ever have mustered. That's a part of what makes Welles the more interesting person, and the greater artist. Gravity and fatigue do not guarantee quality. But it's evident that the money and the triumph never much impressed Welles. He suspected he was that good;

the film was no more than confirmation. Selznick was truly terrified of his great project, and helped surround it with such obstacles that only super-human efforts got the film done. And Selznick cared about Hollywood's esteem, about beating his competitors, and about getting his hands on a packet of money.

But as Irene Selznick had guessed in her gloomy way, the closer David got to unimaginable success the closer he was to disaster. For she had inherited or learned her father's suspicion that David lacked character. But then how could anyone have ever run a studio if she persisted in hold-ing to tests of character?

David Selznick won Best Picture two years in a row, with *Gone With the Wind* and *Rebecca*. He had the stars Vivien Leigh, Joan Fontaine, and Ingrid Bergman under some kind of contract, as well as Alfred Hitchcock. He plunged into a strange mixture of egomania and depression—the one because he was such a master, the other because he had nothing left to achieve. He stopped making films. He was dismayed by the large drama of the war. He gathered money, he became a kind of agent (to rival his brother), he dwindled into being a studio head. The obsessiveness one needs to make pictures, or art, or whatever, was not there. He had always made product.

It may help to fix on that distinction by putting it this way: if a writer is writing a book and falls out of love with it, he or she can abandon it, burn it, forget it. You can stop if the art is not working to your own satisfaction. A product is more merciless. Once started you cannot get out of it—the machine is running, contracts must play out, consequences take their course.

Selznick gambled more. He also elected to take the profits from his picture. In the few years after its release, he gathered close to $3 million—the great killing of his life—and you can argue that he never survived it. He became a moneyed person such as he had not been before. He gam-bled more and lost more heavily. And he gambled with life. Where previ-ously he had flirtations and flings with many women, he found Jennifer Jones and was entrapped by her helplessness (her need to be looked after) and his defiant wish to make a great star of her. She was about as opposite to Irene as anyone could be, and that must have been a part of the attrac-tion. Irene saw the threat, and was furious and vengeful in quite terrible ways, for her own liberator had now betrayed himself.

Like others at this time, Selznick felt squeezed by the tax laws. Rather than lose more than 70 percent of his booty to the government, he looked for a capital gain. That meant liquidating his own company, and taking the profit in that form. He persuaded his partner, Jock Whitney, into that action. Whitney himself remarried at this time and gave up his Hollywood allegiances, so he was prepared to follow David's lead, but he was as close to Irene as he was to her errant husband. They had talked about David's self-destructiveness (Selznick was also on the verge of a nervous breakdown in these years; he was under professional care, an experience that found grotesque bloom in the movie *Spellbound*).

Initially, at least, there was a benign conspiracy between Jock and Irene to protect David from himself. Then there was Myron, a small but proud stockholder in Selznick International, but dying now from the effects of booze. His agency was breaking up. Still, as he had all his life, he warned David not to be an idiot—don't sell, he said, don't let that picture go.

Something else contributed to the tension: raw wealth. When David had married Irene, he had married upward: the Selznicks were broke, the Mayers were not. L.B. would have mentioned it. With the generosity that is also proprietary, Mayer embarked on a gesture to help make his daughters and their husbands secure. For Mayer had become a substantial shareholder in the 1935 merger of Twentieth Century and Fox. (No one ever questioned this, and Mayer does not seem to have intruded on the other studio's affairs, but the leverage was there.) He decided to give portions of the stock to Irene, to David, to Edie, and to her husband, William Goetz. David refused the offer, unwilling to be beholden to Mayer (this from the man who had to go to him later asking for Gable). So Irene got David's share, too. And in the late thirties, she gained tremendously on their dividends with the result that, by 1940, she was a lot richer than David. That was another reason why he took *GWTW* profits—because he couldn't stand her nagging over his gambling, or her implied superiority. Irene's way of implying could lower the temperature in a room.

So the situation in 1942 is as follows: David unstable, manic-depressive, infatuated with Jennifer Jones, an open faucet with cash; Irene, wronged, vengeful, conspiratorial, capitalistic, and very wary of great assets being squandered. She was her father's daughter, and for a woman who craved emotional force behind her, that was the home to go to.

Another significant event occurred in 1944. Irene's father decided, at long last, to end his own marriage. That risked Irene's anger at her mother being betrayed. But it also brought father and daughter closer in their shared admission of romantic failure. Not the least marvel of Hollywood is the story of how conservative people began to lead more reckless lives, as if the movies and the war's turmoil had swayed them. Mayer had his eye on the starlet Ann Miller, but she steered clear of marriage, and that role fell to a bit-part player, Lorena Danker.

David believed he had to sell his share in *Gone With the Wind*. He persuaded Jock Whitney of the sense of it all. And Jock agreed to buy out David's share. David sold his 44.9 percent share in the movie to Jock for $400,000 and for accounts receivable that later amounted to $304,000. For $704,000, he got rid of his great creation.

We can be fair: $700,000 in 1942 was a fat sum on top of what David had already taken from the film. I doubt if any producer had ever done better. But no one had been more eloquent about *Gone With the Wind* being different. There was much of the world where the film had not played yet. It's unfair to expect him to have had our knowledge of what was still to come. Selznick was a business entrepreneur of rare feeling, but not a genius. The one business mind close to him and certainly brilliant was Myron's, and Myron said don't sell. But remember this: in 1946, as the first contract with Loew's ended, the 50-50 ownership of the film's income was to change. Thereafter it would be 75 percent to Selznick, 25 percent to Loew's.

A little less than a year later, Jock Whitney and his sister (Joan Payson) decided to sell off their shares in *GWTW*. Between them, they had 86 percent of the picture. They did not get just twice what they had paid David. They got $2.2 million. You might guess that they pushed the price higher by auctioning it off, by causing the kind of business stir in this property that anyone else would have thought to raise. No, they sold it quietly without warning or auction. They sold it to M-G-M. And in the difficult years that faced the film business, that studio took considerable comfort from the ongoing revenues from the film.

In 1945, Irene threw David out of the house. She decided to give up Hollywood. She went to live in New York and she became a producer on Broadway. Her father surely helped her, and her old friend Jock Whitney was an investor in her first coup, *A Streetcar Named Desire*. The divorce came along in time, and David eventually married Jennifer Jones.

Louis B. Mayer did not die until 1957, several years after he had been fired by Metro and by Nick Schenck. But L.B. was secure, and when he died it turned out that his will was his last great melodramatic gesture. It excluded Edie—she had displeased L.B.; she had associated with Democrats, among other things. Irene inherited, as did her two sons, and she had control over the $5 million left as the Mayer Foundation. In time, honoring his wishes, she would pledge much of that money to medicine, the career she wished she had been allowed to take up for herself.

Follow the money.

things, Los Angeles was subject to fire, landslide, flood, drought, and earthquake. It is a whimsical place to build a city. Or a fictitious place. Still is: I am writing this passage just days after the worst fires in California history, those of late October 2003, in Simi Valley, near Lake Arrowhead and around San Diego. On the maps in the *New York Times,* the red patches look like a planned attack on L.A. itself. There's a weird symmetry with the other maps in the news, the ones of Iraq.

Cities are unstoppable. Sooner or later on the bare land there are going to be clutches of population. The fort, the mission, or the camp will swell. It will build a library, a concert hall, a restaurant or two; a red-light district, a slum, a rancid edge of town. Fritz Lang's *Metropolis,* just like King Vidor's *The Crowd,* had shown both the daunting achievement of a city and its unavoidable dangers. City buildings can tumble down on your heads. The sewers can overflow. The poor can rise, like rats, to reclaim the air. And there is loneliness at work in a city, just as nagging as rats.

At about 5 p.m. on March 10, 1933 (six days after FDR took the oath; less than a month after the Reichstag fire in Germany), an earthquake hit Long Beach, to the south of Los Angeles. More than fifty people were killed and the shock interrupted a meeting at the Roosevelt Hotel of leading movie executives attempting to deal with the current financial crisis. FDR was about to close the banks. The studios were considering pay cuts. Louis B. Mayer was one of the people there. He hurried out of the hotel, got in his car, and drove west, toward Santa Monica. But he thought to stop by at the Beverly Wilshire hotel where his daughter Irene was living with David Selznick and their infant son Jeffrey, as they waited for their new house to be built.

L.B. saw Irene standing on the sidewalk, with Jeffrey in a shawl. "Where's David?" he asked. No one quite knew (not for the first or last time). So it was the father who rescued the daughter and the grandson. He was the man for an emergency. You can see it as a scene—the way Mayer saw everything. A couple of years later, L.B. and Irving dreamed up the notion of *San Francisco,* a gorgeous love story set in San Francisco in 1906. Jeanette MacDonald is the clergyman's daughter who becomes a saloon singer; Spencer Tracy is the priest forever trying to get his old chum, Blackie (Clark Gable), to do the right thing. And wham! The earthquake hits and then love finds a way and those San Franciscans, they just build their city up again, in the American way. And in Frank Gehry's Walt Disney Concert Hall—another event of the fall of 2003—the very facets of the building look like silver flames. Los Angeles has nerve, cheek, or is it wit?

Somewhere a guy can get a decent meal . . . or two. Orson Welles eating, observed by cohort Paul Stewart (*Gary Rosen*)

16 · OUR TOWN

There have always been earthquakes in Southern California, of course. By 1933, there were universities in Los Angeles with the equipment to register such things, and with enough experience in geology and weather to be quite clear about it: in the ordinary nature of

Mayer loved *San Francisco,* and he had a soft spot for MacDonald, too. He knew it was a winner when he saw the preview. It had cost $1.3 million (in 1936), but it made well over $2 million. By then, the Selznicks' home on Summit Drive was being lived in. The economy had started to improve and those first instincts to quit a city where earthquakes can happen had passed over. *San Francisco* played very well in California. Why not? It was an early dynamic in moviegoing that we, the chumps, would pay money to test our own fears, to imagine our courage. And there was also that stealthy possibility growing that reality was not all it had been cracked up to be, that it might be something that stayed on a screen—like the screen where, one day, airliners slice into towers one morning in New York and we wonder what movie that was.

An audience at the movies wants it both ways, and the cunning thing about the medium is that it seems to promise such a deal. We want adventure, danger, romance; we want desire made bright like flesh. It can come in the guise of *Chinatown, Psycho,* or *Casablanca.* We want to be Jake Gittes, prowling along on the trail of the great intrigue; or Rick and Ilse, bathed in the tough velvet light they used to make at Warner Brothers. And we want to be . . . Norman Bates? Well, that one's trickier. If we felt we were Marion Crane at the start of that film, we do have a shock coming. Because at the movies we also expect to be warm, comfortable, secure in the dark, and safe. Isn't that what a nickel or ten dollars buys? And at our movies, monsters, from Norman Bates to Hannibal Lecter, become as familiar as old uncles with naughty habits.

When foreigners marvel at so many guns in American households, they are given answers that refer to colonial history, the perilous frontier, and the second amendment to the Constitution. Those answers seldom admit that guns also represent adventure, and the country's reluctance to give up its own romance. The great role of the Western, in Hollywood history and America's uncertain maturation, is as a parable of excitement, action, prowess becoming law. But there is sometimes a dismay in the Western, too. It is there in *Cimarron,* where the classic land rush is prelude to the building of a dull city that the hero cannot abide. So he moves on. But once such wanderers reached the Pacific they stopped, or went back to the desolate reality and fantasy wealth of Nevada. That roaming is the wistful energy in Sam Peckinpah's films, with those wild bunches who'd sooner die than settle or grow up.

And so, in time, development reached Los Angeles, with all its threat of domesticity. The population of greater L.A. was a million in 1915 and 3.5 million by 1933. In less than a hundred years, the place shifted from the brazen piracy of William Mulholland pointing to the water and telling the young city, There it is—take it, to one kind of practitioner or another counseling metropolitan anxiety with Prozac: Here it is—take one a day.

Just as the major studios had their start-up in Los Angeles in the space of a few years, so it's touching to see the raw city outfitting itself with attributes in a rush. It has worked, more or less, but at a speed that makes us think less of evolution than the quick dissolve, or the cut.

University campuses sprang into being. The University of Southern California, founded in 1880, kept growing, absorbing Exposition Park and then the old Coliseum, itself enlarged for the 1932 Olympic Games (a big step forward in Angeleno self-respect). UCLA, begun as the State Normal School in 1881, expanded in the 1920s when the Janss Corporation (a developer) gave 200 acres of upper Westwood at a knockdown price.

The Hollywood Bowl was dedicated in 1922 and the Los Angeles Philharmonic Orchestra was established a couple of years later. In 1881, the *Los Angeles Times* began business. A few years later, Harry Chandler joined the paper and married the boss's daughter, and so the Chandler dynasty began. In the same downtown area where the paper printed, the Biltmore Hotel was put up in 1923, and three years later the Los Angeles Central Library was erected. L.A. was generally a low-slung city (in part because of earthquake fears), but City Hall went up in 1926–28, twenty-eight stories, and Bullock's Wilshire rose the next year (John and Donald Parkinson were architects on both), a deco palace with a ten-story tower. Racing began at Santa Anita in 1934; that's where Seabiscuit would become a Western hero.

Was there a Southern California style, or even a Western style? Well, there was Spanish, and adobe, and there was the Fritz Lang-like open interior of the Bradbury Building (done in 1893 by George H. Wyman), and used by Joseph Losey in his 1950 remake of Lang's *M*. Union Station was redone in the 1930s as the essential entry point for the city—the end of a four-day train ride from New York—in a mix of Spanish and Streamline Moderne. But other styles were happily copied. The Venice development, south of Santa Monica, came with gondolas and Italianate buildings. Grauman's Chinese Theater and the Mayan Theater were exactly what the names promised. Griffith Park was a vast wilderness, fading into the real wildness north of L.A. with the Observatory standing for knowledge (and waiting for James Dean in *Rebel Without a Cause*). There was a Victorian gothic church copied from an original in Dorking, Surrey. There were buildings meant as dreams or jokes. The influence of décor was profound: it meant not just that you could copy a mood or an atmosphere, but that if you didn't like it, you could tear it down and start again. Begin again. It's what the movies do every week—and threaten twenty-four times every second. The greatest fantasy of all is power over humdrum reality—redo it! Long before Las Vegas, buildings and neighborhoods could be deliberately themed, and then rewritten. One of the most disturbing feelings I had on September 11, watching the screen, was that our fun films had taught us the merriment, the liberty even, of seeing enormous buildings huffed and puffed away.

We are still torn between the fun and liberty of rebuilding and the helpless loss of integrity or of common sense that may accompany it. Listen to one eastern commentator, Edmund Wilson, in 1932, horrified by the riot in styles, yet nearly ecstatic in disdain:

> The residential people of Los Angeles . . . like to express their motivation in homes that symphonize their favorite historical films, their best-beloved movie actresses, their luckiest numerological combinations or their previous incarnation in old Greece, romantic Egypt, quaint Sussex or among the priestesses of old India. Here you will see a Pekinese pagoda made of fresh and crackly peanut brittle—there a snow-white marshmallow igloo—there a toothsome pink nougat in the Florentine manner.

It's as perishable and unnourishing as candy. So who cares if it all slides away in the next earthquake?

There are numerous ways to trace the growth of Los Angeles as it becomes a city of eight million people and more, many of whom are unattached to the movies, do not actually watch movies, but who are engaged in the full American range of business enterprises, legal and illegal. Yet the city cannot let the movies go as its shaping force. That is one reason why in the East there are still disapproving legends about the flimsiness and the silliness of a city that is so many grim square miles of concrete and process. It is why anyone coming into L.A. by air is still likely to take a descending swoop along the line of the northern hills on the way into LAX so that they may read the caption HOLLYWOOD. It's so like those abject western mining towns that put a white initial as big as a house on the town slag heap, as if kids might forget where they lived.

Of course, once the sign read HOLLYWOODLAND, the advertisement for a real estate development in the canyon below, put up in 1923. The letters were wood and painted white, and they were breaking up by 1932 when a young woman who hadn't made it in pictures, Peg Entwistle, took the rugged climb up the steep slopes of Mount Lee and then up the fifty-foot-high "H" and threw herself off. That same letter was later blown down by the wind. The sign was a bad joke until 1978 when a committee was formed to save and restore it. At $27,000 a letter, it was redone, with stars buying a letter each. That director's cut turned it into plain HOLLY-WOOD and now the letters are sheet metal, with elaborate supports.

It was in 1907 that a developer named Burton O. Green opened a sub-division called Beverly Hills. The name came from Beverly, Massachu-setts, where President Taft had a holiday home. Five years later, in farming country, but as a bold alternative to the Hollywood Hotel (at Hol-lywood and Highland), the same Burton Green put up the Beverly Hills Hotel. The manager, Margaret Anderson, bought it out in 1920 (for $250,000) and sold it seven years later for $1.5 million. That was the year the Beverly Wilshire Hotel was erected on the site of the old Beverly Hills Speedway.

And it was in 1920 that Douglas Fairbanks bought a hunting lodge and fifteen acres, hired Wallace Neff to do the renovations, and gave it to his new bride, Mary Pickford. It cost $38,000 and the improved house on the Summit Drive site would be called Pickfair, the first great star shrine, a place where hicks could drive by and hope for a glimpse. When Mary died, in 1979, the place changed hands for $10 million.

The sums of money bespoke a boomtown mentality, and money quickly formed its own caste system. Consider Harlean Carpenter, born in Kansas City in 1911. Her parents divorced—Harlean hardly ever saw her father again—and in 1923 the mother moved herself and Harlean to Los Ange-les. The mother wanted to be a movie star. She rented a single room in a Sunset Boulevard house and nagged the father to pay the fees so Harlean could attend the Hollywood School for Girls. The student body there included Irene Mayer, Katherine De Mille, Joel McCrea, and Douglas Fairbanks, Jr. (It took handsome boys, and the Beverly Hills High School did not open until 1927.)

The school uniform didn't work on Harlean the way it did on other girls, and nothing tamed her great blond bangs. She got her education at the right school, but nothing could diminish the contrast between that golden hair (platinum was the word they would use) and her dark, knowing eyes. Her mother married again, to Marino Bello, a gangster. Harlean married herself, at sixteen. She had affairs with other gangsters. She was on her way to being Jean Harlow. She was taken up by Howard Hughes and put under contract at $300 a week. By 1928 she was making movies—comedy shorts, with tiny parts—a gorgeous kid, hanging around until she made *Hell's Angels* and then she had an M-G-M contract, where she made *Red*

Dust and struck sparks with Gable. They were made for each other. Then came *Dinner at Eight,* in the final scene of which the audience hooted when, in a conversation with Marie Dressler, Harlow's character said she was afraid about mechanical progress taking over life. Dressler halted. The camera heeled, like an attentive borzoi, and she studied the superb fruit of Harlow's barely restrained body and said, "Oh my dear, that's something you need never be afraid of."

Harlow was America's slut, and Metro's wild woman at $1,500 a week. In some spasm of madness she married Paul Bern, much older, one of Thalberg's producers (also at $1,500 a week), the kind of man who liked to be the confidant to bad girls, without ever touching them. It's an enduring Hollywood type, often gay, always kind and patient, and sometimes the best friend sex goddesses ever find.

Then on the morning of September 5, 1932, at the Bern-Harlow home on Easton Drive, a dead-end lane off Benedict Canyon, the butler and the cook arrived at 11:30 a.m. to find the house empty except for Bern's corpse, naked, in his dressing room. He had been shot. Harlow wasn't there.

The butler called Harlow's mother. She called Louis B. Mayer. He called the studio head of security, Whitey Hendry (police chief of Culver City before being hired by the studio), and the head of publicity, Howard Strickling. Strickling called a photographer to go to the Easton Drive house. They all gathered there, to be joined by Irving Thalberg and David Selznick. Mayer and Strickling ran the show. They found a notebook Bern kept, with this on one page:

Dearest dear,
　　Unfortunately this is the only way to make good the frightful wrong I have done you and to wipe out my abject humiliation, I love you.
　　　　　　　　　　　　　　　　　　　　　　　　　　　Paul
　　You understand last night was only a comedy.

Mayer wanted to burn the book, but Strickling said it provided a motive. Who knows what else they did to set the scene? At 2:15 p.m. they called the police. And the police apparently made no protest. They were accustomed to the power or priority of Mayer and Strickling. Perhaps they were glad to be the first members of the general public called in. Studio people called it "our town" in those days.

The official verdict was suicide, prompted by Bern's inability to fulfill his marriage. But another possibility loomed, and is now accepted: that Bern had had a previous wife, Dorothy Millette, unstable but abandoned, and that she had driven to Bern's home and killed him. A few days later, Millette's corpse was found in the Sacramento River.

The scandal vindicated Harlow's reputation; it required not so much cover-up as tasteful display. A new contract promoted her to $3,000 a week. *Red Dust* was released in October 1932. There would be another dozen films in just a few years, all at Metro, including *Reckless* (a Selznick production), in which she was required to play an actress whose husband shoots himself. The connection was inescapable, the exploitation naked. She had another brief marriage, to cameraman Hal Rosson, and there was an affair with William Powell. But her studio owned her.

Harlow died in 1937 of uremic poisoning. She was suffering intense abdominal pain, but doctors could not identify the problem. Was it just her alcoholism? they wondered. But she could not urinate. The waste was gathering in her body. Visitors could smell it on her breath and coming off her skin. Nephritis developed. This famous beauty was rotting. With all the retained fluid, her body and then her skull swelled. It was a hideous death, the grisly obverse of her lustrous image.

She had assets of $24,000 and debts (including taxes due) of $76,000. There was an annuity of just over $100,000 left to her mother (this was on William Powell's advice). Still only twenty-six, an international star, she had made fifteen films for M-G-M and forty-two altogether. Her last picture, *Saratoga,* unfinished when she died, so that a body double and a vocal impersonator had to be employed, grossed $3.3 million. Her career is a Nathanael West story, about a sexy girl being worked to death for studio profit, and about the strange way she pioneered not wearing underclothes beneath her tight outfits. Not many imitated Harlow, but she was an incarnation of desire, one of the first who seem utterly modern. Jean Harlow bypassed censorship. Her look, the way she moved, the way she said things—those were like breath on the embers of audience desire. And nearly everyone in her business and her audience put her down as a tramp because of it. It was playing with fire, and in her hair and her skin (always in black-and-white) Harlow does seem about to catch fire. But it was safe sport for the watchers.

In the summer of 2003, Bob Hope died at the age of 100. Katharine Hepburn went a few weeks earlier, at ninety-six. (They actually made one film together, *The Iron Petticoat.*) Both of them were born before Harlean Carpenter, and their deaths were received in a spirit of unflawed love and respect. Were they better people than Harlow, better actors, or simply in more control of themselves? Did they know to keep a precious element of ownership not necessarily found in contracts?

It's hardly the case that Hope and Hepburn did not belong to "our town." Hepburn won four Oscars and was nominated for twelve. Hope virtually invented the job of hosting the Oscars and while he made many jokes about never winning one—"Ladies and Gentlemen, welcome to the Academy Awards, or as it's known in our house, Passover!"—he got three honorary awards to placate an ego as bold as his nose. He and Bing Crosby were the top box office attraction in America throughout the 1940s. Young people today cannot understand the healing effect of those silly, utterly gay and stay-at-home "Road" films they made at Paramount.

Hope had little in the way of credentials, class, or background, except for being English. He had been a middling boxer and a vaudeville song-and-dance man. It wasn't until he was over thirty that he gradually came to the top on Broadway (second lead in *Roberta*), on radio, and then in movies. He was a self-made man, and while he was willing to hire a pla-toon of joke-writers, he preferred to look after business himself. He was tight with his money. He never lived extravagantly. And anything left over he invested in real estate. A grown-up in the thirties, he didn't trust stocks or banks, but he had seen how much Los Angeles was growing, and he relied on that future. His estate may reveal the full truth: don't be shocked if Bob—stupid, cowardly, mortified—Hope turns out to be the richest actor of them all.

Hepburn's is a stranger case, a model of feminist independence and being in charge of yourself. When she got off the train in Pasadena, in July 1932, with her pal Laura Harding (a great heiress), Laura's dog, and enough luggage for a colony, her agent Myron Selznick looked at the fash-ionably dressed cadaver that was Hepburn and marveled that he had won a salary of $1,500 a week for someone so plainly an outsider.

She was set to act with John Barrymore in brother David's *A Bill of Divorcement*. At first, the director, George Cukor, thought her mannered and affected and too Bryn Mawr to please a large public. She looked and sounded like what she was: the child of an old New England family, liberal and modern, well educated, naturally classy, yet sexually her own woman. Hepburn started wearing pants, and she seemed very attached to Laura Harding. She talked to men as if they were equals, and asked no thanks for that generosity. But then she did a reunion scene with Barrymore, and Cukor saw magic. He was her friend for life and together they went on to do *Little Women, Sylvia Scarlett, Holiday, The Philadelphia Story, Keeper of the Flame, Adam's Rib, Pat and Mike,* and *Love Among the Ruins.*

But Cukor's misgivings were not misplaced. Hepburn did alarm the American public. It is possible that she had sex with a few women, but does the great cabinet of desire that is the movies not extend to all versions of love? How is it that for so long the factory system decided there was only one way? And how did it not notice that so many of "their" people swung both ways?

Hepburn was an astute careerist, and inclined to handle her own business deals. But to be sporting, she had an affair with one of her official agents, Leland Hayward; she had a collection of supposedly powerful men with whom she talked man-to-man (John Ford, Howard Hughes, Louis B. Mayer, and John Huston notably), and she got along like a well-oiled bicycle. She often lived in Hollywood, no matter that she had no intention of buying the silly notion that it was the only society on earth. She was reckoned to be box office poison at just about the moment when Jean Harlow was actually succumbing to poison. And Hepburn lived another seventy years to a point where she was probably the most revered example of what a fine old American lady might be. And if not rich—for she came from a family line that abhorred such vulgar labels—she was very comfortable, thank you.

It was at the Bel-Air Country Club one day where Hepburn was playing golf that Howard Hughes landed his small plane on the fairway, took out his clubs, and joined her. She plays golf with the same insouciance in *Bringing Up Baby*. The film business worked hard to equip itself with such things as country clubs and restaurants. For surely, it had to have that thing called sophisticated fun, as well as a fifty-foot name tag.

But the film business didn't own Los Angeles. There had been a city and a snobbery there before them. Louis B. Mayer had not been able to get his girls into private schools like Westlake. And the oldest set of country clubs—the Bel-Air, the Los Angeles, and the Lakeside—were fussy about Jewish applicants. Here, in their own city, was evidence of the great struggle the Jews had in gaining acceptance. So don't underestimate the small social revolution when Jock Whitney, a scion of WASP society, went into partnership with Selznick. And don't forget the sniping comments at Irene and others for social climbing in the smart New York magazines. The first substantial hint of political evasion or loss of character in the Hollywood community was the way some Jews sought to rise above their origins, or engage in the darkest kind of anti-Semitic humor themselves.

There were restaurants and clubs, too. Musso & Frank's Grill opened on Hollywood Boulevard in 1919, and it's there still, trying to preserve the old look and an even older style of cuisine, one that might have been worked out by Walter Brennan's Groot in *Red River* as he fed the cowboys on the cattle drive to Abilene. The original Brown Derby, shaped like the hat, was opened in 1926 on Wilshire. That's where the Cobb salad was invented: Robert Cobb, a co-owner, is supposed to have fashioned a salad of finely chopped vegetables first at the request of actress Gail Patrick. The meat and cheese came later. There were other notable restaurants that followed—Chasen's, Scandia, the Cock 'n' Bull. But in the golden age, none of these establishments aimed for excellence. California had not quite discovered its own command of produce yet, and most dining out looked for decent food and drink, and relative freedom from stargazers and photographers. As late as 1967, when Londoner John Boorman came to town to make *Point Blank,* he noted highballs before dinner, and water with it, but no wine. Thirty years later, the wine lists are impeccable.

There were nightclubs like Ciro's, the Mocambo, and Café Montmartre; there was the Cocoanut Grove in the Ambassador Hotel, built in 1921;° and Yamashiro, on North Sycamore Drive, an exclusive club before it became a restaurant. There were (illegal) gambling clubs, like the Clover Club; and for a time there were Tony Cornero's gambling ships off the Santa Monica shore, far enough away to be free. There was the wicked resort of Agua Caliente, over the Mexican border, with Mexico itself regarded as the natural poor colony to a rich empire. Los Angeles was also a city of brothels: in *L.A. Confidential,* from the James Ellroy novel, there's one in which the girls are picked and surgically enhanced to look like the great stars. The handsome building now housing Miramax, on Sunset, was once in that trade, and there are a few hints of it left in the décor.

One of the fascinating untold stories of Hollywood concerns the interaction between the prostitution business and the "regular" film industry. There were a few men and women who worked in both, and there was a certain amount of weekend pornography—not just screenings for, but the making of such films by studio people. *The Day of the Locust* has a scene at Mrs. Jennings's call house: "She ran her business just as other women run lending libraries, shrewdly and with taste." For $30 a night Mrs. J. would send a girl to your house; she kept 50 percent. One night, at her place, she shows a movie, *Le Predicament de Marie,* in which the maid is debauched by several members of the family she works for. Connoisseurs still hunt for such shady treasures, and try to recognize the Hollywood faces that go with the unexpected nakedness. The Hays Code might have served middle America, but in "our town" there was more liberty. Plus abortionists and doctors who handled such things.

° Legend has it that Valentino, a sometime resident at the hotel, recommended the palm trees used on *The Sheik* for décor at the Cocoanut Grove.

In Raymond Chandler's novel *The Big Sleep* (1939), private eye Philip Marlowe is called in by General Sternwood to tidy up the debts of his daughter Carmen. Next thing you know, it's pornographic pictures. The "case" gets out of hand, rather in the way *Chinatown* slips away from Jake Gittes's control, but these "eyes" are sound men, reliable and cheap, too (Marlowe asks $25 a day and expenses), people you can trust with potential scandal.

When the news of Paul Bern's death came through, Mayer assigned Whitey Hendry and Howard Strickling to run interference. They kept Harlow out of court; by their lights they looked after her; yet that also meant adding a scarlet brushstroke behind the platinum hair. It's an open question whether they were really looking after Harlean Carpenter, as opposed to their contract. Strickling would die famous for the secrets buried with him, and the troubles he had kept out of the press. The care was smothering, and he seldom noticed the real people at issue. Instead, it was a kind of marketing that chose to polish the image or reputation of the players. It also encouraged the stars to think of themselves as children, not ready yet to take responsibility for their own lives.

A Katharine Hepburn would never have dreamed of letting people look after her—unless they were as rich as Howard Hughes. She took responsibility. On the other hand, Jean Harlow was at the mercy of her mother and her stepfather, Marino Bello, who insisted on negotiating on her behalf with Metro. Harlow would have been better off with a good lawyer, and she might have lived a lot longer without her mother's supervision of those last gruesome days. Mayer loved to assure his contract people that they were part of a great family, that he would look after them. But then if you met Mayer's shell-shocked wife, and his daughters, you realized what liability a family could be.

One way of tracking the history of the film business is in the changing ideas about care. Agents had had to fight their way into the contract system, and persuade would-be clients that they could do better for them. In time, those agents began to spread the idea that the major artists, the stars especially, deserved not just a salary, but profit participation, or ownership.

But agents were just the tip of the entourage we have now come to expect that also includes lawyers, publicity people, doctors, coaches, trainers, bodyguards, nannies for the children, gardeners, decorators, purchasers of art. Anything else? Why, of course: as actors proved themselves more intelligent, or "complex," so the psychiatrist would come to their aid.

It is not just that Hollywood people need discreet doctors to perform abortions or correct the line of a nose. Over the years, Los Angeles medicine has been a leader in what is called "wellness," a broad area that can cover good health, good looks, thinness, and that extraordinary subculture of the movies, youthfulness (which is not the same as youth, a realization that comes with any scrutiny of today's Robert Redford). Nowhere in the world has the preservation of skin tone been more closely studied, even if Southern California is also a haven for tanning. Indeed, Doug Fairbanks, eighty years ago, did a lot to pioneer the tanned look as a sign of robust health and glamour. But we knew less about skin cancer then.

Of course, "wellness" is an ambiguous term: it can mean looking young enough still to command $10 million for a picture; or it could refer to a total capacity for life—not just appearance or performance, but the life of the mind, of moral responsibility, for consciousness as a whole. America faces a health problem called obesity, heavily influenced by the mass marketing of junk foods (sold at most movie theaters and couch fodder with TV), by poor education, and by the weakness for instant gratification. Obesity kills people and costs money, but one might think from movies alone that obesity is automatically to be read in moral terms: so many overweight people on screen are villainous, or decadent, or failures (from Oliver Hardy to Sydney Greenstreet). That is not a reliable test in life. Nevertheless, this just touches on the contrary messages that are conveyed by the term "good-looking."

Doctors may advise on diet, and ensure that a client is tested for common illnesses. Cosmetic surgeons can take away wrinkles or skin itself as the signs of aging arrive. Those are common enough practices for movie actors. But the dieting required in some cases is extreme and dangerous—sometimes helped by addictive drugs—in which case the pursuit of wellness itself endangers the whole organism.

The place for psychiatry in Hollywood, it seems to me, is deadlier still. There is hardly anything more shaming of trained intellect than its jargon-ridden defense of fantasy. As readers will have observed I am quite certain about the place of fantasy in the movie experience—of waking dream even. But I hope I have never given any hint that the skilled interpretation of the dream might be therapeutic. Fantasy is a vast self-indulgence; it requires only the owning-up.

Seeing beauty on the screen, plus the erosion of youth, doctors of many minor crafts made their way to Los Angeles. The psychiatric invasion happened a little differently. Many of those people were German and Austrian Jews who took any escape route out of Europe. Maybe a few of them saw the screen's seven-nights-a-week replaying of dream and smelled out their new home. In the early forties, as David Selznick sank into the depression of success, his wife found him psychiatric help in the form of May Romm. She met with him often at first. But when they started on the real course, he alarmed her by cheering up very suddenly. Why? Well, he said, we're talking about me, and this talk is so like a story conference where we discuss motivation. So I'm in my element.

May Romm may have wondered about her own sanity, for, in time, she became the technical advisor on one of the silliest films about her profession, Alfred Hitchcock's *Spellbound*. She got a credit on the film, too, and although she was scolded by colleagues for drawing psychoanalysis into disrepute, she ended up with many Mayers and Selznicks as her patients. It was her business as well as her calling, and she reached a wise insight, that in bringing mental comfort to the people of Hollywood there was a real future, so long as you never threatened your patients with cure.

For here is the remarkable and American thing: just as the beautiful creatures were striving for a lean magnificence that was not far from hysteria, and for a degree of health so bright they hardly required lighting, so they clung to inward disarray and the kind of spectacular unhappiness so often associated with genius in novelettes and romances—as well as in movies like *Lust for Life* (with Kirk Douglas as Vincent van Gogh), *The Hours* (Nicole Kidman as Virginia Woolf), and even *Raging Bull* (Robert De Niro as Jake La Motta).

No, I'm not dismissive of mental illness or personal unhappiness. But I've grown suspicious of the way their mournful celebration has infected and undermined such things as acting and writing in the picture business. And I'm not persuaded that the unfairness of being paid so much money to write or perform nonsense is truly a justifiable reason for lifelong malevolent narcissism (the triumphant view of the self as unsatisfactory). Yes, many selves in Hollywood (as elsewhere) are unsatisfactory: they behave badly, with disregard for others, with helpless selfishness, self-indulgence, and greed. But is it a rare paradox of advanced civilization to have the most beautiful, the most desired, the most highly paid as devils lurching along the ragged line of sanity or order? Or is it humbug?

To say that there are branches of the medical profession whose interest it is to keep the sick alive as long as possible is not mere cynicism. It is the beginning of politics. For surely the culture of celebrity that began and persists in Hollywood is not just a by-product of show business, it is a condition that has influenced our entire society and which finds modern America both uniquely advanced in the mechanics of health and the neuroses of un-wellness, but apparently incapable of taking basic care of its citizens such as nearly every other advanced country manages. (There is material for a very dark comedy now in a United States that provides universal health care in Iraq before it does in its own land. Julia Roberts as the lead doctor?)

To be precise: there are people whose artistic careers and their own sense of responsibility have been waylaid by the plunge into therapy. There is also the dire cult of incoherent earnestness that overtook American acting because of it. I refer to the styles often lumped together as Method, Stanislavskian, or Actors Studio, but which also deserve to be treated as aspects of the way in which certain stars hijacked the film business, boosting their mounting salaries into partial ownership (though without always taking the responsibility that comes with ownership).

There was a moment in *On the Waterfront* when something snapped. It came during the shooting of the famous back-of-the-cab sequence with Marlon Brando and Rod Steiger as brothers caught up in the waterfront rackets. It is a poignant scene where Terry (Brando) blames Charley for all the woes of his life; this is not untypical of that era of Method films in which dismal spoiled babies were always blaming someone else for everything that had gone wrong (see the career of James Dean).

Judge the scene and the whole movie as you will, this was plainly an important scene. Brando and Steiger and the director Elia Kazan were all fellows in the Actors Studio. When it came to the close-ups, Kazan did Brando's first, and there was Steiger, off-camera, feeding him his lines. That is a small courtesy but a tradition in acting; it is part of the fellowship. However, when it came time for Steiger's close-ups, Brando absented himself. He had to see his therapist. Steiger had an assistant giving him the other lines.

That should not have happened. It reveals a selfishness in Brando that is hostile to the very art he seems so immersed in. It is bad manners. But it was a principle of the Method that the actor was to find in himself the nature of his character. In other words, playing someone confused (or worse), the actor was to go as far down that path as possible. His own emotional pain or crisis was used to become that of the character.

I think that is a nonsense that could yet destroy a society, as well as an approach that drags down art or storytelling or entertainment. And when enough people take some malaise as a right, the result is a society in which everyone is acting instead of being. Furthermore, I would offer the suggestion that in American performance art there is no more reliable warning sign of fouled-up intentions than gravid sincerity. If American art is ever to find its way ahead, playfulness (the teasing interaction of reality and artifice) is a more promising road than the realism of self-pity. Thus the genre of drama in American film is so much less rewarding than comedy, and acting is so much less promising a basis for the show than writing. But the uncertainty that inspires Method acting has time and again replaced the work of writers with gasping hesitation, vagueness, and the animal sigh that actors believe signals profundity.

Marlon Brando is a tragedy in American life. It is not simply that he was an actor of such potential, such extraordinary skill and inventiveness. He was also naturally blessed with a sense of mischief (if not quite wit) and a reveling in pretense for its own sake. You can see this in things as diverse as *Desiree* and *Guys and Dolls,* or *The Godfather* and *The Missouri Breaks.* But Brando had a childhood in which he decided he was not loved, and then the circumstances where he could use that to explain all kinds of mistakes, disaster, and bad luck that befell him and those around him. Famously, he fell out of love with acting and with Hollywood, and in time he grew into the bloated wreck that is the opposite of his youth and the American ideal for actors.

There may be wit and satire in that (the same sort of thing happened with that other superb rebel, Orson Welles). But Brando was never smart or articulate enough to be a reasoned voice of protest, to be a critic. And so he took on therapy's character, the hurt boy complaining about the system, just as he exploited it with merciless financial demands, no matter that his actual participation on films became increasingly like that of a saboteur. Consider this progress:

1947	*A Streetcar Named Desire,* on stage—$550 a week
1950	*The Men,* first film—$40,000
1951	*Streetcar,* the movie—$80,000
1952	*Viva Zapata!*—$100,000
1953	*Julius Caesar*—$40,000
1954	*On the Waterfront*—$125,000
1954	*Desiree*—$125,000
1955	*Guys and Dolls*—$200,000
1957	*Sayonara*—$300,000 + 10% of profits
1960	*The Fugitive Kind*—$1 million
1961	*One-Eyed Jacks,* acting and directing—$500,000
1962	*Mutiny on the Bounty*—$500,000 + 10% of the gross + $10,000 a week expenses + $5,000 a day for every day over schedule
1962	Sells his company to Universal for $1 million + MCA stock and agrees to do five films at $270,000 each

1969	*Burn!*—$750,000
1972	*The Godfather*—$100,000 + 10% of profits; then he trades back his percentage for another $100,000
1973	*Last Tango in Paris*—$250,000 + 10% of the gross
1976	*The Missouri Breaks*—$1.25 million + percentage
1978	*Superman* (15 minutes on screen)—$3.7 million + 11.3% of U.S. gross; 5.6% of foreign
1979	*Apocalypse Now*—$1 million + 11.3% of the gross
1980	*The Formula*—$3 million
1990	*The Freshman*—$3.3 million + 11% of the gross
1992	*Christopher Columbus—the Discovery* (10 minutes on screen)—$5 million

This list deserves some comment. It reflects a process of inflation that pervaded the industry, and which nearly every star took advantage of. Moreover, the very titles remind us how good Brando can be—sometimes unexpectedly. Still, there are two significant landmarks. *One-Eyed Jacks* was Brando's deepest immersion in film. It was a project made for his company, which he directed only after he had exhausted Stanley Kubrick. It was Kubrick's feeling that there was no working with Brando, in large part because the actor was emotionally in charge without knowing what he wanted. A few people defend the final film, but the audience loathed it, and Brando himself abandoned it while half-edited, as if it were too much for him.

Following that, he behaved in such a way on *Mutiny on the Bounty* as to bring his professionalism into doubt. He had great power on the picture, yet he was so capricious that the first director, Carol Reed, quit (replaced by Lewis Milestone) and there was a warring spirit in the cast. The picture ran over schedule (for which Brando was rewarded), and it was another disaster—its losses were said to be $10 million. Those two things close together depressed Brando's financial clout—thus the much smaller deal with Universal.

Brando could say that they don't often make good pictures these days, and there's no disputing that. He had argued with weary eloquence about the quagmire of Hollywood and the small army of leeches that attach themselves to every venture. But then note the difference between the man who took a significant pay cut to do *Julius Caesar,* a "difficult" project, and the man who was nearly gleeful about how close he came to destroying *Apocalypse Now.* He might have felt more warmly toward Francis Coppola. After all, Coppola had insisted on him as Vito Corleone when

Paramount had grave doubts. And it was not Coppola who made Brando trade away profits on that film for more money up front. Brando had panicked, but then felt bitter about Coppola and turned up at the Philippines location fatter than his own deal. He had not even read the Conrad novella, *Heart of Darkness,* in preparation. And he then used his "doubts" to delay the film even further.

It was lousy manners, and part of the career progress that allows you to shift from making movies to making deals. Brando had been a great actor, albeit one very vulnerable to bad material, misguided ventures, and weak directors. And, like so many actors, he had never demonstrated the business acumen or the stamina to take over a picture with pleasure and advantage to the movie. Thus his increased demands for rewards were linked to a distressing abdication.

That is the larger point to make about "our town": the degree to which, high and low, people in pictures are doing what they do for the money, to stay in work. Remember William Holden as Joe Gillis in *Sunset Blvd.*—a great performance, in that Joe's self-pity is held at arm's length from the appeal of the actor. Holden is brave enough to show Joe's malaise for what it is. First casting had been Montgomery Clift, who dropped out because he was advised that it would hurt his image to be seen "in love with" a much older woman. This was good fortune for writer-director Billy Wilder, for Clift would have made Gillis insidiously charming instead of a desperate scrambler. You would have wanted to save Clift (that was his trick); Holden knows that Gillis is beyond salvation.

Gillis, a screenwriter, is broke, and without a job (he is very close to the Pat Hobby character invented by Scott Fitzgerald in a series of very funny short stories). He resembles the majority of members of the Writers Guild: a writer in name only and in the $100 a year dues (today's rate) he owes to the Guild. He is also facing that gravest of disasters in Los Angeles. Without a car, he cannot make the journey to the various studios to offer his feeble pitches. And so, to save the car, he turns into that Sunset Boulevard driveway and begins to become the fall guy in his last script. It's a sardonic self-portrait in that Wilder had begun as a writer, and had faith that writers can carry to fruition some vivid new story or angle that refreshes the whole medium. He realized, however, that he could only safeguard his own scripts (and take proper advantage of them) by becoming a producer.

So now picture a later Joe Gillis. It is 2000 or so, and this Joe is a modest success in Hollywood. He has some good credits, and he gets new assignments. He is, of course, a member of the Writers Guild, and as such—so long as he keeps working—he enjoys the Guild health plan (it covers dental), the pension scheme (Joe is in his fifties), and death benefits. And because of the Guild's steady pressure to raise the respectability of the writer, and because of Joe's agent's endeavors, Joe can get $350,000 for a script. In return, he owes the Guild $100 a year plus 1.5 percent of his gross earnings.

Now let's do a little gentle math on Joe. He has a house in Santa Monica, one he bought seven years ago (at the time of his second marriage). He got it for $850,000 then, and with refinancing his monthly mortgage payment is $5,000 (though he now owes $970,000 on the house). Thanks to Jarvis-Gann (Proposition 13 it was called), Joe pays only about $8,500 a year in property taxes. But the state has suffered in other ways because of Proposition 13: it has lost the quality public schools it once had.

This hits Joe quite sharply. He had a first wife and a divorce, and although California is a no-fault state, the judge nailed him. He pays alimony of $5,000 a month. He has a nineteen-year-old at Dartmouth (that's $40,000 a year if you count plane tickets) and a fifteen-year-old in a private high school ($25,000). Then he has a six-year-old by the second marriage ($15,000 a year at a Montessori school).

Joe also likes to keep a small office in Venice; he works better there, and he has learned that a man deserves a private life. The office and his secretary (just three days a week) run him $25,000 a year.

Are you counting?

Mortgage	$60,000
Alimony	60,000
Schools	80,000
Property tax	8,500
Agent's 10%	35,000
Guild	5,350
Office	25,000
IRS/FICA	40,000
Total	$313,850

I forgot to mention the therapy: not for Joe (he bears up), but the two older kids go once a week and that is $14,000 a year. Now his second wife is saying it's unfair that the six-year-old doesn't go, too.

So far the expenses are $327,000, against income this year of $350,000. Joe is lucky. He has work and a nice house and three kids who are all sound of body if inert in the mind. He has a little left over for a vacation. But the second wife (she is a lot younger than he is) wants to open a dance studio that could be very capital-greedy in its first few years. And Joe really needs a new car. Living in Santa Monica, his drives to the studios are rough and getting rougher. His Volvo is creaking. He has his eye on something just a bit spiffier.

Look, he's in trouble, which is why he is considering this second job, a moonlighting polish called *Bases Loaded* about a girls' softball team. It doesn't really need writing, so much as catching the way teenagers talk in the mall. And Joe has traded on having teenagers—he talks to them incessantly; it troubles them, but he has the latest slang. It's not going to be anything Joe will be proud of, but he needs the second check. It's that or some TV stuff. He is a Hollywood writer, and he doesn't own his own copyright. As Joe says when he's talking to people in the business: "Whenever I hear 'our town,' I think it's a lot more theirs than mine."

Postscript: Anyone living in Hollywood will have detected an extra irony in the equation of Joe's economy. If he does better, his fiscal parameters will expand to keep him pinched. His house, on Montana, is rather shabby. To mix usefully with the A-list people, he needs to live in Beverly Hills. That is not going to happen at under $2.5 million. In turn that would push his mortgage payments to $120,000 a year. To say nothing of staff—he's going to need a housekeeper, a gardener, and catering services from time to time.

This is not all. The new house and the A-list evenings lead to another wife, and another alimony contract. So refigure his numbers against an annual income of $1 million:

Mortgage	$120,000
Taxes/FICA	150,000
Alimony (1)	60,000
Alimony (2)	100,000 (wife #2 was used to a better life)
Property tax	25,000
Agent	100,000
Guild dues	15,000
Office (improved)	50,000
Education	100,000
Therapy	50,000 (wife #2 now demands it)
Lawyers (see above)	50,000
House staff	80,000

| Entertainment | 100,000 (the housewarming makes the columns and launches wife #3's business as a wardrobe advisor) |

This total comes to $1 million. As the accountant points out, that leaves the accountant unpaid. It also leaves nothing for a holiday or Joe's need for a car that he can decently park beside those of Steven Spielberg and Bruce Willis. Joe is still on the edge. I am told that he seldom passes a pool (he has his own now—pool services, $199.99 a week) without a troubled glance.

Joe lives in another trap. At his standard of living, he cannot yield to even his own great ideas, supposing he has them. Suppose he thinks of a lovely, simple story; the whole arc of it comes to him as he knots his tie. But it's a small film, a little gem. How small? Well, it could happen—Joe knows a start-up company that would fund it (at a modest level). Joe could write it, and direct it (the thing he's always dreamed about), for $200,000—two thirds of that deferred. Here it is: the apple of his eye.

But he can't do it. He can't afford to step down. He needs projects of a certain size. Maybe his wife or a child (I like that better) taunts him: "You're only doing it for the money, Dad!" He protests. He argues. He turns angry. He is a writer, isn't he? But when he sleeps, he has a dream in which God (or is it his agent?) comes to him—they are sitting up on Mulholland, surveying the city on a warm night—and says: "Here's the deal. You can make the film you want, the film of your best moments—for nothing. Or, we'll never make another film you touch, but we'll give you $2 million a year."

Noir became them: Lauren Bacall and Humphrey Bogart in Howard Hawks's *To Have and Have Not*, 1944 *(Private Collection)*

17 · THE DARKNESS AND THE LIGHT

Big close-up on a man's face, half-lit—the rest is shadow, the lovely shadow that was blooming on-screen by 1945. There is no need for music, the character can carry the message. He speaks quietly, as if to himself, with that rare, naïve authenticity taken for granted after forty years of movies. (Even animated characters emoted by then—look at Bambi.) The voice is low and husky; it has known troubles:

Like most of the soldiers who came back, I expected a world suddenly reformed. I hoped and believed that the blood and death and confusion of World War II would result in a regeneration of mankind. . . . If men could cooperate in war, how much better they could work together in peace.

I was wrong. I learned that a thousand bucks under the table was the formula for buying a new car. I learned that the real estate squeeze was on for the servicemen. I discovered that the rich had got just a little richer and a lot of the poor had done a pretty good job of grabbing a quick buck. I discovered the world was almost the same and perhaps a little worse.

Yes, it might be the Dana Andrews character in *The Best Years of Our Lives*. But it's not a character—it's a person. It's Ronald Reagan (in his book *Where's the Rest of Me*) failing to recall that the farthest he'd been on his military service was Fort Mason, San Francisco, and already perhaps unsure whether the wartime promos he often narrated were fact or fiction. Years later, those films, like *Rear Gunner*, came back in his political colloquies as dramas he'd actually participated in. Most of Reagan's service had been at Fort Roach, in Culver City—the old Hal Roach studio, its new uniformed inmates sometimes called "Fort Wacky."

At the movies, we take these transitions for granted: we switch the dark on or the light off as part of the automatic process. Or is it the other way around? Once upon a time, I know, mothers would lament that boys gave up glorious sun-filled days for the deliberate dark. What did they mean by that? Well, worlds, of course, for they were alert to the vast metaphorical alchemy that was at work. We hold darkness and light as precious fundamentals, indicative of profound and unalterable meanings.

Extraordinary changes afflicted American movies in the years just after the war, but they were part of a shift in society itself. In 1947, a quarter of American households still lacked running water, though they would clamor for getting television first. Ronald Reagan rolled over from being an actor and what he called "a hemophiliac liberal" to being a player. For many of those who had run the business (in their own minds, at least), the damage seemed apocalyptic. They lost their power, and even their livelihood. Some died, bewildered by the cruel changes. You can even argue that American movies began to die—not that death was final or definitive, not in a medium that had brought the dead back whenever it felt there was money to be made out of rescue. (A vibrant ghostliness has always been available; and while it seems playful, or foolish, don't underestimate how surely it points at part of film's secret nature: fantasy transcends death.) But it was part of the blindness, or the narrowness, of overturned moguls in that they thought the real apocalypses of the age were occurring inside their business, as insults or injuries to them.

So the immediate history of the movies after the war has to include the rapturous surge in audience numbers, and the sickening decline that follows, and the Paramount decision—the 1948 antitrust legislation by which the production/distribution business was no longer permitted to own theaters. It has also to cover the growing dread of Communism in the country, and the way in which the movies were made a focus for recrimination. It has to grasp the daring of so many pictures of this era, and the discovery of a new genre, film noir, so vital to America that Americans could find no name for it. And it has to include the thing called television.

But in all of those areas, we should remember that phrase "after the war," and all it meant, for there were apocalypses greater than those registered in Los Angeles or reported in *Variety*. And in terms of history, our movies are not simply a business or an art. They are a mass medium, reshaped in the need to help the masses understand their world (or ignore it, for that amounts to a dangerous warped "understanding," too). In other words, no book about the movies can be honest historically without some attempt to fathom the feelings of the crowd. What we are dealing with here is the way in which America—and even the entire, hopeful people of the world—sees its ties to others and the passage of time.

Because I was there—not in America, but in my Astoria and Regal, parts of an empire America was only gradually coming to appreciate, let me put it this way: Nothing in life in those first years after the war felt as good as being at the movies. Not on the suburban high street, not on buses or on the Underground, not in queues for this food or that, not in churches or other large gatherings, certainly not in family situations. I wonder if that sounds naïve?

Since 1914, the world in which I lived had become increasingly accustomed to anxiety. It was in that summer, after all, that a British statesman was supposed to have said, "The lamps are going out all over Europe." That didn't just mean that "our" embassies were closing; it was a warning that civilization was shutting down. And as with so many twentieth-century warnings, its gloom proved modest or limited. Of course, I am also talking about the essential history of the movies, for *The Birth of a Nation* comes at nearly the same time as the European killing ground is opened—not just a factory for corpses, but an extermination scheme for social structure, for hope, for humanism even.

Is that going too far? Is it too simplistic? (Remember that the early movies—Chaplin's above all—are open to exactly the same rebuke.)

Maybe, but you do not grasp or come close to the modern history of France, Britain, Germany, and Russia without knowing how thoroughly the Great War annihilated the social structure and the character of those nations. Then recollect that the gap in years between the close of the Great War and the start of the Second World War is only twenty-one years, the same as the gap between the coming to power of Ronald Reagan and September 11, 2001. It is so slight. Yet it was filled with the worst economic depression of modern times, with the rise of Communism and Fascism as enormous political realities (as opposed to smoking-room philosophies), and with the growing certainty that the Great War would have to be resumed.

That is a nutshell history of twenty-one years, and the nut is poisoned. Other things did happen. Still, I think I judge the public mood correctly, and I think that that anxiety is inseparable from the success and sway of the movies. The dark of "entertainment" was an alternative to harsh, painful daylight outside, and a condition in which people felt powerless to intervene. But that also presupposes a large failure in democracy (or whatever you want to call our evolved form of government), for even if people knew that the world was going wrong, they felt helpless with the slide or the sinking. Movies took your mind off that, perhaps; they nurtured the dreaminess, the opting for fantasy as the last inviolable freedom in free nations; they gave comfort and community at the same time. But they were also perceived—grudgingly, vaguely, or half-consciously—as an evasion or an avoidance. We had an inkling that fantasy was either shameful or less than the proper field of exercise for human beings.

But war provides for the unexpected and enforced company of strangers, and of all the versions that took—from being in regiments or being in camps, to being in burial pits or sleeping side by side in the Underground railway stations—being at a movie theater was the most uplifting. That's what I mean by saying it was the best place to be: there was something about the warm company of strangers that embodied the experience of war and the sense of survival, or even victory. You can call it unduly sentimental, or even wishful thinking, but I believe there was community in London movie houses just after the war, a kind of reaffirmation or reunion.

In which case, I know the perfect scene to illustrate that mood. It is in William Wyler's *The Best Years of Our Lives* (a title that was held in high, but solemn, earnest), and comes quite early in the film. Fredric March is back from the war, after years away with every fear of ultimate separation. He approaches the front door. His kids are joyous. One of them is Teresa

Wright. But he is a surprise: his wife, Myrna Loy, doesn't realize who it is, or what the moment means, until she hears the hush, the dramatic silence, and feels the expectation, and knows what it must mean.

The Best Years of Our Lives was photographed by Gregg Toland (the man who shot *Kane*), and in a way it employs the same camera style. There is a long shot rich in domestic deep focus as March and Loy see each other from different ends of a corridor. The depth is totally authentic; it has no hint of the social and psychic challenge that always threatens to pull spaces apart in *Citizen Kane*, a film in which megalomania challenges or warps real space. This household incident is middle America, as ordinary as it is moving—you feel the joy of March and Loy depicted in such a shot. It is a movie moment, to be sure, yet it is humbled by its own subject, human feeling. And there is a way in which the numbed, tender reunion of these two quite plain people, edging along the corridor toward embrace, is exactly like the reunion that occurred in cinemas for two full years after the war.

I like Wyler's *The Best Years of Our Lives,* not just for its decency, its care, its prosaic accuracy, its quality of acting and writing, nor even for its striking sense of how far the home front had become less than fit for heroes, or survivors. It is not in the same class as *Citizen Kane* as a work of art, but *The Best Years of Our Lives* was a box office triumph, the winner of many Oscars. That moment is a defense—no, more than that, a vindication—of what movies might do for us. All of us. It won Best Picture for 1946, and was proof that "Best Picture" can mean something as important as greatness in art. No one should forget that *Best Years* spoke for 1946 with a directness that helps reveal film's eloquence as a kind of history.

As always in film, the numbers vary a little: some claim that as many as a hundred million tickets were sold weekly in the United States in that postwar mood. More conservative accounting says 85 million, and upward. Why not? The standards of 1946 were too modest to want to show the orgy (or the unease) that March and Loy might have discovered, together again in their bedroom (though film was headed that way). So it's quite likely that, after a while, that couple might have gone back to the movies, to rediscover one of life's ordinary pleasures before they were parted—and in so doing, unwittingly repledge their faith at a church dedicated to the love and understanding between those who are forever apart (I mean those on the screen and those in the seats).

There were films in those years, 1945–47, filled with the pleasures of reassurance and reunion: *The Bells of St. Mary's; Henry V* (which, for Britain, spoke to an alleged tradition of martial glory); *It's a Wonderful*

Life (where an angel teaches the lesson of value in every life, no matter how humble); *The Jolson Story* (show business forever!); *Life with Father* (the family forever!); *Objective, Burma!* (G.I.s forever!—but trouble in Britain because of its suggestion that the United States alone had fought the war); *Pride of the Marines* (the Marines forever!); *Road to Utopia* (Bing and Bob forever!—the celebration of those odd friendships war can produce); and *The Big Sleep* (that superb tribute to romantic fantasy and just being with a movie, a film that opened as the idyllic Bogart-Bacall love story was revealed to the public, as if to say that life and the screen might be a continuum).

But wait a minute. That was not the whole story. If *The Big Sleep* seemed enchanted, if its two chatty lovers glowed with charisma, still the glow was like that of two cigarettes surrounded by darkness. *The Big Sleep* was sublime, yet it was peopled with liars, cheats, and killers, and its darkness trailed off into disorder and madness. George Bailey was redeemed eventually in *It's a Wonderful Life,* but only after that haunting vision of a world without him in which a lovely small town became Pottersville, or Poisonville. Capra's film said it was cheerful—it had Christmas, bells, and assurances of reassurance—but within the movie a bomb had gone off, and its remnants were darkness.

There was more: with two films in a row, *Double Indemnity* (1944) and *The Lost Weekend* (1945), Billy Wilder took the shine off Paramount. The first did the unthinkable, bringing James M. Cain to the American screen, in ways that Cain himself found admirable. You could say it was simply a crime melodrama, done with great sardonic wit—the talk was so funny— but it was also a film that relished human corruption, man's weakness for a femme fatale, and the holes in the insurance business.° *The Lost Weekend* went further: it was a very graphic study of alcoholism, with only modest room for hope at the end. Don't forget that a lot of people drank to get through the war, those in action and those at home. Don't minimize *The Lost Weekend:* it is still startling. And it was Best Picture of 1945.

The Lost Weekend had cost $1.25 million, and at Santa Barbara previews in early 1945 it was greeted first with ridicule, then with revulsion. A studio executive admitted, "We make a bad one now and then." There were rumors that gangster Frank Costello had offered a lot of money to

---

°Cain's novel had had the names "Walter Huff" and "Phyllis Nirdlinger" for its leads. Wilder went instead for Walter Neff and Phyllis Dietrichson—the latter was a joke on Marlene's type of screen character, while the former, for the inside few, echoed Wallace Neff, the most favored architect in town for Hollywood society.

have the film destroyed so that the liquor trade would not be offended. The picture was shelved, and Wilder went off to war-torn Europe to work for the Publicity and Psychological Warfare Section. A Berliner once, he saw enough horrors to drive anyone to drink. This, suddenly, was the real world and one he had been lucky (or smart) enough to avoid.

Wilder came back to America changed, tougher, more cynical. He was divorced. That was part of war's pattern, too. *The Lost Weekend* had picked up a new score (by Miklos Rosza, using a theremin), but something else had happened. Previews were going better. Was the world more grown-up? Still, Paramount opened the film in London first and used the rave reviews it received there to help make it a hit in America. It did $4.5 million at the domestic box office.

Also in 1945, Warners had retrieved Joan Crawford's career with *Mildred Pierce* (another Cain adaptation). Regarded as washed up by M-G-M, Crawford at last won her Oscar playing a desperate working mother who is betrayed by her odious daughter Veda (Ann Blyth). *Mildred Pierce,* I suggest, is a great American picture, ravishing looking in its black-and-white, one that takes on Cain's unique sense of how strongly money drives life— another film by Michael Curtiz. But this is also a picture that pours scorn on hard work, women who try to be independent, daughters, suburbia, and the American way. If I'd been a Red-hunter in the late forties, I'd have had it high on my list of films that did dirt on the American dream.

There are others as dark, or darker: *Leave Her to Heaven,* in Technicolor, in which Gene Tierney (sweetheart material) plays a monster of selfishness, letting a child drown and hurling herself downstairs to abort a pregnancy. It did $5.54 million in 1945. Then there are *Crossfire* and *Gentleman's Agreement* (both 1947, the first as sharp as the second is dull), but both admitting to anti-Semitism in America. Or *Notorious* which, if it ends happily, has the first satisfying sado-masochistic love affair in Hitchcock's work. There is Chaplin's *Monsieur Verdoux* (1947)—about a serial killer of wives—by far his most baleful movie. There is Fritz Lang's *The Woman in the Window* (1945), a perfect barbed trap for voyeurs and fantasists. There is *The Killers* (1946), by Robert Siodmak, adapted from Ernest Hemingway, and an unflinchingly fatalistic vision.

Something to note about this harsh list is how many genres are implicated: the women's picture, the romance, the drama, the comedy even. (Why not throw in Olivier's 1948 *Hamlet*—Shakespeare, of course, but in exactly the same drugged, low-key black-and-white we know from noir, and just as intrigued by the neurotic predicament of a man who can't quite pull the trigger. *Hamlet* was a class act, to be sure, and Best Picture of

1948. Five years in a row, 1945–49, Best Picture went to noirish or socially critical films—*The Lost Weekend, The Best Years of Our Lives, Gentleman's Agreement, Hamlet,* and *All the King's Men.*)

It's a Wonderful Life has even been seen as the start of a Christmas genre. Of the films listed above, only *Crossfire, The Killers,* and *Double Indemnity* (and perhaps *The Woman in the Window*) rate as film noir for purists. But that's a warning against purity, for "noir" has been damaged or confined by those fans who demand urban criminal violence and slut women to feel fulfilled. It may be that noir began in a way of photographing that was as economical as it was moody (less light meant less money on décor—an important wartime consideration when studios faced limits on construction material).

Where did noir come from? It's an intriguing question and one still not adequately answered, despite the quantity of writing that wallows in that noir mood. Don't rule out the influence of Germanic modes from the twenties, if only because there were, by the early forties, so many European refugees (writers, directors, cameramen, designers, actors) working in Hollywood. Don't forget the impact of French films of the late thirties, especially those of Marcel Carné. His *Le Jour Se Lève* (1939, called *Daybreak* in the United States) was such a success that it was remade in Hollywood in 1947 as *The Long Night* (there's a fascinating difference between the two titles, enough to show how French irony seldom registers stateside). Finally, don't underestimate the influence *Citizen Kane* had had on anyone whose art and craft was cinematography. The film was a box office flop, but filmmakers were absorbed by it. A landmark in so much, *Kane* is a turning point in the opening up of a noir sensibility.

Equally, don't forget that from the forties onward, Los Angeles was much beset by psychoanalysis, and the growing intellectual interest in guilt, depression, and nightmare. Don't leave out of consideration the great number of broken families, and the "illicit" love affairs entered into in the course of breakup. And don't eliminate the impact, the memory, or the mere thought of a war's ultimate damage, the concentration camps and the startling introduction of the atomic bomb. Don't forget the vibrant black insolence in bop, or the psychotic energy of abstract expressionism—think of Robert Mitchum looking at Franz Kline, listening to Charlie Parker.

It's clear that pessimistic material and anxious attitudes were creeping into American film well before the end of the Second World War. But with the discovery of the price of peace and the terrible suffering of the Jews, an existential distress fell upon the world, weighed down by the worry that war might not be over yet. You can argue that nothing has yet shifted it: we are still trying to live with the extraordinary death culture of Nazism. Why should Hollywood be left out of that eclipse entirely, no matter how sheltered it liked to keep itself? How could Hollywood Jews not need to admit their very mixed feelings at having survived, and prospered, when nearly every potent Hollywood family discovered names of relatives listed in the dire clerical accounting of Auschwitz, Dachau, and Treblinka. There was work in Bel Air for kindly analysts.

I have so far listed as noir films only major pictures. But I want to stress how deeply noir impulses lay in the common imagination—that of the audience as well as the filmmakers. *Mildred Pierce,* for instance, offered in 1945 when many American women were in new businesses of their own, just to survive while the men were away, sighs and seems to say, It doesn't make any difference, why bother, for there is something malign in human nature or luck that will undermine enterprise and hope. Of course, not every film was so bleak. Look instead at David Selznick's very beautiful and touching *Since You Went Away,* which is all about Claudette Colbert, Jennifer Jones, and Shirley Temple coping in the absence of men. That, too, looks like a film noir (it was photographed by the great, if slow, Stanley Cortez, who had done *The Magnificent Ambersons* and who would do *The Night of the Hunter* for Charles Laughton). But the mood is entirely that of innocent, ardent, flawless hope, and assurance that when the war ends everything will revert to calm and order.

For good and ill, *Since You Went Away* was Selznick's film and vision, though he had much to talk to a shrink about when he was screwing Jennifer Jones while she had scenes of tender parting from her real husband, Robert Walker, who plays a soldier who goes off to war and will not return. The authorship of *Mildred Pierce* is harder to pin down. We give James M. Cain credit, as well as studio production chief Hal Wallis, producer Jerry Wald, and director Michael Curtiz. But there's an energy and a central feeling that comes simply from the wounded eyes of Joan Crawford and that look that says, Fuck Metro. This time I'm showing them! And *Since You Went Away* is a film of historical interest, while *Mildred Pierce* works. You can see it tonight and get a kick out of the authentic, pragmatic severity.

On the other hand, if you were to see *Detour,* you might kill yourself. That is a different kind of noir, one hailed by the purists—and me, too. *Detour* was shot in 1945 in six days by Edgar G. Ulmer, who had been born in Vienna, in 1904, and who had worked as an assistant to F. W. Murnau on *The Last Laugh, Faust,* and then in America on *Sunrise* and *Tabu.*

He made it eventually as a Hollywood director, but on B-pictures (or lower)—hence the crazy schedule on *Detour,* a sixty-nine-minute movie that starts with a meeting on the road to Los Angeles and culminates in a sick sexual bond that can only be resolved in murder. As the critic Myron Meisel wrote: "*Detour* . . . employs only three sets, plus a car driving interminably in front of an unceasing back-projection machine. The story is beneath trash: a musician is hitchhiking out to California to marry his girl, only to become inextricably entangled in a web of circumstance and fate. *Detour* is an exercise in sustained perversity."

Part of that malign energy is hurled in the face of movie conventions: The guy has a girl; a song stands for their happiness—don't they deserve a happy ending? Don't they, hell! A curdled malice rears up, like the vision of pulp writer Jim Thompson, which knows they deserve nothing but fate's lousiest tricks, as delivered by an actress named Ann Savage, one of the true monsters in American film.

You can say that *Detour* comes out of German training and tradition, yet the film is intensely American in its settings, its characters, and its hard-nosed despair. As a matter of fact, it was so quickly and cheaply shot—apparently for $40,000—that it doesn't have a lot of classic noir scenes. That very mannered look would have required talent and money, and *Detour* is in too much of a hurry for such niceties. It comes from Producers Releasing Corporation (PRC), an outfit set up by Ben Judell to furnish filler for the bottom half of double bills and supported by producer Leon Fromkess. That *Detour* is so abrasive, so outrageous, so offensive, so beautiful—take your pick, but note that this range of descriptions is a new kind of choice in American film because the only question asked of Ulmer was, Can you give me something in six days?*

Many of the famous noir films come out of that kind of crazy proposition. You can argue that it was the shabby end of the business, but one that had serious lessons for the art. The movie-going public of the golden age loved double bills. When Selznick went to Riverside to sneak preview *Gone With the Wind* in September 1939, he sneaked his four-hour work-in-progress in the middle of a double bill. That audience loved *GWTW,* but when it was over many patrons insisted on seeing the top-of-the-bill picture that had been delayed.

The distribution business was based on the success or failure of the first feature: the variable percentage of box office returns was calculated on the

---

*Recent research has raised the possibility that Ulmer actually shared the direction with Lew Landers.

A-picture. The B-picture was booked for a guaranteed flat rate, and not a generous one, but that guarantee was enough to stimulate a second tier of movie studio, the B studios, or Poverty Row (there were many derisive names) where a modest profit was predictable if the films could be made cheaply enough. Thus the history of outfits like Monogram, Republic, and PRC.

There's no need to romanticize Poverty Row. Much of its product was worse than dull, especially the routine Westerns. At the same time, ordinary production standards at the major studios were already "expensive." They reflected generous payment to the talent. A film could be made for far less than that average and very comfortable figure, if only someone as imaginative (if "difficult") as Edgar G. Ulmer could be found to work at that level.

Todd McCarthy and Charles Flynn did crucial research for their book, *Kings of the Bs,* which showed that in the 1940s Monogram made 402 pictures. In that period, their average profit was only $1,932! Though in 1947 their per-picture profit rose to $12,996. It was a workable business, as long as budgets were not exceeded, and as long as kids, problem cases, or whoever was unlikely to get work elsewhere could be employed. One of their classics was *Dillinger* (1945), produced by the King brothers, written by Philip Yordan, directed by Max Nosseck, and starring Lawrence Tierney (an icon of the B noir) as the hoodlum. According to Yordan, *Dillinger,* at seventy minutes, cost $65,000, and went on to do so well that it made $4 million on its flat-rate income (about as much as *The Lost Weekend*). It was such a crossover hit that Yordan was nominated for Original Screenplay—he lost, of course, because Monogram had no clout at the Academy Awards. The Oscar he lost went to Richard Schweizer for *Marie-Louise,* a Swiss movie that has vanished. *Dillinger* still plays in noir festivals, and still feels brutal, brutish, and smart.

Ironically, in view of these rich, shining fields of human misery and corruption, not to say the tacit celebration of *Dillinger,* Yordan in an interview recollected that *Dillinger* also raised objections in that there was an unwritten agreement among the major studios not to make gangster pictures until the end of the war, because they might depress morale and give a misleading impression of America. This is not a tall story. You will not find many gangster pictures made in Hollywood during the war years. Crime existed then only as a small, domestic aberration. (It had been a problem for Jimmy Cagney's development.)

Thus, it's very notable how swiftly, after the peace, that the notion of organized or professional crime came back into fashion, especially at the

B-picture level. Furthermore, what does it say of wartime experiences that the warped cop or the weak hero was now a favorite character, a man with power, authority, even a gun, yet poisoned within by bitterness, violence, and melancholy? To take just a few examples important to noir: the startling collusion of Van Heflin (fake hero) and Robert Ryan (dark avenger) in Fred Zinnemann's *Act of Violence* (1949), made for M-G-M; the vicious cop played by Robert Ryan in Nicholas Ray's *On Dangerous Ground* (1952), done for R.K.O.; Van Heflin's rogue cop in Joseph Losey's *The Prowler* (1951), made for Columbia; John Garfield's lawyer who has sold out to the mob in Abraham Polonsky's *Force of Evil* (1948); Dana Andrews as the romantic hero who turns sleazy in Otto Preminger's *Fallen Angel* (1945),—a type pursued in two other Andrews-Preminger collaborations, *Laura* (1944) and *Where the Sidewalk Ends* (1950); Orson Welles as the friend who proves to be the Devil in *The Third Man* (1949); to say nothing of Fred MacMurray's insurance man in *Double Indemnity*, who is setting up a client for murder.

In noir, and in the rather more interesting films on the fringes of noir, yet infected by it, something like mistrust enters into the organism of American film. It is a narrative unreliability, and an atmospheric uncertainty. It means being prepared to abandon happy endings and monotonously likable characters. But those shifts are commercial, too, for identification and reassurance had been essential to the old business philosophy. That's what makes the postwar moment so fascinating, for it is not as if a sudden decline in business prompted introspection or self-conscious doubts. These were the glory days. The profits of every studio surged, and it was as possible for every mogul to feel the old days were back as it was for any child to feel community in a movie theater.

Yet something ominous persists, and even if it is vague, it is a signal factor in the rise of noir mistrust. It's there before the end of the war so you cannot simply attribute it to the hideous photographs of concentration camps or the verbal accounts of the new heat of destruction that had become possible. It's as if the experience of war as a whole—of being in service, of seeing the incompetence of officers, the Army, and the nation as a whole—had bred doubts or more mature attitudes about what it was to be American. Was the public growing up? Hollywood would not dare arrange a conference to investigate that very loaded question, but I think the speculation was there. Not too many of the moguls were alert enough, or sufficiently self-critical, to ask themselves whether they had lost touch with the public pulse, but a lot of the young writers and directors were of that mind.

Take a picture like Nicholas Ray's *They Live by Night*, one of the great American debuts, shot in 1947, though not released until 1949. Why? Its maker, RKO, was confused by the picture. It was very noir, yet very realistic—it had a rural setting, unsmart people, and a haunting naturalism in much of the décor and the shooting. True, it had Farley Granger in the lead, and Granger seemed to come from the makeup room and nowhere else, but *They Live by Night* was a fatalistic account of two helpless young lovers who lack every advantage—no money, no education, no home, no running water, no structure—and so they become hunted criminals. There was an unforced, world-weary fatalism to it, and a bleak social criticism that no longer was a sucker for easy answers.

You can feel the same thing a few years later in the attitudes of James Dean in Ray's *Rebel Without a Cause* (1955). That twenty-four-year-old high school kid knows that too much of what he's getting from school and parents is bullshit. Despite that film's title, he does have a cause, or an intelligence; he has begun to see the absurd pipe dream of Americana and, by implication, the way Hollywood has contributed to that. It's a feeling that maybe, after all, life is not a bowl of cherries but cold, sour soup. I don't want to make too much of Ray's earnest yet fragile movies, or even the whole body of work we call noir, but there is this moment after the war when the thinking in pictures begins to turn adult, disillusioned, tough, and wry.

It's as if the quality of written fiction had been picked up by the movies. At the end of *The Third Man*, Carol Reed held the camera's implacable gaze as Alida Valli walked past Joseph Cotten, superior, defiant, and proud, and far too strong to let sentimentality creep in. It was only in the acidic Graham Greene novella that the two characters held hands and settled for a "movie-like" reconciliation.

The Third Man was an English film officially, yet two main characters were American and the film is a masterpiece in that noir photographic style that was sweeping America. So it's very striking to see how little David Selznick, its American co-producer, grasped the moral realism or the behavioral toughness of the picture. During production he was always trying to push it into the safe corners of mystery or romance. How could it work, he asked, with an idiot for a hero and a villain who was the personification of charm? Those were not the old Hollywood rules. So the film could only work if, somehow, you could believe that in real life heroes and villains didn't come from Central Casting. Selznick found the narrative confusing and the tone off-putting. How could such darkness be enlightening? The only thing he understood about the film was that when it was a hit the money was real money.

Yet only a few years before, in the era of *Gone With the Wind* and *Rebecca,* you could have argued that no one in Hollywood had a surer sense of popular taste than Selznick. He regarded himself, with unabashed confidence still, as the best of Hollywood's young generation. He thought himself infinitely more up to date than Louis B. Mayer or the other dinosaurs of that generation. He was still full of ideas: that he could make a great star out of Jennifer Jones; that a vital way ahead lay in European co-production; that television, coming up over the horizon, was a natural part of his business, not an enemy; that when he came to open *Duel in the Sun*—that fevered Western meant to top *Gone With the Wind*—he would open it not in one theater first and then gradually going wider, but all at once in as many theaters as he could grab (a brand-new strategy in 1946).

There were brilliant insights mixed in with all those hopes. But in the late forties, Selznick came apart. *Duel in the Sun* was a smash hit, but it only broke even. Jennifer Jones proved far more complicated than being just a great star. And Europe was so tricky when you got there. In short, in only a few years, Selznick lost his brashness, his nerve, and his relationship with the public. He turned depressive.

In 1951, he was with Ben Hecht—the writer who had worked on so many of his films, and rescued so many of them—chatting on a studio back lot. Hecht told the story in his autobiography:

" 'Hollywood's like Egypt,' said David, 'full of crumbled pyramids. It'll never come back. It'll just keep on crumbling until finally the wind blows the last studio prop across the sands.'

"And now that the tumult was gone, what had the movies been? A flood of claptrap, he insisted, that had helped bitch up the world and that had consumed the fine talents of thousands of men like ourselves.

" 'A few good movies,' said David. 'Thirty years—and one good movie in three years is the record. Ten out of ten thousand. There might have been good movies if there had been no movie industry, Hollywood might have become the center of a new human expression if it hadn't been grabbed by a little group of bookkeepers and turned into a junk industry.' "

Alert: this very page is impregnated with pinches of salt for those readers who may feel the need. This lament is soulful and self-pitying; it is a speech Hecht might have written for Norman Maine in Selznick's *A Star Is Born* (1937). And it is far more plausible as something coming from Hecht's head. He was a writer who liked to think that his genius had been stifled by Hollywood and by its dreadful habit of giving him so much money. But Selznick might have said it—he talked like grandiose movies;

he had an unfailing instinct for curtain lines; and he was sorry for himself and pretty damn sure about something he had lost.

And so we turn to the sorry history of all that his old Hollywood lost in those years between 1944 and 1951, that era that began with more people lining up for movie tickets than anyone had ever counted before. In the mid-thirties, boosted by an Oscar for *Dangerous* and horrified at the roles Warner Brothers offered her, Bette Davis came to a crisis. The studio offered her *God's Country and the Woman,* in which she was supposed to be a lady lumberjack. The woman whose temper was key to her nervy screen presence snapped. She remembered the situation in her book, *The Lonely Life:*

> I was . . . unfulfilled and further compliance would only have destroyed the career I had so far built. Warners seemed bent on undoing all my work. It was impossible to control their vandalism; but the least I could do was to restrain from collaborating with them. I couldn't and wouldn't play this part. This time it was final. The very contract system that once offered me such security had become stultifying.

So she dashed off to Europe to flirt with productions there. The studio suspended her, which they claimed was their right in the standard seven-year contract. The duration of the suspension (without pay) would then be added on to the end of the seven-year sentence.

Bette was sued in the London courts by Warners, and she lost, paying $50,000 out of her own pocket. But the result was another kind of Bette Davis picture: headstrong independence bucking the system. She was called "a naughty little girl" in court, but the condescension helped make a heroine out of her. Once tamed, she found that Warners recompensed her for the legal costs and gave her better roles. In the years at Warner after the dispute, she got *Marked Woman, Jezebel, Dark Victory, Juarez, The Private Lives of Elizabeth and Essex,* and *The Letter.* She could complain about the Warners and the way the studio favored its male stars, but her case had dramatized her public image as well as the films. In truth, her battle had better results than the struggles of Jimmy Cagney, which she studied carefully.

Actors and actresses often found fault with the bad scripts offered them. And while they could take some comfort in their own large salaries, there was a small band of quarrelsome agents who were pointing out that stars often carried pictures but seldom enjoyed any part of their profits. Well, of course not, the studios retorted, but neither do you carry any of the risk. It was a good enough answer for the moment, in part because few actors had been educated in business or legal matters. But there were exceptions; there were talents who stood to share in the booty of their pictures.

At some time in the early forties, Olivia de Havilland became possessed by the Bette Davis bug. This was a surprise as de Havilland was generally thought of as nice, decent, amiable, a good trouper—she was a natural Melanie, never considered for Scarlett. She was popular, and she had seemed happy enough for years at Warners playing second fiddle to Davis and being Errol Flynn's ladylove. Then family intruded. De Havilland had a younger sister, known as Joan Fontaine. Some even said that Joan was the more beautiful. Olivia had been a working actress first, but then, somehow, Joan had passed her in the career race. Fontaine had been nominated for an Oscar for *Rebecca* (a brilliant performance); then, having lost, she won the following year for a rather less impressive job in *Suspicion* (both films by Hitchcock, of course). For her part, Olivia had been nominated once in support, for *Gone With the Wind* (losing to Hattie McDaniel—not the easiest blow to take), and then as Best Actress for *Hold Back the Dawn*, when she lost again—to Joan.

I'm not saying that this rivalry dominated her decision, but the great cause of liberty is not compromised by petty promptings. Olivia's contract was with Warners, too, and she despised the things she was being offered. On one occasion, she was in a conversation with her agent, Lew Wasserman, and with a young actor who was becoming more and more involved in the Screen Actors Guild, Ronald Reagan (who was married then to Jane Wyman, another actress at Warners who had had her problems with the studio). De Havilland was lamenting the strictness of the seven-year contract when Wasserman said he believed there was an old Californian statute that claimed contracts exceeding seven years amounted to slavery. I doubt that Wasserman "believed" that or idly suggested it. I suspect he directed the event and the action that de Havilland then took in court.

To be precise, de Havilland refused to act in a remake of *The Animal Kingdom* (eventually done as *One More Tomorrow,* with Ann Sheridan). She was suspended, for the sixth time. She brought suit and the studio then requested every other studio not to hire her. But in March 1944 the court found for her; a few months later the California Supreme Court upheld the verdict. The victory was modest: henceforth, no suspension time could be added on to the seven years. What that really meant was that studios might as well listen to the feelings of their talent.

In response, Warners made her play Charlotte Brontë in the dreadful but very enjoyable *Devotion* (Ida Lupino is Emily), and after that de Havilland was a freelance. Some argued that the collective system cold-shouldered her; it's true that she worked less. But less also meant winning an Oscar for *To Each His Own* (directed by Mitchell Leisen); as twins in *The Dark Mirror,* a good noir; the very splashy role of the mad woman in *The Snake Pit* (still an uncomfortable picture); and another Oscar for *The Heiress* (directed by William Wyler, with Montgomery Clift and Ralph Richardson). Reward enough, I think; in addition, by then Fontaine was in pictures called *You Gotta Stay Happy* and *Born to Be Bad.*

De Havilland makes a pretty story. The other legal defeat of the time was far more damaging for Hollywood, but far duller. By the mid-thirties, at least, the picture business had been integrated in that several major sources of production not only distributed their own product but owned theaters, too. This monopoly applied to M-G-M, Warner Brothers, Twentieth Century–Fox, Paramount, and RKO. This was not only a power lock that led to block-booking and blind-bidding practices being imposed on all other theater chains, it was also, as I said earlier, a closed system such as made the arrangement of accounts so much easier. Block-booking was the practice by which a studio would dangle before an exhibitor one or two prize films, so long as a dozen other, poorer pictures were taken, too. Blind-bidding was the expectation that theaters would agree to terms (the rental split) on pictures without even having the chance to see them. To equate this with a publishing scenario, an independent bookseller in the sticks would get a publisher's hot books only if he also took every other title on the list; and he had to agree to pay a set percentage of revenue without a chance to read any of the books.

The iniquity of this system, the un-Americanness of it, had been talked about since the early thirties. For this reason, a small New Jersey company brought suit against Warners in 1933. The action had swollen and been endlessly delayed by studio lawyering and by payoffs in Washington. There may be no better proof of the diligence, the ferocity, and the self-protectiveness of Hollywood than that it actually managed to delay the final decision on the matter until 1948. Think of the plunder in those intervening years, and open an accounting book on all the situations in which, with skill or something else, Hollywood has broken the laws of America.

It was in 1948, at last, that Justice William O. Douglas delivered the final judgment by which these monopolies were ordered to dispose of their theatrical holdings—though, even then, they were given—or rather they took—five years to make the separation.

This blow was fiscal and structural, and it was also against popular odds—the studios reckoned that the decision had been delayed or fudged so long, it would never arrive. But it was also emotional for the old men who still ran the studios, for they had all begun as theater operatives. Hence, their sense of the public; it was their roots. But nothing prepared them for the shock that came with the numbers. Not only had the theaters been the cast-iron guarantee of cash flow (and where there is raw cash flow there is a question mark over accounting), but they (the buildings or urban property) were collateral when it came to raising money from the banks; they were another source of income from the sale of refreshments; and they accounted for something like 90 percent of the money spent by studios.

To make matters worse, it was within months of the Paramount decision that the business began to realize that something was happening with the audience. By 1948, audience numbers were beginning to decline. Had the postwar euphoria worn off? Were too many of those new families now encumbered with babies so that a trip to the movies was less likely? In America, especially, there was a move out of urban centers to the suburbs, and most of the older movie theaters had been built in desirable urban centers. Was it even the case that the growing gloom or pessimism of the product was beginning to disturb people? There would be those who made it their business to make that claim, and to insist that Hollywood had turned un-American.

The commonest reason given for the decline is the great fallacy that television was keeping people at home. But there is a clear gap—as much as three years—between the drop-off in cinema audiences and the way in which television became a domestic appliance in America.

Television had been demonstrated in the late 1930s, notably at the 1939 New York World's Fair, but there were not the funds for the manufacture of sets until after the war. A TV set then could cost $600—enough money for a car, or even a house in some parts of the country. By the end of 1948, there were still only a million sets in domestic use. By 1950, that number was 12 million; by 1954, 38 million. There is not the least doubt in any mind that this great rival eventually ate away at theatrical audiences, just as, decades later, it would come around to being the unexpected rescuer of the picture business. It's true that in 1948 a few bright people in pictures saw the threat, though many more believed it was going to be surmounted without any difficulty. What's more important to stress is that the American audience had faltered in its automatic adoration (or acceptance) of movies. The business system might not yet resemble abandoned or forgotten pyramids, but the mania had lost energy. Did that therefore give any promise of a new place for reason?

Perhaps there were hopes. The late forties are a pregnant, developing moment in Hollywood history. But there was another threat in the air, as ridiculous as it was cruel, as specious as it would be damaging. It took as its stance the outlandish notion that Hollywood (and its masters?) had been less than positive about America. Or about life! But in doing so, it shattered every uncertain hope that Hollywood once had been a shared business, a community, a family. All of a sudden, every paranoid foreboding in film noir found a real monster at the door, twice as troubling as any femme fatale or even that piercing emblem of noir menace, Robert Ryan.

The face of Alfred Hitchcock in the San Francisco night (© *Lucy Gray, 1998*)

18 · IN A LONELY PLACE

It is a testing time for irony, 1947 and '48. For just as Hollywood is compelled to admit and remedy a criminal strategy essential to its business, in an issue over which it has prevaricated, bluffed, bullied, bribed, and avoided for fifteen years, so it identifies and punishes crimes that are somewhere between fantastical and absurd, crimes so specious that the truer injustice lies in the craven fact that they were ever charged. To be quick about this part of it, the campaign of the House Committee on Un-American Activities was unconstitutional, and in its punishment, the blacklist, it was illegal. Yet in practice, in the years during which the studios very gradually followed the orders of the Supreme Court in the Paramount decision, many Hollywood careers were halted, a climate of fear was established, and the prospect of an adult attitude in American pictures was set back.

The blacklist may be no more, but scoundrels and idiots in office still bandy about the notion of things being "un-American" or "expecting too much" of audiences. Do not ask, in the chill of Homeland Security, how long we must wait for a black comedy in which our security agencies neglected crucial, tapped telephone calls because they lack the agents who speak the languages of the enemy. (Isn't it a begging sequel to *Dumb and Dumber?*) And as the insistence on the "greatness" of the United States becomes more extreme, so the taste for self-criticism dies. As if a country founded on the philosophies of America ever needed to stoop to "un-American" as a test. How swiftly the ideal of multitudes and diversity shrank to a haunted hope for conformity. For by 1947, the history of Hollywood cannot be judged properly without considering the malaise of the United States. What happens in the crisis called the blacklist is an opting for false security over real thinking, and a preference for money over ideas or openness. More than any committee charged to look after Americanness could ever calculate, the principles of the country were damaged. For here is the ultimate test in it all: You cannot make the kind of enormous appeal to human imagination that is involved in the movies, and then settle for patriotism, profit, or their combined strength as the only way to live. In other words, there were forces in America, business and political, that felt the danger of too many open, critical movies. We have not yet reversed that trend.

Follow the money. The monopolistic vertical integration of the movie business, as well as denying choice and freedom in countless local situations, had remorselessly helped establish the wealth of the business leaders. The less-powerful elements had been screwed, the public had been deprived. After the Paramount decision came down, forlorn damage suits were brought for over $600 million. Hardly a penny changed hands. The history of the medium had been founded on illegal practice and extortion. Thus the studios had accrued far more money than was their right, at a time when the talent had as yet found no reliable way of participating in the profits.

The disparities open to the public gaze offended many of the talented people, and left them indignant over the tricks that were going unseen. To take just one example, consider *Casablanca*, not just Best Picture for 1943 and a "universal favorite," but a picture that still impresses so many of us as typical of what movies can do—in this case, tell an appealing human story in which one human sacrifice (Rick giving up Ilse) can easily be extrapolated into the altruism that may win the war. Yes, it's loaded with white lies, yet somehow, I think, they stop short of the feeling that we have been defrauded. You can argue that *Casablanca* helped the wartime morale (especially when its opening coincided with the Allied relief of that North African port). You can say the public still loves *Casablanca*. You can also say the public should heed one of its writers, Julius Epstein, and his opinion that it was just "slick shit."

But look at it another way: on a picture that cost close to $1 million, Bogart was paid $36,667; Ingrid Bergman got $25,000 (her salary under her Selznick contract; she was loaned to Warners in a straight swap for Olivia de Havilland); Claude Rains got $22,000; Paul Henreid and Conrad Veidt got $25,000 each; Marcel Dalio—the great actor from Renoir's films, the Marquis in *La Règle du Jeu*—got $667 as the croupier (for eight days' work).

The original play was purchased for $20,000; all the writers—and there were several—earned about $53,000 collectively; director Michael Curtiz got $73,400.

The cost of film stock was $8,000; $10,500 went to developing and printing it. The camera crew as a whole was paid $10,873—just think of the look of *Casablanca* and the fluidity of the moving camera; allow that Curtiz may have "designed" such things, but still and all movies are a photographic art. Set builders got $18,000. Makeup and hairdressing took $9,100. The cutters got $4,630. There were other costs, of course, on a picture that shot for eight weeks.

There's nothing untoward or scandalous in these figures. They are typical, as is the fact that the budget was topped off with "general studio overhead," a sum of $223,822. By the standards of Los Angeles in 1942, those craftspeople or technicians were being paid well. The actors were being paid at a level regarded by the public as luxurious or plutocratic. Yet the routine overhead charge was roughly equal to the money paid to the entire cast and the director.

There was need for an overhead charge as in any business accounting: the studio property in Burbank had to be kept up; its services—like the canteen, the legal department, the groundskeeping—had to be maintained.

The executive salaries had to be met. And yet every Warner Brothers picture made in 1942 carried an overhead fee that was usually 35 percent of the direct costs of production.

Casablanca could have flopped—there were Warner Brothers pictures in 1942 that did, though not many. In fact, it earned domestic rentals in its first release of a little over $3 million—the portion of box office returned to the studio in the U.S. market. There was a war on, as the picture observed, but as time went by foreign revenue would be added in. By 1955, the revenue figure on *Casablanca* was up to $6.8 million.

That was nearly fifty years ago. Many readers will have been born in the years since, and how often have they seen *Casablanca*? It was in 1956 that Jack Warner made the decision to sell nearly all Warners films made before 1948 to United Artists for $21 million. Later on, most of those films were acquired by the television magnate Ted Turner, who is now a large shareholder in the conglomerate that decided it would call itself just plain old Time Warner instead of AOL Time Warner, after upstart America Online had taken over the media empire. In short, *Casablanca*, every day of every year, continues to bring in more money to its line of ownership, with all the same old talk about not mattering a hill of beans. It is too complicated a trail to pursue but I don't doubt that *Casablanca* has earned close to $20 million in profit.

That may not sound like a huge sum of money when so many films today do those numbers in their first week of opening. But $20 million in 1942 was prodigious—and 3.33 percent of the modest damages claimed by injured parties in 1948 because of illegal monopolistic practices in the business. I believe that for decades moviegoers have been encouraged to overlook the elements of business. (When *Casablanca* opened, the public had no knowledge of its numbers.) It's like calling Rick in *Casablanca* an anti-fascist hero when he is also, plainly, the proprietor of a casino where, even if he has to pay an "overhead" fee to Major Strasser, still he has a croupier who can make the roulette wheel bring up any number he wants.

It's not quite enough that *Casablanca* still "works" if that functioning only distracts us from all the falsehoods embedded in the picture. It is a blithe romance: I wonder what real concentration camp inmates would think to be told that Paul Henreid was one of them? What has the image of Rick done to American overconfidence and even to American leaders? What does the film say about our arrogant regard for places like North Africa, a world that has no voice in the film? A very large part of this book's concern is looking at the film as a whole, which means acknowledging its heady impact still, while seeing that "slick shit" is pretty good criticism, and remarking on the absence from the business process of those who truly made the film. I don't know where to place "authorship" of *Casablanca*. Maybe a dozen people have a good claim on it. Maybe it is best regarded as the product of a skilled but anonymous system, in which case maybe there is a thing called collaborative art—or maybe as Colonel Jack Warner might have said in 1942–43, it's just the family of Warner Brothers doing it all. But that claim surely bumps against the disproportion in benefit from the film, and the odious way in which the Colonel (among others) would soon turn on his family.

Many movie laborers and technicians lost advantage during the war years. In the thirties, a carpenter in pictures, say, had earned $6 more a week than a carpenter in regular construction. But as military factories set up in Los Angeles in great number they offered wages to compete with the studios. The movie men were squeezed, yet their unions had to respect the pledge the American Federation of Labor had given to Roosevelt not to strike as long as the war lasted. And if you couldn't strike, what was the real point in negotiating?

The great majority of movie craftsmen were part of IATSE. Despite its daunting name, this union had been small for many years until the mid-thirties, when it was effectively taken over by two rogues: Willie Bioff, a Chicago gangster, and George Browne, who had organized stagehands in Chicago. They moved to Hollywood as a team and they recruited busily. Membership rose from just over 150 to 12,000, and Bioff/Browne used their projectionists (also part of IATSE) as a blunt threat to the studios. So they got marginally better deals for their workers, but each man also got $50,000 apiece from the major studios to guarantee labor peace.

Where did that money come from? From overhead, of course. But the truth was wilder still. When Bioff made his proposition in April 1936, to Nicholas Schenck, among others, he asked for $2 million from each studio. Schenck laughed. Bioff went away and came back another day. "A million?" he asked. That a settlement on $50,000 was reached seems crazy—perhaps the studio guys wanted to keep Bioff around for color—but Mayer and Thalberg were in on the agreement. Bioff's last feeble retort was to insist that the payoff be tax-free (he knew the Capone story).

It didn't last. Robert Montgomery, in his capacity as president of the Screen Actors Guild, stuck a private detective on Bioff and turned up enough dirt to secure a twenty-year jail sentence for him and Browne. Joe Schenck, Nick's brother, also went to prison for serving as bagman in some of these arrangements (the official charge was tax evasion). Nick preferred to give up his brother before he would betray Louis B. Mayer.

This sentencing occurred in 1941, just as union liberty was shelved. But IATSE members were disillusioned, and very tempted by the formation of an alternative crafts union, the Conference of Studio Unions, founded in early 1945 by Herbert Sorrell. (Bioff and Sorrell appear in few books about Hollywood, yet their part in the history is crucial.)

Sorrell's chief selling point for the CSU was easy: it was honest and it would be pro-labor in practice. It would get a better deal for its members, and why not if the business was doing so well? IATSE was put under new leadership, that of Roy Brewer, and he had no alternative but to make the obvious response: the CSU was infiltrated by Communists! It didn't matter whether this was true, and who could tell anyway? At this period in Hollywood history so many Communist party members were FBI plants that real numbers were hard to establish.

There followed a series of strikes in 1945–47 in which the CSU and IATSE were trawling for members and a kind of integrity. Warners had been made a test case and there was fighting in the streets in Burbank as pickets were set up. The Writers Guild supported the CSU; the actors followed IATSE. Production was halted on several occasions. Money was lost. IATSE was accused of being a studio front. The CSU was condemned for its Red allegiances. This is the climatic background to the first ominous moves from the House Un-American Activities Committee.

In part, the Committee put such stress on the movies, and the suggestion that they were tainted, because of the old fear that the new medium of the twentieth century was so potent it had to be dangerous. The establishment was nervous about any force that might reach all the people. It still is. Then there was the known history of an attempt, directed from Moscow, to place people in the picture business in the late thirties. Don't forget the character of the union official Brimmer in *The Last Tycoon* (Jack Nicholson in the movie).

It says a lot for Fitzgerald's instincts, and for Monroe Stahr's Americanness, that they both treat Brimmer so well: he's an organizer, from New York, critical, alert, ready to gain any advantage—yet Spencer Tracy could have played him. He asks Stahr why the producers don't support the Anti-Nazi League, and Stahr dismisses that as just a hobbyhorse of the writers: "Writers are children—even in normal times they can't keep their minds on their work." You can read the rest for yourself, but the two men have a good talk, and it all suggests that an Irving Thalberg in 1936 was no more alarmed by a Brimmer than by a Bioff. Indeed, Stahr sees it as perfectly legal to be a Communist, and to try to organize the film business (Stahr was trying to organize it himself), though he does seem to rely on the selfish immaturity of his children to resist that pressure.

Another reason for picking on the movies has been offered by Victor Navasky, one of the scholars of the blacklist era, in his book *Naming Names:*

> But if its [Hollywood's] inhabitants were in the business of manufacturing our dreams, they were also in the habit of living them. Not only their salaries but also their cars, pools, breasts, alimony payments, mansions, muscles, psychiatrists' bills, talents, and images were, like the images on the silver screen, larger than life. HUAC saw a chance to bask in the publicity glow of Hollywood's stars.

I'm sure that's right, yet I suspect Navasky's language speaks for a kind of East Coast academic and intellectual upbringing that had always found Hollywood suspect and soft—fatuous, even. Just as right, but maybe closer to the new anxiety in Hollywood, was the studio fear that Communist strikes could interrupt the smooth flow of production and consumption. Long before there had been a House Un-American Activities Committee, the founders of the movie business had striven to impress onlookers (and themselves) that they were no longer Russian, Polish, Hungarian, or whatever—above all that they were not Jewish. No, they were American, and they put up Christmas trees to prove it. Mayer had even asserted that his own birthday was July 4.

It was in the fall of 1947, under chairman J. Parnell Thomas, that HUAC called its first "witnesses," a pathetic parade of "friendly" voices, most of them pretty powerful but all as troubled by Red seepage as people who cannot sleep. One such figure was Jack Warner, so recently a "Colonel," the most active of the brothers Warner. He gave every indication of being ready to inform on any member of the Warners family he could think of: he named Howard Koch, one of the writers on *Casablanca* (and on *The Letter,* among other Warners hits), only to find that Koch had no history as a Communist. But he disliked Koch because the writer had been vocal during a recent strike.

The potential for malice and vengeance was already apparent. Official Hollywood made throat-clearing noises about the opportunism of it all. The Association of Motion Picture Producers (AMPP) said, "We are tired of having irresponsible charges made again and again and again and not sustained." There was in prospect a list of "unfriendly" witnesses—eight writers, one director, and one producer—subpoenaed, and likely to face tougher scrutiny.

In Beverly Hills there was anticipatory concern, and a group of people met one night at Ira Gershwin's house and formed what became known as the Committee for the First Amendment (CFA). Their point was as sound and strong as it was simple: the First Amendment to the Constitution permitted Americans to hold and express an open range of political opinions. As Lauren Bacall said later, "There was no talk of Communism—from our point of view, Communism had nothing to do with it. It had to do with the Hitlerian tactics being employed."

A representative group elected to go to Washington to demonstrate their feelings. It included John Huston, Danny Kaye, Paul Henreid, Evelyn Keyes, Larry Adler, Gene Kelly, Bacall, and Bogart. They took their venture very seriously: the women in the party agreed to wear skirts rather than slacks so as not to alarm middle America. They gave press conferences and made a big show of their trip East. They were burning with sincerity and, as actors, their experience was that that mode had always served them well. The inevitable confusion of politics and movie celebrity was under way. That was another reason why the Committee had struck at picture people. It wasn't that they were American royalty; they were the most obvious bearers of the American message.

Many people from the CFA attended the "unfriendly hearings," and they said they were shocked and disturbed. The ten men pilloried were Ring Lardner, Jr. (who had written the Hepburn-Tracy film *Woman of the Year*); Albert Maltz (who had written *Pride of the Marines* and *Destination Tokyo*); Lester Cole and Alvah Bessie (who had collaborated on *Objective, Burma!*); Samuel Ornitz (a novelist); Dalton Trumbo (the writer on *Kitty Foyle* and *Thirty Seconds over Tokyo*); John Howard Lawson (who had worked on two Bogart pictures, *Sahara* and *Action in the North Atlantic*); Herbert Biberman (who had directed *Meet Nero Wolfe*); and Edward Dmytryk, the director, and Adrian Scott, the writer-producer, of *Crossfire*.

Yes, all of the above had been members of the Communist party at some time. But I list the credits to show how steadily this group had worked on mainline, patriotic films. Even where a hint of radicalism appears in the work, as in *Woman of the Year*, which begins to suggest that women are as valuable as men, the ending of that film capitulates tidily and has Hepburn melt into Tracy's loyal and unquestioning support. (Billy Wilder tossed off the remark—characteristic of his urge to sacrifice a great deal for a laugh—that only two of the ten were talented, and the rest were just unfriendly.)

To pick one picture, *Crossfire* was a movie that America could be proud of. Constructed as a noir thriller, it has Robert Young as a cop and Robert Mitchum as a soldier, tracking down a murderer who proves to be the anti-Semitic Robert Ryan. *Crossfire* was a very good example of the noir pictures made at RKO under the production control of Dore Schary. It is also typical of the kind of postwar movie I have alluded to that uses a familiar genre to address pressing social realities. It is beautifully made: the photography, by J. Roy Hunt, is still referred to in textbooks; the writing, by Scott and John Paxton, is flawless; and the playing, by Ryan and Gloria Grahame, especially, is magnificent.

And Hollywood approved of it: on a budget of $250,000, with earnings of $1.3 million, it was RKO's biggest picture of the year. It was nominated for Best Picture, and lost to *Gentleman's Agreement* (also about anti-Semitism, but slack, preachy, and dull); it had other Oscar nominations for its screenplay and for Robert Ryan. The National Board of Review voted it one of the best pictures of the year. Over fifty years later it still plays, and works, with Mitchum's drowsy, laconic delivery as much a model of "cool" as the Miles Davis recordings about to happen, and a sturdy safeguard against hysteria in the American grain.

If only Dmytryk, Scott, and the others could have handled themselves as well in front of HUAC. There are disputes still over those ugly hearings, and every reason to think that Parnell Thomas and others (Richard Nixon was on the Committee, too) were determined on trouble. There are even suggestions that Communist lawyers advised the ten's untidy response to be more sure of getting its martyrs. What one longs for, in hindsight, is the record of a strong, dignified reliance on the First Amendment's principles. What actually happened seemed evasive, blustering, scared, disorganized, and verbose. There was no plan, no trust in law, no dignity. Perhaps the ten really were scared, and as lonely and naïve as most writers, even those who deal in hard-boiled stuff.

The Bogarts of the world faced the same problem. It was far easier facing down Major Strasser when people like the Epstein brothers (Julius and Philip) had written your lines. You could sound like the modern knight in armor, risking life for $25 a day, in *The Big Sleep*, when you had Jules Furthman and Faulkner being brave for you. Bogart blinked. His own advisers, lawyer Morgan Maree and agent Sam Jaffe, warned him of the risks. Bogart had just signed a new independent contract. At last, he stood to make some real money as a producer-participant in his own pictures, instead of just that $36,667 from *Casablanca*. His future, he was told, was in jeopardy.

This is the greatest movie hero of that moment. This is Bogey. The ten had not behaved well in Washington; they hadn't acted with Bogart's grace under fire on screen. But the issues remained exactly the same, except that now the ugliness of the threat was too plain to be written off. The ten faced contempt charges and jail time. A blacklist was shaping up, utterly contrary to California law, through which anyone suspected of Communist ties might be kept from working. Still, Bogart was persuaded to go public in contrition:

> I went to Washington because I thought fellow Americans were being deprived of their constitutional rights, and for that reason alone.
>
> That trip was ill-advised, even foolish, I am very ready to admit. At the time it seemed like the thing to do.

His stance was neither ill-advised nor foolish, but Bogart's stepping down was more effective in America's real life than all his borrowed gestures could be in fiction. By 1949, the ten were in jail. Lardner and Cole were sent to the penitentiary at Danbury, Connecticut, where they found Parnell Thomas as a fellow inmate, convicted for taking kickbacks. Camp Wacky again.

The American motion picture industry willfully attacked itself in perhaps its finest moment. It victimized many talented people and deprived itself and its audience of what they might do. And it hardly grasped how far its cowardice, its stupidity, and its profound un-Americanness helped to break down the bonds between the movie and the audience. Our common vision of the blacklist remains that of individual melodrama: John Garfield died too early; Elia Kazan traded away honor for a successful career. There's truth in both those claims, but they are small beside the way in which the studios, those household corporate names, declined to stand up for their own people and the law of the land.

What did we lose? Well, take two cases. Abraham Polonsky was born in New York in 1910, the child of Russian Jewish immigrants. He graduated from City College and from Columbia Law School and he was until the end of his days a brilliant, fast mind, a cunning arguer, a wit, a storyteller, and a sexpot. He joined the Communist Party because of the Spanish Civil War and for all I know he was a member until his death. He wrote two novels (one under his own name) and during the war he served in the Office of Strategic Services.

Hollywood was interested in him and he went there after the war, hired as a $2,000-a-week writer. He sold a new small company, Enterprise, on a boxing picture that became *Body and Soul*, with Garfield in the lead and Robert Rossen directing. It's pretty good, pretty tough, and pretty sentimental at the same time; indeed, it's an old genre made tart by the postwar attitude. It's nowhere near as good as the next film, *Force of Evil*, which Polonsky wrote and directed for Enterprise—and which M-G-M released!

Force of Evil is a film noir (just seventy-eight minutes long) in which Garfield plays a smart lawyer who works for the Mob and helps organize the numbers racket. He is redeemed in the movie thanks to a love relationship and the death of his brother at the hands of the Mob (there are several hints of *On the Waterfront* here). Those are Hollywood tricks, of course, but what is different is the harsh analysis of corrupt power, some of it accomplished in the visuals, some in the dialogue that is often blank verse. I think you can see a Communist influence in the picture's trenchant, acid view of capitalism, and I think that any capitalist system anxious to endure would be grateful for the criticism.

It is a terrific movie, one of the best first films ever made in America. And, yes, it is subversive. But art is allowed to be. And what was M-G-M doing with it in 1948 if they didn't think they could make a buck on it? Polonsky was very soon blacklisted. He did TV work under pseudonyms; he scripted the 1959 movie *Odds Against Tomorrow*, anonymously; and he did not come back to pictures under his own name until the script for *Madigan* (1968), and *Tell Them Willie Boy Is Here* (1969), which he wrote and directed. Later still, he did a script for *Guilty by Suspicion*, in which Robert De Niro plays a director who is ruined by false accusations of having been a Communist. That was 1991, when the history of paranoia was, supposedly, over. But Polonsky took his name off the film (and Frenchman Bertrand Tavernier opted out of directing) because he had wanted the De Niro character to be a real Communist and because the whole approach was, well, slick shit again. So *Guilty by Suspicion* ended up "written and directed by" its producer, Irwin Winkler.

Times had changed, but courage was still rare. Polonsky was freer to work now; his promise was a bad joke; but he held to old principles. Not that he was ever doctrinaire or unamusing. Polonsky could be very sharp on how the Party in old Hollywood had been a kind of club for well-heeled do-gooders. Nor did he ever see any prospect of making a truly radical film there:

> One of the great discussions that used to go on all the time was: Should I be in Hollywood, and should I be writing movies? Or should I, say, do documentaries? Or should I try to make films apart from Hollywood that

would in some way deal with the theoretical basis of why we are in fact in the Communist Party? This dilemma was not solved, and it couldn't be solved, because it was artificial and didn't exist. Filmmaking in the major studios is the prime way that film art exists. That doesn't mean that film, as an art form, doesn't exist apart from the studios. But when you want to get into making movies . . . then there's only one thing to do: you try to make feature films for studios. . . . It may end in the total defeat of every impulse that the writer, the director, and the actor has. But the fact of the matter is, that's the only choice.

Polonsky made these remarks near the end of his life (he died in 1999), after *Guilty by Suspicion* and his experience overseas. He is talking about Hollywood still, but his comments cover filmmaking on a far wider scale. What Polonsky knew was that he had lost out to stupidity and worse, and the audience had lost, too. But there were limits to what might have been achieved.

Then consider Joseph Losey, born in La Crosse, Wisconsin, in 1909, and educated at Dartmouth and Harvard—another very smart kid. He worked in theater for years and after war service (making films for Frank Capra) he directed the first production (in Los Angeles) of Brecht's *Galileo,* with Charles Laughton. At that point, RKO and Dore Schary hired Losey to make his first film: *The Boy with Green Hair,* produced by Adrian Scott, an adroit fairy tale about conformity and being different. It launched Losey on a series of fascinating low-budget pictures: *The Lawless,* about Chicanos; *The Prowler,* a very fine noir about a rogue cop, produced by Sam Spiegel and with Dalton Trumbo as a writer; *M,* a remake of the Fritz Lang picture, with David Wayne as the killer—an outstanding and still neglected movie; and *The Big Night,* with Ring Lardner, Jr., among its writers.

Losey, too, had joined the Communist party and found it dispiriting: "a lot of meaningless so-called Marxist classes which were a bore and which never had any practical result either in terms of the films that were made or the films that weren't made or anything else. The Hollywood left had no influence on Hollywood excepting possibly in the Writers' Guild and I was not a writer."

One day, perhaps, someone may write a great comedy on those Marxist cell meetings where young Communists slip in and out of the pool, in and out of bed, and where their magnificent cars line the drive like steel topiary. Why did no one, in 1947 or in the following years, ever think to ask, What is the Communist influence in pictures? In Hollywood movies? In

Astaire and Rogers? In the Marx Brothers (there's that name)? In all this happiness, the bright living rooms as spacious as halls, the family cohesion, the natural certainty of virtue? Or was this just a version of East Coast revenge, like having the atomic bomb tests held in Nevada because the place had gone gonzo on divorce and gambling?

Losey could be very practical. He said always that he believed that if, in the worst moments, enough people had stood up and said, Sure, I'm a Communist, so what?, the whole frenzy could have been blown away. We'll never know. But perhaps we'll be given other chances to test the mettle of American pragmatism.

Certain that he was about to be blacklisted, Losey went to Europe, where he had hard years, doing hack work in television, making commercials, and working under pseudonyms: as "Joseph Walton," he directed *The Intimate Stranger* (with Howard Koch on the script, but known as "Peter Howard"). Losey stuck in England and learned to examine that country in the way he had once studied America. The result was that he became one of the best English social critics (often with Harold Pinter as his writer) on films like *Blind Date, The Criminal, The Servant, Accident, The Go-Between.*

I doubt that anything as dark or emotionally complex as *The Servant* could be made in America even now. It suggests that a certain amount of Marxism (if channelled through Dartmouth and Harvard) might benefit any nation's cinema. But very few blacklist victims turned their misfortune to such good ends, and few moviemakers have ever gained such an insight into a new home.

*   *   *

The most serious damage done by the blacklist occurred in the early fifties, and it coincided with the picture business's policy of economizing. Starting in 1948, the attendance figures began to fall. By the early fifties, it was evident how far television was accelerating the decline. When contracts were terminated, or dropped, in the aftermath of HUAC exposure (or the mere suggestion of involvement), it was something the industry had already been in the habit of doing, having been laying off workers at all levels—craftsmen, actors, writers—for a couple of years. The form termination letters were already in hand. The contract system had met its ultimate enemy: loss of business confidence. So the studios had no compelling reason to be brave with HUAC, to stand by the law, or even to live up to their frequent protestations of family kinship. They had another reason for keeping quiet: the Paramount decision of 1948 was not rigorously enforced. Paramount did not separate itself from its theaters until the last day of 1949. At M-G-M, Fox, and Warners the final breaks came in 1952 and 1953. In other words, the studios were all in debt to the government.

Is it ironic then that the blacklist is so seldom attributed to the studios, and so often to Washington, to people like Parnell Thomas and Joseph McCarthy, and to finks like Elia Kazan? Or is it part of Hollywood's history of irresponsibility?

Look at it this way: in 1999, the Academy proposed to give Elia Kazan an Oscar for lifetime achievement. By then, Kazan was ninety and in poor health, but he was fighter enough still to attend the ceremony and take his statuette (proffered by Martin Scorsese and Robert De Niro). Outside the theater there were busy demonstrations against the award and against Kazan. He had already had Oscars for directing (for *Gentleman's Agreement* and *On the Waterfront*) and three other nominations. More than that, in 1952, Kazan, briefly a Communist in the thirties, had chosen to give names to HUAC. He would admit to two reasons for that: he had come to loathe and despise Communism, and he wanted to work.

Kazan is a tricky case, just as he was always a very complex man—which is nearly palpable in his book *A Life,* one of the most revealing ever written about a show business or artistic career. He was an inspiring director of actors, and a driving force behind the naturalism known as Actors Studio style. His influence was intense, on stage and screen. In addition, he went from being a rather ordinary filmmaker (*Boomerang, Gentleman's Agreement, Pinky*) to a director of passionate melodramas that were vital in the emotional reawakening of the 1950s (*East of Eden, Wild River, Splendor in the Grass*). Moreover, I believe that he found himself as a director—found his own ego—in the crisis of testifying to HUAC and betraying old associates.

The Oscar in 1999 was unnecessary and provocative. Yet it spoke to the moral blindness of the Academy and the picture business. I would have been very happy if Kazan had taken the opportunity to apologize to those he damaged and offended (some of whom were still alive). He did not do that; like John Wayne in *The Searchers,* he may have believed that apologizing was a sign of weakness—we are all horribly subject to those wicked fortune cookie axioms.

But far more important than contrition from Kazan would have been the appearance of elder statesmen figures from the Academy and from the picture business (I would have proposed Lew Wasserman and Bob Hope) to say something like this: Tonight, we recognize responsibility for a great crime. Because of misjudgment, cowardice, and raw economic fear, the essential parties to this business [they would be named] undermined the law, denied people working opportunities, and in some cases hastened their deaths. It is too late for rescue or remedy, but we apologize. We do this because of the responsibility we bear, but also because we want to be a respected part of the ongoing experience that is American.

No, it didn't happen. You are dreaming. But the picture business is supposed to be about dreams, isn't it?

In calling this chapter "In a Lonely Place," I am not only building toward the film of that name, I am thinking about a kind of alienation that begins within the film business itself, and in its relations with America. Yes, it is vague and far-reaching, but it is part of the whole equation, and not to be avoided just because it is elusive. Indeed, it is all the more important because the disenchantment with Hollywood also predicts a similar lack of caring in the relationship between the American people and their government. Suppose the two are connected? Suppose that in its most concerted and potent effort to tell itself stories, America has lost interest in fact, in history, and even in meaning and consequence?

The loneliness was actual, and you can feel it in Los Angeles if you're waiting for a call that will tell you whether a project is on or off. Consider two lonely people: Joe Gillis and Norma Desmond from *Sunset Blvd.* Gillis has no job: he is typical of the thousands who were unemployed in Hollywood by 1950; he has no family, no ties. Norma Desmond is alone in other ways. She lives in a mansion cut off from Sunset Boulevard, in a forgotten palace where she tries to maintain her past. She has strange ties: her ex-husband and onetime director is her butler; her monkey has just died. Her car, a magnificent relic, is on blocks. She is crazy, or acting crazy—why not, she's an actress? Joe is so alone it's nagging at him in ways he doesn't notice (he's dead, but still talking to himself because he thinks he's a storyteller).

Sunset Blvd., we all agree, is a great Hollywood movie, yet trickier than Elia Kazan. It is also the proper continuation of the career of Billy Wilder, last seen with *Double Indemnity* and *The Lost Weekend*, those startlingly pessimistic pictures.

There had been movies about Hollywood before and few of them were simply rose-colored. In Selznick's *A Star Is Born* (1937), we see the ruin of careers and the viciousness of characters like the press agent. Still, *A Star Is Born* was made by people who loved Hollywood, and who trusted that the public felt the same way. By about 1950, no one was prepared to maintain that trust. In the era of *Confidential* magazine, real intrusions were being made into the sordid private lives of movie celebrities. You may hear about the golden age being afraid of gossip columnists Louella Parsons and Hedda Hopper, but the risk was small and the pain usually fell on those picked out by the studios as ripe for demise. But in the fifties, in magazines, you can begin to feel a tougher edge in reporting—it's the attitude that made Marilyn Monroe's life so hellish. And it was exacerbated by the way in which fewer and fewer of the stars were still under long-term contract and protected by the publicity office. Stars were on their own. They might make more money, but they were more vulnerable.

A book played a part in this. *The New Yorker* sent a young writer, Lillian Ross, to stay close to John Huston as he tried to make *The Red Badge of Courage* for M-G-M. She was small, quiet, and she sat in the corner. She kept her head down and copied whatever people said. The result was *Picture,* a slim book, but like a knife to the business and so startling that her eavesdropping has hardly been permitted since. For the first time, readers could hear the tough-guy attitude and the uneducated talk of famous moguls. Here is Louis B. Mayer himself, in charge still, technically, but resolutely opposed to *The Red Badge of Courage,* which his new Thalberg, Dore Schary, wants to make. He is talking to his cohort, Arthur Freed, the maker of so many great musicals, the way Joe Gillis talks to the water in Norma Desmond's swimming pool:

> Between you and I and the lamppost, the smart alecks around here don't know the difference between the heart and the gutter. They don't want to listen to you. Marie Dressler! Who thought you could take a fat old lady and make her a star? I did it. And Wally Beery. And Lionel Barrymore. The audience knows. Look at the receipts. Give the audience what they want? No, not good enough.

Arthur Freed ventures a thought—"Thoreau said most of us lead lives of quiet desperation. Pictures should make you feel better not worse"— but Mayer is not diverted:

> *The Red Badge of Courage.* A million and a half. Maybe more. What for? There's no story, I was against it. They wanted to make it. I don't say no. John Huston. He was going to do *Quo Vadis.* What he wanted to do to the picture! No heart. His idea was he'd throw the Christians to the lions. That's all. I begged him to change his ideas. I got down on my hands and knees to him. I sang "Mammy" to him. I showed him the meaning of

heart. I crawled to him on hands and knees. "Ma-a-ammy!" With tears. No! No heart! He thanked me for taking him off the picture. Now he wants *The Red Badge of Courage*. Dore Schary wants it. All right, I'll watch. I don't say no, but I wouldn't make that picture with Sam Goldwyn's money.

That was 1950. L.B. was at least sixty-five, whichever birthday you used. And he let it be known that he was allowing *The Red Badge* to slip by in order to teach Dore Schary a lesson. Mayer was dangerous still. That same year, he attended a preview screening of *Sunset Blvd*. There was much praise for the film. From the outset so many people were taken with the novelty, the "daring," and the unrestrained comeback by Gloria Swanson. Not Mayer. Outside the screening room on the Paramount lot, he yelled at Wilder, "You bastard! You have disgraced the industry that made and fed you! You should be tarred and feathered and run out of Hollywood!"

It didn't work that way. Wilder and his partner, writer-producer Charles Brackett (the president of the Academy then), got eleven nominations and three Oscars. Their film had cost about $1.7 million, and its first-run income was only $2 million (Mayer had guessed something—though a standard now, *Sunset Blvd*. was received warily in 1950). For that job as writer-director, Wilder received approximately $300,000 (as opposed to $70,000 on *Double Indemnity*). But he was troubled, and it was after *Sunset* that he terminated his partnership with Charles Brackett. Was that to have more creative freedom, or a better cut on the deals?

In the Oscars that year, *Sunset Blvd*. lost out for Best Picture and direction to Joseph L. Mankiewicz's *All About Eve*. The pictures were not dissimilar, even if Margo Channing was saner than Norma Desmond. Both pictures examined the hothouse of show business, the way it smothered real life—and both pictures (show biz champs themselves) took a lofty, sardonic view of the proceedings. Mayer had been shocked, but if you look closely, *Sunset Blvd*. does not actually bite the feeding hand. There is one foolish minor producer (the Fred Clark character), but otherwise the movie world is filled with people as earnest as the Nancy Olson scriptwriter and Cecil B. De Mille himself. Norma has gone mad on her own, it has nothing to do with the system that has made and unmade her. Like much of Wilder's work, *Sunset Blvd*. is cruel when it wants to be—to Norma, to the history of Erich von Stroheim, and to failures in general. But Hollywood success goes undisputed. Billy Wilder was a testament to how well it worked.

There were other films that needled Hollywood, or treated it more harshly. *The Bad and the Beautiful* (1952) was actually made at M-G-M, with that fascinating wanderer, John Houseman, producing. It's an exposé of Hollywood, and a veiled portrait of David Selznick, if that's how you want to read it. Its producer figure, Jonathan Shields, is one of Kirk Douglas's smiling scoundrels—a manipulator, a liar, a dog, "bad" even; he's the only person in the film who comes close to deserving that label. But at the end of the film, the three people he has most wronged are gathered around a telephone, spellbound by his old unreliable charm and the prospect of another movie. What the film comes to, really, in a very entertaining way, is having your cake and eating it.

One tougher film is *The Big Knife* (1955), directed by Robert Aldrich from the play by Clifford Odets, in which an agonized Jack Palance plays a movie star driven to suicide, with Rod Steiger as a ranting, corrupt mogul. Although lesser known, *The Star* (1952) has Bette Davis trying to put her personal life together after her career as a star is over, not a thing at which Davis succeeded in real life. And best of them all is *In a Lonely Place* (1950).

Which brings us back to Bogart. When Bogart made *The Maltese Falcon, High Sierra,* and *Casablanca* (his turning years at Warners), he was contracted for about $63,000 a year. (He more than doubled that by doing endorsements—for clothes, and for cigarettes, the way he was killing himself.) *Casablanca* transformed his deal: after that, it went up to $195,000 a year. And that's when his life turned into a movie, as he met Lauren Bacall on *To Have and Have Not.*

The sweetness of nineteen and forty-five—but the problems, too. After *To Have and Have Not* and *The Big Sleep,* their two films for Howard Hawks, Bogart's salary went up to $467,000 a year. Bacall rose from $100 a week to $1,000. That's what the couple had to lose, especially after Bogart's divorce settlement with his third wife, Mayo Methot, which allegedly took more than half of what he had. I stress these details because unless you've been there you can't measure the pain of being told—on your way to Washington—that the whole hill of beans might be in jeopardy.

But Bogart listened to advice. He was at his peak, it seemed, firmly established as the ideal sour hero for the postwar mood. Yes, his salary was up, but suppose he had a portion of his films. Suppose he had had a percentage of *Casablanca* or *The Big Sleep.* So he formed his own company, Santana, with his manager, Morgan Maree, and Robert Lord, a writer-producer from Warners. *Santana* was the name of the yacht Bogart had just bought (from Dick Powell) for $50,000, more than he'd been paid for being Rick Blaine.

In a Lonely Place is usually categorized as film noir, and that's fair enough. But as with the best film noirs, it bleeds into other genres, too, notably the love story. Dixon Steele (Bogart) is a Hollywood screenwriter, successful but cynical: he no longer believes that the system employing him will do good work, so the anger of frustration burns in him, and it is close to violence. He falls in love with Laurel Gray (Gloria Grahame) just as he becomes the leading suspect in a killing.

The novel on which the picture is based (by Dorothy B. Hughes) has Dixon as the real killer. But the subtlety of the film version is that Dixon is in fact innocent. It's just that he *could* be a killer, and may be soon, and that Laurel's love is crushed when she sees this. Because Hollywood is not the direct object of attention, it becomes a suggestive metaphor for Dix's warped state. The title grows in meaning through the film so that it covers not just the infinite condition of paranoia, but the atmosphere of Hollywood as a whole, and the unlikelihood of honest work.

The film has other complications. The producer in Bogart wanted Bacall to play Laurel, but that would have thrown the audience for a misleading loop. As Warners wouldn't let Bacall do the film, Nicholas Ray cast his wife, Gloria Grahame, instead. And then their marriage broke down during the filming. Ray would claim later that Bogart-Bacall and Ray-Grahame were matched pairs: there was a similar age gap, both wives were promiscuous, both men were sometimes driven to anger. (Bogart had been banned from a couple of clubs for fighting, just like Dix.)

See the film, and see how, for once, the pathos and the cruelty in Bogart's eyes were allied and going somewhere. The film was a flop, and in time Bogart would go back to studio assignments, weary of the extra burden of owning himself. But in this one film, he and Ray (never better) had mapped out a loneliness, a paranoia, that you can still cut with a knife as easily as you can the seared tuna at any of the great restaurants in L.A.

Cahiers du Cinéma, February 1959, with a scene from *Vertigo.* The top and bottom bands were bright yellow. *(Lucy Gray)*

19 · "WHAT IS CINEMA?"

Nobody even gave him a going away party. When the amazing event happened, in the summer of 1951, hardly anyone at M-G-M was aware of it. One person looked out of a window and saw the stocky figure of Louis B. Mayer, alone, waiting at the gate. What was he doing there? In fact, as he was driving away, he had been told no, not in your usual car, that's a studio car. So he had been further humiliated, standing there in the sun, waiting for another car to be driven in from his home, to take him away.

How had it happened? In the most immediate sense, Mayer had told his old boss, his hated "friend" Nick Schenck, to choose between Mayer and Dore Schary, the "kid" who had been brought over from RKO in 1948 to be head of production at Metro. Schary and Mayer had had their disagreements, but Mayer had allowed himself to be finessed. Once upon a time, he would have stopped *The Red Badge of Courage;* now it was rope for Schary to hang himself. But the inside lesson was that Schenck wanted to get rid of Mayer, and found time on his side. The old man was losing touch. As his first biographer, Bosley Crowther, would note in 1960:

> His authority as a showman relied upon insistence on qualities of sentiment and make-believe that were nothing short of "corny" in the postwar age. . . . More fatal for him, however, was the fact that his strength was based upon the maintenance of a large productive capacity that no company could any longer afford.

Some say Mayer was emboldened by a promise that he could take over Warners. But that plan collapsed. (Was Jack Warner a party to Nick Schenck's plot?) Mayer made blustering talk about getting into independent production. He dreamed for years of doing *Joseph and His Brethren*—it was his own story, he told himself. But it never came to pass. Instead, Mayer had lawyers sit down with M-G-M to settle his contract: he retained rights to 10 percent of the ongoing profits on every film made at M-G-M since 1924. In 1951 the lawyers decided that this was worth $2.6 million. Mayer pulled his last strings to get a clause added to the tax legislation so that his payoff would be assessed as capital gain, not income, a 50 percent difference.

Between 1948 and 1957, weekly movie attendance in the United States dropped by more than half, from 100 million to 40 million (by then the population was 170 million). This made for alterations in the structure of the business more shocking than Mayer's departure. Consider the case of RKO. Never a major studio, and subject to regular convulsions in ownership, RKO looms large in film history. From its earliest days, it had had to concentrate on economy, style, and imagination. It had to its credit the brief regime of David Selznick (which produced *A Bill of Divorcement, King Kong,* and *Little Women*), the Astaire-Rogers musicals (perhaps the ultimate movie balance of luxury and modesty), comedies like *Bringing Up Baby*, adventures like *Gunga Din*, mysteries like *Suspicion*, the dazzling B-pictures made by producer Val Lewton (*Cat People*, for instance, in 1942, for $134,000), the film noir cycle (*The Boy with Green Hair, They Live by Night, Crossfire, Out of the Past*)—to say nothing of *Citizen Kane* and *The Magnificent Ambersons*.

Like the rest of Hollywood, RKO had heady years right after the war (that was what persuaded M-G-M to hire Dore Schary). In the years 1946–47, it had profits of $19 million. But then in 1948, control of the studio was purchased by Howard Hughes for $8.8 million. During the next seven years, the operation fell apart, thanks to overall trends and the caprices of Hughes himself, who variously tried to display women he adored and make fatuous epics like *The Conqueror* (John Wayne as a Genghis Khan–like Mongol; cost $6 million, domestic gross $4 million). In 1955, Hughes backed away, selling the studio to General Tire, and then in 1957 the studio lot was sold to the television company Desilu.

In 1940, on an RKO stage, the contract actress Lucille Ball had bumped into Cuban bandleader Desi Arnaz. They formed Desilu years later, after she had been dropped by RKO and by the movie business in general. But their noisy marriage helped inspire the idea of a new television show, *I Love Lucy*, in which Ball played the scatterbrain housewife who longed to be in show business while Desi was a successful businessman. Desi was in charge, the producer, and he made sure they had a good concept and good writers. He then elected to deliver the show to CBS not live but on film—precious, lasting film. He and Lucy paid for the pilot themselves and Desi accepted the very tough deal of delivering each half-hour episode for $26,000. He hired Karl Freund to be director of photography, a sign of the times. Freund was from Bohemia and the German film industry. He had worked for Murnau and Fritz Lang on *The Last Laugh* and *Metropolis*. In America, he had done the Bela Lugosi *Dracula*, *Camille* (with Garbo and Robert Taylor), and the stormy noir mood of *Key Largo*. *I Love Lucy* required a brassy domestic high key. For Freund it was dull work. But it was a steady job.

I Love Lucy first aired on October 15, 1951. For three years it was the nation's number one show. Because it was on film, it was able to go into syndication, where it still plays. The two stars took an annual salary at first of only $35,000 each, but by 1953 Desilu had revenue of $6 million. By 1957, when they bought the RKO studio for $6.15 million, they used the space to produce many more television series. In 1967, Gulf & Western bought Desilu for $17 million. Yet again, the principle of owning your work had been proven.

The penetration of a show like *I Love Lucy* was twofold: popular with immediate viewers, it also prompted more people to buy television sets. By 1956–57, 85 percent of United States homes had at least one set. More than that, it was reported that those sets were being watched for five hours a day. Do the numbers: with a population in 1957 of about 170 million, this means that about 135 million people were seeing the equivalent of at least two films a day. Yet in theaters, an audience of less than a quarter of that number was attending one picture a week.

Of course, the home audience wasn't simply seeing "movies" (though movies were part of it as the studios made what were at first absurdly generous deals leasing their library to television). They—we, the people— were undergoing the most drastic change to common experience since safe home electricity: we were seeing fiction and nonfiction, commercials and public information, news and fantasy, all in the same small, grainy image—and muddling through. Nor were we necessarily "seeing," for whereas attention is taken for granted at the movies, along with a compulsive visual force, television is a home system. It is "on" rather than "off"; and it often goes on with mere presence. We don't have to attend to it; we hear it as we do other ambient things, even the extraordinary mixture of things we may deem fit for privacy. It is a mass medium, but one that permits inattention and indolence. Indeed, it may be as much a comforter as a communicator. And so, subtly, a message has been communicated to us about our minds, our response, and our value. Television suits a world that says Sure, these things are happening, but you don't have to notice them or ask why there's no need to pay attention or take part. You need not be involved. And if you don't quickly like one channel, switch to another. Go back and forth. Become a kind of random editing machine. You are in the world to have your time passed, as if it were your waste.

It is part of the fundamental cultural indifference of television that we have done so little educationally to attend to it. After all, we know now— and we have had the better part of fifty years to digest this—that our children (which means ourselves, not just because we are the first generation of children to grow up with TV, but because TV is a medium that asks us to be childlike) spend more time watching (or merely being present) as moving imagery plays in front of them than they do reading or writing. As I write, there is modish alarm in the *New York Times* that infants, babies, blink their way through hours of television a day. Yet our education is still largely based on what words mean, how they fit together grammatically. Against that, how many of us have ever had any education in the nature of moving imagery, its grammar, its laws or lawlessness, or how the naïve viewer is expected to distinguish news from fantasy, art from deception?

The movie business tried to defy television. It had rejected the chance of coopting the new medium, and making it an extension of movies. It retaliated by refusing to show television sets in domestic interiors. Then it responded by making its own screen bigger, or more novel. It also set up a kind of class structure suggesting that movie might be a higher form than television, an attitude that persisted for decades in defiance of every observable reality, including money.

It's natural to ask how that trick was achieved. Did movies after *Lucy,* say, become so much better? I don't think the warmest fan could argue that. No, there is only one significant change that had an influence: the movies became more lucrative, for a few. If you recollect that this was accomplished in the face of a massive decline in the audience, to the point that by around 1970 most movie companies were in the red, you can see what astonishing magic remained. I use the word "magic" with some irony here, but how else do we describe so thorough a disguise of reality?

Let me try another "joke" on you: If in 1950 you were disposed to search out some utterly un-American act, some monument to subversion, you need look no further than the tall, elegant person of Lew Wasserman.

Though mentioned before, Wasserman has rather crept up on us. Born in Cleveland in 1913, Louis Wasserman was the son of Russian Jews who had only been in America a few years. The family was poor. Louis sold candy in movies at the age of twelve, and by fifteen he was an usher at the Palace theater. As a young man he joined the Music Corporation of America (MCA), an agency that concentrated on the music business. MCA had been founded by Jules Caesar Stein in 1924 in Chicago. Stein and MCA (despite vigorous denials later, by which time Stein had become a leading American and a famous philanthropist) owed their rise to an intimate association with Chicago gangsters and to the occasional use of their persuasive powers.

I say this simply to stress the age-old association between show business and organized crime, a natural exploitation of a cash business that became more socially acceptable as crime organized itself into a business. The adjective "organized" before crime is the key. America has shown every kind of paternal patience and social optimism with crime, so long as it promises to get organized. Thus it tolerated the fairly rapid progress of Las Vegas from a mobster's paradise to an all-American family resort. It is unruly crime, passionate crime, wild, impoverished, mad crime we disapprove of and punish most diligently.

MCA was not very much into the movies until 1940, when Stein posted Wasserman to Hollywood. Over the next ten years, Wasserman built the agency into the dominating force in a business that, as it broke up, needed some new organizing impetus. As the studios lost funds and confidence and their leaders (they began to die; they lost touch), so Lew Wasserman began to be perceived as the sharpest man in town.

In 1940, MCA had had three top clients: Richard Dix, Hattie McDaniel, and Ronald Reagan, none of whom was remotely top. But Wasserman recruited fiercely and he picked up the pieces as Myron Selznick's agency collapsed in the early forties, prior to Myron's death. Then, in 1945, he persuaded Leland Hayward and Nat Deverich (whose business had spun off from Myron's earlier) to join him. By the late forties, MCA had an estimated seven hundred contracts with leading movie personalities.

The next step was to alter the basis on which stars were employed. As star contracts lapsed, and as studios found more need to make one-off production deals for this or that project, so an agent heaven opened up. MCA could negotiate from scratch. As mentioned earlier, James Stewart, a Wasserman client, had become a big star in the early forties, his appeal enhanced by his authentic war record—actually flying bomber raids to a point of nervous collapse. Universal wanted him to play the lead in two pictures, the Western *Winchester '73*, and the stage hit *Harvey*, about a man whose best friend is an invisible white rabbit. Wasserman asked for $200,000 per picture, only to be told that the studio was short of cash at that moment. So he switched his request: Hold the money; instead we'll take 50 percent of the profits. Universal agreed. *Winchester '73* was a hit, and the beginning of a series of Westerns with Stewart, directed by Anthony Mann; over the next few years Stewart took away at least $750,000 on the Western alone, spread out over several years to ease the tax burden.

As we've seen, this was not the start of profit participation, but it was a crucial deal, very public and influential. Of course, it hinged on profit: in a way, the studios could tell themselves they were getting a safer deal. Still, as time went on, Wasserman did begin to slip in, and beef up, the up-front guarantee on such contracts. By then it was too late for the studios: they were paying in advance and later on as well, and sometimes they found that on one picture they had bargained away an unreasonable chunk of their profits. Moreover, it could be the case that all the people in on the profits were MCA clients. The studios might be wilting, but the agencies were picking up control.

A further measure of Wasserman's acumen concerns television. In its early years, television production was centered in New York in a way that alarmed West Coast–based actors who were losing movie work. In 1952 MCA approached the Screen Actors Guild with a proposal: anxious to set up a California television production industry and to help local actors, MCA was prepared to negotiate for something SAG foresaw as a coming issue—re-use or residual payments. Early on, it was evident that television was likely to show hit series over and over again, if only to fill air time. Yet the first contracts in TV called for a once-only payment to actors. Why was MCA ready to be so obliging? Well, it had one other card in its hand: it wanted to set up its own subsidiary, Revue Productions, as a television producer, even though doing so would conflict with the standing ban against agencies being directly involved in production.

I hope this doesn't sound too technical. There is always a danger in business matters that drastic alterations of the law can be made to sound "technical." The regulation against agents being producers was, and still is, a protection against an unholy conflict of interests. SAG yielded to the MCA proposition, and signed off on a waiver that excluded MCA and Revue from the customary operating ban. The key officials of SAG at that time were MCA clients Walter Pidgeon and Ronald Reagan.

The Revue waiver, or shall we say the Revue exception (for it was granted to no other agency or production company), proved monumental. The advantage lasted seven years before the courts caught up with it, time for MCA to establish its citadel position in television production, and to run so many shows in which they were hiring their own clients (while pulling back 10 percent of their salaries). Revue became a company with annual revenue of $50 million.

In 1962, the Department of Justice did investigate the MCA monopoly in a Los Angeles court. Reagan was called as a witness, and, when the most embarrassing questions were put to him he said "I don't honestly recall" (a line he would use in other stories) because he felt he must have been up in Montana at the time making a Western. Alas, film scholarship did not obtain among the attorneys: *Cattle Queen of Montana* was in fact filmed two years later—1954, the same year that MCA gave Reagan the career boost of hosting *General Electric Theater.* No one would have believed it then, but Reagan was destined to be *the* man on television, otherwise known as the President of the United States.

Not that the movie studios gave in to television, but they may have erred in taking the natural response of old patriarchs hustled by a new medium: they determined to be bigger, more spectacular, more boastful than ever. Thus, while live television drama explored the small, the natural, the ordinary lives neglected by movies (especially in the use of writers like Paddy Chayefsky, Rod Serling, and Reginald Rose), so the movies flexed their muscles and went in for screen enlargement. In 3-D (tried before and given up on) cinema became the art of people shooting arrows, tossing scarves, or even spitting at the camera. As used by its pioneer, Twentieth Century–Fox, CinemaScope simply widened some pretty staid epics (like *The Robe* and *Desiree*) and the road-show musicals (*The King and I, Carousel, South Pacific*—done in Todd AO). All of those films were hits. The audience was stopped in its tracks by size, and, apparently, by the word of the Lord: *The Ten Commandments* (in VistaVision) showed C. B. De Mille back again for one last time, unchastened and no closer to being grown up. But a few years earlier he had won Best Picture for *The Greatest Show on Earth,* a circus movie that cheerfully defied its own title. Charlton Heston was De Mille's new star, and he would have another huge Biblical success—for M-G-M and William Wyler—in *Ben-Hur.*

Heston was one of the new stars of the era, most of whom arrived after 1945, full of energy and hardly aware at first how much the medium was shifting. But they wanted to be film stars, not TV people, and in time several of them became their own producers: Heston, Burt Lancaster, Kirk Douglas, Gregory Peck, Robert Mitchum, William Holden, Montgomery Clift, and even Marlon Brando, Rock Hudson, and Tony Curtis. The new female stars were not as actively involved in production, but in hindsight the fifties could hardly be equalled for its class of new actresses, some nearly erupting with censored sex, some all the more suggestive for being ladylike.

There's Monroe, of course, who seemed caught up in an impossible battle with censorship whereby she yearned to take off her clothes, and then distribute her skin like gifts for poor children. But was that actually sexier than Grace Kelly in *To Catch a Thief* asking Cary Grant whether he preferred a thigh or a breast? Then there was Audrey Hepburn (the gamin of the moment), Doris Day (everybody's chum), Susan Hayward (the emotional powerhouse), Ava Gardner, Deborah Kerr, and the fully-grown Elizabeth Taylor, whose violet eyes inspired lasers, and maybe the most ambitious of them all.

To picture those actresses is, in most cases, to see them in color—the way they were born, of course, and thus, allegedly, truer to life. That rea-

soning was often used in the steady capitulation to color that occurred in
the 1950s. I am not an enemy of color—how else should films as varied
and good as *Lust for Life, Funny Face, East of Eden, The Searchers,
Shane,* or *Singin' in the Rain* have been done? There have always been
movies that required color because of the dramatic material, because of
the story or the places involved, and even because of the color of a
woman's hair. But color was less reasonable than dogmatic. It was automatic because, until 1964, it was something television lacked.

Many color processes—I have to single out Fox's De Luxe Color—were
harsh and restricted. None of them was remotely comparable to the glory
of Technicolor. That process (it is not just a synonym for color) lasted from
the mid-thirties to the mid-fifties, involving three different strips of film,
great care in hand printing, and extra expense. It also permitted a range of
colors that some called "painterly" and which some audiences (it was
alleged) believed was not "lifelike." On the other hand, Technicolor is the
medium in which we have *Gone With the Wind, The Red Shoes, Duel in
the Sun, Leave Her to Heaven, An American in Paris, She Wore a Yellow
Ribbon, Samson and Delilah, Henry V, Black Narcissus, The Pirate,* and
Meet Me in St. Louis.

I could go on. I love Technicolor for its expressiveness, its moist alive-
ness, its damson and crème brûlée mix as lipstick meets cheek, and its passion—because it is, often, better than life. Art is meant to be. There is
another virtue to Technicolor, one with large fiscal consequences. Technicolor lasts. Prints from the late thirties have not yet begun to deteriorate,
whereas most of the color schemes that replaced it do begin to fade, to
turn pink or blue, in twenty years. Thus the color negatives of modern
films are largely useless. And that is a lost investment as well as squandered beauty. The original Technicolor is no more: the remnants of the
process went to China, but it was truly reliant on craftsmen and now neither the equipment nor the talent exists to work with it.

So, in the 1950s, for shortsighted commercial reasons, the film business
deprived itself of its greatest color system and began the trend that would
make black-and-white close to illegal. Today, it is the tragic case that one
can hardly get young audiences to sit still for pictures if they are not in
color. The beauty of black-and-white, its uniquely photographic magic,
have been given up in all cases except those where a very deliberate director insists on the old form, even if it restricts the film commercially.

Black-and-white remained viable in the fifties, and it distinguished
some of the best films of the decade: *Sunset Blvd.;* George Stevens's *A
Place in the Sun,* in which the romance between Clift and Taylor loses

nothing, but where the foreboding and the fatalism need the noir look; *From Here to Eternity,* Fred Zinnemann's triumphant rendering of the James Jones novel for Columbia, when everyone advised that the book was unfilmable; Fritz Lang's classic *The Big Heat; Sweet Smell of Success,* not just a drastic reappraisal of newspapers, but of two popular stars, Tony Curtis and Burt Lancaster; *Twelve Angry Men,* Sidney Lumet's debut as a film director, and one of those TV dramas that were remade for the big screen; Robert Aldrich's *Kiss Me Deadly,* a scathing treatment of Mickey Spillane's Mike Hammer character that is both film noir and social criticism; *Men in War,* by Anthony Mann, a study of combat in Korea that seems to me far more intellectually interesting than the following year's vaunted *The Bridge on the River Kwai;* Otto Preminger's *Anatomy of a Murder,* perhaps the first movie in our reeducation about legal proceedings, with the mood of a game dispelling hopes of justice; *Touch of Evil,* Orson Welles's return to Los Angeles (and to that then-rotting suburb, Venice), a move prompted by Charlton Heston, who was already the star of the movie; that early suave promise from Stanley Kubrick, *The Killing;* and *The Night of the Hunter.*

Of all these black-and-white films, *The Night of the Hunter* is the exception. All the others (except for *Touch of Evil*) did somewhere between well and very well at the box office. *The Night of the Hunter* was a disaster. Yet history has redeemed it, and helped illustrate the place for a new kind of production setup.

Paul Gregory had been an agent at the William Morris Agency, but he was impatient to be his own master and to be more involved with artistic ventures. To that end, he became business manager to the actor Charles Laughton and arranged a successful reading tour for him. Laughton confessed along the way how much he had always wanted to direct a film. Gregory said he had the same desire. Not long after that, Gregory saw the galleys for a forthcoming novel, *The Night of the Hunter,* by Davis Grubb. It was rural, set in the thirties, gothic, spooky, and fascinating. Both men liked it and decided that it would be their picture.

Laughton was very famous, of course, but he did not intend to act in the picture. So Gregory had great difficulty setting the project up, especially because the two men had agreed that Robert Mitchum would be ideal in the lead role of "Preacher" Harry Powell, pervert, killer, monster, and stepfather to a Hansel and Gretel who know where the stolen money is hidden.

The only deal that Gregory could make was at United Artists, which was still serving as the releasing organization for independent ventures. But

UA could offer only $600,000 to make the picture. I don't know the details beyond the fact that former film critic and novelist and present drunk James Agee was paid $30,000 to do a screenplay that Laughton was obliged to rewrite.° It's unlikely that Mitchum worked then for under $100,000, though that unpredictable man, often deliberately insolent to any suggestion of taking work seriously, was very attached to this project and to Laughton. Laughton must have had another $100,000 to survive. Gregory took something. The cast also included Shelley Winters and Lillian Gish. Stanley Cortez did the photography. The novel had to be purchased. Above-the-line costs must have been $300,000, leaving the same sum for the shooting—with a novice director and a famously studied cameraman.

Edgar Ulmer might have done the whole thing in ten days at half the cost (though I doubt Mitchum would have gone out on a limb for an Ulmer). The saving wouldn't have mattered. The film opened to mixed reviews and it did no business. What that means, alas, is that after the theaters had taken their nut, after the costs of minimal advertising and making prints had been covered, and after United Artists had taken its percentage, there may have been nothing left. Gregory and Laughton had planned next to do Norman Mailer's *The Naked and the Dead.* Gregory had bought the rights. There was a script on which Laughton and Mailer had collaborated. But then the always insecure Laughton lost heart as *Hunter* flopped. The project moved on (with Gregory still an attached name) to become a Warner Brothers movie, directed by Raoul Walsh, with a screenplay by Denis and Terry Sanders (who had worked on *The Night of the Hunter*).

It doesn't matter. A few years ago at the Castro Theater in San Francisco I was privileged to introduce a screening of the picture as part of a series of films selected and preserved for the Library of Congress. That was and is very nice, and a record of how highly Laughton's only directorial effort is regarded today. (The Library of Congress does not preserve every film made in the land of movies. I suppose they see that as a province the business should look after.)

I am trying to track the business trends and the artistic prospects of the 1950s, when the movie industry was feeling very insecure. In popular estimate, the fifties are sometimes written off as a very dull time, the Eisenhower years, with people clinging to prosperity and security, and using

---

°Agee's screenplay has recently been discovered—nearly three hundred pages, highly literary, but with moments that figure exactly in the film.

television (among other things) to assert that everything was okay. On the other hand, the fifties saw superb jazz and the start of rock-and-roll; it saw a pressing need for a new kind of candor, evident all over the place, but notably (for our purposes) in the publication of Norman Mailer's *The Deer Park,* a pungent Hollywood novel that regarded the place as a ferment of greed and corruption (Mailer had spent a lot of time there). There were stirrings.

And there were great American films. Above and beyond the pictures I have mentioned so far, there were the works of Nicholas Ray—uneven always, jittery, overemotional, but often piercingly alert to the uneasy society and the steady diet of public and private lies. I'm thinking of *Rebel Without a Cause, Bigger Than Life,* and *Bitter Victory,* all of which, incidentally, showed that a man with a great eye could take CinemaScope and make widescreen as beautiful and dynamic in two dimensions as Frank Lloyd Wright had the horizontal in three (Ray had studied with Wright). Ray was near the end of his tether personally. A gambler, a drug-taker, a fantasist—let's face it, a mess—he would collapse at the end of the decade as he settled for disastrous big paydays. But he had moments in the fifties that confronted everyday realities in America.

Then there is Alfred Hitchcock, a world unto himself in so many ways. Indeed, he hardly seems to have noticed the experience of being in America, beyond enjoying the more sophisticated facilities of the Hollywood studios. He was engaged in his own equation of film and suspense, as if it were a private mathematics. But in the fifties, he comes forth with what I think are his masterpieces—*Rear Window, Vertigo,* and *North by Northwest.* Yes, all were in pretty color, yet with that sublime hint of poison in the prettiness. Two of them were hits, one a flop; all with the kind of starry personae Hitch liked—he didn't really want to have to direct actors in the way of a Kazan. Hitch reckoned casting was 90 percent. The other 10? Showing up. But *Rear Window* and *Vertigo* are much more than such an attitude suggests. They are thrillers, yes. They are mechanical operations, if you like. But they are also reflections on the very art or mathematics that obsesses Hitch: They are about looking, fantasizing, and what happens when the reality and the fantasy clash. *Vertigo* above all is a morbid analysis of fantasy involvement, and its resolution is not pretty or comforting. These films are something new and more disturbing than even *Psycho.* For they begin to ask the question: What have movies done to us?

Billy Wilder (who directed Charles Laughton in 1957 in that shameless throwback and potboiler, *Witness for the Prosecution*) said that he found *The Night of the Hunter* too strange—Laughton should have started his career with something simpler. But Laughton was beyond simplicity or career planning. For good and ill, he was in love with film. He had done it for its own sake, a terrible freedom to which Wilder seldom committed.

This is not to belittle Wilder, who was one of Hollywood's great survivors in the very difficult age of the fifties. But a closer look at Wilder's record (and the structure of his films) shows how far he was carried along on the rush of the decade. On *Double Indemnity,* made for Paramount in 1944, Wilder had earned $70,000, while $100,000 each went to Barbara Stanwyck, Fred MacMurray, and Edward G. Robinson. The film cost $972,000.

The film was a hit; so was *The Lost Weekend.* And so was *Sunset Blvd.,* where the money went out as follows: $21,000 to William Holden; Gloria Swanson got $50,000; producer Charles Brackett earned $130,000; and Wilder as co-writer and director got $301,000. Total budget: $1.75 million.

In the fifties, Wilder had another big hit with *Stalag 17,* and a moderate hit with *The Seven Year Itch.* Equally, *Ace in the Hole* and *The Spirit of St. Louis* did not do very well. Never mind, by the time Wilder came to make *Some Like It Hot* this was the deal: Marilyn Monroe got $300,000 against 10 percent of the gross after it reached $4 million; Tony Curtis and Jack Lemmon got $100,000 each plus 5 percent of the gross after it reached $2 million. Wilder got $200,000 plus 17.5 percent of the gross after it reached twice the cost of the picture, and 20 percent if the gross went $1 million past break-even point. That movie cost $2.88 million (half a million over budget), and had been an independent production of the Mirisch Brothers and the Ashton Company released through United Artists. It is said that Wilder came away with over $1 million.

I stress *Some Like It Hot* for several reasons. It seems to me Wilder's peak, and at once his most completely sardonic and exhilarated film. In gender confusion, it was decades ahead of its time. But it was not nominated for Best Picture; it did get a Best Director nomination and Lemmon was nominated for Best Actor, but not Curtis (because he was the more complete babe of the pair?). A year later, *The Apartment*—made on the same terms, and another great success—did win Best Picture. It happens that way sometimes. I think *The Apartment* is strained today, and very uneasy in its attempt to make a nasty situation palatable; Wilder had a habit of taking sour material and sugaring it up for the audience. Whereas *Some Like It Hot* is perfect, divine and profane, surreal and a movie about the movies. It is another version of *Vertigo,* albeit hilarious, in which the characters, the plot, and the scenes are not offered as a reality so much as a distillation of the thousands of films we have seen all our life.

Nor do I begrudge Wilder that $1 million in participation. He deserved it; he earned it. And Wilder, a very civilized connoisseur, put all his spare money into a superb art collection, auctioned eventually for $32.6 million ($14 million of that went in taxes). He showed me those pictures one day, telling stories about them, pointing out details, rediscovering them as he looked again. I thought deep down that the famous moviemaker was in awe of these small, fabulous works. Their stillness seemed to soothe him.

But remember that $500,000 overrun on *Some Like It Hot*—more than half the total cost of *Double Indemnity*. Stories claimed that Monroe's lateness accounted for some of that. But it was also a mark of how on independent pictures budgets were exceeded—to get it right, to indulge the actors, because this was a unique venture as opposed to a routine product. And because, working without studio contracts, people needed more support—makeup, drivers, assistants, backup, yes-men such as the system had not allowed before. Everyone was getting paid better, but because the profit factor meant so much a Wilder would repeat a scene until he judged it correct. The expert director begins to take artistic care. And the strain of being co-writer, director, and producer starts to tell.

Wilder enjoyed great success from 1944 to 1964, the year of *Irma La Douce*. That grossed $9.5 million on its first run and earned Wilder $1.2 million. But the Mirisch Brothers and United Artists, those who actually raised the money, went off with only $400,000. Then Wilder lost his touch, or his luck—who knows which comes first? Who knows when the pressures of keeping control, of being patient with the idiots, the swine, and the enemies, of maintaining your own record of success, become so draining that an artist thinks to protect his assets rather than his art? *Kiss Me, Stupid* had greatness in its outline, but in 1964 it was as offensive as anything Wilder had dared—an untempered sneer in the public's face. Then Peter Sellers dropped out of the cast, and in the confusion Wilder didn't have to be so daring. He was nearing sixty—when does peace ever come?

Then, in 1971, Wilder at last got to make the picture of his dreams, *The Private Life of Sherlock Holmes*, a melancholy view of the great detective and his solitude. Once more, it was for Mirisch and United Artists. He had a great deal, with Peter O'Toole as Holmes and Sellers as Dr. Watson. Then that cast dissolved. There were delays. Freshness perhaps congealed. The picture got made and Wilder believed it needed three and a half hours. No one any longer talked as fast as Stanwyck and MacMurray had managed in *Double Indemnity*. Did they take themselves more solemnly? The picture grossed only $1 million. But it had cost $10 million.

Yes, it was twenty-five years later, but that was ten times the cost of *Double Indemnity*. You can credit inflation, simply—or was it that by 1971 so much of the energy went into making the deal that the picture suffered?

Once upon a time directors had told stories about being assigned to a big picture a couple of days in advance. But that pressure was exhilarating, and it relied on the collective craft in a studio crew that knew how to photograph the house stars. Today, a director (not necessarily skilled at such maneuvers) may take a year or more finding a cast that can come together at the same time, in a location that is "economically viable." Think of *Cold Mountain,* very late in its day, having to give up North Carolina for Romania, and then notice the creeping discontent in its reviews that the film somehow lacked authenticity. And remember the chance on *Gone With the Wind* that George Cukor went cold on those very melodramatic scenes because he was shooting them for a couple of years in advance. Melodrama is best taken quickly, like bitter medicine or sweet pastries.

That loss on *Sherlock Holmes* could have wiped out the profit on *Irma La Douce, The Apartment, Some Like It Hot,* and others. But Lew Wasserman and the community of agents never did contracts in which the filmmakers had to cover the losses, or reap the profits. And full ownership requires both.

*　*　*

Ownership, authorship, cultural possession? It makes for an intriguing triangulation, especially if you take as your disputed territory Yosemite, the great library of the blues, or the history of the movies. I spoke of the Library of Congress earlier. It has the largest film and television archive in the world—well over 300,000 titles. However, the Library does not have a statutory right to deposit for all films and television programs, as it does for books, newspapers, and magazines. In 1995, James H. Billington, the Librarian of Congress, wrote that "the moving picture is not so much an art form as it is the language of our time." I think we know what he means to say by that. Yet, as he also admitted, the Motion Picture and Recorded Sound Division at the Library was only established in 1978, half of all feature films made before 1950 have been lost, and the federal funds granted to film preservation have declined in actual value.

Of course, these funds began to be granted far too late, but what does that reveal of Washington's attitude? Simply that film was a rather trashy commodity, not quite worthy of space in the Library of Congress, something better left to the care of its raffish businessmen. To an astonishing degree, the great age of movies in America went on without academic or intellectual mediation. There were many fan magazines, most of them generated by the business itself. There were the several show business gossip columns. Films were reviewed, but reviewing had not yet become an important part of the nation's discourse. There was hardly any coverage of film at universities or colleges (with the notable exception of the film program at USC, which goes back to 1927—Thalberg was an early guest lecturer). There was nothing like a serious magazine of film commentary. It was as if fallout was occurring before anyone had yet identified the toxic (or fertilizing) properties in fallout. *Vertigo* is now one of the most discussed of American films, but when it opened, in 1958, there was hardly any talk about what it meant.

It wasn't an absolute desert. The British Film Institute was established in 1933. In 1935, the Museum of Modern Art in New York set up a Department of Film, where the English-born Iris Barry led the fight. There was a handful of pioneer writers on film by the forties: James Agee (at *The Nation* and *Time*); Manny Farber (at *The New Republic* and *The Nation*); and Otis Ferguson (at *The New Republic*). But even Agee, the most widely read, was anxious to get into his "real writing" or into movies themselves. Thus he pioneered the tricky path of reviewing a director (John Huston) and ending up working for him.

It may be that America's innocence, its lack of critical edge, was an important part of the age of movies. I do not offer that lightly: Could it be that the sensational, the entertaining, the sheer "Wow!" of movies are more important than a library of books? Is there something innate in Americana that prefers the unanalyzed joys of life? Did Pauline Kael have her finger on the pulse when she said (in the 1960s) that if anything could kill the movies it would be letting academe get its hands on them? It was Duke Ellington who opined once that if you had to explain to people what swing was then they didn't swing—but maybe you didn't, either.

Well, by now, academia has its hands full, and William Friedkin may qualify as an emeritus trashpot. So how did such changes come about?

They do such things differently in France. Despite the ruthless way in which Edison and his followers had outstripped French inventors and entrepreneurs like Léon Gaumont and Charles Pathé in the early development of film, cinema had enjoyed a place in French culture that helps illuminate the empty place in America. There was always a commercial cinema in France, but it never felt itself cut off from the cinema of experiment and intellectual outrage. It was regarded as a natural thing that artistically minded people and intellectuals in France loved the movies and took them seriously. Thus you cannot track the history of French cinema without names that are to be found in larger studies of cultural history, too: Louis Feuillade, Marcel L'Herbier, René Clair, Luis Buñuel, Jean Vigo, Jean Cocteau, and, above all, Jean Renoir. Leading writers and composers worked in films—Georges Auric and Jacques Prévert. The movies were discussed as vital to culture.

The Cinémathèque Française was founded in Paris by Henri Langlois and Georges Franju in 1936, a year after MoMA's Film Department, but it is fair to say that Langlois's archive and his showing of films quickly became more central to Parisian life than MoMA has ever managed to be in New York. In 1943, IDHEC (Institut des Hautes Études Cinématographiques) was set up by L'Herbier long before there was a film school in the United States.

Then, in 1951, André Bazin, a critic and teacher, turned his magazine, *La Revue du Cinéma,* into *Cahiers du Cinéma;* and a year later, another magazine, *Positif,* was founded in Lyon (the city of the Lumières). With those two magazines in print, Langlois and Bazin became unofficial godfathers to an unusual band of film critics or writers, many of whom would one day jump into filmmaking itself. These names include François Truffaut, Jean-Luc Godard, Claude Chabrol, Eric Rohmer, and Jacques Rivette, the crest of the French New Wave, a movement to which other figures, such as Alain Resnais, Agnès Varda, Chris Marker, Jacques Demy, and Georges Franju, became attached as they started feature filmmaking at about the same time.

In their indefatigable attempt to see all films ever made, and to distinguish the great from the good, the promising from the acceptable, the atrocious from the useless, these writers fell upon the mainstream of American cinema. Yes, they admired the obvious figures—Chaplin, Griffith, Welles—and, yes, they were alert to the work of those Europeans who had gone to Hollywood—Murnau, Lubitsch, Lang, Renoir, Ulmer. But the thing that astonished America as the news gradually trickled home was that the young French were crazy about Hitchcock, Hawks, Nick Ray, Preminger, Vincente Minnelli, Samuel Fuller, Anthony Mann, Robert Aldrich, and lots of others.

This was not without its humor. In some cases American directors were suddenly plunged into a torrent of praise to which they were absolutely unaccustomed, and which, literally, they did not understand. Movie directors in America had no encouragement to take themselves seriously, not from their employers, not from the public (who hardly knew them), and not from any kind of critical establishment. Now they were "auteurs." There were instances of American directors, on vacation, or on location in Paris, being snapped up by the young men of *Cahiers* for an interview. The questions they were asked sometimes were longer than the answers. To a blazing paragraph of exaltation, the director might say, "I guess so." I believe that Hitchcock (a very quick learner) picked up a way of talking about his films from those French interviews. The first-ever book on Hitch was written in 1957 by Chabrol and Rohmer; a few years later Truffaut did a pioneering career-long interview book (to which every director has since aspired). I suspect that Nicholas Ray was thrown a little further off balance by the unbridled celebration he received from people such as Jean-Luc Godard (not always the most generous of men).

The young French critics of the fifties were more often right than wrong. Truffaut, I think, was a better critic than filmmaker. But the cultural shock was resisted. In *Sight and Sound,* the magazine of the British Film Institute, a famous article asked "Ray or Ray?"—did we prefer the sober humanism of Indian filmmaker Satyajit Ray or the brilliant Hollywood spasms of Nicholas Ray? In America, the French spirit was usually derided—after all, the French liked Jerry Lewis, too, didn't they? (Yes, they did—and so do I!)

The outburst of praise and the larger attempt to rewrite film history (so that the supposedly compromised commercial cinema had its beauties and marvels, too) might not have prevailed but for the impact of the films these critics made. You have to remember that films like *Les Quatre Cents Coups, Tirez sur le Pianiste, Jules et Jim, Les Cousins, Les Bonnes Femmes, À Bout de Souffle, Vivre Sa Vie, Paris Nous Appartient, L'Amour Fou,* and *Ma Nuit Chez Maude* did a great deal to establish the new art houses in America that were springing up to meet a young generation miraculously interested in film history and foreign films.

Yes, other things were happening: it was a student generation aroused by civil rights and then Vietnam, and more than aroused by the new sexual opportunities. There were also good films imported from so many places: from India (the *Apu* trilogy by the other Ray); from Japan (the careers of Kurosawa and Ozu, and the discovery of Mizoguchi, a big *Cahiers* hero); from Italy (Fellini, Antonioni, and Bertolucci); from wherever Luis Buñuel was at the time (*Viridiana, Belle de Jour*); even from Britain (the films of Karel Reisz, John Schlesinger, and Joseph Losey). And Swede Ingmar Bergman, in so many ways film's first Nobel laureate.

In the early sixties, this new interest in film took many exciting forms: disenchanted English teachers in colleges began to offer film courses, and the enrollment was startling. Very quickly, individual courses grew into programs and departments. With black studies and women's studies (and there was overlap) film was the fastest-growing area in American education. As a result, film criticism in newspapers and magazines became more important to their editors. As if the fight had been fixed (it was not), Pauline Kael and Andrew Sarris took opposing corners in a way that pioneered arguments over film all across the country. And there were new repertory cinemas that, along with television's growing use of old movies, allowed the student to go back and see as many classics as possible.

The Film Society of Lincoln Center and the New York Film Festival came into being, initially under the leadership of Richard Roud, who had previously created the London Film Festival. *Film Comment* began to be published in 1964. The American Film Institute was founded in 1967. Andrew Sarris's book *American Cinema* was published in 1968, by which time Pauline Kael was installed at *The New Yorker.*

All of that may sound somewhat esoteric. But then look at it this way. In the early sixties, two young writers at *Esquire,* Robert Benton and David Newman, were so inspired by the early films of François Truffaut that they reckoned to write an American script for him. It concerned a couple of small-time hoodlums from Texas around 1930; Benton was Texan and he knew the story. Truffaut liked the script but doubted his English was sufficient to carry it off. The project moved briefly to Jean-Luc Godard, and then a young American actor, Warren Beatty, heard about it. He was looking to become his own producer.

He bought the script. He started to work on it anew with a friend, Robert Towne, helping him. He enlisted Arthur Penn as a director, a man who, like Kazan, had begun in the theater and who had Kazan's intense rapport with actors. Beatty took the project to Warner Brothers where he was mocked by the old hands, including Jack Warner himself. They gave him grief all the way, especially when he went off on location to Texas. They hated the film he brought back. Their marketing campaign did not help it. But Beatty persevered; that was his great talent, or the most natural. Pauline Kael discovered the film and went into raptures over it. The film did so well in London that Warners was persuaded to rerelease it. *Bonnie and Clyde* became not just a big hit, but a movie that went through young audiences like a first slug of Scotch. It affected clothes, talk, manners. Though set in the thirties it had the feeling of 1966, the most dangerous moment in America young people remembered. Warners was befuddled. Jack Warner, then seventy-five, couldn't grasp it. But *Bonnie and Clyde,* which had cost $2.5 million, was up to $22 million in domestic earnings. It would be $70 million worldwide, eventually.

* * *

So what was cinema? It was the old question of art and business all over again. But now, as "Qu'est-ce que c'est le cinéma?", it was being asked in fresh terms. (That was the title of the four-volume collected writings of André Bazin, published in France between 1958 and 1965, and in American paperback a few years later.)

The question was heard again in *Pierrot le Fou,* the Jean-Luc Godard movie that opened in 1965. Just as that film marked the end of Godard's marriage to the actress Anna Karina (as important to his early work as Gish was to Griffith), so it signals his divorce from American sympathies. Godard was that kind of Frenchman (born Swiss in fact) whose giddy love of America was always likely to be betrayed by real American behavior. So *Pierrot* is, in part, a study in the conflict between American popular culture and the French aesthetic tradition.

From afar, Godard had loved American culture. His first feature film, *À Bout de Souffle,* was dedicated to Monogram Pictures, and it begins with Jean-Paul Belmondo studying a poster of Humphrey Bogart. But from the outset, Godard treated the classicism of American film narrative as a set piece that needed to be destroyed and remade, rather as Cubism had refashioned our sense of appearance. Those films of the early sixties represent a landmark in film history in which an encyclopedic knowledge of American film, and a dismayed fondness, are subjected to the modernity of a kid who can chop up anything, like kids watching TV with a remote control button. Film as a medium has still not advanced beyond Godard's achievement. Most people have not begun to digest Godard's revolution properly: he is still as far ahead of the avant-garde as *Kane* dominates classical filmmaking. Thus *Pierrot le Fou* is a "remake" of *Bonnie and Clyde,* yet made in advance of the Beatty film, in which Bonnie grows bored with Clyde and offs him.

But early on in *Pierrot le Fou,* Belmondo, as a disillusioned Parisian husband and father who has just been stirred by meeting an old girlfriend (Karina), goes to a dreadful salon party. He meets a tough-looking American, drinking Scotch, wearing shades, and very bored. It is Samuel Fuller. He says he is in Paris to make a film of Baudelaire's *Les Fleurs du Mal,* a dream that never came to pass.

Belmondo asks him what the cinema is.

Fuller answers in Godard's words, but with an attitude that might come from a Fuller film: "The film is like a battleground . . . Love . . . Hate . . . Action . . . Violence . . . Death. In one word . . . Emotion."

That is the raw voice of American innocence speaking, and Fuller was exactly the right choice for the brief role. But by 1965, in the sort of collage-movie Godard knew how to make, there were other answers that had to be added, not just some obscure sentence from structuralist criticism, but your good old $22 million. *Pierrot le Fou* cost virtually nothing, and for a few minutes it seemed like the future of film, even in America itself.

You can say that Godard is old hat now—that he deserves no more than his place in the history of foreign art-house cinema. I disagree. *Pierrot le Fou* is still one of the great modern American films, where French words and light have fed Fuller's earth: "Emotion." And the hero and heroine are both dead, daubed in blood or red, gone with the wind. That was 1965, and it was a moment when an austere romantic, Godard, determined that romantic cinema—and even the romance of cinema—was over.

But the business was not finished.

"It's only business." Melodrama joins hands with business strategy—Al Pacino's Michael Corleone is still the model for Hollywood office style. *The Godfather Part II,* 1974 *(Private Collection)*

20 · A FILM WE CAN'T REFUSE

One day in 1958, a young English writer, Gavin Lambert, had lunch at the M-G-M commissary. He was recently over from London, where he had helped edit *Sight and Sound.* But he had become friendly with Nicholas Ray, and Ray had invited him to Los Angeles where he would be a scriptwriter, a helper, and even a lover to Ray. Lambert knew his Hollywood history, and understood the special legend of the Metro canteen, a place where the whole family had once taken lunch together.

This day the place was nearly empty. As far as Lambert could discover, there were only a couple of movies being shot on the lot, one of which was Ray's *Party Girl*. So Lambert observed ships passing under the strip lighting: Robert Taylor, the star of *Party Girl*, and a middle-aged woman on a desultory visit to her old home—it was Greta Garbo. She and Taylor had been screen lovers—immortal, we still like to say—in *Camille* (1937). But twenty-one years later, no one remembered the congruity or thought to reintroduce them.

For the first time in its brief history, old Hollywood was learning the habit of keeping its funeral clothes dry-cleaned. The very creators of the business were exiting: Mayer went in 1957; Jesse Lasky and Harry Cohn in 1958; De Mille in 1959; Mack Sennett in 1960; Joe Schenck died in 1961. In 1965 David O. Selznick had a fatal heart attack while testifying in a legal proceeding to discover whether (or by how much) M-G-M had cheated him on revenue from *Gone With the Wind*.

These were public names still, but the losses were not felt as much as those among actors: Bogart, dead in 1957, Ronald Colman in 1958, Tyrone Power in 1958, struck down on the set of *Solomon and Sheba*, Errol Flynn in 1959, Clark Gable in 1960 (soon after the strain of *The Misfits*), Gary Cooper in 1961, Charles Laughton in 1962. Not one of those men had made it to seventy. Thus every departure seemed premature and shocking, as well as an early warning of what smoking could do to you. On-screen, smoking had stayed heavenly; but the real bodies that carried the message were poisoned.

Yet these famous faces were alive still on the screen, and young. All at once, we seemed to learn the way film had blurred life and death, and made memory material. A novelist, Norman Mailer, noticed this sly shift in a rich essay on film theory:

> Think of a favorite uncle who is gone. Does the apparatus of the mind which flashes his picture before us act in another fashion if we ask for a flash of Humphrey Bogart next. . . . Film seems part of the mechanism of memory, or at the least, a most peculiar annex to memory. Film is a phenomenon whose resemblance to death has been ignored for too long.

Just as the movies began to die, it seemed, so the logic arose in which they had never been alive, only lifelike.

There were two other deaths, not readily associated with the list above, that were more moving still to the public. On September 30, 1955, after completing just three big films, James Dean was wiped out in his new Porsche on a California back road. He was on his way to a motor race, and he was twenty-four. In a way his career had been so sudden that he had always been twenty-four, and always is forever. His life was muddled and short; his future is beyond accounting, even if it begs for speculation. But he was an authentic star and the one above all who indicated a rich new territory of filmmaking—movies that flattered the unhappy youth of America. The teenage audience was not predominant in 1955; significant spending money had not yet passed down to teenagers. But Dean embodied a way of standing, of dressing, of scowling that is not over yet. And his cult (the marketing of his image and those of his followers after his death) was of profound commercial importance. Like a ghost, Dean rides alongside Peter Fonda and Dennis Hopper in *Easy Rider* (1969), to say nothing of this abiding model of life that began to take hold: of staying twenty-four forever.

On August 5, 1962, at the age of thirty-six, Marilyn Monroe was found dead, naked, in her own bed. That was her fit location, but in every other way her scenario had gone wrong. There's no need now to argue her quality as an actress, or the degree to which she was a victim of a cruel system or her own worst enemy. What was clear, immediately, on hearing of her death, was the way in which this lovely girl had meant something, anything, to everyone—whether she liked it or not; whether or not she had the faintest idea of how to control the wild circus. It may be that her life had always been closer to metaphor than reality, and that can help kill you. But she had been photographed to death: she was a genius or a ruler in still pictures; and yet, like the famous savage, she seemed to have lost her soul to the lens. She was the first modern celebrity (as opposed to star), and she did her bit to spread celebrity around, like honey or poison, in politics. She seemed to require rescue, and over the years everyone from husbands Joe DiMaggio and Arthur Miller to biographers Norman Mailer and Joyce Carol Oates tried that job. But the real question that lingers is how we define the prison of fame, and where we place Monroe as the hapless saint of being mad from the movies.

People blamed Twentieth Century–Fox for Monroe's death, the studio that had at last run out of patience with her. And over the years, nearly every other segment of our society, from the federal government to the Mafia, has been listed among the suspects. But maybe that says more about the breadth of her appeal than actual lethal intent. And don't leave her out when blame is assigned. So many of the decisions were her own, even if her mind was a working example of change. Still, Marilyn Monroe has come to represent an uncertainty that many of us share: Is this kind of life, with its lunatic fame and iconography, really what America is about?

May I remind you, too, that that very sturdy babe, Elizabeth Taylor, nearly died. There may even have been those executives at Fox who offered discreet prayers that she might slip away at the London Clinic, so that the grotesque travesty of *Cleopatra* could be written off against insurance.

This was the most famous film of the early 1960s, the epitome of misguidedness. For the story of Caesar, Antony, and the queen of Egypt had been set up by Fox, and assigned to studio space at Pinewood, England. Walter Wanger was to produce. Rouben Mamoulian was to direct. Lawrence Durrell was to do the screenplay. Rex Harrison was Caesar, Richard Burton was Marc Antony, and, for a very famous $1 million, Taylor was Cleopatra (first thoughts had Joan Collins in the part). Technically, Brando had beaten Taylor to the million mark, but in a secret deal (out of shame?), whereas the million to Taylor was boasted about as a proof of grandeur.

The shooting began in September 1960, only to be intruded on by the customary winter habits of English weather, the lack of fluency in the script, the very traditional approach of Mamoulian, and the uncertain health of Taylor. The troubles mounted: Mamoulian was dismissed; Joseph L. Mankiewicz was hired as his replacement, with orders to redo the script as necessary. By March 1961, Taylor was in a coma in the London Clinic—bulletins from within said that she was close to death.

Taylor survived—survival would turn out to be her most enduring role—London-on-the-Mediterranean was abandoned, and the project was reassigned to studios in Rome. And then in August 1962, its demented overrun (the budget had passed $30 million) required the return of Darryl F. Zanuck. In 1956, Zanuck, the founder and chief executive of Twentieth Century–Fox, had stepped down from control to go to Europe, the better to cultivate his love life and to produce such wayward pictures as *The Sun Also Rises* and *The Roots of Heaven,* culminating in his dream project, *The Longest Day* (about D-day). He had left the studio under the leadership of Spyros Skouras (a trusted veteran, though his English was still shaky), and the flops had been many.

Zanuck was still only sixty, but *The Longest Day* (1962) was a smash hit: it cost $8 million, but it had rentals of $17.5 million. The Fox board understood cash flow and it voted Zanuck back as the new chief. He could only drag *Cleopatra* into the light. Also released in 1962, it had cost $44 million, and it earned rental income of about $25 million. That was a lot of money to take in, but $44 million was a huge investment—about ten times the cost of *Gone With the Wind,* a little over twenty years later. And whereas *Gone With the Wind* had been about brave people surviving, *Cleopatra* was about the ultimate demise of vain celebrity. Once made, *Gone With the Wind* seemed essential and emblematic, whereas *Cleopatra* was a metaphor for ruin.

All of this took place in 1962, and at the studio that had fired Marilyn Monroe just weeks before her death. The public relations was terrible, though in fairness Taylor had done all she could to justify the investment in herself and to keep *Cleopatra* in the public eye with her riotous love affair with Richard Burton (another threshold for celebrity "culture," and a story that would have its sequels). More than that, a major studio was in tatters (Fox had lost $80 million in four years), enough for anyone to wonder whether the business as a whole could survive.

That Fox was still on its knees (as opposed to prostrate) was due largely to the sale in the late fifties (under Skouras) of about 200 acres of its back lot for real estate development (sold to the Aluminum Corporation of America, better known as ALCOA). This area is still known as Century City, and it brought the studio revenue of $43 million. That looked tremendous in terms of cash flow, and was a signal transition in the L.A. landscape. But the revenue was modest in the long term and it showed the studio's disinclination to develop the land themselves, or their failure to appreciate how in the last hundred years nothing in L.A. has been as profitable as land.

The financial climate was changing by 1960. Old studio space, once purchased so cheaply, could no longer be in constant use, not even by turning over sound stages to television production. Forty-four million dollars for a picture was way out of line, but $1 million for a star was quickly aped. The costs of production shot up again: *The Fall of the Roman Empire* (1964), done in Spain, cost $20 million; *55 Days at Peking* (1963) went over $10 million. Those were both Samuel Bronston productions, and Bronston was typical of freelance production outfits, set on epic movies that were filmed in cheaper locations. Bronston made five pictures one after the other—*King of Kings, El Cid, 55 Days, The Fall of the Roman Empire,* and *Circus World.* Nicholas Ray and Anthony Mann directed four of them, for a lot of money before they grew too old, yet sadly removed from the America they knew. Only one film, *El Cid,* was a hit, but its earnings were wiped out by losses on the other four.

The lesson was clear: big pictures could kill the entire enterprise behind them. But the naïve urge to overwhelm television was still strong, and there were big stars (like Charlton Heston) who could enjoy immense paydays in the initial optimism. Sometimes the plan worked. In 1960, Kirk Douglas's independent production company Bryna made *Spartacus,* adapted from a novel by the Communist Howard Fast, and employing Dalton Trumbo (after a decade blacklisted) and the young Stanley Kubrick in the days when it was still possible to regard him as a hustler and an opportunist. *Spartacus* was blown along on Douglas's unrivalled ego and resolve. (In one famous scene, all the rebels declare, "I am Spartacus," to defy identification of their leader by the wicked Romans. It's only an evil rumor that some actors actually shouted "I am Kirk Douglas!") That picture earned rentals of $14 million.

It may be useful to say what "rentals" means in the age of Hollywood that followed the separation of theaters and studios. The American box office has a gross income—that is, every last cent paid for tickets (and some actors have a percentage deal that starts on the first dollar of that gross). But theaters are permitted to subtract their "nut" (their basic running costs) from the gross, plus the percentage of box office revenue that has been allotted to them in the deal that places a picture at particular theaters. That percentage will likely be small, maybe as little as 10 percent, in the first weeks of a smash film; it can become much more generous later. The "rentals" are the sum of money passed on by theaters to the film's distributor.

Ben-Hur had succeeded in 1959 (rentals of $36 million and eleven Oscars). Throw in *The Bridge on the River Kwai, Lawrence of Arabia, The Guns of Navarone* from the same years. But then note the casualty list: not just the Bronston pictures and *Cleopatra,* but *The Greatest Story Ever Told, Doctor Dolittle, Mutiny on the Bounty, The Bible,* and *Waterloo.* In the course of the 1960s, against original costs, those movies lost over $100 million. John Wayne made a large personal stand with his production of *The Alamo,* a film that stood for so many of his ideals. Budgeted at $7.5 million, its costs crept up to $12 million as Wayne succumbed to the urge to get everything "right." It earned rentals of about $15 million eventually, but because of the deals undertaken to get it shot he never made a cent of profit from it. And many people (Mexicans foremost) reckoned it had everything "wrong."

Try seeing any of those films today—only *Lawrence,* I think, stands the test, and still leaves too many questions unanswered if you are of a mood to wonder why Alec Guinness and Anthony Quinn can play Arabs, and how modern-day Iraq was carved out of the First World War (or are those two kinds of indifference mutually sustaining?). The rest are painfully archaic, far more wearisome than any number of classics from the thirties and forties, or even the following films, made in the same short period, 1958–62, and indicative of new ideas that were springing up even in America: *Vertigo, Touch of Evil, Anatomy of a Murder, Rio Bravo, Some Like It Hot, Psycho, The Hustler, Splendor in the Grass, Lolita, The Manchurian Candidate, Days of Wine and Roses.* All those films together cost less than *Cleopatra.* Not every one was a hit. Yet their collected profits must be close to $25 million.

What I'm getting at is not just that modest production was a safer policy to pursue, but that smaller subjects were invariably more interesting. All the pictures in that second group, save for *Rio Bravo* (Hawks remained in paradise) and *Some Like It Hot,* are downbeat or depressing. They question the probity of the law, the reliability of gender, mother love, the importance of winning, the American political process, and a cocktail or three before dinner. They question the mindless comfort of the movies. Nevertheless, most found an audience and a place in history. Of course, most of the films in this list were made against the grain of Hollywood, and disturbed some Americans. Initially released by Paramount (under Hitchcock's contract there), even in script form *Psycho* alarmed the studio. This led to the downfall of longtime executive Y. Frank Freeman, and the film being coaxed away to Universal (a maneuver Lew Wasserman engineered). It became the biggest profit-maker in the group.

Against the whole idea of a motel murder, of corpses kept "alive," and of Janet Leigh being ogled in her underwear and then knifed off the screen, there remained a Hollywood pledged to the old order. Nothing spoke for it more clearly than *The Sound of Music,* a Twentieth Century–Fox rendering of the Rodgers and Hammerstein musical, with Julie Andrews as maybe the least likely pinup for 1965. With rental income of $72 million, it officially passed *Gone With the Wind* as the biggest grosser of film history. To some of us, that picture seemed moribund on first viewing, but truly the gap between Julie Andrews and the military buildup in Vietnam was no greater than the gulf of understanding between Adolf Hitler and Shirley Temple. But Julie Andrews was, theoretically, an adult.

Of course, it set off trends: after the sugary *Sound of Music* and *Mary Poppins,* Andrews had savage reversals and sour medicine with *Star!* and *Darling Lili.* And the widescreen musical ground to inertia after *My Fair Lady* (Best Picture for 1964, but a film that cost far more than it earned), *Doctor Dolittle, Camelot,* and *Hello, Dolly!* For the best part of thirty years now, the American movie musical has been in retreat, though during those same years, young people's habit of music has grown out of all proportion. Musicals are now rare, and Baz Luhrmann's *Moulin Rouge* was really an Australian film, but there have been dramatic movies that employ music in fresh ways—the great Jacques Demy–Michel Legrand pictures of the early sixties (*Lola, Baie des Anges, Les Parapluies de Cherbourg*), plus *American Graffiti, Nashville; New York, New York; Saturday Night Fever, The Singing Detective* and *Pennies from Heaven* (the English originals, please, made for television with Dennis Potter undiluted), *One from the Heart, Casino,* as well as several films by Woody Allen. To say nothing of animated features, many of which have supplied the nominees for the Academy's Best Song category in recent years.

But if you love the musical, and regard it as an essential American form, then it is all the more striking that the cinema has neglected the works of Stephen Sondheim.

*   *   *

Imagine the scene as the lawyers for Twentieth Century–Fox sat down with those from ALCOA to discuss the sale of more than half the Fox lot. There is, obviously, haggling over the final price, and no doubt the Fox lawyers staggered out of the room, grim yet proud, with the whispered glee, We got them up to 43—as in millions of dollars. That may have been more than the Fox board expected—$43 million in the late fifties was a lot of money. So why did no one ask, Where's the zero?—as in $430 million.

We are talking about the whole equation here, as well as all that land between Olympic and Santa Monica Boulevards, and between Century Park West and Avenue of the Stars. Today, that plot is one of the centers of the commercial world, with hotels, restaurants, and shopping *in excelsis Deo.* If you care to compute (just for fun) the rental income from that plot in over forty years, just bear in mind that when the estate of Myron Selznick's daughter, Joan, was settled, it was found that in her self-imposed exile (and worse) at Laguna Beach she had been receiving $1 million a year as rental from Neiman Marcus—the store had built on the land that once housed the Myron Selznick Agency. Of course, by the late eighties, when Joan died, that $1 million a year was out of line with going rates. It needed to be renegotiated. But Joan had not taken care of her own affairs. She was not like her father. My guess is that $430 million could have been criticized for tameness and lack of vision.

But the history of Hollywood is often that of deferring vision for an appealing bit of cash up front. There is a grand old Hollywood story in which a veteran of the business is having lunch with his accountant. The veteran is only picking at his food, but the accountant is sure that he has uplifting news. "George," he says, "according to latest estimates, the value of your house [just off Benedict Canyon] is now—conservatively, mind— at $6.5 million."

"Really?" says George, not one atom improved.

"How about that?"

"Sure," sighs George. "Arthur, can I ask you something?"

"Ask. Aren't we from way back?"

"I guess we are. Could you let me have a hundred?"

There's a pause, as if George has just admitted the passing away of an ex-wife, or a household pet. Arthur would like a hint before responding. It doesn't come.

"Of course, I could!" says Arthur. He takes out his checkbook.

"In cash," says George. "Fifty'll do."

To which you could add that parking in Century City seldom goes over $30, even with a long lunch.

Yes, that's made up, but here's a real-life story that attests to the same kind of thing. The story is told by Steven Bach, one of the new generation of Hollywood executives in the 1970s. He noticed this:

Nobody ever realized the value of ancillary rights before the mid-1970s. I remember being in an office at Paramount ten years ago, and seeing a framed Xeroxed check for $10 million. Very impressive. It was for the sale of the entire pre–1948 Paramount feature library to Universal-MCA. But who ended up with the better deal? Ten million dollars isn't worth ten million dollars anymore, but the value of film libraries has skyrocketed. Who do the networks and cable people and videodisc people come to for the best libraries? Of course—the majors.

The pattern is hideously clear, and it has to be set against every piece of folklore that those movie moguls were accomplished businessmen, instead of innately reactionary guys who could never resist immediate cash. The Lumière brothers thought they had a white elephant. Griffith fancied he was making an art instead of a business. The reception for both sound and color was suspicious and self-destructive, yet it was as nothing compared with the bizarre decision to challenge television (instead of owning it).

Even after the domestic delight in television was there for any idiot to behold, the guardians of the great film libraries began to sell their backlist to television networks for peanuts. But peanuts in hand. It is as if, in the late forties and the fifties, the executives remaining in charge somehow doubted that television was going to catch on, and as if they failed to see that one of the gnawing insecurities for those who owned TV stations was how to find enough things to broadcast, to fill the airwaves so that audiences didn't turn off or switch the channel. A movie could fill two hours, just like that—no production costs, no residual payments, and once you'd got the rights to the movie you could show it as often as you liked. Yes, that's right: the movies were sold off to TV (often in perpetuity) in job lots, without any recognition of how large an audience they might win. The attitude that dictated selling the lot (as opposed to leasing it out, acre by acre) said, Get rid of the movies, all of them, for the best up-front bit of cash you can squeeze. The land and the movies should have been owned. But the studios begrudged the storage space needed for all those cans of film, and the trouble required to keep them at the proper temperature and to let them be exercised (reels of film need to be run every now and then, so as not to get brittle).

Put it this way: all of Paramount's sound films before 1948 for $10 million—that's the early Marx Brothers, Mae West, W. C. Fields, Hope and Crosby; it's *Trouble in Paradise, Shanghai Express, Lives of a Bengal Lancer, The Lady Eve, Morocco* (and *Road to Morocco*); *Swing High, Swing Low; Double Indemnity, Going My Way, For Whom the Bell Tolls, The Lost Weekend.* It's madness—yet the check was photocopied, framed, and put up to impress people.

To be polite about it, there was a crisis of leadership increasingly evident in the 1950s. It was illustrated by the simultaneous surge in television viewing and the decline in cinema attendance, and by the demise of a generation of people who had made the movies. But what they had made, in great part, was a very lucky business that could hardly fail in its first decades. And already, a new wave of agents and independent-minded stars had foreseen the shape of things to come: a panorama of independent productions where the talent had an increasing fiscal involvement in its own pictures. One other thing is worth stressing: though America fell giddily in love with television, it retained its affection for the movies.

There's a business logic that says, of course, what happens in the fifties is that the audience shows itself happy to sit at home and watch the stories on a small screen. So be it. Let us act accordingly. The logical end of that thinking—and it's still there, pressing to be heeded—is that a new movie could play all over the world on the same day, on television. Think of the benefits: the huge investment in theaters can be liquidated; the movie plays immediately so that the investment in its production can be recouped at one blow; and the urgent fears of piracy would be circumvented, for piracy means that for far-flung markets someone steals a movie's image on video and starts selling it before its official release.

There's another consequence to this futurism: that in the same time-span "everybody" might see the same thing. What that could do for internationalism, for the global village or for the spirit of interaction and sharing in the world is untold. Of course, it's what the World Wide Web now claims to offer. But the great majority of messages and offers that go under that flag are pretty drab compared with, say, *Star Wars, E.T., The Godfather,* or *Titanic,* all at once, everywhere, especially if you add to the equation the kind of high-definition home television that is possible already and which could work on a screen the size of a wall.

This could come to pass, or something close to it, financed by advertising, by cable subscription, by license fee, by pay-per-view. But something else was also evident by the sixties—a very large minority of Americans, maybe as "few" as 25 million a week, still elected to go to theaters, to the big screen, to that strange "paradise" where Hopper's usherette lives. More than that, by the sixties it was also emerging that that 25 million or so was more slanted toward the educated, the critically minded, and the alert portions of society than ever before. As I said previously, this was the dawning of an age of film culture in America, as colleges and universities began to take on the subject, and as the appetite for reappraising American film history was satisfied by the wealth of old movies appearing on the small screen.

I do not want to sentimentalize the sixties, but still I believe that there was a narrow window (from about 1967 to about 1975) in which the prospect of a grown-up American cinema (I cannot really use the word "adult," because that was getting its erection, too) came into being. All manner of things affected it. There was the disintegration, physically and morally, of the old mogul order. I've talked already about the troubles Warner Brothers had in digesting, let alone selling, *Bonnie and Clyde.* It is a rare thing to own a medium, only to see a new film, one that you loathe, turn into a tremendous success (it's like Mayer seeing *Sunset Blvd.*). So I think it's no accident that in 1967, the year of *Bonnie and Clyde,* Jack Warner sold off the studio to a company called Seven Arts, run by Eliot and Kenneth Hyman.

This was the new development in the sixties: in 1962, Universal yielded and was purchased by MCA, passing into the hands of Lew Wasserman, yesterday's agent and therefore the notional enemy to the studios. In 1966, Paramount became a subsidiary of Gulf & Western. Two years later, a mogul from the next-door showtime, Kirk Kerkorian, a casino/hotel owner from Las Vegas, gained control of M-G-M for $80 million, whereupon he held an immense and tragic sale of studio assets—costumes, properties, and so on—to help fund the first MGM Grand Hotel in Vegas (the one that burned down in 1980). As for the office files, a mine for scholarship such as can scarcely be conceived, he had them burned.

So the executive class was on the ropes, and quite desperate to clutch at anything that worked. There was also a new young generation, the first that had ever been to film school, that knew the history of the medium, that was hip to the tumult of the sixties, that knew its Godard, Antonioni, and Fellini as well as its Hawks and Hitchcock. Correspondingly, those kids—they were called brats sometimes—had an audience of students with something like the same preparation. And because television catered safely to the audience that did not wish to be troubled, so it was easier for American movies to pick up some of the alluring traits of foreign films— nudity, sex, bad language, grim material. In a way, it began to be assumed that if you were willing to go out at night you were already on the road to depravity.

All of those factors are "fun" if you like—real, provable, and anecdotal. But of far greater importance is the way in which these are also the years in which America began to confront some of its own flaws. The coverall of being the greatest country on earth was no longer quite sufficient. The start of the civil rights movement was the deepest lesson in the sins of racism.

In the late sixties and the early seventies, I suppose, optimists and reformists could cheer themselves up at beholding the careers of such new movie stars as Sidney Poitier, Cicely Tyson, and Bill Cosby. Blacks were no longer confined to playing servants, sidekicks, and obliging supports to the white system of society and government. They might even be surly, arrogant, and sexually aggressive in the blaxploitation films. Over the years, they might be outrageous comedians or satirists of Americana, figures like Richard Pryor and the young Eddie Murphy. Not that far off was a time when anyone would need to list several blacks among the best actors alive in America—Denzel Washington, Morgan Freeman, Andre Braugher, Alfre Woodard.

But that last paragraph is also, alas, a measure of the unearned ease with which white liberals can congratulate themselves on "improvement." In 1939, David Selznick was happy and proud that Hattie McDaniel should be the first black performer to win an Oscar, for *Gone With the Wind*. Yet he had bowed to pressures from Atlanta's civic authorities that

McDaniel not be part of the premiere celebrations, and on the night of the Academy Awards he permitted his actress to sit in a corner of the room at a small table for two, as opposed to being at the *GWTW* table.

So, yes, it was good to see and hear Richard Pryor, yet note how uneasily Hollywood fitted him into its scenarios, and see the toll that his pioneering fame took on him. By the seventies, several things were clear enough for liberalism to be guarded in its hopes: blacks had not begun to penetrate the money-gathering or decision-making process in Hollywood. There was vigor, rhythm, and sauce in some blaxploitation films, but those were still regarded as black flavors and the genre as a whole was a ghetto. I am not sure that anything in the seventies (or since) has done more than enlarge and humanize the servant role indicated for blacks, in our pictures and in our society. Let me add this: it is also painfully clear by the seventies that jazz, a magnificent black art, seldom lucrative enough to pay a decent living, but radiant with black ideas, sentiments, and attitudes, was dying, and was being replaced by middle-class white kids who liked to sound black and bad and make a fortune at it. "Improvement" can be a deadly thing.

On the other hand, the dire adventure in Vietnam (where blacks were overrepresented) clearly suggested that Americans should have studied history, politics, and even courtesy before they made such drastic policy. The several assassinations, followed by Nixon's presidential assault on the Constitution, made it easier to perceive the real perils to America, and to see that they *were* American, as opposed to foreign or un-American. The havoc on campuses raised so many issues pertaining to curriculum, discipline, liberty, and purpose in education. And as it became available, so sex infected everything in that heady era before AIDS when sexuality and education meant nearly the same thing.

No one should be misled into thinking that American film during this nervy age was all advanced, doubt-filled, or brilliant. This was the time of such happy hits as *Planet of the Apes, Butch Cassidy and the Sundance Kid* (which was cunningly hip, though actually antique), *Patton* (which Nixon watched several times through the dark night of his soul), *True Grit, Airport, Love Story, The Poseidon Adventure, The Sting,* and *The Towering Inferno.*

To utter more of a disclaimer still, the film which, dollar for dollar, exerted the most pull on Hollywood, and which probably ensured deals for more people than the mini-skirt, was *Easy Rider,* one of the worst acclaimed films ever made in America. This was the dream project of Dennis Hopper and Peter Fonda, who naturally enough expected that their road movie would appeal to the independent producer Roger Corman, who had given a start to many kids, and who had reaped from *The Wild Angels,* a film budgeted at $350,000, rentals of $5 million.

But Corman hedged: *Easy Rider* seemed unduly expensive at $350,000 and he was uncertain of the boys as directors and unwilling to make it himself. Whereupon a young actor who had his eye on a supporting part in the film directed them toward Bert Schneider and Bob Rafelson. Their Ray-Bert company had just invented the Monkees and was cash rich. On the spot, they wrote a check for $360,000 to make *Easy Rider.* The actor—his name was Jack Nicholson—got the part. *Easy Rider* went on to earn well over $30 million. It was quickly talked about as the most profitable film ever made, and as fatuous evidence that kids could do no wrong. *Easy Rider* became the vouchsafe in arguments with what was left of the old Hollywood that you did not need to spend several million dollars to get a movie.

In partnership with Steve Blauner, Schneider and Rafelson formed the BBS Company, the plan of which was to let newcomers (like themselves) make films for no more than $1 million each. These films were to be released by Columbia, because Bert was the son of Abe Schneider, who was president of that studio after Harry Cohn's death. The results were enough to make up for *Easy Rider.* Rafelson directed *Five Easy Pieces* and *The King of Marvin Gardens;* Nicholson made his directorial debut with *Drive, He Said;* Henry Jaglom did *A Safe Place;* and Peter Bogdanovich directed his second film, *The Last Picture Show.* Five films—two flops, one in the middle and two significant hits—and three of them, *Five Easy Pieces, The King of Marvin Gardens,* and *The Last Picture Show,* that seem to me exemplary works of modest art and intelligent entertainment.

All five pictures have less than positive or happy endings. None of them features characters who are simply appealing and to be identified with. Instead, the people are real, awkward, untidy, difficult—they are people from life. Without being gloomy or depressive, the films are portraits of ordinary life in difficult times. As a group, they are a model for what a small studio could produce and remain successful, and it was an echo of the golden age. For the notion of trading some misses against rich hits had always been part of Thalberg's logic. It was just that the material at BBS was so much tougher and more lifelike than anything Thalberg would have dared.

Bogdanovich was an interesting member of the new generation. Born in Kingston, New York, in 1939, he had studied acting with Stella Adler before becoming a film critic and scholar. He wrote about film for *Esquire,* and he had curated seasons on Hawks and Hitchcock at the Museum of

Modern Art. He would also make a documentary film about John Ford. But before that, apprenticed to Roger Corman, he had taken some old footage, some sets, and a few days of Boris Karloff's time to make a remarkable debut, *Targets,* which is both an effective thriller and a meditation on violence in America.

On the strength of *The Last Picture Show,* Bogdanovich leaped ahead and had two real hits with *What's Up, Doc?,* a screwball comedy with Barbra Streisand and Ryan O'Neal, which took in $28 million on a budget of $4 million; and *Paper Moon,* a fond tribute to the rural world of some of John Ford's films of the 1930s. I'm not sure if anyone has made a better three in a row—certainly not many people as young in the game. Very sympathetic to the films of Jean Renoir, Bogdanovich also resembled the French New Wave directors in that he had made the shift from critic to director with astonishing aplomb.

Robert Altman was fifteen years older, out of Kansas City, from an arduous preparation in industrial filmmaking and television, before he had his first (and so far only) hit with *M.A.S.H.* (1970). Under cover of concerning itself with the Korean War, here was a movie about Vietnam's demoralization, and the steady revelation that America in unison or uniform was a model of disorder not far from madness. The humor was cheerful; the human grouping was still Hawksian; but Altman's wandering style, his multilayered soundtrack, and his almost random use of focus-pulling in group shots suggested the seething wildness of wars that went under the rubric of fraudulent communiqués—until it was too late. Over the next few years, Altman made a series of films that revelled in that untidiness and in the dreamy dismantling of so many American genres: *McCabe & Mrs. Miller* ruined our hopes for Western entrepreneurs; *The Long Goodbye,* with that tune that will not go away, and the superb, lazy Elliott Gould, was Philip Marlowe dissolved in acid; *California Split* was one of the first true studies on screen of the lost soul of gambling; and then there was *Nashville.*

Not one of those films after *M.A.S.H* did well, or cost too much. But they were the subjects of a debate that went beyond criticism and which was helped along by Pauline Kael's early assumption that *Nashville* was a masterpiece in an age of assassinations (it was a musical, too), but viewers should take great care in deciding whether it is a tragedy or a comedy. In the end, like a city, it is what we choose to see or remember.

I don't want to hurry so much that I neglect movies I love still—and here in the early seventies we are at what looks like the last great love affair. Alan J. Pakula made *Klute* and *The Parallax View.* Martin Scorsese delivered *Mean Streets* and *Taxi Driver.* Milos Forman (a refugee from

Czech tyranny who was droll enough to notice absence of freedom in the United States, too) made *Taking Off* and *One Flew Over the Cuckoo's Nest*. Hal Ashby, trained as an editor, made *Harold and Maude, The Last Detail,* and *Shampoo*. Terrence Malick's *Badlands* was one of the great debuts in American film. The very able Sidney Lumet would make *Dog Day Afternoon* and *Network*. John Boorman made *Deliverance*. From a script by Paddy Chayefsky, Arthur Hiller made *The Hospital,* a lethally funny account of American social benevolence collapsing in its own bureaucratic chaos.

In 1974, at Paramount, Evans, Towne, Polanski, and Nicholson made *Chinatown*.

The telling point is that, more or less, all of these films could have been BBS productions. Not many of them were extravagant even if actors like Jack Nicholson could hardly resist their advisers telling them that they deserved more money: on *Five Easy Pieces* he had worked for scale upfront, with profit points if the picture did well, which it did; but by the mid-seventies, he was up to $1 million, and that was just the beginning. The approach was consistently grown-up, as witness the decision to take *Chinatown* to a darker resolution than even its writer had intended; as witness the nearly macabre dissonance of "Hooray for Hollywood!" at the end of *The Long Goodbye;* it's there in the feeling to *The Last Picture Show* that so many hopes in life get snuffed out, and that the small Texan movie house will show *Red River* no more.

It's not that these films are endless parades of misery. On the contrary, they are movies that generally evince fondness for people, for actors, and performance—just think of Ben Johnson in *The Last Picture Show,* Sterling Hayden in *The Long Goodbye,* Ruth Gordon in *Harold and Maude,* Sissy Spacek in *Badlands,* Jane Fonda in *Klute.* But to think of those performances is to note a new line of people, more eccentric, wilder, yet more ordinary or helpless than people in the golden age of Hollywood. It's the difference between Bogart and Gould as Philip Marlowe (and there is space to love them both), and Altman's realization that in decency and taste you can't quite run the Bogart act any longer.

There is humor in these films—the "screwing like a Chinaman" routine from *Chinatown* is timeless. There is light and air and place—the endless prairie in *Badlands;* the snowbound township in *McCabe & Mrs. Miller;* Atlantic City in winter of *The King of Marvin Gardens.* There is sadness, to be sure, and I think it is absolutely vital that every so often that sadness drifts off the immediate story and begins to become a fog over America as a whole. But that is what art does.

In so many of those films there is Nicholson, a rallying ground, a charmer and a backtalk specialist, a presence as encouraging as that of Jean Renoir in *La Règle du Jeu*. I don't think I'm alone in the feeling from those years of watching a group at work, a new generation—and about time, too, for those directors who had made up the pantheon at *Cahiers du Cinéma* were dead or dying. And Nicholson has not given up on us yet (as Brando did). A very rich and rather lonely man, perhaps, Jack Nicholson cannot be fooled on the toughness of the world, and still he conjures up unexpected, worthwhile films—*The Pledge, About Schmidt, Something's Gotta Give*—and still he has that grin that goes back to Gable and says that loving stars isn't crazy.

Of course, I have still to come to what I see as the most notable film of the era, the one that became for a moment the most successful picture of all time and is still the model for that inspiring notion that one can make a great film and a big hit at the same time.

Francis Ford Coppola was born in Detroit in 1939, but he grew up around New York because his father was a flautist with Arturo Toscanini's NBC Symphony Orchestra. I'm not sure that an American filmmaker had ever been raised in so creatively minded a family, a point worth making if only to counter the widespread notion that hard knocks, dogged professionalism, and bitterness are the only training for pictures. None of that hurts, but there is a place for idealism, and for good and ill Francis has struggled with his idealism, and with the clash it makes with traits that are closer to that of a Michael Corleone. Coppola—as much as Chaplin, Hawks, Welles, and Sturges—is an enormous muddle of a man. Again, this is not the sole test or a guarantee of talent, but it's a signal that art may lurk in those dark woods.

Coppola was new in another way: he had been to film school. After Hofstra (where he worked in theater), he went to the UCLA film school, and it was while there that he met Walter Murch and George Lucas, both of whom were studying film at USC. They became friends and a team even in their youthful enthusiasm about the need to shrug off the moribund ways of Hollywood. One demonstration of that was moving to northern California. All three still live there and they are friends. Murch is one of the greatest editors and sound artists in the history of film, and Lucas is . . . well, we'll come to that, but you know what I mean.

In the late sixties, Coppola made his beginnings: he worked for Roger Corman (like so many others); he directed a couple of films, including *The Rain People,* that road movie on which he and Murch and Lucas really discovered northern California; and he established himself as a screenwriter with *Patton*. Setting up shop as American Zoetrope, Coppola and Murch helped Lucas make his first film, *THX 1138*, in the Bay area, in 1970–71. It was a very doomy piece of science fiction and such a flop as to threaten the new group with ruin. They owed their backer, Warner Brothers, over $300,000.

So Coppola needed the chance, from Paramount, to direct *The Godfather*. It was a close-run thing. A lot of clout at the studio felt that it was beyond Coppola. For weeks as he worked they kept another director around, ready to take over. The casting raised many problems, and it was only through perseverance that Coppola kept Brando and Al Pacino— both roles were hotly pursued by just about every actor you can think of. The shooting was beset with difficulties, from the jitters at Paramount to the rather baleful attentions of real-life gangsters, very interested to see how they might be portrayed.

To make *The Godfather* (which included doing the screenplay with Mario Puzo, author of the book), Coppola received $125,000 plus 6 percent of the rentals returned to Paramount. The movie went over budget: it ended up costing $6 million. It was a big, long picture with a large cast and period re-creation. Equally, it was a movie on which the cast was paid moderately: Brando got $200,000 (in the end). Pacino, James Caan, Robert Duvall, and Diane Keaton were all early in their careers. I doubt that the above-the-line costs came close to $1 million.

The results were extraordinary. *The Godfather* opened March 11, 1972, and people came to see it. Because the film did not have a wide release immediately, there was a steady flowering across the nation: for example, its tenth week was its biggest grossing period ($3.1 million). The reviews were good, but the marketing was built so that word of mouth encouraged the real size of the audience. People heard they had to see it, and so they waited anxiously for it to come to their part of the country. It was a picture talked about at dinner parties as well as in bars and on buses. None of which was remarkable—that had always been the way in which pictures were sold. But in the end, on its first run, *The Godfather* had domestic rentals of $85 million, with about $150 million worldwide. It displaced *The Sound of Music* as the "most successful" film of all time. At the next Academy Awards it took Best Picture, Best Actor, and Best Adapted Screenplay (though not Best Director—that went to Bob Fosse for *Cabaret*). Paramount made arrangements for it to be sold to NBC for television viewing, spread over two nights, for $10 million—just like the check that Steven Bach had seen on the wall for everything the studio had done before 1948.

So what is *The Godfather*, apart from a terrific American movie? Is it the unified vision and work of one man? Of course not. It needs Brando and the way his hand flutters; it needs the untamed energy of Jimmy Caan and the mounting stillness of Al Pacino. It needs the somber color range of brown through gray and black that Gordon Willis achieved. It took an overnight rewrite from Robert Towne. It needed, at the end, a merciful conclusion from Walter Murch's editing. It would not be as it is without Nino Rota's music or Dean Tavoularis's design. Come to that, what do you lose if there is no Abe Vigoda, no Sterling Hayden, no Alex Rocco, no Simonetta Stefanelli (she bears the persimmon breasts of Apollonia)?

I am talking about the nature of collaboration or company, and I could make the same kind of listing for every good picture ever made. And I suspect that nearly every person I've listed (as well as all the others, even the production executive at Paramount, Robert Evans, who, someone said, was wrong on every key decision on the film) would say that Francis made it all possible. He brought them together. He saw the shape within the Puzo book. He gave liberty to every talent, yet organized them all, too.

He made it a film about family, a subject on which he had very mixed feelings himself. He permitted, or he did not prevent, the gradual awareness in some viewers that this was a film about Nixon and America in which Michael Corleone becomes a kind of presidential surrogate. But that's a point at which commentary begins to realize that great films—all films—also belong to their viewers, to the audience.

In other words, the great collaboration needs us. It needs our involvement, our feelings, our intelligence, just as much as our dollars. And to that extent *The Godfather* has passed into the bloodstream and the nervous system of America. It is us, and in 1972, maybe more powerfully than at any other time, it was made clear that an American movie might speak to everyone.

Of course, if that were so, then the exhilaration of company was not everything. You had to see, too, that we and our America are not far from the heart of darkness. For what was happening at the movies, and maybe it was something no one intended, was that as we gazed at the stillness of Michael Corleone (and it was evil making him calm), so we were enchanted by it, wanted to be him, or to be a part of his family.

Two ways of seeing. Melinda Dillon and Cary Guffey in Steven Spielberg's *Close Encounters of the Third Kind,* 1977 *(Private Collection)*

21 · RIGHT BEFORE YOUR EYES

A couple of nights ago (2003), I took my fourteen-year-old son Nicholas to see *The Matrix Revolutions,* the third and "final" offering in the *Matrix* trilogy. I introduce Nicholas at this point in the book because as we waited for the film to start (he was impatient in that lovely way), he said that he had been thinking of film as a career. I was similarly inclined at fourteen, and nearly fifty years later I am not sure whether what happened was a "career," a ruined life, or something in between. His comment made me realize that this book is for Nicholas and his generation. And to the extent that, among film critics, I may sometimes be regarded as a doomsayer about where modern film is going, I introduce my own son as a character witness and as a measure of good will. I want the movies to be marvelous so that he might ride along on their momentum. And since the *Matrix* trilogy has become a small habit for the two of us, I am happy to repeat the following story.

When we went to see *The Matrix,* the original, in 1999, when he was ten, I turned to him half an hour into the film and whispered something to the effect that I couldn't understand what the movie was about. "It doesn't matter," he hissed. "Just watch it!" It was like sitting next to Pauline Kael again, and, as with much of what she had to say, it was both intimidating and instinctive criticism. Later I was reminded of that feeling when I read Antonia Quirke's remarkable short book on *Jaws,* part of the British Film Institute's lively series of monographs, where, in discussing the mounting excitement of Steven Spielberg's 1975 movie, she says:

> Right before our eyes Spielberg is inventing the almost aggressive purposelessness of his Indiana Jones mode. *Jaws* is perhaps the most tonally comprehensive thriller ever made—sheer exhilaration at lacking an agenda or a subject in any classical dramatic sense. The film is sometimes nothing more than a dance to music. Spielberg never meant anything really. But neither did Fred Astaire.

There were moments of "pure cinema" in those heady days of the early seventies. I can watch over and over again as Altman finds fresh ways of filling the Panavision frame in *The Long Goodbye* without ever crowding it, and as Elliott Gould simply lends himself to passing time (there is no other way to put it). There are so many passages from Sam Peckinpah's *Pat Garrett & Billy the Kid* that I put up on the screen at home as balm, as beauty, rather in the way I might play the last moments of Mahler's Ninth over and over again, or stand gazing at some pictures by Lucian Freud or Pierre Bonnard.

Peckinpah wasn't one of the gang of brats who made the late sixties and early seventies interesting. He was too vengeful and self-destructive a loner for that. But he was a key figure of the times, able to do a very early Vietnam allegory (*Major Dundee*), a sublime song to disorder and honor (*The Wild Bunch*), and then, in *Pat Garrett,* a retelling of a classic tale that was both more historically accurate than any other and a parable of how to tell a story when the syndicate was out to ruin you (and the syndicate in New Mexico in 1881 was Hollywood in 1972, in Sam's paranoid eyes, and always out to screw him).

There was much to be alarmed about in Peckinpah: the hateful misogyny; the perilous closeness to letting "beauty" eclipse the damage in violence; the drugs; his childishness. But *Pat Garrett* is surely a great American film, filled with rue for all the liberties that are being lost, and about as ecstatic on the screen as Ophüls, Mizoguchi, or Renoir himself. Peckinpah could be crippled by his own paranoia (like Hemingway was), yet he had something of Astaire's grace, too. When Garrett is out on his own and he sees a raft coming down the river, and he and that stranger exchange wary shots and the brief terror of aimed weapons—well, that was America in a moment.

There were other weird figures from the early seventies, one of whom, William Friedkin, could do no wrong for a few years. *The French Connection* heralded the impact of *The Godfather* in that it was Best Picture and a super-hit for 1971: it had rentals of $26 million, and you could argue, if you wished, that it reckoned drugs were a Bad Thing and the police good guys. Except that Friedkin didn't really seem to care, not when the whole thing was an inspired chase set to a clunking piano note, and not when Fernando Rey took one step aside from the world of Buñuel to be the sweetest, dandyish villain you could ever wish for. The dance he and Gene Hackman did getting on and off the subway, that was worth including in the new musical.

Two years later, Friedkin was back with *The Exorcist*, which did $66 million and was nominated for Best Picture (it lost to *The Sting*). I dislike *The Exorcist,* and I found it a warning sign (along with a lot from Brian De Palma) of the dangers in a furious cinematic talent "putting the audience through it" (a Hitchcock phrase) without purpose, or without the nagging moral anxiety that activated Hitch. You see, I don't think Friedkin believes in the Devil (or one more potent than himself; there are resemblances), or cares about him. I think he found exorcism a pretext for gross-out and he calculated that there was an audience for it, or a crowd ready to be challenged. (Can you watch this? Can you keep your eyes open?) Maybe I'm too much of an atheist to stand religion being so trashed. Maybe I'm a stick-in-the-mud, but I felt the cynicism of the venture, and I could only worry how some people with unsettled minds might feel on seeing the film.

The matter of cynicism and violence, or even material that turns on evil, is not casual, though sometimes American movies have made it feel so. The breakdown in censorship that began in the late sixties has surely permitted far more in the way of violence than sex (not that the two are always separate). For good and ill, I think that *Psycho* now stands revealed as a turning point in attitudes to the horrific. *Psycho* itself had many sequels.

And the modern craze for franchising, for telling the same story over and over, can be seen in *The Omen* (started in 1976), *Halloween* (started in 1978), *Friday the 13th* (started in 1980), *The Evil Dead* (1983), *Alien* (1979), and, of course, *The Texas Chain Saw Massacre* (1974).

I don't mean to lump all of these together. The first *Alien* was beautifully made, and that monster deserves a place alongside the classic demons of narrative history. John Carpenter, who started *Halloween,* is very skilled, very funny, and fond of people. In many of those series, the threatened woman—played by Sigourney Weaver or Jamie Lee Curtis—became an authentic feminist heroine. Some of the films are much better than others. But the generality of all the franchises—earning huge sums of money from teenage audiences—is climatic. It raises questions about the fit age for seeing such things, the larger influence of the screen on our behavior, and the way in which ever more exaggerated bloodletting has sometimes lost contact with character, story, and credibility. The *Scream* series (begun in 1996) is at best a camp pastiche of horror, and at worst a bunch of movies that encourage you to risk no emotional investment in the screen's action, because that action is a deliberate, mocking travesty.

I share in most arguments against censorship, whether we think of film as an art or a business. The spirit of America's First Amendment is always to reach out for liberty of expression, though the definers of those rights were also intent upon achieving a wide range of arguments and expressions. I grant too the difficulty of proving either the noxious or the beneficial effects of watching movies, though in other walks of life we do take for granted some things we cannot prove, like night following day, and the presence of weapons assisting the incidence of violence.

I have tried to stress that the whole equation must extend to the poetic or fearsome expressiveness of the screen, and to the unique condition of its audience, that of the voyeur fantasist. In other words, it's crucial to stress how far our basic way of watching is itself furtive, or dark, or out of the mainstream of experience. Nor would any film enthusiast seek to diminish the effectiveness of film, whether it is "everyone" jumping at the end of De Palma's *Carrie,* when the pale hand reaches out of the grave, or the way some feet start tapping to the rhythm of Leni Riefenstahl's *Triumph of the Will.*

Take that last film, a "documentary" record of the Nazi Party rallies at Nuremberg in 1934 which was actually used as propaganda (or advertisement) to the German people in the years preceding the Second World War. It doesn't really matter whether Riefenstahl was a Nazi herself, or a fascist in her heart. She was very talented; if there is beauty in some of Peckinpah, there is beauty in *Triumph of the Will*—the beauty of composition, movement, rhythm, and conveyed exhilaration. That's why your soul may start pulsing to the beauty, which doesn't mean that you are a Nazi, but suggests you might have been if you'd been born in unluckier times. And that is the historical revelation to be found in this hateful film.

It doesn't really matter now whether or not we ban *Triumph of the Will*. Riefenstahl was effectively blacklisted from moviemaking for the last fifty years of her prolonged but rather empty life. The damage was done in the thirties, and no, you can't measure it. We can't even prove that a given percentage of the SS saw and liked the film. But in *our* dislike of the film— and for God's sake, let us hold on to that dislike—aren't we admitting that the pulse of the screen can pass into the body and mind of the spectator? We are affected by what we see. How does a movie have any chance of being art if that is not the case?

If we were cast back in time and put in charge of Germany in the thirties, would we not ban the film? Would we not assassinate Hitler if we had the chance—that is the starting point of Fritz Lang's icy *Man Hunt*, of course. So isn't it reasonable to exercise some moderate controls?

Let me turn to one alleged "control" which I take as an indictment of modern America. To avoid federal or state intervention in filmgoing, the MPAA has always promoted self-censorship. That began with the Hays Code, and we are agreed that that Code became absurd. That's why it fell into disuse. But the MPAA now regulates our rating system, which likes to present itself as a model of concern fit to reassure parents of children at the movies. I think that is humbug. The rating system is a cover for the sale of as many tickets as possible.

Consider the R rating. The terms of an R-rated film are that no one under the age of seventeen shall see it without a parent or guardian, or someone acting in those roles. In essence, you might conclude that that measure is based on the common understanding that there are some films unfit for people under seventeen. Films like *In the Cut, The Silence of the Lambs, The Blair Witch Project, The Texas Chain Saw Massacre, Hannibal, Last Tango in Paris, The Deer Hunter, The Exorcist, Deliverance, The Ring, Boogie Nights.*

I've made that list generous to start you thinking. Not long ago I was in a packed theater watching *Hannibal*. A child was crying. I'd guess she was no more than three. Perhaps she was hungry, sick, or distressed to see Anthony Hopkins in such material. She was with her parents. But what does "with" mean in the dark, when looming above you, twenty feet high, someone is eating another's brain? I have tried to stress, as a strength or a power in the medium, how certainly we are alone at the movies (as well as caught in the crowd). What hypocrisy can take comfort that a screaming child is not in terror of something seen (and misunderstood) on the screen? It is the cant that will sacrifice so much to sell tickets, and the three-year-old has to be paid for, too.

This goes on all the time now. My son Nicholas pursues R films, and if he is precocious in some respects that doesn't mean he isn't tender and innocent in others. He could not get in to *The Matrix: Revolutions* without me. So I was "with" him; we did talk about it afterward. But I was only with him in the way that I could be told, Be quiet—just watch. Some Rs are harder than others. Some theaters frequently let kids in to see Rs without an older person. In most other countries, a real age limit is imposed and enforced: not even with her entire family can a European three-year-old see *The Silence of the Lambs*. What freedom of business is it that is being protected in the United States? Shall we start with greed and the liberty to be indifferent to the customer, along with the cynical discounting of the power of your own medium?

*   *   *

The Godfather was such a success, for everyone, that Paramount was eager for more. But now Coppola was respected: like Michael Corleone, he had risen from being the raw kid to the father figure in one sweep of action—the concluding passage to the first film, the marriage of murder and baptism, a triumph of editing, yet just a touch glib in the way it put *a* next to *z* and asked us to recompose the moral alphabet. Even there, in that masterpiece, there was a hint of: Well, if film *can* do this, why *not* do it? (Beneath it all, the movie seemed to yearn for this new family power.)

So Coppola could lay out terms to Paramount: He wanted to make *The Conversation* first, a small, melancholy film, one that he felt very personally, a study in loneliness. Then he would do the *Godfather* sequel, but with himself as producer and director, and for $1 million and 13 percent of the rentals. It was a bid he couldn't refuse making; not to have protected himself in that way would have been timid in that context. Not to have sought a much higher salary was not playing the game.

Everything turned out pretty well. *The Conversation* is an unnerving film. The second part of *The Godfather* was bold enough to cover not just the future of the Corleones but their backstory, too. In so many ways, the sequel is more intellectually challenging than the first film. And when they were both done, for television, it was possible to reconstruct the narrative line chronologically so that a real epic was visible. Many people today think of those two films as one, so that De Niro's gestures, after the fact, seem father to the Brando who had gone before him. The achievement in terms of craft, in acting, in sustained suspense has not been surpassed. But the ambiguity of the central evil of Michael was greater still. Coppola had been driven in part to show that he did not mean to glamorize the Corleones; that accusation had been made in commentary on the first film. But I think it's clear now that that reformist urge was subtly defeated by Pacino's great calm and by the way the movie is drawn to stillness. In watching evil, it was so hard not to be fascinated. It was another signal of the medium, above and beyond the intent of its artists.

The Godfather Part II won Best Picture for 1974 (*The Conversation* and *Chinatown* were among its rivals), and this time Coppola won Best Director. But the very sophisticated sequel did less well: the film cost $13 million (more than twice the original, for everyone now had to be better paid), but its rentals were only $28 million (less than a third of the original).

This was still an excellent return. Paramount would have gone for a Part III then and there. But Coppola was now intent on founding his own empire. He returned to northern California, ready to launch all manner of artistic ventures, including what would become *Apocalypse Now,* something he regarded initially as a relaxation, a picnic-in-the-country movie, after the intense effort of the two parts of *The Godfather.*

Something else had happened in the meantime. George Lucas had set up *American Graffiti* at Universal, a story about young people growing up in the Modesto area (where Lucas had been born), with a great deal of popular music from the sixties. The film had a $750,000 budget and a young cast of relative unknowns. It also had Francis and Zoetrope as godfathers for 10 percent of the profits. And in a final struggle with Universal it had been Francis who backed the film and fought the idea of cutting it. Again, that was proof of younger minds knowing what the public wanted: *American Graffiti* opened in August 1973 (it was a summer-night-out film for kids, a fairly new concept) and it had rentals of over $40 million.

In hindsight, for the picture business, *American Graffiti* was a more instructive film than both parts of *The Godfather.* The studios were passing under the control of conglomerates that put them in the charge of young, statistically minded business experts. One of their central conclusions was that whereas, by 1973, 40 percent of the American population was in the age range 12–29, that grouping made up 73 percent of those who went to the movies. The vindication that came with *American Graffiti* was that the people on the screen looked like the people in the audience. The film had come from a youth department set up at Universal by Lew Wasserman with Ned Tanen in charge. Wasserman had no great taste for youth, and few creative instincts; he shut down the youth department just before *American Graffiti* opened. But if he couldn't watch that film, he could read the numbers. And he had a picture coming that might prove the case.

Steven Spielberg had been born in Cincinnati in 1947, and raised in Phoenix. He made home movies as a kid, including *Firelight*—140 minutes long and a teenage foray into science fiction. It was a short film, *Amblin'*, made in 1969 at California State College, that got him under contract to Universal. Aged twenty-four (just like Welles with *Kane*), he did a TV-movie, *Duel*, about a motorist in the desert being pursued by a monstrous truck. It was mad but compulsive, a dream shot and cut with rare aplomb. Vehicles also played a large part in his first theatrical feature, *The Sugarland Express* (1974), a raw-nerve melodrama that used Goldie Hawn very well. And that's when Universal, through the production team of David Brown and Richard Zanuck (Darryl's son), offered him the Peter Benchley novel *Jaws*, about a Long Island summer resort terrorized by a rogue shark.

Spielberg went to the re-location of Martha's Vineyard with a budget of $3.5 million and a screenplay by Benchley and Carl Gottlieb. His deal to direct was very modest: he had no points. The film was beset with problems: filming on the water is famously hazardous; the mechanical shark, nicknamed "Bruce," proved an intractable piece of rubber, hated by everyone; Spielberg sometimes seemed at a loss. Sidney Shainberg, Wasserman's most trusted lieutenant, went to the Vineyard and talked to Spielberg. The budget was out of control. Did Spielberg still feel he could pull it off? The kid said yes, and Universal agreed to give him his head— and a budget that went to $10 million. This was not just brave (for they had considered cutting their losses); it was a sign that once committed to a picture, there was no turning back. Few films get shelved before they are finished—not because that decision would be other than prudent, but because Hollywood is so scared of seeming scared of the gamble.

It is a distinctive quality of a work of art that, late in the day, Degas might have burned a canvas, Hemingway may have contrived to lose the briefcase holding a precious but insoluble manuscript. Beyond such anecdotage there is the decision by the artist to decide he has been wasting his time, exploring a dead end. Ironically, that courage is often rewarded, for it so strengthens the character of the work that in the next attempt gold is uncovered. An artist can say, if only to himself, "Not good enough." In the movies, publicity takes over, to hide mistakes.

Jaws delivered. It had its male grouping (not far from the world of Hawks) and three vivid performances. It received a decisive edit from Verna Fields, and in John Williams's score it found a way of identifying and signaling the character of the shark. Plus, it touched upon everyone's primitive fear of the water and what lurks there.

Is *Jaws* "about" anything? I appreciate Antonia Quirke's ecstatic hope that it might not be, that it might be just a matter of motion, light, color, music, and rhythm. She amply demonstrates that it can be seen or described that way, and I realize how close that comes to the certainty that sense matters so much less than watching. But I think it is very hard for an American film to be about nothing, just as it is rare in that kind of moviemaking for nothing to happen.

So, gently, I have to say that I think there is a certain schoolboy suspicion of bureaucracy in *Jaws*—the degrees of dishonesty by which the resort leaders try to cover up their problem. Spielberg has always had that earnest wariness about adult wrongdoing, though it is probably more suited to *Jaws* than to *Schindler's List*. There is also embedded in the film a notion of heroism: the rugged (if not encrusted) valor of Quint (Robert Shaw) runs off a little on Roy Scheider's hydrophobic police chief. And it's good to be brave, and conquer the beast. There are even some film critics who surmised that this was a comic book *Moby Dick*, or a rubber shark as the new version of that ill-tempered truck in *Duel*.

None of this is very significant, I agree. But even if a film is that flimsy, still there are other "abouts" waiting to pounce, and quite shark-like in their way. Quirke's book on *Jaws* is brilliant film commentary—if you are content with lopsided equations. Her book says nothing about the way Universal made the picture, not simply in trusting Spielberg to finish it, but in identifying what it was. For the studio, and for Wasserman, it was "about" $100 million and changing the business. And *Jaws* is historically crucial to the extent that its lasting meaning is the money it made.

Wasserman looked at the film and how it tested and saw the light of a new kind of marketing. He foresaw that there were ad "bites" (it's the only word) ideally suited to television advertising. He then guessed that, instead of opening *Jaws* in the kind of gradual release pattern that prevailed, he might flood the nation with it. He would open it in several hundred theaters at once (actually 409, a number that spells death and restraint today). And he would spend almost a million dollars on television advertising, in spots aimed at the teenage audience that was lining up for a summer on the beach. He would make a craze of the film, and in filling so many theaters at once he would outflank any critical response that might note how silly the whole thing was. He judged that *Jaws* and a poster image of the creature's open mouth was a perfect ad—what else did a film need to be about but that terrific adrenaline shot? One critic, Molly Haskell, said that she "felt like a rat being given shock treatment."

Jaws did $2.5 million its first week, and then $4.3 million in the second. In each of its first six weeks it did better than *The Godfather* had done in any week. In its first run, it earned $129 million, and it was clear that many kids were going back to see it several times. In this surfeit, Universal gave Spielberg 2.5 percent of the profits. He would do better later. *Jaws* was the new champion movie, for a couple of years.

I don't mean to rush history, not when those years cover the last scuttling from Saigon, the likely arrival of AIDS in America, the bicentennial, the death of Mao Tse-tung, as well as *One Flew over the Cuckoo's Nest, Nashville, All the President's Men, Network, Taxi Driver,* and *Annie Hall.* It was not that American film was ignoring the world, but a film was coming that brought a bounty enough to presage oblivion, despite the fact that a man playing the role of president chose to employ its name for a "defense system" that not even Industrial Light and Magic could actually manufacture.

On an outline treatment, George Lucas had tried to sell *Star Wars* in the months before *American Graffiti* opened. Major enterprises like United Artists and Universal passed on it. Lew Wasserman refused even to talk about the fourteen-page treatment, but then when *Star Wars* opened he blamed his assistant, Ned Tanen, for passing and putting the project in turnaround (making it available to other studios, if they refunded all the conceivable costs so far). As Wasserman often said himself, it wasn't that he had power so much as relationships.

So Lucas ended up at Twentieth Century–Fox, still a studio with fiscal crises like no other. In May 1973, on a development deal, Lucas and his partner, Gary Kurtz, got $10,000 to do a script. It was agreed that the studio and the filmmakers would share merchandising rights—a very vague concept in 1973. The script was approved but the studio required research on the special effects it referred to. Lucas and Kurtz did that research on their own money.

By the spring of 1976, Fox had granted the project a budget of $10 million for production. Of that, nearly $4 million went to special effects, and another $1.5 million on sets. The above-the-line costs were only $750,000, which covered Lucas, Kurtz, and the cast, though Alec Guinness had a wrinkle.

The film cost $11 million, but along the way, instead of taking more money, Lucas persuaded Fox to give him the merchandising rights. From the outset, Lucas had seen *Star Wars* as a collection of toys that a child might like to own. All he had managed in addition to making the film was to win the rights to those toys, to souvenirs and clothes, to related concessions at fast-food places, and all the rest. He also had the rights to all sequels. Taken as a whole, this deserves to be regarded as the most decisive negotiation ever carried out in Hollywood.

Not that Fox went hungry. Three years after the film opened, Fox could report a worldwide gross of $510 million. Half of that stayed with the exhibitors. Fox got their distribution fee (30 percent of the rentals): $75 million. They also picked up another $88.5 million. Lucas and Kurtz had $55 million. And Alec Guinness, on 2.25 percent of the profits, came away with $3.3 million (the biggest payday in a great actor's career). Needless to say, *Star Wars* was the new champion. And in addition to all that, Lucasfilm had the profits from the merchandising deals. What reason did he have to doubt his teenage wisdom, that the film business was run by rogues and idiots?

Clearly, it didn't matter what any critics thought of *Star Wars*. One of the signal changes in the seventies was the way in which critics in America first won power, then lost it. A lot of critics thought the picture was fun, pretty, exciting, and a perfect switchback ride. There was even talk that its heroics were derived from the "thought" of that odd philosopher Joseph Campbell. Others observed that the experience of the movie was very like the sensations incurred in playing pinball or the video games that were beginning to appear in theater lobbies and other amusement arcades. The screen was flagrantly electronic. Yes, there were real actors there, but so much of the imagery was fabricated. Nothing looked or smelled like life. Which may be one reason why it appealed so much to those children of all ages rather alarmed by life.

Spielberg and Lucas were friends to Coppola's generation. Indeed, Lucas had had Francis as his spokesman and protector, for George was not nearly as articulate as Coppola. With reason, Spielberg and Lucas felt themselves part of the film school movement that had begun in the early seventies, and they both found it a little harsh when it was suggested that their seminal works of 1975 and 1977 initiated changes in the film business beyond recognition. Not that it was their fault, but in indicating the ways in which direction did not really matter (and both men, I suggest, were crucially more producers than directors) they helped to fold up the brief eminence of directors in American film. Above all, of course, they brought confidence back to the business after years of collapse and they alerted a new generation of conglomerates to the "neatness" of having a film studio as part of their synergistic way of doing business. Nothing has ever mattered more than that confidence: it is the mania that drives gambling.

I have nothing to say about *Star Wars*. To the extent that I have written about movies, it has been because I felt there was enough of art (or the attempt at it) in some films to justify the effort—to justify the excitement I had felt in the dark. But there is nothing to be said about *Star Wars* because there is not enough in it: the fullest response is "Wow!" or pressing the repeat button. It is, for good and ill, sensational. And I like sensations, like hot water on my back or salt on my tongue. But in recent times there are too many occasions when new films do not deserve the space or the paper it would take, let alone the effort. They defy critical response or verbal enquiry. They are beyond examination. It is a discredit both to a newspaper like the *New York Times* and to film as a whole that every film is reviewed, and surely it is time for the community to note the compromise whereby in a year the *Times*, say, earns over $85 million from movie advertising. For the advertising is the real news, more significant than the reviews, because the ads measure the clout of the picture. And that is all that so many of them seek to have.

* * *

There is one more story from the seventies to be told, nowhere near as drastic as the impact of *Jaws* and *Star Wars*, yet immensely significant. Michael Cimino was born in New York in 1943. He studied architecture and art history at Yale before drifting into documentary film and going out to Hollywood in 1971. He started working on screenplays; with Steven Bochco (later a key figure in television production) he co-wrote *Silent Running*. Then he did a Clint Eastwood picture, *Magnum Force,* and in the way of Clint's cut-rate empire he was engaged to direct and write the likable *Thunderbolt and Lightfoot* (1974).

Nothing in Cimino's career seemed like preparation for *The Deer Hunter* (1978). There is a good deal that can be said against that film: that its three guys from Pennsylvania are too old to be summoned into the military; that the view of the Viet Cong is racist and politically hostile; that the patriotism of the film is cold-blooded and superimposed; that the inner credo of manly honor it lives by is fascistic; and that the mountains they go to are clearly in the Pacific Northwest, not a drive from coal country. There's something to every charge, so Cimino remains somewhere between a genius and a charlatan. But at least here we are talking about serious things. (And I'm not sure whether the final difficulty in settling on genius or charlatan doesn't apply to all the best personalities in this book—that's a sign of how strenuous the whole equation is. Being true to yourself is not enough. You have to keep faith with mixed motives.)

At the same time, I remember my first viewing of *The Deer Hunter* (in a large, packed theater in Boston) where the feeling of community was akin to that of all of us being in the same prison. There were cries of protest, and other cries of shared pain. In the lobby afterward people seemed pale and stricken by the emotional onslaught of the film. Maybe the history was shaky, but this was history written in lightning again. The movie was an event and a way of compelling Americans to start talking about Vietnam.

I was from the outset a great admirer. Political details aside, I saw an epic and tragic vision about America's determination to overawe rather than understand the alien world—indeed, the historical errors rather proved that point. I thought the re-creation of the steelmaking community was both theatrical and realistic in the best way, with amazing fruits to be found in the use of brilliant actors playing unintelligent people. The switch from America to Vietnam was as thrilling and sickening as any tonal shift in great music. And the suspense in Vietnam, the moral anxiety as well as the physical tension, was unequalled. Overall, the transition from the bravado guys in the bar singing "Can't Take My Eyes Off of You" to the hushed rendering of "God Bless America" by the survivors was beautiful and mysterious.

The Deer Hunter still seems that way to me: it is securely on my list of American movie events, by which I mean those films that aspired to the whole equation, to be show business and art at the same time. The movie had cost about $15 million, and it earned about $29 million for Universal. It won the Oscar for Best Picture and Best Director. In doing so it defeated *Coming Home,* a more politically correct Vietnam film and far to the left, but one that is hardly remembered today.

Before it was released, *The Deer Hunter* was shown to key executives at United Artists to whom Cimino had proposed his next picture. Steven Bach, who was then head of worldwide production at United Artists, offered his reaction in his book *Final Cut:*

Cimino's version of Vietnam was hallucinatory and fascinating. The Russian roulette sequences were so appalling and powerful that like later audiences, we were torn between voyeuristic fascination and a compulsion to avert our eyes; the poignance of homecoming seemed honestly felt, for all its *The Best Years of Our Lives* familiarity; and even the first hour's wedding party sequence—daringly attenuated—seemed a tour de force of filmmaking.

This was a moment in America when the culture was disposed to make heroes of film directors—so many new kids had taken hold of American film. Cimino was but the latest, and one of the most striking in that *The Deer Hunter* came without warning.

By the late seventies, not all the kid directors were doing so well. Nor were they making pictures for under a million dollars apiece, for modest salaries. They had become national figures. Some of them were very rich indeed, which only left the others a little envious, or very envious. Their marriages had likely come under strain, or broken apart. Some of them had become caught up in disastrous drug habits. And some of them had behaved like monsters, megalomaniacs, and children, as if they really believed that directors were gods.

Others have charted the lapses and the breakdowns; you can tell by looking at faltering filmographies, and by careers that ground to a halt. Let's just say that Michael Cimino took it for granted that it was his artistic duty to be lofty, arrogant, difficult, and even "impossible" in his talks with United Artists. His strategy on his new film was to demand every right of script, casting, location, and cut (at vast expense) while behaving like a very rich kid who was doing it all on his own infinite resources. In this, Bach began to see a kind of nihilism that affected the final picture and undercut its required sympathy for the characters.

This is not a small point, that the culture may have gone so far as to encourage young directors in the belief that they should film the insides of their own heads. David Selznick committed every one of Cimino's sins on *Gone With the Wind*—he took that gamble—but he loved Scarlett O'Hara. I don't mean he slept with Vivien Leigh (I doubt she ever slept), but he shared his caring with us. It is very basic as a tactic, but it made *Wind* blow for decades.

Cimino had an idea for a Western based on the events of the Johnson County cattle wars in Wyoming. It was a story of the struggle between the old interests of the cattle ranchers and those of the immigrant newcomers.

It was rich versus poor. It would be called *Heaven's Gate*. From the outset, his vision lacked burningly needy characters, like the guys (and the women) in *The Deer Hunter*.

Of course, we have the film that emerged—and a very interesting picture it is—and we have Bach's brave, candid book about it, *Final Cut*. But we don't have United Artists as it once was.

The full story is in *Final Cut*. When United Artists decided to make the film, their first commitment was for $1.7 million. This covered $500,000 to Cimino to direct, $850,000 to Kris Kristofferson to act, $250,000 for the script, and $100,000 for Christopher Walken. A final budget of $7.5 million was talked about.

It grew. Cimino insisted on Isabelle Huppert as the female lead, threatening that, if thwarted, he would simply ship the whole project over to Warners. The revised budget was over $11 million, and UA could tell that many items were hopelessly vague. It was as if, in Cimino's mind, the picture was alive, growing, infinite, and so it proved to be, once the large crew reached its location in the West—the far West, so that travel times made shooting time that much more elusive. Indeed, Cimino had found spots so beautiful and so remote that the whole crew might spend (and be paid for) four hours' driving a day. The film was out of control. Bach is very honest (since the control was his) about the errors made, but recollect these things: the script was strong; Cimino was spellbinding; UA wanted a masterpiece and a blockbuster—they had never gone into this expecting an "ordinary" film. They had good reason to guess they were being strung along, exploited, and put in jeopardy. A Thalberg might have cut his losses and withdrawn. Cimino, however, had contractual rights on final cut: he owned a thing he had not paid for. UA played the game—after all, *Star Wars* had earned over half a billion across the world. *Heaven's Gate* seemed so much more important in prospect.

And it's not that *Heaven's Gate* is a bad film, though at 219 minutes it had hideous problems, including an obstacle-like twenty-minute opening sequence that could have been dropped in its entirety. It was intensely beautiful and often very moving; it had an undoubted historical sweep and it was one of those few Westerns that made clear the connection between the legendary era and modern times. At $7.5 million it would have been a bargain; even at $11 million, it was a likely venture. But in the end it cost $44 million, because, more or less, a willful and secretive "artist" had been allowed to make it up as he went along while a studio was caught in indecision. He was always calling for retakes—not right after the first take, but days later. He exposed about 1.5 million feet of film, and printed about 1.3 million feet. It was the Stroheim story all over again.

The film opened very badly in America. Playing in more than eight hundred theaters—notice how that trend was growing—it earned a little over a million dollars. The ticket revenue was not even covering the theater expenses. And then it fell off. The reviews were very bad, and ridiculous, but there was already an appetite for vengeance among critics at the medium that had bypassed them, and at the onset of extravagance and personal plunder by some leading practitioners. Indeed, you could feel the ways in which the American public as a whole no longer liked or approved of Hollywood. *Heaven's Gate* was the victim of that malevolence, and United Artists fell with it. Bach and several others had to resign.

*   *   *

It's interesting to see the different paths taken by Bach and Cimino since then. Bach, sooner or later, resolved that to be a motion picture executive was not his calling, or his best fun. In fact, I'm sure that he would have been rehired in the roundabout way of things that controls the film business. Yes, there are dramatic dismissals and there is talk of "disgrace" here or there, but the atmosphere of the club actually prevails. Whatever fault (or credit) lay in Bach's corner for *Heaven's Gate* was quickly offset in 1985 when he published *Final Cut,* so lucid and fair an account of what had happened to be required reading for anyone intending to be another Bach or another Cimino.

So Bach moved on and found that he enjoyed writing: he has since delivered excellent biographies of Marlene Dietrich, Moss Hart, and Leni Riefenstahl. In addition, he has become a teacher, most often at Bennington and Columbia, not just an occasional visiting teacher, but for the long term. I don't think any other executive of his importance has ever done such a thing. He is a friend to this author, too, and someone whose talk has enriched this book over the years. I think we share a mixture of delight, wonder, dismay, and horror at the passage of American movies, along with the conviction that they have amounted to a "weather system" (or whatever) so far-reaching and influential that it has to be talked about.

Michael Cimino has become a character from legend. He, too, might have expected to be outlawed for his "disgrace." But we have realized by now that Hollywood is far more inclined to blackball its ingenious members than its true liabilities. Cimino worked on. He directed *The Year of the Dragon* (1985), *The Sicilian* (1987), *The Desperate Hours* (1990), *The Sunchaser* (1996). Little in those films suggested that the Cimino of *The Deer Hunter* was alive, let alone awake. Of course, he might yet revive, but those later films were all made under such changed circumstances, which would have had to include the exhausted respect for Cimino as an artist or anyone to be trusted.

There have been lurid personal rumors about Michael Cimino not really worth repeating. He had a novel published in France. He might have a comeback, he might not. But I'm not sure he has to. For instance, in the years of Cimino's "retreat" from eminence, no one in Hollywood was more powerful than the agent Michael Ovitz. Not only did he represent so many of the best, or highest-paid talents, but he packaged entire films. He had more say than anyone in town over what got made. At last, this power ended, as if the world became bored with him, whereupon it was apparent that Ovitz had exerted this tremendous authority without an atom of authorship. He will be forgotten. His place in history will become increasingly hard to comprehend. But the mystery of *The Deer Hunter* will endure and strike people afresh, I believe. In the years since *Heaven's Gate* you can argue that we have been ushered into a drabness that has gone on far too long for comfort. But have no doubt about real power—it is on the screen, and it is the traces left by lepers like Sturges, Welles, Ray, and Cimino.

Unless one day those films are simply left to rot, in the way RKO once shipped all the footage from *The Magnificent Ambersons,* all the cut material, out to sea and threw it away. There are monsters, and there is monstrousness.

There is a world beyond the movies. John Gutmann, "Portrait of Count Basie," 1939
(© 1998 Center for Creative Photography, University of Arizona Foundation)

22 · THAT'S ALL, FOLKS?

Sooner or later, people ask, "Where are the movies going?" To which the first useful answer is, "Where have they been?" That's what this book has tried to cover, on the shared assumption that our movies matter; that they might represent us—or mislead us. They are one of the few subjects on which all of us can join in the conversation. Film offers a kind of universal right, like stepping out of doors, looking at the sky, feeling the air and wondering what the weather will be. In which case, it's a warning maybe that in the dark there is no weather.

Some say our movies are better than ever: from 2000 to 2002, the domestic theatrical box office rose from under $8 billion to over $9 billion, while DVD revenue climbed from $1.4 billion in 1999 to $11 billion in 2002. When Hollywood recites such facts the loss of self-criticism is its version of the flat national confidence—that we are the greatest of countries, and that God is with us. (Which is teasingly close to the dreadful lines Arabs have always been given in Hollywood pictures—or American politics. On a quiet night, you can still hear Anthony Quinn saying them.)

Over Christmas 2003, I was at a dinner party where people told stories of whether or not they had yet managed to get into the third part of *The Lord of the Rings.* I asked the table about something often referred to in this book: How many Americans go to the movies? In 1947, with a population of nearly 150 million, American movie theaters sold 100 million tickets a week. Today, when the population is more like 270 million, we sell 25 million tickets a week. That means that less than 10 percent of Americans go to the movies. No one at the dinner quite realized how alone they were.

But our dinner-table conversation had interesting sidebars. One was about two high school students at the Castro theater in San Francisco watching a one-night-only revival of *The Godfather,* a film they had never seen on the big screen. Upstairs, two nine-year-olds occupied themselves for the three hours of dinner by playing some video game. One of those nine-year-olds is mine and I would guess that over the Christmas period he spent thirty hours at one video game or another, as fully engaged with the screen as if it were a car he was driving. And in some cases those video games will be derivatives of movies, owned by the same conglomerate deploying what it calls synergy. It's not so much that movies are dead as that history has already passed them by.

The annual turnover for video games in the United States is now $28 billion, and rising by 20 percent annually. Those games are not too many worlds away from *The Lord of the Rings:* their light and their air are electronic; their battles are immense and unending; the games can be played seemingly forever, and they often embody a quest that will never be satisfied. Their imagery seems to be engraved in metal.

Let's look at some other numbers. In the years since the Paramount decision, film exhibition has become a very testing occupation. In the early 1970s, weekly ticket sales slipped as low as 15 million, a number that could not sustain many of the theaters. Further, the existing theaters were now in the "wrong" places. The downtown palaces were in areas often shunned and dangerous at night. The population had moved out to the suburbs, and it was developing the habit of shopping at malls on the edges of cities. Those had become the inviting locations for new, smaller theater buildings, often in complexes—six screens, a dozen, maybe twenty or more, a supposedly bounteous gathering of choices, economizing on projection services (have you ever watched a film break down, and found there was no human being in the booth?), backed up by restaurants and parking. And as the picture business rallied in the eighties and nineties, so a number of exhibition chains invested heavily in these new multiplexes. Films and franchises were so heavily promoted on television advertising that they might open across the nation at several thousand screens, and with a fresh starting time every twenty minutes at your megaplex: the *Batman* franchise; the *Jurassic Park* movies; *Titanic; Independence Day; The Matrix* and its brood—the alleged events of modern moviegoing. *The Passion of the Christ,* printed in blood.

Those theater chains made bids for the upcoming pictures. And when you recollect that Hollywood now makes about 200 movies a year, compared with between 500 and 700 in the golden age, you can easily see the pressure to get the pictures that will perform. To get those "hot" pictures, the chains must agree to return to the studios rental money of as much as 90 percent of their total revenue in the opening weeks of a film's appearance. Those percentages start to slide in the theaters' favor as time goes by, getting to a 50–50 split or even something more advantageous to theaters.

In turn, that is why you are likely to have to pay $7 a head to get popcorn and a drink. Those costs are lurid, and they hardly attest to the intelligence of moviegoers as a whole, but they are crucial to the success of the exhibition business. And this has been all the more so in the recent development whereby the "hot" pictures may open very big, but seldom sustain. In 2003, for instance, it was common for big movies to drop off by as much as 60 percent from their first week to the second. The Trojan War, they say, lasted a decade, but in 2004 *Troy* lost half its audience from one week to the next.

That stress follows an unfortunate overbuilding of theaters, or installation of screens. The more Hollywood talked about its own boom in the eighties and nineties (so much a matter of inflation, with a very modest lift in attendance figures), the more reckless theater construction there was. In the years from 1995 to 1999, the number of screens in the United States went from 27,800 to 37,100. Many of those screens were as small as their rooms, and they were once part of benevolent promises by which multiplexes would reserve some screens for foreign films, independent pictures, or even revivals of classics. Any moviegoer knows how seldom that is the case, and he or she will also know the loneliness of the movie rooms at so many times. For in truth the exhibition business has closed in on the weekend and such holiday seasons as Christmas/New Year and school vacation times. Today's moviegoer hardly expects good pictures at other times of the year. As for daytime screenings—at reduced, pensioner rates (often with the theater's heating turned off)—they can be tests of endurance and solitude.

Even so, the glut of theaters was disastrous for exhibition. Around the year 2000 many chains went bankrupt, many new operations closed, and projection as a service continued to deteriorate. Ticket prices went up. Theaters started to show commercials. The cost of "refreshments" soared.

The larger perspective on moviegoing, the principle that fewer than 10 percent of Americans go, supports the common attitude that moviegoing is for teenagers now, the social group that is most eager to get out of the house, and the one that exerts an increasing influence on the nature and subject of our big pictures. In truth, I think many of the parental generations share that urge to get out sometimes, just as many older people still cherish memories of the communal experience of moviegoing. One reason for the success of the *Lord of the Rings* trilogy was the understanding that different generations could enjoy those films with comfort and pleasure.

Yet it's also premature to say that movies are dead, even if one may sympathize with everyone from Norma Desmond to Pauline Kael, or from David Selznick to Jean-Luc Godard, in the suspicion that a warming age of entertainment and companionship has passed. I understand the feelings of critics asked to come up with the ten best films of any year, who say, Ten? Ten's a lot!, and those more generous spirits whose thumbs grow as long as Pinocchio's nose from overrating a lot of pictures—because they want the medium to do well, and because they'd like to feel good about it.

When Charlie Rose does a show on *The Matrix Reloaded* for an hour it isn't just because he reckons to get high viewing figures. He hopes against hope that *The Matrix Reloaded* may be as Important as producer Joel Silver and his young assistants have been telling him. Rose sniffs the air like a loyal retriever, one who never learns that some masters can't shoot straight, but he wants to smell the musk of a champion movie that, for a weekend, drives out all other scents.

So *The Matrix Reloaded* did $121 million in its first week, $53 million in the second, $21 million in the third. By the sixth week it was scraping the bottom of the barrel at $5 million. When Nicholas and I saw *Reloaded*—

we were there on the first weekend—we could tell after half an hour that the air was going out of the balloon. The packed room went still and dead, then restless. Being at the movies in 2003 was a diet of disappointment and lost concentration. When the third part, *Revolutions,* opened only a few months later, it started off at $50 million—in effect, it lost its opening weekend.

I know, these numbers are still so awesome as to defy belief. Maybe that's not the worst response if you recollect that the opening week of *The Godfather,* more than thirty years ago, was only $568,000—1 percent of *The Matrix Revolutions.* And one of the most interesting changes in movies since 1972 is that our newspapers now carry these figures every Monday morning, as if they expected us to believe them, to understand them, and to reckon that movies are better than ever. Of course, some newspapers belong to the ownership that controls the business, and most newspapers could not function without movie advertising.

Newspapers say they run the numbers because readers are interested, but that may only underline the way the "reader" has grown more cynical toward the movies. If something works for us, if it moves us, do we worry about the numbers? It would be attractive to answer "no," but would modern America rather trust the numbers as an imprint of success than its own nerve endings? Has "art" succumbed to the money-measuring system? Would you want the score on your own orgasm, on your "love"?

We don't have to swallow the hype. We can question the compromised ownership. We may realize that some movies are made for the toys and the video games that will trade on their characters. Is that why those characters are written hard, small, and plastic? We may learn that the Monday morning figures are based on a few samples controlled by the picture business itself. We may still have enough respect for the English language and for the grossness in marketing to recall that, only days before the *Matrix Revolutions*'s numbers came through, the story in the same papers included this remark from Alan Horn, president of Warner Brothers Entertainment, announcing the international opening of *Revolutions* in forty-three languages and on 10,013 screens, all on the same day: "It's showmanship. We think it's theatrical, it's fun, it's exciting. We talk about having event movies at Warner Brothers, and this is a way to further event-ize our movies."

But not just his movies, or theirs—ours, too. After all, we are "folks." And there were folks in advance of *Revolutions* who said they—that Time Warner operation in the sky—were doing the wrong thing. The figures on *Reloaded* made it clear: *Matrix*-heads were jaded. Don't hit them again too soon. Wait until spring, at least. But why should Alan Horn and his associates not be wrong and stupid—and greedy: perhaps cash flow overwhelmed every other thought. That big enterprise in the sky has not been floating along as predicted. Is it America Online or on loan?

Let me add this, just to test your faith in the business and our media of record. The 10,013 screens and forty-three countries stuff was reported on November 5, 2003. Yet by November 10, the numbers had swollen to 18,000 screens and ninety-six countries. As if anyone in the United States of America, apart from lifelong stamp collectors, could name ninety-six countries.

Still, folks are folks, and we are, barely, a culture that wants to have a useful sense of what "ours" might mean. Like Charlie Rose, we all hope that something like congregation or community exists. I noticed that in the first week of showings of *The Matrix Revolutions*, *The Godfather* and *The Godfather Part II* played on cable television. I started watching, and I was held; I wanted to go through the process again. Can anyone credit that thirty years from now there will be an audience for the three parts of *The Matrix*, anywhere? Even if Keanu Reeves is our president by then?

* * *

Of course, inflation has kidnapped the numbers, not just the economic inflation that killed modesty in the eighties and nineties but the new way in which the picture business pays itself. In 1982, the average ticket price in the United States was $2.94; today it is about $5.80. In which case it might be excusable if the average cost of movies had doubled. In truth, the increase has been far greater—it's close to four or five times. Over the years of increase, desperate alarms have been sounded by the industry because of this. When *Dick Tracy* opened in 1990 the production chief at Disney, Jeffrey Katzenberg, said its costs were excessive because they seriously endangered the film's profitability. In turn, the people who pushed the costs higher, not least Michael Ovitz and Creative Artists Agency, pointed to the way the box office ticket was no longer an adequate way of appraising a film's potential. Not only was there television money to be factored in, from the early eighties onward there was the rental income on videocassettes and later DVDs, to say nothing of the enlarged international market—enlarged not just in its most immediate terms of figures that measure population with easy access to theaters, but in the way the international conglomerates in control of movies could reach those audiences. These days, some so-called American movies are actually made for foreign companies. And why not? All over the world now, different nationalities have had to accustom themselves to movies made by an America that has scant interest in foreign places.

Stars sometimes get $25 million. A director has been paid $20 million. A script has earned its author $5 million. And the notion persists that the teenage audience wants to see spectacle, combat, and effects such as they have never seen before.

What was once Columbia (and TriStar) is now a part of Sony. Twentieth Century–Fox is part of News Corporation, which means Rupert Murdoch. Warners is a part of Time Warner. Paramount belongs to Viacom. And Universal is the new kid on the NBC/General Electric block.

The Universal story deserves more scrutiny, for it shows the elimination of that last instinct for moviemaking, as opposed to being in charge of a multinational entertainment delivery system. Universal was a part of MCA (after the 1962 deal) and was therefore under the imprimatur of Lew Wasserman. Though Wasserman was seventy-seven in 1990, he remained active in the business and took poker-faced pleasure in being esteemed for his power. We have noted his decisive influence on the scale of *Jaws*'s success. Since that film, his Universal had released *The Deer Hunter* (though it was not of their making and not to Lew's taste), *E.T.* (which became the new box office champion with earnings of $399 million), and *Out of Africa.* The company was very successful, in part because of Wasserman's exceptional managerial tightness, but also because if your contract with the studio gave you participation points on a profitable film, you might still have to outlive Lew to see green money. And it was also known as the last studio that might be receptive to interesting or difficult projects.

Early in 1990, MCA bought Geffen Records (the brainchild of David Geffen) for $545 million; Geffen acquired ten million shares in MCA. In a business world then rife with takeovers (many of them hostile) the aging Wasserman (who had a hunch that a catastrophic economic depression was at hand; that is how approaching death feels to the great, sometimes) began to entertain thoughts of selling MCA.

In so many ways conservative and restrained, Wasserman thought to have one great emotional splurge before he died. It was as if the cleric wanted to wear a coat of many colors for a day. He could die in immaculate power, or he could make a deal that impressed everyone in the world. It was on that uncertain basis, and because of the legendary (if not occult) properties of synergy that might be exploited by an international merger of show business and electronics, that MCA began to get into bed with the Japanese corporation Matsushita Electric Industrial Company. The Japanese wanted product to be sold on their hardware.

The dance and the deal lasted over six months in 1990, with Michael Ovitz performing the uncanny role of go-between. Indeed, key people at MCA occasionally worried that they had never met anyone at Matsushita, that their information was simply what Ovitz told them. Did Ovitz know what the Japanese intended? Was he being straightforward? How had he inserted himself in a position of such power? Well, Ovitz had an earnest admiration for Japanese business and philosophy (like Tom Cruise at the end of *The Last Samurai*) and he had helped Sony in its takeover of Columbia. But no one could credit that Ovitz was doing all of this for the sake of international cooperation. He had carved out a role for himself that made him seem necessary. His great eminence was a living definition of how business power had replaced creative vitality, no matter that pictures were a business that had always refused to be businesslike two quarters in a row.

In September 1990, Ovitz indicated to MCA that Matsushita had a purchase plan that valued the MCA shares at between $75 and $90 each. That news leaked, pushing up the MCA stock price. Some at MCA congratulated themselves with the thought that Lew could probably get it up to $100 a share. But when the parties eventually met, Matsushita offered $60 a share. Ovitz told Wasserman that he had only learned of that price just before the offer.

This is where you realize how irrational and unbusinesslike the deal was, and how overwhelmed even the "cool" Wasserman was by dreams of cash when his own ten million MCA shares had cost him about three cents apiece. MCA refused $60 and Matsushita came back at $64. Over the Thanksgiving weekend, they went to $66. Accepted. It was part of the deal that the MCA management would stay in place—that covered Wasserman, but it really meant Sid Sheinberg, who would begin to take over. Sheinberg would be paid $8.6 million a year to run MCA and he got more than $110 million for his stock. Wasserman could have cashed out at $327 million, but he was like Louis B. Mayer: Why pay the capital gains tax? So his deal had his stock converted into Matsushita stock, and that gave him annual dividend income of $28.6 million.

Alas, being rich is a bleak calling. Wasserman had never been as good at spending money as he had been at squeezing it out of unnoticed flaps of juice in the business. Mayer had at least hoped to make a great film of his own (and remember, he had kept "Over the Rainbow" in the picture). Wasserman's mind never reached to that extreme. He found himself just another suit at the corporation. He had no power anymore. Matsushita grew unhappy with its new property. The Japanese economy went into shock. Wasserman made noises about buying back the company—*his* company. But his discovery of the importance of ownership came too late. Matsushita sold to Seagram, instead, which lost money; Seagram sold to Vivendi, which lost so much more money that no one really elected to bid for MCA when Vivendi sought escape. Until, at last, General Electric stepped in. In the dozen years since the great sale, the property had become somewhere between a phantom and a white elephant.

Lew Wasserman died in 2002. He was worth half a billion more or less, but he knew he had ruined his own company. (Marcus Loew had been worth more in 1927, when he died, and hardly anyone now knows who Loew was.) When it had mattered, in 1990, the man who had made MCA, and helped make presidents, too (no matter the party, so long as they were presidents), had yielded to greed just like any hustler from Cleveland.

When Wasserman died, there was a wistful newspaper cartoon by Paul Conrad in which the double-O in the HOLLYWOOD sign was replaced by Wasserman's trademark black horn-rimmed spectacles. I wonder if Conrad intended the allusion to "the eyes of Doctor T. J. Eckleburg" in Fitzgerald's *The Great Gatsby,* a poster that hangs above a valley of ashes halfway between West Egg and New York, as well as hanging over everything in the story like foreboding:

> The eyes of Doctor T. J. Eckleburg are blue and gigantic—their retinas are one yard high. They look out of no face, but, instead, from a pair of enormous yellow spectacles which pass over a non-existent nose. Evidently some wild wag of an oculist set them there to fatten his practice in the borough of Queens, and then sank down himself into eternal blindness, or forgot them and moved away. But his eyes, dimmed a little by many paintless days, under sun and rain, brood on over the solemn dumping ground.

Remind yourself that *The Great Gatsby* is set in 1925. It's not that our urban wastelands have changed so much, but where is the pitiless, poetic observation now to match Fitzgerald's? Or such an intuition about how much seeing and being seen were about to mean in the culture?

Yet history has moved on already. If we argue that the age of movies altered when television arrived, that puts a useful stress on how much visibility mattered from, say, 1914 to 1954. After all, the condition of the movie house is intense: I know Weegee snapped several patrons asleep, and others wrapped in each other, but his most arresting pictures are of customers nearly attached to the screen, hanging on, if not for dear life, then for the sake of desire. At the movies, we were all as alert as watchmen on the line, and I think it's possible that in those years the power of attention grew in filmgoers. They learned to see more, and that acuity was linked to the maturing of directorial style.

But half an hour of television will let you realize you don't have to watch in the same way. In part, that's the ceaseless pressure of household interruption, be it a visitor, dinner, a telephone call, the nearness of boredom. It's exactly because people don't turn the TV set off when they're not locked in attention that we know watching is secondary—to the vague sharing in on-ness, or to the coexistence that is sometimes called "radio with pictures."

It follows that TV's small frame is a minor aspect of why its picture is seldom beautiful, or atmospheric, or magical, or whatever word you want to use to denote response to the visual. Television has no style—it is on/off; it is "information." (In passing, I have to ask what this has done to the old experience of moviegoing that has been channeled into DVDs? If that TV screen never trades in beauty how do we suddenly see it in, say, a DVD by Fritz Lang, Max Ophüls or Nicholas Ray? Or do we see just the plan for beauty, the academic indicator?)

The intrusion on our culture by the movies had many repercussions. Let me mention two. In that loose period from 1914 to 1954, there was a renewed determination among writers of fiction to make us see. You can find this in Hemingway, Dos Passos, Graham Greene, Simenon, and even Nabokov, novelists who are sometimes called "cinematic," but who are actually stimulated by the fresh emphasis on the visual, and who may have found it a welcome alternative to the inwardness of Henry James, James Joyce, and Robert Musil. Hemingway and Greene are also examples of "important" writers who might also be "best sellers," and surely that happy coincidence is impressed by the movies' promise of reaching "everyone."

At a more mundane level, we all became more conscious of being seen. The force of the movies reminds us of visual meaning. Look at photographs from the years since 1914, and who can deny the steady stress on individuality, color, stylishness, personality (and thus meaning) in the way people try to refine their appearance. But then add to costume, looks, and cosmetics the ways in which ordinary people may have become more self-conscious about the signals they give about feeling and meaning. The movies taught us to read faces, and so faces are more alert, more contrived, and more actorly. We do not have to approve of this, or enjoy it, but it's hard to escape.

The next implication may be contested. But I offer it because its imprint is profound. Consider the experience of young people from the fifties onward, by which I mean the startling increase in hours spent watching as TV came to the fore. Take it at a modest level (watching four hours a day is the equivalent of more than seven hundred movies a year!) and the result is nearly hysterical. It sooner or later shattered the integrity of movies as a medium. So kids coming of age in the sixties and seventies were so used to moving imagery, and to their repetitive narrative models, that they could no longer take them seriously.

This phenomenon has several different names—one is "camp" (and it can overlap with the gay mockery of stale social and narrative habits, as witness Gore Vidal's novel *Myra Breckinridge,* and *Some Like It Hot*). It can be "ironic," as if to say that appearance has become an absurdist disguise—Antonioni's *Blowup* is a key work in that mood. But the most widespread consequence is the disinclination of young audiences today to take movie stories seriously, or even to believe in them. Perhaps you need to have children to appreciate this shift properly, but for the past twenty years or so it has been evident that the essential young audience flinches from being moved at the movies. They prefer motion, spectacle, novelty, and a readiness for the visible to exceed reality. Thus the feeling that cinema is a visual form that gives us things never seen or known in life.

* * *

Where did that shift come from? In the early 1960s, following the triumph of *Psycho,* Hitchcock cast around for what to do next. He settled on the Daphne du Maurier short story "The Birds," thirty-seven pages in length, about a peasant family in Cornwall at a moment when birds seem to attack humanity. Hitch considered writers to join him on the project, and he approached the novelist James Kennaway, who had just had an Oscar nomination for adapting his own novel, *Tunes of Glory.* Kennaway read the story, came to a meeting, and said, this is how to do it—we never see one bird!

Politely, no doubt, Hitchcock told Kennaway that their relationship was over. For Hitch wasn't greatly concerned over why the birds attacked, or what might come of it. He saw that the lives of the people under attack might need to be fleshed out, so that an audience cared. But the reason why he was making the film was because of the challenge of showing the birds and making them seem as hostile and as dangerous as, well, Soviet missiles in Cuba (*The Birds* opened in 1963; the end of the world was a hot topic).

The Birds was an illustration of what was to come. Hitchcock was a common man in many ways—that was his strength as an entertainer. He was practical, coarse, dirty-minded, down-to-earth and intent on whether things worked, whether they played, whether the audience fell for the trick. He was not much given to beliefs beyond his intense dedication to film. I don't think he entertained any notion that birds (or for that matter tomatoes; he was a greengrocer's son) might attack human society. Nor was he intrigued by the allegorical possibilities of such a conflict. He wanted to find out if he could make the far-fetched situation work, if audiences would be afraid. Kennaway's approach was not daft—it was the old Val Lewton approach to horror or suspense, to show the face that is seeing the dread thing rather than the thing itself—but it was not what Hitchcock was after.

Hitchcock in the past had been both a master of film magic and a servant to plausibility. In the shower scene in *Psycho,* the fragmentation of his shooting and editing (all preconceived) made us share the feeling of being trapped under that shower. Part of *Psycho's* power is in the ordinariness of Janet Leigh's Marion Crane, and the plain motel setting. The lack of wonder in everything offsets the superlative outrage.

The Birds was shot in 1962, when you got what you filmed. If you wanted a trick, or an impossible thing, then you had to contrive it before the lens. You could paint birds onto the celluloid. You could film a bird against a matte screen and then match that image into a shot of a room. You could use stuffed birds (a man should have a hobby). You could use trained birds. You could gather thousands of helpless birds and throw them at Tippi Hedren until you had enough jabs, bites, beaks, cuts, and wounded eyes to build a scene. *The Birds* was a marvel in its day for its extent of trickery (and cruelty to an actress). Although it earned $5 million, that meant not much profit because the cost of all the avian detail had amounted to $3.3 million.

The film is powerful still, especially in its ambivalence toward Tippi Hedren, a strange, rather drained model-turned-actress who became perilously adorable in Hitch's eyes. It's clear that he was ready to give up his settled life if she would have him. The voyeuristic lust he had visited imaginatively in earlier films on Joan Fontaine, Ingrid Bergman, Grace Kelly, Kim Novak, Vera Miles, and Eva Marie Saint broke out into the open. But Hedren saw just a fat old man.

For me, that tension or tragedy is more intriguing than the manipulation of the birds—though that is well done, too, if that's what you like. But I think *The Birds* is at its best in depicting the relationship between the characters played by Hedren and Jessica Tandy.

In 1964, when he was only eighteen, Steven Spielberg made that home movie, *Firelight,* which plainly quotes from *The Birds.* And then, a few years later, Spielberg found himself at Universal, the studio that had become the workplace of Hitchcock and Lew Wasserman—and Wasserman, as we have seen, was vital in aiding Spielberg's career. But *The Birds,* I think, and the example of Hitchcock were even more instructive to the young man. Which brings us to the career of one of the last candidates in the short list of those who may have understood the whole equation.

No one discussing *Jaws* has ever credited the threat of giant sharks like that, though real sharks do attack. Spielberg believed in making the trick work. A couple of years after *Jaws,* he made a film I much prefer, *Close Encounters of the Third Kind.* At that time he was asked if he himself believed in unidentified flying objects. No, he said, but he believed in those people who saw them. Especially if they'd put out $2.50 for a ticket.

Close Encounters was initially budgeted at $2.7 million (that was Spielberg's own estimate). But at every turn, the costs rose. Remember this in thinking of *Heaven's Gate*: in the end, *Close Encounters* cost over $19 million, and had Columbia board members in panic; they said they would never have given the go-ahead if they had known what was going to happen. But the picture then earned $77 million, and it seems to me, still, a wonder. Yes, the famous light shows are spectacular—though they're dull, too (light is a greater wonder than its shows). What drives the picture forward is Spielberg's affection for common human faces (Richard Dreyfuss, Melinda Dillon, Cary Guffey) being made nearly angelic by the light and the kind of knowledge it portends. Here is proof that the most special effect in movies is always the human face when its mind is being changed.

After that, Spielberg was untouchable. Not even the colossal failure of *1941* made him less desirable. He has become the embodiment of every dream Hollywood would like to have for itself, and there's no irony in the name of the company he formed in 1995 (with Jeffrey Katzenberg and David Geffen), DreamWorks—it works for him.*

And for millions. For me, however, he is the object of mixed feelings— I hope never again to be caught in the same room as *The Color Purple, Always, Hook,* anything to do with *Jurassic Park,* or *A.I.* I'm a good sport with *Raiders of the Lost Ark* and its franchise. I love *Close Encounters,*

---

*Periodically, newspapers ask whether DreamWorks has been a success or not. But they forget their own doubts over whether it would survive. It has had ups and downs, good luck and bad, but it has lasted in the business. It will be turned into money soon, no doubt. Too many investors want the comfort of liquidity. So what? A more telling question is, did it cramp Spielberg or simply coincide with his fatigue?

Poltergeist (on which he is not credited as director, Tobe Hooper is), *Empire of the Sun* (his best film), and the first half of *Minority Report*. I can hardly think of a movie more likely to sustain arguments over the fatal banality of "great film" today than *Schindler's List*. Much of that movie is impeccable and very intriguing; but crucial things in it—like the girl in the red coat—are not just disastrous, but enough to leave one believing in a schizoid chasm in the director's soul. Of course, the ultimate proof of that division is the way in which he could make *Jurassic Park* and *Schindler's List* at the same time. It is like composing Mahler's Ninth and commercial jingles on the same day.

Schindler's List is well acted, well made; it is in so many ways a model of serious film. And yet, in its need to dramatize, it reveals a helpless immaturity. As Leon Wieseltier put it, "*Schindler's List* proves again that, for Spielberg, there is a power in the world that is greater than good and greater than evil, and it is the movies. He is hardly alone in this cineaste's theodicy." There it is, the accusation that could dissolve film culture, even the terrible insistence in a Quentin Tarantino to stay a kid—because the world is for kids? Alas, it is so much more.

But this chasm is so indicative of the contrary forces in the equation I am talking about. No one else has the shameless energy to lunge forward as artist and showman at the same time, and to believe or hope that the two might become one. The results with Spielberg are as awesomely cataclysmic as his commercial record is great, and Spielberg has produced or enabled many notable films (*Back to the Future* and *Who Framed Roger Rabbit?*). He is not quite human in the way such prodigious effort seems unaccompanied by neurosis. Yet I don't think he has made a great film, unless it is *Empire of the Sun*. How many attempts does he require? But you could make a case for *Jaws, Close Encounters,* and *E.T.* being among the great American movie events. *The Terminal* is Chaplinesque.

It's unfair to charge Spielberg with simply flattering the predominant teenage audience. Yes, he is often drawn to children as emblems of potential, but children are not teenagers, and *Empire of the Sun* and *Schindler's List* are adult material. It is his sometime colleague, George Lucas (the producer on the Indiana Jones films), who has chosen to cater to that audience so singlemindedly. Lucas is probably richer even than Spielberg, and that's because he takes the trouble to be, and because the *Star Wars* audience has stayed loyal to that very odd saga, no matter that Lucas's own enthusiasm for film seems to have deserted him.

I mean that in two significant ways. The man who directed *American Graffiti* and *Star Wars* was having fun. It was hardly serious fun, but there was a verve to those pictures. Then for twenty years or so Lucas stopped directing to concentrate on business. When he came back, with *The Phantom Menace* and *Attack of the Clones,* the verve was gone. Few devotees of the series will tell you any different. How much of that falloff in verve is thanks to the other departure from film, the one that increasingly favors the digital projection of computer-generated imagery—everything you could conceive of under the rubric of Lucas's highly successful company, Industrial Light and Magic?

Spielberg is often his companion in that pursuit. For who can now deny the loss of natural light, of skin tones, of real place, and common but precious things in our movies, to be replaced by the gorgeous imagery of things that never have been and never will be? And which may fade as color does.

* * *

Even the business record of conglomerate Hollywood is very mixed. The international market ("foreign" as Hollywood used to put it) has become increasingly potent. Above all, the conglomerates have the means to smother the world with their product. Throwing *The Matrix Reloaded* everywhere at once is one sign of that, and whereas it topped out at $280 million in the domestic market, it did $455 million in foreign. There's no doubt that young people in many parts of the world—in Asia, especially— have a ready appetite for the kind of special effects fantasy that has become a dominant American genre in recent years. But some of those countries, and their filmmakers especially, are bitter that the local mass marketing (now regularly linked to merchandising and fast-food outlets) has done severe damage to their native filmmaking. Over the last twenty years, even France has complained of this pressure. And here we are talking about something more than the result of global competition among fellow capitalists. We are talking about the effective imposition of American attitudes, many of which are deplored by the elders and the governing classes in foreign countries.

The scale of the enterprise goes further still, and has done so ever since the invention of home video. For, belatedly, in the late seventies, technology found a way to compete with television in the provision of cheap tapes and home video players. Do not be surprised to hear that, in the early days of that innovation, the movie business was fiercely resistant. At nearly every turn, movie technology has had to overcome the wretched thinking of industry leaders. None other than Jack Valenti, president of the MPAA since before some filmmakers were born (thirty-seven years), testified to Congress: "I say to you that the VCR is to the American film producer and the American public as the Boston Strangler is to the woman home alone."°

He feared that the scoundrel public would record tapes off the television, though in thirty years I still doubt that enough Americans have learned to use the VCR. What he never foresaw was the extent of the market to come in the sale and rental of videotapes, and later DVDs. The figures vary, of course, but in general nowadays the picture business counts on at least 40 percent of its total earnings coming from home video.

If we apply those figures to *The Matrix Reloaded,* the bald sum of revenue looks approximately like this:

Domestic theatrical	$280 million
Foreign theatrical	455 million
Home video	270 million
Total	$1.005 billion

There are those who ask, Why take Hollywood seriously any longer? Why waste time on event-ized nonsense aimed at teenagers? Why cling to any hope that a zoo for dinosaurs is going to produce anything worth discussing? With plenty of good reasons, those people say that we should all concentrate on the worthy foreign films (God knows, they need every bit of support they can get) and that area of work known as "American independent film."

That's a tempting strategy and worth attending to. At least since the moment of John Cassavetes and *Shadows* (1960), there has been an urge by some to make movies in America that "Hollywood" would not make. On the whole, these pictures have been low-budget, unglamorous, difficult, and ingenious in their willingness to take on unusual subject matter and novel forms. Some of them have even been made in Los Angeles, with talent crossing over from much more expensive ventures.

The list of distinguished work in this vein is long and well worth pondering: John Sayles (*Return of the Secaucus Seven, Matewan, Lone Star*); Jim Jarmusch (*Stranger Than Paradise, Down by Law, Dead Man*); Abel Ferrara (*Bad Lieutenant, The Funeral*); Nancy Savoca (*True Love, Dogfight*); Gus Van Sant, Jr. (*Mala Noche, Drugstore Cowboy, My Own Private Idaho*); Spike Lee (*Do the Right Thing, Malcolm X*); James Toback

----

°At last, albeit slowly, in 2004 Valenti receded, to be replaced by Dan Glickman.

(*Fingers, Two Girls and a Guy*); Steven Soderbergh (*sex, lies, & videotape, Kafka*); Mike Figgis (*Leaving Las Vegas, Timecode*); the Coen brothers (*Blood Simple, Fargo*); David Lynch (*Eraserhead, Blue Velvet, Mulholland Dr.*); Paul Thomas Anderson (*Boogie Nights, Magnolia*).

That selection is far from exhaustive, yet already it has reached out enough to include a few names more conventionally placed in "establishment" cinema: Paul Schrader (*Affliction, Auto Focus*); Martin Scorsese (*Raging Bull, The Last Temptation of Christ, Gangs of New York*); Francis Coppola (*Apocalypse Now, One from the Heart*); Woody Allen . . . Stanley Kubrick?

In other words, the bigger your list the more carefully you have to ask yourself what you mean by "independent." Of all the films named in the two previous paragraphs, which was the more independent? Was it *Return of the Secaucus Seven* because it cost the least? (The legendary figure is $40,000, and by now the legend is too sacred for any revision.) Did $40,000 introduce unquestionable limitations and restrictions? Or is it that John Sayles simply sees the world in endless two-shots of people talking together? You could call such an approach artistic vision, though long ago I came to the conclusion that it meant some of the dullest respectable filmmaking around.

Or was it *Apocalypse Now* (final cost over $30 million), where in the calamities and exigencies of production, some of which Coppola may have caused himself, he assumed all the burden of debt and the ultimate fiscal responsibility. To this day, Coppola owns both *Apocalypse Now* and *One from the Heart*, famous problems or "disasters" in their day, yet works of undoubted personal artistic ambition where the artist took on the debt load (and suffered for it), held on to the film, and in the case of *Apocalypse Now* revisited it some twenty years later and brought out a version, *Apocalypse Now Redux*, that is a valuable reworking of first thoughts. Further, after *One from the Heart* failed, and Zoetrope was compelled to abandon its Hollywood studio, Coppola is certain that none other than Lew Wasserman put out the word that he was not to be helped.

Sooner or later, "independence" leads to the question of ownership, and that is fundamental. I could easily argue that *The Birth of a Nation, Gone With the Wind,* and *Citizen Kane* are models of American independence. They are the unfettered, uncompromised vision of their makers: D. W. Griffith, David Selznick, and Orson Welles. Of the three, Welles was probably the most liberated, because by temperament he hardly ever paid attention to money (his strength and his weakness). But all three were restricted in one vital way: they could not release or distribute their own films. Griffith traded the rights away, and was screwed, but hardly cared. Welles let the system handle his movie. And in time Selznick did actually set up his own releasing organization (on *Duel in the Sun*) and was ruined by the overhead. And yet, the most independent of recent movies, paid for by its maker, and once without distribution, was *The Passion of the Christ*.

At some point, every filmmaker has to make a deal with the big money (to get the film distributed). Independence is a state of mind. I suspect that James Toback would have been as personal and selfish (I mean that in the best sense; artists must be selfish to exist) if, say, a major studio had given him $10 million to make *Fingers* (and done their best to watch over him) or if, as it actually happened, a perfume company, Fabergé, had said here's a million dollars, go away and do something.

That policy has worked very well in film history (even if the sum of money slides). It seems to me profoundly enlightened to throw a bit of cash at kids and say, Go do your best and your worst. It worked pretty well with Edgar Ulmer, with the kids who made films for BBS, and with *Citizen Kane*. Moreover, in any kind of factory system, where a distributor, at least, has a roster of films to spread out through the year, isn't it politic to have a few films so cheap they can hardly fail to make a profit? Why then has an alleged business taken on the mindset of gambling, which is to neglect the small, safer bets and go always for the long shots and that dream of a huge killing? The answer in essence is because every now and then a long shot pays off and does so in such bounty that no one can get that greed out of his head. Never forget that Stroheim said, no, not *McTeague*—call the movie *Greed*! They are doing it for the money.

Our list of independents included several people who try to have it both ways. Soderbergh's *sex, lies, & videotape* was an independent film. His diary on its making recounts his own moves from film courses at Louisiana State University to Los Angeles, screenwriting and trying to hustle up a deal. At last, Larry Estes and RCA/Columbia agreed to finance the picture for $1.1 million. Soderbergh himself was paid $37,000 (Directors Guild scale) to write, direct, and edit. He was not intruded on by hostile forces— if you don't count casting problems, the short shooting schedule, and whatever limitations he encountered in his own imagination.

The film got into the Park City festival (Sundance), and then it won the Palme d'Or at Cannes. At that point, it was bought for distribution by Miramax, a small company founded in 1979 by the brothers Harvey and Bob Weinstein, initially as a distributor of foreign, art-house, or independent pictures, and then, gradually, as a small production company.

Harvey Weinstein was born in Buffalo in 1952—and the buffalo is only one of the brave, menacing animals with whom he has been compared. He is a lion and a bull, too, a big man who tends to wear an open-necked white shirt with his business suit. There is no one in the business today who so embodies the bullying strength of a Mayer and the taste of Thalberg crammed into one person. He can be boisterous, aggressive, crude, and domineering; he is also smart, very alert to talent and quality, and more prepared to back his hunch on a difficult idea than anyone else around. He could have been the acclaimed producer of *The Lord of the Rings* and *Fahrenheit 9/11* if his Disney bosses were bolder.

Don't forget that he and Bob once made a movie together, *Playing for Keeps*. It wasn't good, but it shows their respect for the medium and the craft. In their earliest days, Miramax measured its success in terms of foreign-language pictures that played well in America (among them, *Pelle the Conqueror* and *Cinema Paradiso*). But then they began to concentrate on the American independent movie, in ways that quickly advanced into the mainstream. They bought *sex, lies, & videotape* for $1 million up front and a million's worth of guaranteed advertising. At the time Soderbergh wondered if his picture could ever cover that advance, but it ended up earning about $24 million in the United States alone. That was modest money beside *Batman*, but it was still more proof that a moderate, discerning audience was waiting for interesting material.

In 1993, for about $100 million, the brothers sold Miramax to the Disney corporation, while retaining their executive positions and a great deal of autonomy. And the company has steadily developed so that it is now regularly listed as being in competition with the major studios. Miramax won Best Picture for 1996 with *The English Patient* (a project rescued for Anthony Minghella and Saul Zaentz when other "major" studios dropped it and Miramax stepped in with a deal that still owes money to Minghella and others). There's a risk that independence can be quickly coopted by the mainstream.

But the Miramax record is very suggestive: time and again they have taken up unlikely causes, let directors work on them in relative freedom, and then done as smart a job at promotion as anyone in Hollywood today. Their list includes *Pulp Fiction, Emma, The Wings of the Dove, Good Will Hunting, Shakespeare in Love, The Cider House Rules, Chocolat, Iris, In the Bedroom, The Talented Mr. Ripley, Gangs of New York, The Human Stain,* and *Cold Mountain.*

Harvey Weinstein gathers tall stories about himself as easily as he has scripts submitted nowadays. Some of the stories fit. He has shelved pictures once bought; he has leaned on the editing; he has sometimes entered into the recutting himself—the way Kane completes Jed Leland's damning review of Susan Alexander's "performance." Harvey Weinstein is exactly what the picture business in America now deserves—a gambler, a hustler, a man of taste, and so riotously confused by his own mixture that he attracts attention. He makes his business seem as big as he is. He cannot save the business on his own; nor can he kill it. He must expect and bear up under the wicked stories, most of which are funny, but we must give thanks for him. In a time of great stress, he has made the American independent movie a viable genre. You don't have to like them all. You can't forget the creeping elitism of a kind of cinema that relates to literary novels. But then see something like *Monster* or *The Fog of War* or *Magnolia,* and know that things could be worse.

Soderbergh was one director launched beyond his dreams by Miramax. He says in his diary that he hopes *sex, lies, & videotape* will not prove to be the best film he ever makes. So far, that's an open issue. But Soderbergh likes to pick and choose (one for them, one for me). He hopes to make his films as well as America's. Others have tried that and done well enough over the years, but it's tricky, and you are always subject to the economics we sketched out for Joe Gillis whereby you live up to the level of your hits. *Ocean's 11* would count as that (though no one reckons it matched *sex, lies, & videotape*). A Soderbergh may remember caution and not scale upward, but wives and children, not to mention ex-wives and ex-children, are far less wise. Of course, there's *Erin Brockovich,* a film about being very independent-minded, an entertainment—I'd call it a great American movie—that earned $125 million when Soderbergh was no longer working for scale. There is a moment in the life of the American artist (or most of them) when he learns economics and realty values.

Whereas Griffith and Welles and many others (for good or ill) did it for the thing itself, and knew that they had used up all their luck already inasmuch as someone (it didn't matter who) had put up $200,000, $650,000, or $1 million for them to take their shot. And if you don't have that money yourself (Chaplin had it, Coppola could borrow it, Spielberg and Lucas have it now), you are, more or less, saying to the world, Well, I would like to be an artist, but I would like to take that risk on someone else's money. That is unfair, it is un-American, and in the end it is deeply pernicious, for it encourages the notion that you can make art without taking total responsibility. You can't. And in movies, truly, it doesn't work that way.

* * *

But do the movies have to be an art form? Aren't they good enough already? Weren't they at their best and sometimes just miraculous before we thought of saying "art"? Isn't there something specially important in the way they are close to art but not quite there? It may even be that the movies, in their proximity to art and their redefinition of success, have corrupted the essential ingredients of art—its solitariness, its insignificance, its detachment from response or reward. Art is an elitist concept—it has to be—and the cheerful but dogged egalitarianism of America has confused its nature and its austerity. The movies, with their Monday numbers, have aided the fallacy that only expensive art is valuable.

We have a thriving subculture of "independent" American movies that makes an impact on America as a whole roughly equivalent to that of the modern literary novel. I encourage it, I sometimes enjoy it, and I think it's what a country like America has earned. These are the films sincere viewers marry, whereas, once upon a time, movies were a lifetime of one-night stands. Put that way, independence sounds so much more defensible. But don't give up the idea of fatal attraction, or basic instinct, or. . . . Occasionally, something happens in the dark that sets off an explosion. One example is David Lynch's *Blue Velvet,* a film that was and wasn't "independent." It was paid for by one of the ancient whores of the picture business, Dino de Laurentiis, who liked Lynch and felt he owed him one. So he gave him a few million to do *Blue Velvet,* which I think Lynch would allow he was able to do without any undue pressure. Lynch seems to me the one genius of the modern era, and somehow with *Blue Velvet* he made a film that was a dream, a psychic parable, a fantasy, an excursion into art, that broke through into the mainstream. *Mulholland Dr.* is as good a film, but it didn't quite cross over. The thrilling thing about *Blue Velvet* was the way in which it got to the raw mass of the people. It's a kind of danger you can smell in the dark, and once sampled, there's no other game in town. Some middle Americans came out of *Blue Velvet* feeling dirty, and I am of the faith that believes that this kind of infection is very necessary, and much more gently done by movies than by the dismay of foreign wars.

Why? Because the sensation carries us back to that earliest primitive intuition: that in a world where "art" (whether it is Henry James or Darren Aronofsky) is too demanding or austere for "everyone," here is a medium that could move or reach anyone, Henry James or Homer Simpson. It's the convicts in *Sullivan's Travels* laughing at Mickey Mouse in what may be the only freedom or community left to them. It's the hush at the close of *The Godfather* as we begin to realize how far Michael Corleone has invaded us. It's wanting to be there that early morning in Texas, wanting to be one of the circle of cowboys in the great panning shot in *Red River* before Wayne tells Clift to take them to Missouri.

It's very important to America, and to the extent that the United States now imposes itself on the whole world in so many ways—friendly and not—it's vital to the world. I don't know where the movie is going: I've suggested some ways or some pressures, and I suspect that technology will lead the way. It has a life of its own. But that is already a crushing admission about a country as idealistic as America: technology gave us nuclear weapons and they simply do not go back in their bottle. Nothing manages them save understanding and imagination. And film can be essential to that, for it is one of the few media still able to bind us all together.

I regret the way that America has elected to make films for its bluntest section of society and in ways that flatter them, and we have to recognize how much that is being done for the money. We have to find another way of measuring ourselves. And film is one of the few ways that might be done. Here and now, a twenty-four-hour period in which the people of the Middle East and the people of the United States simply watched a television record of that day in the other place—call it unmediated documentary—could be the most radical jolt to malice and political idiocy that we possess. So much in our films—American films now—supports the worst views held of us in other parts of the world: that we are combat-ready, aggressive, adolescent, greedy, sensationalists without humor, depth, or imagination, rampant devotees of technology (as opposed to enlightenment).

I am alarmed and mystified by the way film and still photography have so fallen in love with digital imagery that they are prepared to abandon that once-essential—and was it sacred?—reliance on light. There is much evidence that digital imagery will not last; literally, it may fade away, erasing the collective memory of family snapshots as well as history's archive. There is also a deadness in digital (it seems to me) that may mark a fatal arrogance prepared to forget that equation in which light kept photography lifelike. I have a hunch that future generations may see this shift as fateful in the progress of fantasy overwhelming reality, or of reason succumbing to desire.

My wife Lucy went to see Richard Curtis's *Love Actually,* on my recommendation. Not that I think it's a great film, or unflawed. It's actually pie-in-the-sky, unhindered fantasy and so contrived as to risk being sickly cute. But it's well made, funny, touching, and very, very movie-like. I can imagine anyone responding to it. I think the usherette in Hopper's painting would have liked it as much as Lucy did. She came back happy and she said the theater had been packed. It is a British film, but Americans were lapping it up. And my wife said: "It's a date film. The place was full of couples. When are today's movies going to regain that old habit they had, of getting us to the point of fucking?"

The more I thought about that, the wiser it seemed. For it harks back to that excitement or anticipation whereby audiences believed films belonged to them—not to a cocksure business, but to a mass of people struggling with their own desires. The thing I call movie may be dead now, or antique. It may have greater futures than I can imagine. But I begin to see that in history the thing we call the golden age of movies was a dream that perhaps helped people negotiate a very grave test.

Let me try to spell that out. Around 1900, several alarming confrontations were emerging in world history. On the one hand, statism was building, and as states found themselves in charge of dramatically mounting populations, who could tell what powers they would need—military or police control; urban organization; directed economies; totalitarian systems; social engineering?

At the same time, there were intense pressures on the human being to be more inward, more unique, more independent—universal education; suffrage; the discovery of the unconscious mind; a world of science in which people might be able to survive beyond the "regular" term of life; that pursuit-of-happiness thing; and a culture in which individualism was valued.

We have not worked these things out yet. We may fail. There are too many people, on the left and the right, who are so frightened by the clash that they would sooner take the law into their own tense hands than trust liberty to work out its untidy destiny. We are all perplexed about when to act, and when to wait—the going to war in 1939 is the most forceful instance of that; and any subsequent war carries some risk of obliteration. So it becomes more apparent and disconcerting that this dilemma is the more pitiless because we are living with the last shreds of organized religion or comfort.

The great American movie radiated the confidence and the energy that were required to take on the vast new continent. There is nothing more American than the confrontation of the Western hero and the open space that challenges him. But the same sense of exuberance exists in *His Girl Friday,* with Cary Grant and Rosalind Russell exchanging insults. There was once an ease and good nature and a lyrical expression of behavior in American films that shrugged off all the stupid orthodoxies about "happy endings." It knew not to wait for endings, but to trust to the moment. And maybe no moments are so fine, as beautiful and as free from "meaning" as the way Astaire moves, over the course of thirty years in American pictures, doing "Pick Yourself Up" with Ginger Rogers in *Swing Time;* "Begin the Beguine" with Eleanor Powell in *Broadway Melody of 1940;* or "All of You" with Cyd Charisse in *Silk Stockings.* Or pick your own moments.

The confidence cracked after World War II. But even in the age of increasingly unhappy endings, the American movie maintained its courage, its grace, its optimism. Jimmy Stewart survives in *It's a Wonderful Life*—an angel saves him—but we are not spared the terrible sense of the hole in life and Bedford Falls that he might have left had he killed himself. And even in *Chinatown,* where the rapist of his state and his own daughter survives, Noah Cross has met a fair match in the sour charm of Jack Nicholson, a screen presence who knows he can't dance, but tells himself that Fred wasn't much of an actor either.

It's time for America to live through its age of downbeat answers—just as few filmmakers now could offer one of those great spacious trips from the old Western and forget the damage done in the real West. By instinct, John Ford sensed the necessary loneliness of those old heroes in the new age when he closed the doors on Ethan Edwards in *The Searchers* and consigned him forever to the great blast of space.

I have a last story that also has to do with space. It occurred a few years ago and it was a turning point in my relations with movies. I was in a 747 flying from London to San Francisco. That plane arcs northward over Scotland; it touches Iceland and Greenland; and then comes in over the extraordinary mix of land and water that is northern Canada. I had a window seat at 39,000 feet on a day of such prodigious sunshine that you could see the columns of cloud and the lacework of ice far below. Why bother to say that it was beautiful? Why not admit that the exhilaration of flying is akin to the feeling you get when Charlie Parker or Louis Armstrong plays, or Fred Astaire dances. Except that, how many times are you going to fly that route on such a day?

And then the flight attendants asked the company on board to lower the blinds so that some dreadful contemporary movie could be projected in maybe the worst conditions a movie is ever seen. And most people—slaves to indifferent screens, today—did as they were told and gave up the majesty of cloud citadels over Greenland.

"Forget it, Jake. It's Chinatown."

NOTES ON SOURCES

1 · THE GAMBLE AND THE LOST RIGHTS

I have quoted from the introduction and the script of *Chinatown: A Screenplay* by Robert Towne (Santa Barbara, California: Neville Publishing, 1983); and I have read Towne's own script for *The Two Jakes* (draft of February 27, 1985), begun but never finished. Other valuable Towne material is in John Brady, *The Craft of the Screenwriter* (New York: Simon & Schuster, 1981), and a piece I wrote, "Trouble in Chinatown," *Vanity Fair*, November 1985. In addition, I have consulted Patrick McGilligan, *Jack's Life: A Biography of Jack Nicholson* (New York: Norton, 1994); Roman Polanski, *Roman* (New York: Morrow, 1984); and Robert Evans, *The Kid Stays in the Picture* (New York: Hyperion, 1994).

2 · MAYER AND THALBERG

The story of Louis B. Mayer has been offered in *Hollywood Rajah: The Life and Times of Louis B. Mayer* (New York: Holt, Rinehart and Winston, 1960) and Charles Higham, *Merchant of Dreams* (New York: Donald Fine, 1993), but I look forward to Scott Eyman's book in progress, which is likely to be the best. More vital in many ways is Irene Mayer Selznick, *A Private View* (New York: Knopf, 1983). Other valuable sources are Samuel Marx, *Mayer and Thalberg* (New York: Random House, 1975); Bob Thomas, *Thalberg* (New York: Doubleday, 1969); and Gavin Lambert, *Norma Shearer* (New York: Knopf, 1990). The Selznick side of the story is described in my book *Showman: The Life of David O. Selznick* (New York: Knopf, 1992). Another useful book is Neal Gabler, *An Empire of Their Own* (New York: Crown, 1988).

3 · THE PLACE

On Thalberg, see the books cited for chapter 2. The literature on California is enormous, and in many ways it is more thoughtful than writing on the movies. I have benefited from Carey McWilliams, *Southern California Country: An Island on the Land* (New York: Duell, Sloan and Pearce, 1946); Reyner Banham, *Los Angeles: The Architecture of Four Ecologies* (New York: Harper & Row, 1971); Norman M. Klein, *The History of Forgetting: Los Angeles and the Erasure of Memory* (London: Verso, 1997); Mike Davis, *City of Quartz* (London: Verso, 1990); and Marc Reisner, *Cadillac Desert* (New York: Viking, 1986), and *A Dangerous Place: California's Unsettling Fate* (New York: Pantheon, 2003). On the light, try Lawrence Weschler, "L.A. Glows," *The New Yorker,* February 23, 1998. And then there is the work of Joan Didion—the novel *Play It As It Lays* (New York: Farrar, Straus and Giroux, 1970), and nonfiction books *Slouching Towards Bethlehem* (New York: Farrar, Straus and Giroux, 1968), *The White Album* (New York: Simon & Schuster, 1979), and *Where I Was From* (New York: Knopf, 2003). The most thorough book on Wyatt Earp is Allen Barra, *Inventing Wyatt Earp: His Life and Many Legends* (New York: Carroll & Graf, 1998). The Gary Cooper story came from Niven Busch. Bob and Baker are characters in Stewart Edward White's novel *The Rules of the Game* (New York: Grosset & Dunlap, 1910). Frank Capra's life sends one to his autobiography, *The Name Above the Title* (New York: Macmillan, 1971). The fond corrective to that is Joseph McBride, *Frank Capra: The Catastrophe of Success* (New York: Simon & Schuster, 1992). Lenore Coffee on early Hollywood is *Storyline: Recollections of a Hollywood Screenwriter* (London: Cassell, 1973). Similar stories are in Agnes de Mille, *Dance to the Piper* (Boston: Little, Brown, 1952). On M. F. K. Fisher, see especially *Among Friends* (New York: Knopf, 1970). On gambling and Nevada, see David Thomson, *In Nevada: The Land, the People, God and Chance* (New York: Knopf, 1999). On the making of *The Ten Commandments,* see Cecil B. De Mille, *Autobiography* (Englewood, New Jersey: Prentice-Hall, 1959).

4 · TO BE IN AN AUDIENCE

On the earliest history of the discovery of movies and the phenomenon of their performance, I recommend: Charles Musser, *The Emergence of Cinema: The American Screen to 1907* (New York: Scribner's, 1990), and *Before the Nickelodeon: Edwin S. Porter and the Edison Manufacturing Company* (Berkeley: University of California Press, 1991); Jacques Rittaud-Hutinet, *Le Cinéma des Origines: Les Frères Lumières et Leurs Operateurs* (Seyssel, France: Editions du Champ Valon, 1985); Alan Trachtenberg, *The Incorporation of America: Culture and Society in the Gilded Age* (New York: Hill & Wang, 1982); Jay Leyda, *Kino* (London: Allen & Unwin, 1960); John Frazer, *Artificially Arranged Scenes: The Films of Georges Méliès* (Boston: G. K. Hall, 1979); W. K. L. Dickson and Antonia Dickson, *History of the Kinetograph, Kinetoscope and Kineto-Phonograph* (1895), reprinted (New York: MoMA, 2000); W. K. L. Dickson, *Biograph in Battle* (London: Fisher & Unwin, 1901); Robert Conot, *A Streak of Luck: The Life and Legend of Thomas Alva Edison* (New York: Seaview, 1979); Paolo Cherchi Usai, *The Death of Cinema: History, Cultural Memory and the Digital Dark Age* (London: BFI, 2001); Rebecca Solnit, *River of Shadows: Eadweard Muybridge and the Technological Wild West* (New York: Viking, 2003); and Vachel Lindsay, *The Art of the Moving Picture* (New York: Macmillan, 1922).

5 · CHARLIE

Charles Chaplin's *My Autobiography* (London: The Bodley Head, 1964) is neither reliable nor readable—but it's Charlie, and fascinating. Better books are David Robinson, *Chaplin: His Life and Art* (New York: McGraw-Hill, 1985) and Kenneth S. Lynn, *Charlie Chaplin and His Times* (New York: Simon & Schuster, 1997). Lita Grey Chaplin (with Morton Cooper) wrote *My Life with Chaplin: An Intimate Memoir* (New York: Bernard Geis, 1966). The key book on United Artists is Tino Balio, *United Artists: The Company Built by the Stars* (Madison: University of Wisconsin Press, 1976). The Buster Keaton story can be pursued in Rudi Blesh, *Keaton* (New York: Macmillan, 1966); David Robinson, *Buster Keaton* (London: Secker & Warburg, 1970); and Tom Dardis, *Keaton: The Man Who Wouldn't Lie Down* (New York: Scribner's, 1979).

6 · BY A NOSE

Josef von Sternberg's instruction to Marlene Dietrich comes in his unique autobiography, *Fun in a Chinese Laundry* (New York: Macmillan, 1965). Amplification can be found in Andrew Sarris, *The Films of Josef von Sternberg* (New York: MoMA, 1966), and Steven Bach, *Marlene Dietrich: Life and Legend* (New York: Morrow, 1992). There are already books on Nicole Kidman—most usefully, Lucy Ellis and Bryony Sutherland, *Nicole Kidman: The Biography* (London: Aurum Press, 2002).

7 · THE MAN IN THE HAT . . . A WOMAN IN GLOVES

The best book on D. W. Griffith is Richard Schickel, *D. W. Griffith: An American Life* (New York: Simon & Schuster, 1983). The Agee quotes are from *Agee on Film* (New York: McDowell-Obolensky, 1958). The Karl Brown quotes are from Brown, *Adventures with D. W. Griffith* (New York: Farrar, Straus & Giroux, 1973). The Griffith quote on his rural life is from *The Man Who Invented Hollywood: The Autobiography of D. W. Griffith* (Louisville: Touchstone, 1972). Michael Thomas's screenplay for *Indecent Exposure* (still not made) was shown to me by its producer, Edward Pressman. In turn, it is based on David McClintick, *Indecent Exposure* (New York: Morrow, 1982), the classic account of the David Begelman affair.

8 · STROHEIM AND SEEING MONEY

The original was Frank Norris, *McTeague: A Story of San Francisco* (New York: Blix, 1899), but I have quoted from the Penguin edition which has a good introduction by Kenneth Starr and includes the Kenneth Rexroth observations. The reconstruction (which would benefit from more editorial work) is Herman G. Weinberg, *The Complete "Greed"* (New York: Dutton, 1973). The best book on Norris is Franklin Dickerson Walker, *Frank Norris* (Garden City, New York: Russell & Russell, 1932); and the most complete biography on Stroheim is Richard Koszarski, *The Man You Loved to Hate: Erich von Stroheim and Hollywood* (New York: Oxford University Press, 1983). There is also Thomas Quinn Curtiss, *Von Stroheim* (New York: Farrar, Straus & Giroux, 1971), and Jonathan Rosenbaum, *Greed* (London: BFI Publishing, 1993). The Irene Mayer report comes from Selznick: *A Private View.*

9 · THE FRENZY ON THE WALL

The chapter title comes from Jean-Paul Sartre, *Words* (Greenwich, Connecticut: Fawcett, 1966). On the surrealists, see Paul Hammond, *The Shadow and Its Shadow: Surrealist Writing on Cinema* (London: BFI, 1978). On early film history, see Musser, *The Emergence of Cinema;* Eileen Bowser, *The Transformation of Cinema, 1907–1915* (New York: Scribner's, 1990); and Richard Koszarski, *An Evening's Entertainment: The Age of the Silent Feature Picture, 1915–1928* (New York: Scribner's, 1990). The M-G-M figures are from Marx, *Mayer and Thalberg.* See also Budd Schulberg, *Moving Pictures: Memoirs of a Hollywood Prince* (New York: Stein & Day, 1981), and Maurice Rapf, *Back Lot: Growing Up with the Movies* (Lanham, Maryland: Scarecrow, 1999). Los Angeles in the twenties and thirties can be tracked in Kevin Starr, *Material Dreams: Southern California Through the 1920s* (New York: Oxford University Press, 1990), and in Nathanael West, *The Day of the Locust* (New York: Random House, 1939).

10 · RESPECT

On West, see Jay Martin, *Nathanael West: The Art of His Life* (New York: Farrar, Straus & Giroux, 1970). Huston's driving is in Lawrence Grobel, *The Hustons* (New York: Scribner's, 1989); and Gable's is in Higham, *Merchant of Dreams.* The Clint Eastwood parking saga is told in Patrick McGilligan, *Clint: The Life and Legend* (London: HarperCollins, 1999). Mayer's house comes from Crowther, *Hollywood Rajah;* Higham, *Merchant of Dreams;* and Selznick, *A Private View.* On Crawford, see Bob Thomas, *Joan Crawford* (New York: Simon & Schuster, 1978). On the Arbuckle case, see David Yallop, *The Day the Laughter Stopped* (New York: St. Martin's, 1976). On William Desmond Taylor, see Robert Giroux, *A Deed of Death* (New York: Knopf, 1990). On Hays, see Will Hays, *Memoirs* (New York: Doubleday, 1955) and Tino Balio, ed., *Grand Design: Hollywood as a Modern Business Enterprise, 1930–1939* (New York: Scribner's, 1993). On the Academy, see Koszarski, *An Evening's Entertainment,* and Anthony Holden, *Behind the Oscar* (New York: Simon & Schuster, 1993).

11 · AT THE PARADISE

On Hopper, see Gail Levin, *Edward Hopper: An Intimate Biography* (New York: Knopf, 1995). On sound, see Scott Eyman, *The Speed of Sound: Hollywood and the Talkie Revolution* (New York: Simon & Schuster, 1997). On Dietrich, see Bach, *Marlene,* and Sternberg, *Fun in a Chinese Laundry.* On Murch, see Michael Ondaatje, *The Conversations* (New York: Knopf, 2002).

12 · THE FACTORY

On *The Big Parade,* see King Vidor, *A Tree Is a Tree* (New York: Harcourt, Brace, 1953); Marx, *Mayer and Thalberg;* and Raymond Durgnat and Scott Simmon, *King Vidor, American* (Berkeley: University of California Press, 1988). On Garbo, see Barry Paris, *Garbo* (New York: Knopf, 1995); Alexander Walker, *Garbo: A Portrait* (New York: Macmillan, 1980); and Raymond Daum, *Walking with Garbo* (New York: Harper-Collins, 1991). The Mankiewicz cable to Hecht is in Pauline Kael, *The Citizen Kane Book* (Boston: Little, Brown, 1971). On Hecht, see Ben Hecht, *A Child of the Century* (New York: Simon & Schuster, 1954). On Mankiewicz, see Richard Meryman, *Mank: The Wit, World and Life of Herman Mankiewicz* (New York: Morrow, 1978). For O'Toole, see Michael Freedland, *Peter O'Toole* (London: W. H. Allen, 1983). On Cagney, see John McCabe, *Cagney* (New York: Knopf, 1997); *Cagney by Cagney* (New York: Doubleday, 1967); and Patrick McGilligan, *Cagney: The Actor as Auteur* (New York: Barnes, 1975). On Garland, see Gerald Clarke, *Get Happy: The Life of Judy Garland* (New York: Random House, 2000). On *Gone With the Wind,* see Thomson, *Showman* (New York: Knopf, 1992); for *The Rules of the Game,* just see the film. On Sternberg, see his *Fun in a Chinese Laundry.* On Welles, see David Thomson, *Rosebud: The Story of Orson Welles* (New York: Knopf, 1996), and Peter Bogdanovich, *This Is Orson Welles* (New York: Harper Collins, 1992).

13 · VIABLE BUSINESS

On Cagney, see previous chapter. On M-G-M, see Higham, *Merchant of Dreams,* and Marx, *Mayer and Thalberg.* On Fox, see Aubrey Solomon, *Twentieth Century–Fox: A Corporate and Financial History* (Metuchen, New Jersey: Scarecrow, 1988). Constance Collier is *Harlequinade* (London: John Lane, 1929). Karl Brown is *Adventures with D. W. Griffith.* On Hollywood in the thirties, see Joel W. Finler, *The Hollywood Story* (London: Wallflower, 2003), which is full of facts and figures. On Myron Selznick, see Mary Mallory, "Agent Provocateur: The Tradition and Influence of Myron Selznick on the Motion Picture Talent Agency Business" (MA thesis, University of Texas at Austin) and Thomson, *Showman*. On Lew Wasserman, see Connie Bruck, *When Hollywood Had a King* (New York: Simon & Schuster, 2003), and Kathleen Sharp, *Mr. & Mrs. Hollywood: Edie and Lew Wasserman and Their Entertainment Empire* (New York: Carroll & Graf, 2003).

14 · GOLDEN?

On attendance, see Finler, *The Hollywood Story*. On Capra, see *The Name Above the Title*, and McBride, *Frank Capra: The Catastrophe of Success*. On *It's a Wonderful Life*, see Jeanine Basinger, *The It's a Wonderful Life Book* (New York: Knopf, 1986). On *The Best Years of Our Lives*, see A. Scott Berg, *Goldwyn* (New York: Knopf, 1989). On Preston Sturges, see Diane Jacobs, *Christmas in July: The Life and Art of Preston Sturges* (Berkeley: University of California Press, 1992) and *Preston Sturges by Preston Sturges* (New York: Simon & Schuster, 1990). On Fritz Lang, see Patrick McGilligan, *Fritz Lang: Nature of the Beast* (New York: St. Martin's, 1997), and Peter Bogdanovich, *Fritz Lang in America* (London: Studio Vista, 1967). On Howard Hawks, see Todd McCarthy, *Howard Hawks: The Grey Fox of Hollywood* (New York: Grove Press, 1997); Slim Keith, *Slim: Memories of a Rich and Imperfect Life* (New York: Simon & Schuster, 1990); and Joseph McBride, *Hawks on Hawks* (Berkeley: University of California Press, 1982).

15 · DIVORCE, HOLLYWOOD STYLE

On the Hawks marriage, see Slim Keith, *Slim*, and McCarthy, *Howard Hawks*. On divorce figures, see U.S. Census. Cavell is Stanley Cavell, *Pursuits of Happiness* (Cambridge: Harvard University Press, 1981); see also James Harvey, *Romantic Comedy in Hollywood* (New York: Knopf, 1987). On the Selznick story, see Selznick, *A Private View;* Thomson, *Showman;* and Ron Haver, *David O. Selznick's Hollywood* (New York: Knopf, 1980). The Bette Davis quote is in Davis, *The Lonely Life* (New York: Putnam, 1962). On Whitney, see E. J. Kahn Jr., *Jock: The Life and Times of John Hay Whitney* (New York: Doubleday, 1981).

16 · OUR TOWN

On L.A. in the thirties, see Starr, *Material Dreams;* Selznick, *A Private View;* Bruce Henstell, *Sunshine and Wealth: Los Angeles in the Twenties and Thirties* (San Francisco: Chronicle Books, 1984); and Charles Moore et al., *The City Observed: Los Angeles* (New York: Random House, 1984). Edmund Wilson is *The American Jitters* (New York: Scribner's, 1932). On Harlow, see David Stenn, *Bombshell* (New York: Doubleday, 1993), and Samuel Marx and Joyce Vanderveen, *Deadly Illusions: Jean Harlow and the Murder of Paul Bern* (New York: Random House, 1990). On Hepburn, see *Me: Stories of My Life*

(New York: Knopf, 1991) and Barbara Leaming, *Katharine Hepburn* (New York: Crown, 1995). On Brando, see Peter Manso, *Brando: The Biography* (New York: Hyperion, 1994), and Marlon Brando, *Brando: Songs My Mother Taught Me* (New York: Random House, 1994).

17 · THE DARKNESS AND THE LIGHT

Reagan is *Where's the Rest of Me?* (New York: Dell, 1965). On *Double Indemnity*, see Richard Schickel, *Double Indemnity* (London: BFI, 1992). On Wilder, see Ed Sikov, *On Sunset Boulevard: The Life and Times of Billy Wilder* (New York: Hyperion, 1998). On film noir, see Raymond Borde and Etienne Chaumeton, *A Panorama of American Film Noir* (original, 1955; San Francisco: City Lights, 2002); Alain Silver and Elizabeth Ward, eds., *Film Noir: An Encyclopedic Reference to the American Style* (Woodstock, New York: Overlook, 1996); and Eddie Muller, *Dark City: The Lost World of Film Noir* (New York: St. Martin's, 1998). On *Detour,* see Myron Meisel, "Edgar G. Ulmer: The Primacy of the Visual" in *Kings of the Bs* (New York: Dutton, 1975). On Nicholas Ray, see Bernard Eisenschitz, *Nicholas Ray: An American Journey* (London: Faber, 1993). Hecht and Selznick is from Hecht, *A Child of the Century.* Davis is *The Lonely Life.*

18 · IN A LONELY PLACE

On *Casablanca*, see Aljean Harmetz, *Round Up the Usual Suspects* (New York: Hyperion, 1992) and Rudy Behlmer, ed., *Inside Warner Bros., 1935–1951* (New York: Simon & Schuster, 1985). On the blacklist and HUAC, see Larry Ceplair and Steven Englund, *The Inquisition in Hollywood: Politics in the Film Community, 1930–1960* (Garden City, New York: Anchor, 1980); Victor Navasky, *Naming Names* (New York: Viking, 1980); and Patrick McGilligan and Paul Buhle, eds., *Tender Comrades: A Backstory of the Hollywood Blacklist* (New York: St. Martin's, 1997). On Bogart, see Lauren Bacall, *Lauren Bacall by Myself* (New York: Knopf, 1979), and A. M. Sperber and Eric Lax, *Bogart* (New York: Morrow, 1997). On Polonsky, see Paul Buhle and Dave Wagner, *A Very Dangerous Citizen: Abraham Lincoln Polonsky and the Hollywood Left* (Berkeley: University of California Press, 2001). On Losey, see David Caute, *Joseph Losey: A Revenge on Life* (New York: Oxford University Press, 1994), and Michel Ciment, *Conversations with Losey* (London: Methuen, 1985). On Kazan, see Elia Kazan, *A Life* (New York: Knopf, 1988). On M-G-M, see Lillian Ross, *Picture* (New York: Avon, 1952), and Dore Schary, *Heyday* (Boston: Little, Brown, 1979).

19 · "WHAT IS CINEMA?"

On Mayer, see Crowther, *Hollywood Rajah*, and Schary, *Heyday.* On Lucille Ball, see Stefan Kanfer, *Ball of Fire: The Tumultuous Life and Comic Art of Lucille Ball* (New

York: Knopf, 2003). On Wasserman, see Bruck, *When Hollywood Had a King,* and Sharp, *Mr. and Mrs. Hollywood.* On Reagan, see also Dan Moldea, *Dark Victory: Ronald Reagan, MCA and the Mob* (New York: Viking, 1986). On *The Night of the Hunter,* see Preston Neal Jones, *Heaven & Hell To Play With: The Filming of "The Night of the Hunter"* (New York: Limelight, 2002), and Simon Callow, *Charles Laughton: A Difficult Actor* (London: Methuen, 1987). On Hitchcock, see Patrick McGilligan, *Alfred Hitchcock: A Life in Darkness and Light* (New York: Regan, 2003). On Wilder, see Sikov, *On Sunset Boulevard.* On the Cinémathèque, see Richard Roud, *A Passion for Films: Henri Langlois and the Cinémathèque Française* (New York: Viking, 1983). On Bazin, see Andre Bazin, *What is Cinema,* 2 vols. (Berkeley: University of California Press, 1967–71). See also, Jim Hillier, ed., *Cahiers du Cinema: The 1950s* (Cambridge: Harvard University Press, 1985); Michel Ciment and Larry Kardish, eds., *Positif 50 Years* (New York: MoMA, 2003); Colin MacCabe, *Godard* (London: Bloomsbury, 2003); and Antoine de Baecque and Serge Toubiana, *Truffaut* (New York: Knopf, 1999).

20 · A FILM WE CAN'T REFUSE

For Gavin Lambert, see "From a Hollywood Notebook," *Sight and Sound,* Spring 1959. On Norman Mailer, see "A Course in Filmmaking," *Maidstone: A Mystery* (New York: Signet, 1971). On Fox, see Mel Gussow, *Don't Say Yes Until I Finish Talking: A Biography of Darryl F. Zanuck* (New York: Doubleday, 1971), and John Gregory Dunne, *The Studio* (New York: Farrar, Straus & Giroux, 1969). Steven Bach on ancillary rights, see David Pirie, ed., *Anatomy of the Movies* (London: Windward, 1981). On the seventies, see Peter Biskind, *Easy Riders, Raging Bulls* (New York: Simon & Schuster, 1998); Michael Pye and Lynda Myles, *The Movie Brats: How the Film Generation Took Over Hollywood* (New York: Holt, Rinehart and Winston, 1979); and Julia Phillips, *You'll Never Eat Lunch in This Town Again* (New York: Random House, 1991). On Altman, see Patrick McGilligan, *Robert Altman: Jumping Off the Cliff* (New York: St. Martin's, 1989). On Coppola, see Peter Cowie, *Coppola* (London: Andre Deutsch, 1989); Cowie, *The Godfather Book* (London: Faber, 1997); and Eleanor Coppola, *Notes* (New York: Simon & Schuster, 1979)—the best book by a film director's wife.

21 · RIGHT BEFORE YOUR EYES

On *Jaws,* see Antonia Quirke, *Jaws* (London: BFI Publishing, 2002); Carl Gottlieb, *The Jaws Log* (New York: Dell, 1975); and Joseph McBride, *Steven Spielberg: A Biography* (New York: Simon & Schuster, 1997). On Peckinpah, see David Weddle, *If They Move . . . Kill 'Em!: The Life and Times of Sam Peckinpah* (New York: Grove, 1994). On Coppola, see previous chapter. On Lucas, see Dale Pollock, *Skywalking: The Life and Films of George Lucas* (New York: Harmony, 1983), and Charles Champlin, *George Lucas: The Creative Impulse* (New York: Abrams, 1992). On Cimino, see Steven Bach, *Final Cut* (New York: Morrow, 1985).

22 · THAT'S ALL, FOLKS?

News reports and figures on current films are from the *New York Times*. On Wasserman and Universal, see Bruck, *When Hollywood Had a King*, and Sharp, *Mr. & Mrs. Hollywood*. On Hitchcock, see McGilligan, *Alfred Hitchcock*. On Spielberg, see McBride, *Steven Spielberg;* also, see David Thomson, "Presenting Enamelware," *Film Comment*, March–April 1994 and Leon Wieseltier, *The New Republic*, January 24, 1994. On the independent movement and Miramax, see Peter Biskind, *Down and Dirty Pictures: Miramax, Sundance and the Rise of Independent Film* (New York: Simon & Schuster, 2004). On Soderbergh, see Steven Soderbergh, *sex, lies and videotape* (New York: Harper & Row, 1990). On Lynch, see Chris Rodley, ed., *Lynch on Lynch* (London: Faber, 1997).

FURTHER READING

There are a few other books that are essential reading, and very entertaining:

Anger, Kenneth. *Hollywood Babylon.* San Francisco: Straight Arrow, 1975.

Boorman, John. *Money into Light: The Emerald Forest Diaries.* London: Faber, 1985.

Dunne, John Gregory. *Monster: Living off the Big Screen.* New York: Random House, 1997.

Friedrich, Otto. *City of Nets: A Portrait of Hollywood in the 1940s.* New York: Harper & Row, 1986.

Haskell, Molly. *From Reverence to Rape: The Treatment of Women in the Movies.* New York: Holt, Rinehart and Winston, 1974.

Hayward, Brooke. *Haywire.* New York: Knopf, 1977.

Mailer, Norman. *The Deer Park.* New York: Putnam, 1955.

McGilligan, Patrick, ed. *Backstory: Interviews with Screenwriters.* 3 vols. Berkeley: University of California Press, 1986, 1991, 1997.

Puttnam, David. *Movies and Money.* London: HarperCollins, 1997.

Sanders, James. *Celluloid Skyline: New York and the Movies.* New York: Knopf, 2001.

Sarris, Andrew. *The American Cinema, Directors and Directions, 1929–1968.* New York: Dutton, 1968.

———. *"You Ain't Heard Nothin' Yet": The American Talking Film, History and Memory, 1927–1949.* New York: Oxford University Press, 1998.

Schatz, Thomas. *The Genius of the System: Hollywood Filmmaking in the Studio Era.* New York: Pantheon, 1988.

In Cottage Grove, a small town in Oregon, there is a mural that commemorates the local making of *The General* in 1926. As far as I know, it is the only memorial in the United States to Buster Keaton. (© *Lucy Gray, 2004*)

ACKNOWLEDGMENTS

The turning point for me was 1981, the year in which my wife and I elected to live in California. For that was the moment at which it began to be less possible to sit back and watch the films of America as if they were artistic messages from a far country. They might be good or bad (as it seemed to the observer), but there was no questioning their being or their fundamental assumptions. To be a film critic, I felt, was to judge them as if they were poems sent out to the world by some Wordsworth, or Little Richard. But once in California, I fell in love with the history of the place—with that of Los Angeles, especially—and the strange but wondrous way in which "Hollywood" could hold together the assumptions, the tone, and the very manner of both Wordsworth and Little Richard (and more, much more). Thus began an education in how pictures are made, and why, which I now find more interesting than whether they are "good" or "bad."

So I have to thank the many people who have contributed, in all manner of ways, to that education, in the hope that this is a book some of them would enjoy reading: Maurice Rapf, Arthur Mayer, Bob Rafelson, Michael Powell, Martin Scorsese, Harry and Mary Jane Ufland, Paul Schrader, Peter Bogdanovich, James Toback, Alan Carr, Bernie Brillstein, Francis and Eleanor Coppola, Tom Luddy, Tom Sternberg, Chris Meledandri, Daniel Melnick, Niven Busch, Michael Douglas, Robert Towne, Irene Mayer Selznick, Jeffrey Selznick, Daniel Selznick, Nancy Keith, Fay Wray, Dorothy Hirshon, Marcella Rabwin, John Houseman, Norman Mailer, Philip Kaufman, Edward Pressman, Paula Morgan, Holly Goldberg Sloan, Gary Rosen, Michael Barker, Anthony Minghella, Harvey Weinstein, Pierre Rissient, Bertrand Tavernier, Gavin Lambert, Elvis Mitchell, Patrick McGilligan, Andy Olstein, Virginia Campbell, Richard and Mary Corliss, Richard Jameson and Kathleen Murphy, Andrew Sarris and Molly Haskell, Leon Wieseltier, Steve Wasserman, Max Palevsky, Leslee Dart, Fielder Cook, and Frank Pierson.

Two friends have been especially important: Steven Bach, not just for his own work and example, but for friendship over the years, and for reading the book at an early stage and gently pointing out some howlers; Mark Feeney served the same role, with his own unique diligence and humor, and has been a marvelous conversational companion over the years. I know that I am also in the debt of three remarkable, and remarkably dry, observers of the film scene: Gore Vidal, John Gregory Dunne, and Joan Didion.

My association with Knopf is nearly as old now as my Californian residence, and I have many people to thank there: Bob Gottlieb, the late Lee Goerner, Sonny Mehta, Kathy Hourigan, Kevin Bourke, Iris Weinstein, Kathy Zuckerman, Carol Carson, and John Morrone, who copyedited this book with many red pencils. But above all, I want to thank Jonathan Segal, the editor of the book, its patient backer for years, a terrific stimulus to its text, and an abiding friend.

I am grateful, as ever, to Lorraine Latorraca for the typing and to Victoria Stewart for her library research on the precise numbers attained by many films.

More than ever, I feel the need to see films with people and so I also thank my wife Lucy (for her pictures, too), my sons Nicholas and Zachary and Mathew, and my daughters Kate and Rachel.

INDEX

Italicized page numbers indicate illustrations